The Problem South

The Problem South

Region, Empire, and the
New Liberal State, 1880–1930

NATALIE J. RING

The University of Georgia Press
Athens & London

A portion of this book appeared, in different form, as "Mapping Regional and Imperial Geographies: Tropical Disease in the U.S. South," on pages 297–308 of Alfred W. McCoy's *Colonial Crucible: Empire in the Making of the Modern American State*, © 2009 by the Board of Regents of the University of Wisconsin. Reprinted courtesy of The University of Wisconsin Press. Other portions of this book originally appeared, in different form, as "Inventing the Tropical South: Race, Region, and the Colonial Model," *Mississippi Quarterly: The Journal of Southern Cultures* 56 (Fall 2003): 619–32, and as "Linking Regional and Global Spaces in Pursuit of Southern Distinctiveness," *American Literature* 78 (December 2006): 712–14.

Designed by Walton Harris

Set in 10.5 / 14 Minion Pro

Printed digitally in the United States of America

Library of Congress Cataloging-in-Publication Data

Ring, Natalie J.
The problem South : region, empire, and the new liberal state, 1880–1930 / Natalie J. Ring.
    p.   cm. — (Politics and culture in the twentieth-century South)
Includes bibliographical references and index.
ISBN-13: 978-0-8203-2903-1 (cloth : alk. paper)
ISBN-10: 0-8203-2903-7 (cloth : alk. paper)
ISBN-13: 978-0-8203-4260-3 (pbk. : alk. paper)
ISBN-10: 0-8203-4260-2 (pbk. : alk. paper)
1. Liberalism—Southern States—History. 2. Southern States—Politics and government—1865–1950. 3. Southern States—Social conditions—1865–1945.
4. Southern States—Economic conditions. 5. Southern States—Economic policy.
I. Title.
F215.R56 2012
320.510975—dc23   2011047929

British Library Cataloging-in-Publication Data available

To Jon Daniel

CONTENTS

ILLUSTRATIONS

ACKNOWLEDGMENTS

There are many people, institutions, and associations who made this book possible. The process of researching and writing has taken longer than expected and my memory is weaker; thus I offer a preemptive apology to those I have neglected to acknowledge.

The genesis of this book was the product of a conversation with David G. Gutiérrez, William Deverell, and Douglas Flamming in Los Angeles over lunch. They peppered me with question after question, enabling me to identify a dissertation topic. After many initial dead ends, this meeting turned out to be a pivotal moment. Dave Gutiérrez continued to offer encouragement through doubtful times despite the fact that the subject matter of this book was far outside his field of study. In retrospect, I am very lucky that I landed in southern California to study southern history. The rigorous training I received from Steven Hahn, Rachel N. Klein, and Stephanie McCurry at the University of California, San Diego (UCSD) continues to be priceless. Steven Hahn never lost faith in the significance of this project, from the very beginning as an initial proposal to completion as a book. I cannot thank him enough for his wise advice and unending support. As a dissertation advisor, mentor, and historian he has inspired me. Rachel Klein's unflagging kindness and advocacy during graduate school was inestimable. I am grateful to Stephanie McCurry for encouraging me to "stick to my guns" at the tail end of this process. The history department at UCSD is a jewel. I also learned much from Michael Bernstein, Stanley Chodorow, Michael Meranze, and Michael Parrish. Other faculty at the university, Susan G. Davis and Jonathan Scott Holloway, taught me a lot as well. Special thanks go to Vincente L. Rafael for serving on my dissertation committee with enthusiasm at the last moment. The cohort of graduate students and friends in San Diego made the process more than bearable: Eric Boime, Krista Camenzind, Julie Davidow, Rene Hayden, Linda Heidenreich,

Katrina Hoch, Volker Janssen, Christina Jiménez, David Miller, Katrina Pearson, Démian Pritchard, Leah Schmerl, Sarah Schrank, Gabriela Soto Laveaga, Rita Urquijo-Ruiz, Adam Warren, and H. Mark Wild. Without Linda, Démian, and Gabriela I never would have made it out of graduate school. Daniel Berenberg, Wendy Maxon, Douglas T. McGetchin, and Angela Vergara provided constructive feedback in the dissertation writing class.

In the early stages, my research was funded by the Smithsonian Institution, the American Historical Association, the Rockefeller Archive Center, the Southern Historical Collection at the University of North Carolina at Chapel Hill, and the Copeland Fellow program at Amherst College. I learned much from other fellows at the Smithsonian and always enjoyed "talking southern history" with Pete Daniel. Thank you to David W. Wills and David W. Blight for sponsoring me as a Copeland fellow. I am grateful to the archivists across the United States who have assisted me over the years. I would especially like to thank Thomas Rosenbaum of the Rockefeller Center Archive for his indefatigable commitment to locating new sources while I worked in the archives and Vincent Fitzpatrick, curator of the H. L. Mencken Collection, who made my first "official" visit to an archive and my lone work in the Mencken room a welcome one. Although the project took a slightly different direction, his assistance proved to be extremely useful. At the beginning of this project when I was traveling in Chapel Hill, Fred C. Hobson graciously met me for dinner and listened to me share my thoughts on H. L. Mencken and the critics of the 1920s, even though I was a complete stranger to him. Samuel L. Webb also provided early support and dinner at his home, and I appreciate his best effort to gain me access to the Thomas Heflin Papers at the University of Alabama. Although I did not get to view the Heflin papers, I did discover some invaluable sources in the W. S. Hoole Special Collections that I would not have seen otherwise.

The two years I spent at Tulane University as a visiting assistant professor marked an important moment in my professional development. The opportunity to be a part of the intellectual community at Tulane and live in New Orleans while studying the South was not only serendipitous but inestimable. I was fortunate to have such welcoming colleagues and friends: Laura Rosanne Adderley, George L. Bernstein, James M. Boyden, Rachel Devlin, Kate Haulman, Daniel Hurewitz, Alisa Plant, Lawrence N. Powell, Randy J. Sparks,

Edith Wolfe, Justin Wolfe, and Jacqueline Woodfork. Rosanne Adderley not only introduced me to all that is great about New Orleans culture but she passed on the good will, assistance, and karma of previous dissertators working until the very last minute. Her friendship is a treasure.

I am appreciative of the vibrant interdisciplinary academic community and colleagues I have discovered in the Dallas/Fort Worth area (or those who were just traveling through) including Marco Atzori, Charles Bambach, Charles Bittner, Susan Briante, Matthew Brown, R. Sophie Burton, Gregg Cantrell, Robert T. Chase, Stephanie Cole, Sean Cotter, Meg Cotter-Lynch, R. David Edmunds, J. Michael Farmer, Caitlyn Finlayson, Amy Freund, Jonathan Frome, Shari Goldberg, Charles Hatfield, Benjamin Heber Johnson, Farid Matuk, Alexis McCrossen, Adrienne McLean, Patricia Michaelson, Christopher Morris, Jessica Murphy, Cihan Muslu, Michelle Nickerson, Peter Park, Stephen Rabe, R. Clay Reynolds, Thomas Riccio, Nils Roemer, Mark Rosen, Eric Schlereth, Rainer Schulte, Rebecca Sharpless, Erin A. Smith, F. Todd Smith, Sabrina Starnaman, Theresa Towner, Elizabeth Turner, Jennifer Jensen Wallach, Dennis Walsh, Daniel Wickberg, and Michael Wilson. Many provided support, offered friendship, and/or read my work. Dean Dennis Kratz gave me time off to work on this book and reduced my teaching load at key moments. I am thankful for his assistance. Daniel Wickberg deserves acknowledgment for reading an initial draft. I am incredibly grateful to Stephanie Cole for her sharp, incisive copy editing. Her perceptive commentary made this a far better book. Special thanks go to my dear friends Charles Hatfield and Susan Briante for keeping me sane and laughing.

When I first began thinking about the South in a global milieu, I was fortunate to discover a whole community of literary scholars who were thinking in similar ways. I appreciate their enthusiasm for my scholarship and for welcoming a historian with such graciousness. The stimulating conversations we had at the conference in Puerto Vallarta and the symposium held at the Center for the Study of Southern Culture at the University of Mississippi have influenced this book significantly. Thank you to Hosam Aboul-Ela, Suzanne Bost, Keith Cartwright, Deborah Cohn, Leigh Ann Duck, Judith Jackson Fossett, George B. Handley, Karla Holloway, Suzanne W. Jones, Valérie Loichot, John W. Lowe, John T. Matthews, Kathryn B. McKee, Tara McPherson, Riché Richardson, Scott Romine, Peter Schmidt, Mab Segrest, Barbara Ellen Smith, Jon Smith,

Melanie Benson Taylor, and Annette Trefzer. Jon Smith served as an initial advocate for this project to the University of Georgia Press and I appreciate his early commitment.

I have been fortunate to learn from and enjoy the company of many people at the annual meetings of the Southern Historical Association and other conferences including George Baca, Erin Elizabeth Clune, Jane Dailey, Pete Daniel, Gregory P. Downs, Laura F. Edwards, Watson W. Jennison, Susanna Lee, Daniel S. Margolies, Jeffrey W. McClurken, Joshua D. Rothman, Anne Sarah Rubin, Bryant Simon, Paul S. Sutter, and Kirt von Daake. Scholars who commented on my work at conferences assisted me in sharpening my analysis: Edward L. Ayers, Pete Daniel, Matthew Pratt Guterl, Martha Elizabeth Hodes, Margaret Humphreys, Michael Salman, and Keith Wailoo. I am indebted to William A. Link and the anonymous reader who offered valuable suggestions on how to improve my argument. John David Smith and Bryant Simon also read the entire manuscript and provided useful insights. Nancy Grayson, Beth Snead, and Jon Davies at the University of Georgia Press have been extremely patient and accommodating.

I must thank my professors at Amherst College who inspired me as an undergraduate and sparked my interest in history and American studies. There was a brief moment when I considered a career path in medicine but their enthusiasm was infectious enough to dissuade me. I learned much from Francis G. Couvares, Jan Dizard, Hugh D. Hawkins, N. Gordon Levin, Barry O'Connell, and David W. Wills. The enthusiasm of my own students in the "New Southern Studies" classes kept many of the issues in this book fresh in my mind over the years. Thank you to Ariana Warren for agreeing to be my research assistant.

Finally, Jon Daniel has been with this book for more than half of its life span. As a "history groupie" and partner he has been a persistent champion of my career. I benefited from his willingness to leave the house often so I could write in solitude. His bigheartedness, forbearance, and devotion are more than I deserve. Therefore, I dedicate this book to him.

The Problem South

Regional, National, and Global Designs

> It is true that each section and state and county and township has its own problems—but the particular problems of the part are the general problems of the whole; and the nation, as a nation, is interested in the administration and concerns of the most insignificant members of the body politic.
>
> — ANDREW SLEDD

> There exists among us by ordinary—both North and South—a profound conviction that the South is another land, sharply differentiated from the rest of the American nation, and exhibiting within itself remarkable homogeneity. . . . The peculiar history of the South has so greatly modified it from the general American norm that, when viewed as a whole, it decisively justifies the notion that the country is—not quite a nation within a nation, but the next thing to it.
>
> — W. J. CASH

In 1920 Henry Louis Mencken published a scathing essay titled "The Sahara of the Bozart" in which he derided the American South for its lack of culture, political ignorance, degraded Anglo-Saxon stock, and "vexatious public problems." He remarked, "It is, indeed, amazing to contemplate so vast a vacuity" and concluded that "for all its size and all its wealth and all the 'progress' it babbles of, it is almost as sterile, artistically, intellectually, culturally, as the Sahara Desert." In fact, Mencken added, "It would be impossible in all history to match so complete a drying-up of a civilization." Mencken also compared the South to the foreign lands of Asia Minor, Poland, Portugal, Serbia, Estonia, the Balkans, and China and all but argued that the region lacked American attributes and values.[1] Although an earlier version of this essay drew scant attention in 1917, Mencken's reworking of the piece in 1920 provoked not only a surge of enmity from traditionalists in the South but also a roar of approval from budding critics around the country. Even in the South condemnation of the region was robust. Between 1923 and 1929 southern newspapers as diverse as the *Charleston News and Courier*, *Montgomery Advertiser*, and *Norfolk Virginia Pilot* won Pulitzer Prizes for their editorials on the Ku Klux Klan, lynching, political backwardness, and buffoonish demagogues in the region. In 1924 Paul Green, editor of the *Reviewer* in Chapel Hill, North Carolina, described the "horrible Menckenitis which is now breaking out over the lily-white body of our beautiful South, causing that most somnolent lady to scratch herself publicly in most unseemly parts, yea, even in the capitol [sic] buildings," but he welcomed such an illness since "she has at last called upon the doctor."[2] Throughout the decade Mencken continued to lambaste and ridicule the South for its inadequacies and his work received national attention long after his death. Contemporary historians—as did many journalists and critics in the 1920s and 1930s—typically celebrate Mencken as the forerunner of a vigorous criticism of the South. They have argued that his caustic musings precipitated a wave of copycat South-bashing among nascent liberals in the region and neo-abolitionists in the North.[3] Some critics of the South were content merely to ridicule. Others worked tirelessly to reform.

In addition to Mencken and his imitators, the progenitors of a new regionalism drew attention to the South and its problems and advocated social engineering in response to regional deficiencies. Historians view the establishment of the Institute for Research in Social Science in 1924 at the University of North Carolina at Chapel Hill as evidence of the willingness of social scientists and reformers finally to come to terms with the shortcomings of the South. Four years before the establishment of the institute, the university appointed Howard W. Odum, a sociologist who had grown up in the rural South, to head the School of Public Welfare and the Department of Sociology. Two years later Odum founded the *Journal of Social Forces*, which focused on an assortment of problems in the South. Odum then presided over the new Institute for Research in Social Science, which continued to receive institutional funding well into the 1930s. The new "regionalism" at Chapel Hill aimed to put aside the "sectionalism" of the recent past and promote the integration of the region into the nation.[4] Odum and his fellow sociologists and reformers acknowledged that the South had distinctive problems, but they believed that social scientific research and planning were keys to the region's revitalization. By the 1930s the regionalist movement at Chapel Hill had attracted extensive northern support, and in 1931 the General Education Board of the Rockefeller Foundation made a grant to the Social Science Research Council for a regional study of the South. The foundation chose Odum and historian Benjamin B. Kendrick to lead this massive social study, and their work resulted in the publication of a weighty manifesto titled *Southern Regions of the United States* (1936).

Most scholars view this regionalism and criticism of the South in the 1920s as sui generis, a brief moment in the late New South period in which the nation turned on the region in a fit of unexplained antagonism or developed interest in southern deficiencies following several decades of fervent commitment to reuniting North and South. George Tindall, one of the first historians to address the mythology of the backward South, contrasts the modern "neo-abolitionist image of the benighted South" in the 1920s with the late nineteenth- and early twentieth-century "romantic plantation myth of gentility."[5] However, interest in the "benighted South" or Problem South did not materialize suddenly out of the cultural ether. This book contends that regionalism and national censure of the region in the 1920s in fact followed a long period of fascination with the "southern problem" that began after Reconstruction and paradoxically and problematically occurred alongside the more familiar sentimental symbols of national reconciliation. The image of the South as the nation's problem served an ideological purpose; demarcating the region as a backward space reinforced the hegemony of the nation-state and created a sense of urgency surrounding sectional reunion. National efforts by northern and southern reformers to modernize the South was central to the development of early twentieth-century liberalism and part of the process of nation-state formation. Social scientific investigation of the South's backwardness in the context of Progressivism reflected a liberal faith in social science as a tool of reform and offered a working vocabulary to define and categorize southern problems. This also occurred at a moment in which imperial expansion abroad drew attention to global problems in the arenas of public health, education, agriculture, and race relations.

Beginning roughly in 1880, an array of institutions and people, including northern philanthropists, federal officials, southern liberals, social scientists, national journalists, progressive reformers, clergymen, and academicians, helped fashion an image of the South as a regional, national, and even global problem. This group began to draw attention to the region's poverty, backwardness, and distinctiveness. These efforts often consisted of collaboration between the Rockefeller philanthropies, the Carnegie Corporation, the Southern Education Board, and the U.S. Department of Agriculture, among other groups and institutions. In the 1880s and early 1890s criticism and calls for reform remained subdued partly due to the competing power of the New South creed that promoted industrial progress, racial harmony, and sectional reunion. By the mid- to late 1890s, with the intensification of the Populist Party, a series of economic depressions, the U.S. Senate's investigation into the condition of cotton growers in the South, the multiplying complexities of Jim Crow, and American forays into colonialism, which included public health and educational reform, the image of the South as a problem gained more definition in the national imagination. During the first decade of the twentieth century, attention to the Problem South reached a crescendo and solidly planted the seeds for the regional condemnation and reformist ideology of the 1920s.

The heart of this work focuses on the period between 1900 and 1914, when northern philanthropies, associations of southern liberals, and the federal government targeted the South for what they described as "readjustment" and "uplift," although the interest in southern problems existed in the years before the turn of the century and persisted beyond World War I. The first of these terms, "readjustment," summoned memories of Reconstruction and referred to perceived lingering racial problems, entrenched poverty, and a commitment to rehabilitate the South in the image of the North. The latter term, "uplift," often evoked ideas about racial advancement, colonialism, and global reform in the context of American expansion. At times the words "readjustment" and "uplift" were used interchangeably to describe the need to facilitate the modernization of the South, which often paradoxically seemed to be making great progress while simultaneously remaining in a state of backwardness.

Part of the difficulty lay in the fact that reformers interested in modernizing the South noticed that not all areas of the region suffered equally. Most observers of the region struggled to reconcile what they saw as the paradox of poverty and progress. Was the South an American entity, a part of the nation, or was it a place with its own peculiar problems? The word "progress" evoked the concept of American nationalism, and the word "poverty" marked the idea of southern regionalism. To reconcile this paradox, reformers frequently described the South as moving through a period of extended transition toward a more perfect state of industrial democracy. They invoked the language of sociocultural evolutionism to describe what they identified as the process of southern readjustment. The concept of readjustment proved to be a flexible one, and it permitted people to view the trouble of the South as both a southern and a national problem. In this way the South could be viewed simultaneously as regionally distinctive and American in character. As Edward Ayers and Peter Onuf have demonstrated, American nationalism did not necessarily preclude the continuation of regional or sectional identities and images.[6] The persistence of regionalism in the history of the South's relationship to the rest of the nation is a long one and has never entirely waned. This regionalist ethos can be seen in Thomas Jefferson's observations about the distinctions between North and South; the antebellum travel narratives of countless Americans and overseas travelers to the South such as Frederick Law Olmsted, who perceived the region as a backward alien land apart from the rest of the nation; and the free labor ideology of the Republican Party, which drew distinctions between the independent, enterprising middle class of the North and the backward, lazy poor whites of the South.[7]

The Problem South argues for a wholesale rethinking of what we mean by the idea of sectional reconciliation and posits that the effort to reincorporate the New South into the nation was as much a process of rehabilitation and reform as one of political and cultural reunion.[8] The traditional historical narrative maintains that the hostilities of the Civil War and the dashed hopes of Reconstruction gave way to the powerful forces of sectional reunion in the late nineteenth and early twentieth centuries. White northerners and southerners embraced a culture of reunion marked by a reworking of the historical memory of the Civil War; celebrated the development of a New South gospel of progress, which ironically championed the cult of the Lost Cause; and generated a national literary explosion of romantic images celebrating life in the old plantation South. Yet the phenomenon of cultural reunion was not without challenge, and indeed it reflected a momentary shift in focus rather than a permanent alteration in a broader historical narrative about the South's differentness from the nation. An equally powerful and opposing set of representations of the South as a backward region played counterpoint to the nostalgic image of the reconciled New South and distorted the nation-state's myth-making efforts to construct a more benign social memory of the Civil War and its consequences.

In addition, the imagery of the Problem South was supported by material evidence and had its roots in the social and economic strategies of reform undertaken by a wide range of historical actors. The national goal to reunify the North and South entailed the transformative initiatives of the federal government and the efforts of northern philanthropies working in collaboration with a nascent liberal movement in the South. Actions taken by reformers in response to the South's shortcomings were a constituent part of what Gary Gerstle has identified as "strong-state liberalism." This was a moment in which "liberals turned to the state as an institutional medium capable of reconstructing society and of educating citizens in the task of intelligent living."[9] The consolidation of early twentieth-century liberalism entailed the creation of a persuasive image of regional backwardness that could then be resolved through economic and social reform. Unlike Reconstruction, the readjustment of the South through the use of the regulatory state did not include the use of military troops or the implementation of grand pieces of legislation. Yet it was no less a process of reconstruction.

This image of southern backwardness that developed in the late nineteenth and early twentieth centuries occurred during a period of rapid industrialization, political consolidation, urbanization, and overseas expansion. The rise of corporate capitalism, technological advances, the expansion of the railroad system, and the decline of the farmer in the nation as a whole reflected a shift from a more traditional rural way of living to an urban metropolitan life. As Martin Sklar writes, "In one and the same period were laid down and intermeshed the foundations of the corporate-capitalist economy, of the regulatory state, of internationalist foreign policy, and of modern political liberalism, as they would develop in mutually reinforcing and conflicting ways over the next several decades in the United States."[10] The national tendency to identify economic, racial, and social problems in the South worked to highlight the importance of modernization and the advance of civilization. The attempt to rehabilitate and reconstruct southerners involved efforts to improve the economic welfare of southern cotton growers, develop a healthy labor force by eliminating such diseases as malaria and hookworm, stabilize the "race problem," and educate the southern populace in the hope of creating a more prosperous body of democratic citizens. Poor whites, in particular, were a special target of attention, and anxieties about white racial degeneration often competed with the environmental explanations offered for the seeming backwardness of this group.

More specifically, several circumstances converged in this period that engendered interest in the Problem South. A group of northern and southern liberals contributed to the discourse of the "southern problem," which reached its zenith during the Progressive Era.[11] The rise of a small group of outspoken liberals in the South, including such spokesmen as George Washington Cable, Walter Hines Page, Edgar Gardner Murphy, Charles W. Dabney, John Spencer Bassett, Edwin Mims, and Edwin A. Alderman began to challenge the more traditional reactionary forces in the South. These liberal clergymen, intellectuals, and social reformers were quite vocal, and many of them wound up fleeing the South in search of a tolerable intellectual climate in the North. Liberal reformers pursued educational reform, supported southern industrial progress and sectional reunification, and, for the most part, did not criticize the basic underlying racial structure of the South. Yet their voices produced an undercurrent of criticism that fueled national and popular interest in the "southern problem."[12] Northern philanthropists such as Robert C. Ogden often worked in conjunction with these southern liberals, and they publicized collectively and successfully the shortcomings of the South on a national level. Northern middle-class social clubs (sometimes made up of southern expatriates) gathered to study and discuss the problems of the South, and northern philanthropies such as the Rockefeller Foundation injected significant amounts of money into the region in an attempt to solve the region's social problems. Academics such as Albert Bushnell Hart of Harvard University and Frank Tannenbaum of Columbia University contributed to the literature on southern problems based on travels they had made to the South.

The rise of a prominent black middle-class dedicated to racial uplift also contributed to the discourse on the "southern problem." These black reformers, sometimes in conjunction with white liberal reformers, sought to reform the social lives of working-class and rural black Americans. Black intellectuals such as W. E. B. Du Bois, Kelly Miller, George S. Schuyler, D. Augustus Straker, and Ida B. Wells theorized about the social relationship between whites and blacks and identified problems such as lynching, illiteracy, and poor health. Northern philanthropic organizations such as the George Peabody

Foundation, the Jeanes Foundation, and the General Education Board invested hundreds of thousands of dollars in educational reform for black Americans. As a result of postemancipation efforts to reform African American education, early twentieth-century white southern reformers began to point out that poor illiterate whites in the South suffered from similar deficiencies and deserved equal attention.

In addition, the federal government increasingly took an active interest in the nation's rural problems, which drew attention to the South. In 1895 the U.S. Senate held hearings and issued a long report on the conditions of cotton growers based on extensive testimony and surveys. In 1908 President Theodore Roosevelt established the Commission on Country Life to assess the nature of rural life in the United States. The U.S. Department of Agriculture (USDA) worked for decades to reform the condition of cotton farmers in the South and elsewhere. A global circuit of agricultural reformers traveled and exchanged ideas about rural problems in such places as the southern states, Puerto Rico, Hawaii, the Philippines, China, Japan, and South Africa. Federal intervention in the South may have been minimal in comparison to Reconstruction, but the commitment to reform was no less significant and highlighted the region's worst features thereby encouraging continued involvement. In this context, the use of social scientific knowledge consolidated and legitimized the power of the federal government.

The reliance on social scientific knowledge represented a major conceptual shift in the western intellectual tradition and created a context for talking about and responding to the problems of the South. In the late nineteenth-century theories of sociocultural evolutionism, which generated ideas about the nature of progress, the origins of civilization, and the relationship between civilization and savagery predominated. New forms of social scientific knowledge gaining credence within the European and American intellectual community set the context for discussions about the lack of advancement in the New South.[13] Fascination with the "southern problem" appeared during an era marked by an absolute faith in abundance, progress, and the value of scientific solutions. Paradoxically, the centralization of the federal government destabilized the process of nationalization since the burgeoning liberal state now had the capacity systematically to identify and resolve problems that might hinder the very creation of that liberal state. The consolidation of new scientific vocabularies and models made identification of those problems possible and highlighted distinctions that previously might have been disregarded. The professionalization of such disciplines as sociology, history, economics, political science, anthropology, and medicine created experts interested in surveying, mapping, and analyzing "the South." Reformers relied on scientific experts in the realm of public health, agriculture, education, and race relations to classify and define the backward degraded region in contrast to the industrial progressive nation.[14] They identified the South as a target of "rational interventions" and strove to push the region along a more sophisticated evolutionary path. In the process of reconstructing the South reformers discovered that many of the problems were not only regionally distinctive but of greater magnitude than they had anticipated. The expansion of the regulatory state acted as a powerful microscope, serving to magnify the ills of the region. Persistent interest in resolving the "southern problem" reveals that Progressivism was not a uniform national impulse but a movement with heterogeneous goals rooted in an enduring belief in regional distinctions.[15] In short, the notion of southern distinctiveness was central to Progressive ideology.[16]

It is no coincidence that the interventionist state's efforts to solve the "southern problem" and reformers' increasing reliance on social scientific methodology occurred during the Age of Empire and an expanding global economy. The spatial projection of American power during the height of western imperialism drew attention to the significance of place and infused regionalist discourse with new life. For example, the American discourse surrounding problems such as the "Philippines problem" encouraged some reformers, government experts, and social scientists to think about the South as a particular manifestation of a broader problem around the globe. The annexation of the Philippines in 1900 and subsequent establishment of a colonial government leading to the passage of the Jones Act (1916), where the U.S. government ultimately ceded sovereignty to the Philippines, overlapped with the most intensive wave of southern reform from 1900 to 1914. During the late nineteenth and early twentieth centuries, the United States also turned to the North Atlantic world, and even countries as far away as China and Japan, for borrowed concepts and models of reform. Daniel T. Rodgers has explained how capitalism and the circulation of goods in the Progressive Era tied together a shared set of policy choices, political debates, and intellectual influences. He notes that between the 1890s and World War II Americans "did not swim in problems," rather "they swam in a sudden abundance of solutions, a vast number of them brought over through the Atlantic connection."[17]

The traditional understanding of southern history in this period inevitably frames the trajectory of the South along a North–South binary, but rather than looking at the relationship between the South and the nation on a regional and national scale it is more useful to broaden the units of analysis. It makes more sense to locate southern history in a complex web of intersecting regional, national, and global discourse, practices, and designs. Our understanding of the relationship between the South and the nation shifts as we step back from the simple binary framework that has long dominated the field of southern history.[18] *The Problem South* situates itself within the body of scholarship on global Progressive reform and colonial and postcolonial studies, particularly the recent influence of postcolonialism on the field of southern studies.[19] I use the words "transnational" and "global" interchangeably to capture the movement of peoples, patterns of governance, reform practices, racial ideologies, and social scientific theories that circulated between the United States and other countries including the overseas colonies.[20] Thus, my work is not a true comparative history between the South and other countries.[21] It is a study of the ways in which both discourse and actions taken by reformers constituted a symbiotic relationship and cast the South as a distinctive place in relationship to the rest of the country, even as this reform and rhetoric drew attention to the similarities between the region and transoceanic locales at the peak of empire.

Postcolonial and colonial studies offer a way to understand the paradox of the New South. On the surface, the South does not appear to fit this framework, with the possible exception of Reconstruction.[22] Yet even following Reconstruction, several features of the "southern problem" were colonial in nature or at the very least they were *perceived* to be colonial. First, some areas of the South in the late nineteenth and early twentieth centuries mirrored a colonial economy. The infusion of northern capital, the production of raw materials for the market, and low wages kept these southern areas in an economically subordinate position. I do not mean to suggest that the entire southern economy was colonial in nature. What is more important is that observers of the region sometimes viewed the region as a colonial economy even if it did not always function strictly as a dependent market.[23] For example, New South and national claims that cotton (as a distinctive crop) would generate great wealth for the nation was rooted in a belief in the rich extractive possibilities of the southern states. Second, both northerners and liberal southerners viewed and referred to themselves as missionaries seeking to modernize the South and uplift poor whites and poor blacks. The region became a colossal laboratory for social change and "civilizing missions."[24] Federal and scientific experts officially initiated reform in the region, including efforts from the USDA, including the Bureau of Plant Industry and Bureau of Entomology; the Extension Service's involvement with the Farmers' Cooperative Demonstration Work; and public health workers affiliated with the Rockefeller Sanitary Commission for the Eradication of Hookworm and the International Health Board. These institutions often worked in conjunction with liberal indigenous and expatriate southerners. Third, the South's problems attracted an array of northern, European, and South African travelers who spent weeks to months journeying through the region publicizing its needs and drawing comparisons, even while they marked the region as a retrograde space.[25] All of this took place within the context of American empire, a moment in which America's conceptual and geographic boundaries were quite fluid.[26] At the turn of the century, the South was viewed as both foreign and American, emblematic of backwardness and progress.

Taken from another perspective, the features that underscore the South's distinctiveness are not unique when viewed through the lens of postcolonialism. Indeed, more than fifty years ago, C. Vann Woodward noted that "the South had undergone an experience that it could share with no other part of America—though it is shared by nearly all the peoples of Europe and Asia—the experience of military defeat, occupation, and reconstruction."[27] Jon Smith and Deborah Cohn argue for a more expansive interpretation of Woodward's statement, suggesting that we "define 'America' hemispherically" and "include the African American experience of defeat under slavery," not just the "southern white men's surrender at Appomattox."[28] This book contends that the South was not just a distinctive region in an exceptional country, nor did the South simply mirror problems traditionally thought to be quintessential American problems. It was a region that shared commonalities or perceived commonalities with other countries and cultures. Transnational discourses and parallel practices of reform in public health, agriculture, education, and race relations proffer evidence of the unexceptional relationship the United States had with the South. My goal is to move beyond the framework of American exceptionalism and illuminate historiographical misconceptions about a narrow belief in southern distinctiveness.[29]

In summary, the central paradox of the New South was the fact that persistent poverty and cultural backwardness seemed to go hand-in-hand with progress and the development of national industrial ideas. The case studies in this book demonstrate that sectional reunification was a process of reform and contestation that involved juxtaposing the image of the Problem South with the image of a national industrial democracy. In rethinking the relationship of the North and South at the turn of the century, we can better understand the development of the modern liberal state over the course of the twentieth century and how and why the federal government, often in collaboration with corporations, philanthropies, or reform organizations, justified intervention on the local level at key historical moments. The turn of the century proved to be a significant moment when the welfare and well-being of the South was deemed crucial to the nation's health. Reformers and government experts abandoned a strictly political interest in the region and began to focus on the social and economic deficiencies that had not been resolved as a result of Reconstruction. The rise of corporate liberalism, the consolidation of the regulatory state, the expansion of international foreign policies, and the powerful new tools of social science reinvigorated questions that many thought had been laid to rest: How easily could the South be incorporated into the nation-state? What place would the African American population have in the American nation? Would the region's economy wind up weakening or fortifying the national and international economies? Reformers and federal authorities raised new questions too, such as: What should be done with the growing population of backward poor whites? Emancipation and Reconstruction had failed to resolve completely the question of race, and despite the powerful forces of cultural reunion the issue continued to press upon the American national imagination.

Furthermore, anxieties about the faltering economy, a weak labor force, racial degeneration among whites, waning Anglo-Saxon superiority, the decline of civilization, and the dilemmas associated with the extension of democracy in the South begin to make more sense when we situate them within the context of turn-of-the-century understandings of the tropics and colonial settings. Efforts by colonial administrators and reformers to survey and map unfamiliar topographies paralleled similar practices in the southern states. In short, the wider question being considered was: How does one incorporate a backward region or colonial possession, and at what status, into a modernizing nation? The history of the Problem South demonstrates that liberal social reform and imperial expansion were mutually constitutive.

I would like to offer a note on some of the terms and concepts used in this book such as regionalism, sectionalism, imperialism, colonialism, neo-orientalism, southern, and the South. This book is a story about how a particular idea of the South evolved in the late nineteenth and early twentieth centuries, and I will sometimes refer to the region as such. Prior to 1980, the region was simply thought of as "the South." In the early 1980s some scholars (many of whom were British) began to refer to the region as the American South. In the 1990s other scholars introduced the concept of the U.S. South, noting that the southern states were, in fact, part of a broader hemispheric American South that included the Caribbean, Mexico, Latin America, and South America. As Fred Hobson has written, "In fact, to that more encompassing South, the U.S. South is essentially *el norte*. All is relative, all depends on the point of view" when considering how we define the idea of the South.[30] I recognize that the southern states are diverse with regard to topography, race, economy, politics, and history, and I do not wish to replicate a vision of a monolithic, isolated South. But there will be times when no other vocabulary exists to reference the geographical space that we know as the southern states and so I will often use the phrase "the South." When I need to make it clear that the South, as referred to by the historical actors or myself, is to be understood in a global context I will use the phrase the "U.S. South." To avoid perpetuating a mythological and traditionally unspoken race-specific notion of "southerner," I refer to groups as either black southerners or white southerners where relevant.

In the past two decades, a group of interdisciplinary scholars have revitalized the question of regionalism and the concept of regions as useful categories of historical analysis. These scholars of the "new regional studies" are interested in reworking older models; incorporating familiar methodological frameworks such as race, class, and gender along with region; and, recently, drawing connections between regional communities and global concerns. Much of this literature focuses on the cultural and social construction of regions and regional identity as well as emphasizes the unstable, fluid, and sometimes fragmented nature of regionalism.[31] Of course, the history of the South as an imagined construct is hardly new, and scholars have long debated the existence of regionally distinctive features of the South.[32] Regions, then, are both symbolic and material entities. Notwithstanding the recent interdisciplinary interest in regionalism, the long-standing preoccupation with the distinctiveness debate in the field of southern history has pushed many scholars to declare regionalism a tired, stale tool of analysis and to question whether the concept has possibly outlived its usefulness in the case of the South.[33] In using regionalism as a framework for understanding the place of the New South in the nation-state, I am not interested in reinvesting life in timeworn debates. Much of the scholarship on the South and regionalism in the late nineteenth and early twentieth centuries tends to focus on the evolution and continuation of a regional identity: namely, how southerners collectively viewed themselves as a distinctive region or people. This book explores the development of a *regional image* of the South projected against a national and international backdrop rather than the formation of a specific *regional identity*. It explains how reformers shaped and acted in response to the image of the Problem South but does not attempt to answer the question of whether or not the South was a materially distinctive place or how and why southerners have come to view themselves as different from other Americans.

In the context of American history, regionalism and sectionalism are understood to be opposing concepts. As Howard W. Odum noted in 1934, "regionalism envisages the Nation first, making the national culture and welfare the final arbiter" whereas "sectionalism sees the region first and the nation afterwards."[34] Reformers committed to resolving the problems of the South often viewed sectionalism as an impediment to nation-state formation and considered it provincial, antagonistic, and defensive. In the late nineteenth and early twentieth centuries, sectionalism was typically associated with the South although some liberals blamed the North for harboring sectional proclivities too. Edgar Gardner Murphy, a clergyman, child labor opponent, and educational reformer in Alabama, was quick to point out that the country as a whole tended to view the North as the nation, thereby showing "a Northern sectionalism as offensive as any sectionalism in the southern states."[35] Albert Bushnell Hart, a historian at Harvard University, son of an Ohio abolitionist, and the dissertation adviser of W. E. B. Du Bois, noted that the three regions of the North, Midwest, and West were often lumped together as "the

North" to the exclusion of the South, thereby reinforcing the belief in southern sectionalism.[36]

Regionalism, in this period, did not become subordinate to nationalism; the two conceptual categories existed in close embrace. Regional images help frame national ideologies and each reinforces the contours of the other. Regions as material or ideological entities cannot be divorced from nation-states because the use of the word "region" implies that it is a part of some whole. Scholars of the "new regional studies" make few distinctions between region and section and view them both as destabilizing by nature. They describe something local and particular, and this is always set in contrast to something national and general. The region is often viewed as backward and a potentially catastrophic space, yet it also is considered to be the custodian of tradition. Paradoxically, it is a site of authenticity but reflects a nostalgic yearning for the past. Regionalism tends to be disruptive and discontinuous because the region stands in opposition to the nation and because regions are simultaneously represented as backward and as having something valuable and traditional to contribute to the established whole.[37] Consequently, we cannot begin to understand nation-state formation in the wake of Reconstruction, nor can we account for the paradoxical and entangled existence of the images of the Problem South and the reconciled New South, without the framework of regionalism.[38] The creation of a regional image of the Problem South reflected efforts by the liberal state to fashion a national identity. While "invented traditions" and "imagined communities" play a role in structuring national political culture, defining national citizenship and belonging has as much to do with exclusion and demarcating boundaries as it does with a focus on common memories and shared conventions.[39] The nation-state is partly defined by what it is not.

The process of identifying the "southern problem" was also, in my view, a project of southern neo-orientalism. Indeed, historians and geographers of the South have used Edward Said's theory of Orientalism to understand hegemonic representations of the region generated by northern middle-class travelers as the antithesis of the North.[40] What I mean by the concept of southern neo-orientalism is the way in which the South was marked as the negative antipode of the United States by a large assembly of social scientific, literary, political, and federal commentators who understood and often recognized each other's critical work on the region. Indeed, this group discovered the South much like Said's Orientalists discovered the Orient, and the differences could be easily quantified and marked. The power of southern neo-orientalism lay in its ability to represent itself as the static truth as well as its ability to use binary oppositions, thereby generating a collective understanding of the Other. Recognizable vocabularies, tropes, and impressions helped constitute the idea of the South. Southern neo-orientalism was both an image of the South as well as an extensive body of formal knowledge collected and discussed by the group identified above who often referenced and referred to each other.[41] It lent authority to those interested in reforming the region and remaking it along the lines of the North.

Edward Said's well-known book *Orientalism* influenced the field of colonialism and postcolonialism significantly. Colonialism is a form of imperialism that involves the settlement of people on foreign soil, the exercise of power over the indigenous occupants of the land, and the economic exploitation of the area's resources. As Said has shown, it also involves using discourse and knowledge as tools of control. I understand imperialism as a much broader expression of expansive political, cultural, and economic power of which colonialism is simply one specific modus operandi. *The Problem South* is interested in demonstrating what John McLeod describes as "the ways in which *material reality* and *cultural representations*—the conditions of the world and the knowledge we make about the world—are always intertwined and mutually supportive."[42] Efforts to repair the South's educational deficiencies, reconstruct its public health system, reconcile the "race problem" with the principles of American democracy, cultivate a healthy labor force, and build and sustain an economy capable of generating regional and national wealth resonated with colonial practices initiated in international settings.

One caveat is in order here. The fields of postcolonial and colonial studies as applied to the South are problematic to some degree. The region symbolically and historically has existed as both the colonizer and the colonized.[43] In using these frameworks we have to be very careful not to replicate white southern visions of what came to pass during and after Reconstruction. In this story line, white southerners were the victims of a dominant colonial North that imposed "Negro rule" upon the South, leaving the region prostrate, humiliated, and debased. This conventional narrative celebrates the establishment of "home rule" (white supremacy) in the South and white southerners throwing off triumphantly the yoke of northern oppression. It conveniently neglects to address the context in which this occurred—the unwarranted, systematic, violent domination of black southerners through legal and extralegal means. I do not mean to suggest that white southerners responsible for instituting Jim Crow and disfranchisement are colonial subjects and possible victims. Furthermore, it can be argued that the antebellum South harbored imperial tendencies itself, as reflected in the efforts of wealthy white plantation owners to expand the institution of slavery further West and in proslavery advocates' proposal to enlarge the slave empire through the acquisition of Cuba and parts of Mexico. The danger in using terms such as "postcolonial" and "colonial" is that they are so elastic as to become conceptually useless. The South is not a foreign country nor was it a colonial possession. The South was American, and even though it was viewed as peripheral, it existed geographically within the contiguous borders of the United States. Most Americans certainly assumed that one day (if it had not arrived already) the South would stand on equal footing with the rest of the United States. The same cannot be said for the colonial possessions.

Still, the model of colonialism is a suitable tool for understanding the place of the U.S. South in the late nineteenth and early twentieth centuries. The social and cultural mapping of the region provided a template for reform and much like scholars have noted in other colonial settings the South became a laboratory for modernity. Consideration of the U.S. South as a unique locale warranting reform was not simply sustained by drawing contrasts between the region and the American nation-state. Americans viewed the U.S. South and other foreign countries as parallel aberrant geographical spaces in need of rehabilitation in the colonial world. What this demonstrates is that the U.S. South was clearly not the exception within American exceptionalism.

CHAPTER ONE

The "Southern Problem" and Readjustment

I pause here only to protest against that crudity of impatience with which the world has so largely observed the development of Southern life.

Expecting within the brief period of a generation the entire re-creation of our industrial fortunes and of our political institutions, men have waited to see the whole character of a civilization doffed like an outer garment; the fabric of a new order — involving the deepest issues of memory, of passion, of pride, of racial and social habit — instantly re-created upon a strange loom.

— EDGAR GARDNER MURPHY

Facing back over Southern history is not cheering. Facing forward is trying to the stoutest-hearted optimism. The fallacy in most of our debating is, in fact, the fallacy of willful optimism. We have constantly assumed that there was a solution of each problem as it presented itself, a clearly right thing to do, which could also be done.

— WILLIAM GARROTT BROWN

In the first decade of the twentieth century President Theodore Roosevelt wrote, "The problem of any one part of our great common country should be held to be the problem of all our country."[1] Roosevelt's statement echoed what many Americans had already come to believe, that the southern United States was a problem of great magnitude, and one the nation would do well to resolve. This was not the first time that Americans had set the South apart at odds with the rest of the nation. As early as the eighteenth century, northerners and southerners drew attention to the inherent differences between North and South. During the antebellum period, abolitionists, free labor Republicans, and travelers to the South often portrayed the region in a negative light, emphasizing its backwardness, licentiousness, and extreme poverty. However, in the late nineteenth and early twentieth centuries the problem of the South elicited far greater attention than it ever had before, with the possible exception of Reconstruction. Various social scientists and academics, regional and national associations, northern philanthropies, and federal agencies identified an array of problems and articulated a host of solutions. The South was transformed into a mission field and an immense laboratory for social and cultural change.

Efforts on the part of reformers to draw attention to the South's shortcomings and make them known to the rest of the world generated a discourse about the Problem South that played counterpoint to national progressive ideals. Most Americans understood the nature of the "southern problem"; the phrase conjured up an image of a backward, poverty-stricken region that stood in contrast to the rest of the nation. This discourse on the problem of the South inspired real people and institutions to engage in reform of politics, the economy, and social relations. The development of a set of cultural representations and the inauguration of reform continued to reinforce one another symbiotically. The Problem South was simultaneously a discourse and a material reality acted upon by identifiable groups of people. Although the South itself varied tremendously in terms of topography, racial demography, social relations, labor arrangements, and economic development, people came to view the region as a timeless entity marred by region-wide problems. In his discussion on the problem of the South, Larry J. Griffin argues that "in no other case . . . were social problems so intimately related, even equated, in the public mind to a particular region for so sustained a period of time that the region itself—rather than the objective conditions—became commonly understood as the 'real' problem."[2]

As the introduction to this book notes, the ascendancy of this vision of southern regionalism cannot be divorced from the profound transformations in American society that contributed to a new sense of nationalism. Growing urbanization, the rise of big business, the expansion of the railroad system, new patterns of immigration, revolutionary technological achievements, and the spread of American empire encouraged Americans to reassess the concepts of nation and Americanism. The identification of an array of regional problems peculiar to the South—high rates of illiteracy, diseased bodies, white degeneration, a backward rural economy, and racial tensions — complicated the nationalist project since these southern idiosyncrasies came to be viewed as immutable, essential natural differences. Reformers and government experts found themselves facing seemingly irreconcilable circumstances. Belief in the timeless, distinctive quality of the South's problems ran contrary to the objective of an imagined national community marked by homogeneity, comradeship, and communal experience. Later chapters examine in more detail the nature of some of these specific southern problems.

The traditional historical narrative suggests that sectional reunion between North and South, economic progress, and racial harmony as embodied in the New South creed was the dominant mythology of the late nineteenth and twentieth centuries; but in fact this optimistic mythology was perpetually under assault by the image of the backward Problem South. In reality, the evolution of these two competing mythologies — the Problem South and the reconciled New South — were two sides of the same coin. It was not uncommon for optimistic New South ideologues to offer contradictory assertions about southern progress in their propaganda and to note possible areas of exception or for critics to praise the region for the great strides it had already made. Oftentimes, the two strains of thought coalesced. All agreed that the South had suffered tremendous devastation at the conclusion of the Civil War. No one disputed the importance of integrating the region into the liberal nation-state or the goal of creating a homogeneous American populace in which sectional boundaries did not exist. The boosters and critics shared a fundamental belief in the importance of evolutionary progress toward a higher and better state of being, and they both described the region as moving through a period of extended transition. What they disagreed about was the nature and extent of the progress being made in the South and the degree to which lingering sectionalism impeded it. In short, the questions being dissected were: How new (or like the North) was the New South, if at all? What role would the South play in the nation-state? Would the process of reunification occur with ease and goodwill or be marked by great difficulty? Both critics and boosters grappled with the paradoxical nature of the postbellum South — the fact that poverty and progress seemed to exist simultaneously. In a sense, attention to the Problem South was a variation on the process of sectional reunion and one that proved to be a national project in constant flux.

Finally, the paradox of the New South involved not just the constant strain between the sanguine New South creed and the representation of the backward South but also the struggle to counterbalance the belief that the South was American in spite of regional characteristics that appeared to mirror alien conditions in distant lands. As late as 1913 the *New York Sun* reported that "the South was still regarded by many in the North as a foreign and very turbulent country."[3] Ironically, images of southern regional dysfunction and depictions of the South as a potentially dangerous foreign country were used to shore up the nationalist vision. The identification of regional pathologies played a crucial role in liberal nation-state construction and cannot be separated from the expansion of American empire in the same period. The image of the South — as alien, problematic, and retrograde — served as a foil to the nation-state. Like the alleged backward traits of the overseas colonies and certain Asian countries, the region's economic and social problems were continually measured against American norms. The tendency on the part of reformers and detractors to frequently refer to themselves as missionaries only reinforced the sense of the South as another country. By underscoring un-American values they could illuminate the model of American citizenship even while they worked to reform and erase those very regional differences.

The New South Gospel of Progress

In the 1880s it appeared the emphasis on national reconciliation and industrial progress in the South marked the direction of the future. Most New South ideologues and northern capitalists spoke in glowing terms of the South's admission to the Union. By the 1890s New South boosters and northern capitalists' belief in the successful reunion of the North and South had reached a fever pitch. Together they pointed to certain features of the New South as evidence of this triumphant reconciliation including the rapid economic recovery of the region. They argued that economic distinctions among regions had virtually evaporated and that the South had lost its former distinctive qualities. In 1890 Richard H. Edmonds, editor of the *Manufacturer's Record*, published a pamphlet titled *The South's Redemption: From Poverty to Prosperity*. The caption beneath the title described the development of the New South: "In 1860 the Richest Part of the Country — In 1870 the Poorest — In 1880 Signs of Improvement — In 1889 Regaining the Position of 1860." Edmonds described the South as a cornucopia of wealth and declared that the region was destined to become the "richest country upon the globe." The New South's advantages and resources included its soil, climate, minerals, iron, coal, timber, abundant rainfall, and healthfulness.[4]

Edmonds and other visionaries celebrated the achievements of the post-bellum South and praised the energy and enterprise of a new generation of white southerners struggling to improve their fortunes. The *Manufacturer's Record*, established in 1882 and published in Baltimore, became the mouth-piece for this newfound optimism and a platform from which to defend the South. Businessmen reporting on recent advances in the region wrote glow-ing editorials about southern opulence and prosperity. Frederic Taylor, a lead-ing banker from New York, remarked that while in the South "'we traveled through a continuous and unbroken strain of what has been aptly termed the music of progress — the whirr [sic] of the spindle, the buzz of the saw, the roar of the furnace, and the throb of the locomotive.'" He also praised the efforts of the young men working in the South for change and noted "'the eager, earnest, restless, driving energy which seems to fill them.'"[5] Others were equally sanguine. Richard A. McCurdy, president of the Mutual Life Insurance Company in New York, noted, "The Southern people possess a re-gion unsurpassed on the earth in its natural resources. With the intelligence and energy which characterize them, these resources ought during the next generation to experience a development which will place them among the foremost communities of the civilized world in wealth and happiness."[6] This effervescent belief in southern progress was not simply confined to social commentators but also could also be found in corroborative testimony pro-vided by the federal government. Members of the U.S. Treasury Department, State Department, Department of the Interior, Department of Agriculture, Senate, and House of Representatives all reported on the remarkable com-mercial and industrial growth in the South. Northern capitalists and south-ern apostles of industrial development foresaw a golden age of growth and abundance in the South in cotton manufacturing, coal mining, timber, and the iron industry.[7] Such titles as *How to Get Rich in the South. Telling What to Do, How to Do It, and the Profits Realized* or *Road to Wealth Leads through the South* advertised the promise of the New South for those who would seize the initiative. Countless books, pamphlets, and articles outlining the poten-tial of the New South rejoiced in the modernization of the region and offered endless columns of statistics and detailed charts proving the soundness of their predictions.

Many New South spokesmen described the South as America's new frontier — a replacement for the West, which had already fulfilled its potential. Industrial advancement had been so rapid in the South, Edmonds argued, that prominent capitalists in Europe and America had gone to "spy out the land" and were seeking information on every phase of southern growth. The call was no longer "'Go West, young man,' but 'Go South.'"[8] In 1888, William D. Kelley, a congressman and industrialist from Pennsylvania, published a book titled *The Old South and the New* in which he declared the South "the coming El Dorado of American adventure." Even though he was a former abolitionist and Republican, Kelley's praise of the South's abundant resources and future prospects won him the respect of native white southerners. He became a regular contributor to the *Manufacturer's Record* and his call to conquer the "El Dorado of American adventure" turned out to be a rallying cry for New South boosters who frequently referenced his remarks. Kelley recalled that it was the "building of an empire in the West that relieved and enriched the East." Now that the West had been developed, the United States needed a new field of investment. The country had to find a new and larger market for the surplus in the North, Kelley argued, whether that surplus was in the form of capital, "future productions of labor," or "labor itself." He advocated investment in the New South and considered the region to be more abundant in resources and wealth than even the historical West.[9] Almost two decades later, the *World's Work* published an article titled "The Arisen South" championing a similar sentiment. The first sentence declared boldly, "The present industrial awakening in the Southern States is the most important economic event in our history since the settlement of the West."[10] In many ways, New South rhetoric resonated with nineteenth-century myths about the West as a place where men triumphed over the frontier, extracted precious economic resources, and spread American democratic values. Kelley's use of the word "empire" in describing the development of the West and South was not coincidental. Indeed it presaged by five years the statement issued by Frederick Jackson Turner that "American history has been in large degree the colonization of the Great West" and his suggestion that with the conquering of the frontier the United States must turn to new resources and markets overseas.[11]

While the pro-industrial rhetoric of New South ideologues occasionally flirted with the language of empire and colonization, the proponents of the New South creed stressed the importance of industrial development in minimizing sectional differences and fashioning a unified nation. In that sense, any colonization of the region would be temporary since ultimately the colonized region would be integrated economically into the United States on an equal level. In 1908 Samuel C. Mitchell, professor of history at Richmond College and later president of the University of South Carolina, wrote an article on the "nationalization of southern sentiment" in which he argued that in order to nationalize the South it needed to be industrialized. Mitchell warned of the dangers of provincially, rather than nationally, oriented sections since a provincial region would inevitably be reduced to a state of dependency on the nation-state. He opined that the advancement of industry in the New South would lead to the development of a unified nation-state in which no part was dependent upon the other and all parts were equal.[12] Early twentieth-century conclusions about the role industrial development played in minimizing regional distinctions and creating a national democracy were ideological vestiges of the New South philosophy first articulated in the 1880s. The commitment to the modernization of the South lay in the desire to minimize the region's rural aristocratic tendencies and eliminate its economic reliance on the North. Paradoxically it was possible to talk about the South as a provincial dependent section while championing a unified nation-state rooted in commercial democracy. Thus, it was the *process* of colonization, not a permanent state of colonization, which would enable the country to utilize the resources and wealth of the South as part of the process of nationalization.

Support for commercial development and the abolition of sectionalism led to parallel expressions of exuberance in other regions. Some northerners extolled the development of a New North. In a special issue of the *South Atlantic Quarterly*, the editorial staff (which included Edwin Mims and William G. Glasson) along with Hamilton Wright Mabie, a literary critic and associate editor of *Outlook Magazine*, wrote extensively about the ways in which the North had changed alongside the South. The editors reported that nationalism was strong in the New North and that victory in the Spanish-American War, increasing commercial prosperity, and a strong political party in control of the government fostered a strong patriotism in the North.[13] In his piece, which Mabie described as having been written in "hot haste," the New North had forgiven the Old South and recognized that the "Old South was as high-minded, disinterested, and conscientious as the Old North." The New North also acknowledged that Reconstruction had been a tragic mistake, encouraged the belief that both the North and South shared the initial burden of slavery, and affirmed that all states should have the right to decide their own conditions of citizenship. Mabie celebrated the new spirit of "mutual comprehension and sympathy" that permitted the men of the New South and New North to come together as a nation and put aside the sectionalism of the past.[14] Robert Bingham, a North Carolina educator, believed that the merger of a New North, New South, New East, and New West into a "New National America" would erase the race question and all other problems regarding the South. He concluded that the "evil spirit of sectional America" would dissolve in the twentieth century as residents of the various sections joined forces and celebrated the supremacy of the nation-state.[15] Two years later, with his commitment to the union solidified, Bingham refused an invitation to speak about his experience as a prisoner of war at a meeting of the United Daughters of the Confederacy and resisted seeing Thomas Dixon's popular play *The Clansman* since there was no use in "exhuming a dead and putrid corpse."[16]

Those southerners and northerners who celebrated the great industrial strides being made by the New South tended to view the South as distinctly American. They based their argument on the South's supposed identification with whiteness — a claim that ignored the region's black population and focused attention on the North's immigrant population. Historically, Americans have tended to equate Americanism with whiteness.[17] Henry Grady, one of the most recognized New South spokesmen, declared in a speech before the American Bankers Association in 1883 that the South was "simply a geographic expression" and no longer a land with a peculiar breed of people.[18] Ten years later the *Arena* printed an article boldly declaring "The South is American," in which the author Joshua W. Caldwell concluded that "the strongest, most concentrated force of Americanism is in the South" and that "there is no part of the globe, except the kingdom of England, which is so thoroughly Anglo-Saxon as the South."[19] Holland Thompson, a southern industrialist, argued that what made the South "overwhelmingly American" was its lack of a foreign-born population.[20] Later critics of the New South spokesmen's celebration of whiteness would address two faults with these assertions. First, the great mass of poor whites in the South offered evidence that the Anglo-Saxon race was not as sturdy and superior a stock as in the North. Second, the persistence of interracial sex in the region — a product of continuous contact between two distinct races — pointed to the lack of purity among the races in the South.

When New South ideologues did acknowledge the presence of blacks (a population that was difficult to ignore no matter how hard white southerners tried to erase them from the record), they usually took a less reactionary stance than many of the racial demagogues. New South spokesmen who defended white supremacy believed in the inherent inferiority of southern blacks and had no desire to overturn the basic underlying racial structure of the South. But they also believed the future economic prosperity of the region depended on cooperation between the races. Wallace Putnam Reed from Atlanta, Georgia, writing in the Boston *Independent*, believed that the peculiar racial conditions of the New South could not last forever. Over the course of time racial conflict would "cease to be a disturbing factor" when the increasing white population outnumbered blacks by three to one and the South progressed along commercial and industrial lines.[21] Some of these New South men believed commercial development in the region was the key to solving the "race problem" since each race desired upward mobility. If the races could learn to cooperate with one another, the reduction in racial tensions would permit the New South to progress to a more industrially advanced state like the North. All New South proponents linked racial problems with sectionalism and thus the commitment to nationalism entailed a fervent belief in the fiction of goodwill between the races. This paternalistic component of the New South creed also resonated quite nicely with Booker T. Washington's philosophy of racial uplift and accommodation. Any evidence of racial problems in the South marked the region as distinctive and sectional; likewise, true Americanism or nationalism entailed the absence of any kind of racial hostility or friction.

In general, the New South philosophy's stress on the great industrial strides being made in the South, the importance of sectional reconciliation, the need for racial harmony, and the celebration of the superiority of the Anglo-Saxon race dovetailed rather easily with dominant American values. The New South creed in the 1880s and the culture of reunion in the 1890s rejoiced in the mythology of the romantic plantation South and celebrated the memory of the Civil War, honoring both northern and southern soldiers. Travel literature circulating outside the South promoted vacations in this genteel traditional world, and narratives of reunions between lovers from previously antagonistic sections helped bridge the divide between North and South. These ideologies and mythologies appeared to leave no room for ideas about a Problem South or any sense of paradox. Paul Gaston writes in *The New South Creed* that among the New South ideologues there was "no appreciation of the enigma noted by concerned social critics of the period: the association of poverty with material progress."[22] But, in point of fact, the story of the mythology of the South in the late nineteenth and early twentieth centuries is more complicated and nuanced than the one told by Gaston. Social critics certainly noted the paradox of the New South. The proponents of the New South creed also were aware of the contradictory nature of the region and occasionally sprinkled their optimistic commentary with denunciation of the South's most intractable problems. Often their allusion to southern problems was simply a matter of degree.

Early Hints of the "Southern Question"

In the midst of talk about the New South industrial creed and the reconciliation of North and South, conflicting voices could be heard. The image of a region beset with problems played counterpoint to the New South mythology. Indeed, the paradox of the South was multilayered. Within New South ideology itself, the South could be regionally unique because of its former conquered status and its newly industrialized nature, but also it was simultaneously the most white and American of all sections. On a national level, the South was viewed as being as patriotic and nationalistic as the North, but it was also seen as an undeveloped backward region with residual problems that continually threatened unification of the nation-state. In the late 1870s and 1880s, uneasy detractors began to raise questions about what they identified as the "southern question" or "southern problem." In the beginning, this criticism and concern was faint. Strains of this nascent disapproval reflected the former objectives of Reconstruction as well as the interests of a few southern white liberals and black intellectuals who displayed the courage to speak out against the overwhelming tide of New South optimism. Some of these early skeptics included Albion Tourgée, George Washington Cable, D. Augustus Straker, and Walter Hines Page. Page would go on to become one of the leading proponents of reforming southern problems in the first two decades of the twentieth century.

One of the earliest critics in the post-Reconstruction period was Albion Tourgée, who served in the Union Army and in 1865 moved to Walter Hines Page's home state of North Carolina to purchase a plantation and participate in the new political system. Tourgée became a well-known political figure over the next few decades as he championed black rights, helped redraft the state's constitution in 1868, rewrote state law as a code commissioner, served as state superior court judge, and later argued Homer Plessy's case against segregation before the Supreme Court in *Plessy v. Ferguson* (1896). Throughout his life Tourgée pursued what biographer Mark Elliott has described as "color-blind justice."[23] In addition, Tourgée edited several newspapers over the course of his career and published many novels, including an anonymous account of a "carpetbagger" in North Carolina, *A Fool's Errand by One of the Fools* (1879). In many ways, his writings marked the beginning of liberal northern interest in southern problems in the post-Reconstruction period, although his concern was as much about education and industrial promise as it was a critique of the limits of the Radical Republican agenda. *A Fool's Errand* followed the story of the Fool (Comfort Servosse), a northern Republican, who moves to the South at the end of the Civil War only to discover the cowardice of moderate congressional Republicans who would not commit to using the full force of the federal government in establishing a free labor system, instituting national public education, or thwarting the violent efforts of white southerners' to restrict the civil and political rights of the former slaves. Described by *Appletons' Journal* as "sectional fiction," the book portrayed the North and South as two vastly divergent civilizations.[24] In explaining to a former mentor why Reconstruction was a "magnificent failure," Servosse lamented, "The North and South are simply convenient names for two distinct, hostile, and irreconcilable ideas, — two civilizations they are called, especially at the South. At the North . . . we are apt to speak of the one as civilization, and of the other as a species of barbarism. These two must always be in conflict until the one prevails, and the other fails."[25]

In 1880 Edwin L. Godkin, editor and founder of the northern-based *Nation*, penned an editorial titled "The Southern Question in the Canvass," which opened with a discussion of *A Fool's Errand*. Godkin explained how the novel demonstrated that southern whites would never accept the black man as a political equal, nor did the North have enough political force to "execute reconstruction in the spirit in which it was conceived." The mistake, according to

Tourgée, had been to treat the Southern states as states of the Union rather than as "conquered territories." In short, the existence of southern problems was due to the North's failure to fully colonize the South. Godkin agreed with Tourgée's assertion that the white majority would never cease intimidating black voters, but as a moderate Mugwump Republican who believed in limited government and opposed "waving the bloody-shirt" he did not sanction more federal intrusion. Godkin tried to downplay sectional politics by suggesting that concerned northerners should not treat the southern response to northern interference as "utterly baseless or unreasonable" since "we are asking them to face without fear a problem which no Northern State has ever been called on to face." The solution to the "southern question" involved "infusing courage into the intimidated class" and "bring[ing] Northern opinion to bear directly on the negro voters, in the form of instruction and advice from the lips of Northern men." Working to uplift the character of African Americans in the pursuit of "social and political prosperity" in the South, the editorial argued, would eventually benefit the white race. Godkin went so far as to advocate northern missionary efforts for southern whites, proclaiming "the very least we can do for both whites and blacks, therefore, is to send down some of our best speakers to tell them to their faces in what manner we think they can get out of the very serious fix in which we have placed them."[26] This editorial in the *Nation* foreshadowed the early twentieth-century interest in southern problems, which typically included retreating from an explicit defense of citizenship rights for southern blacks and concentrating on the social and benevolent side of the question through the use of propaganda.

One month later, Godkin published a second essay that focused on "The White Side of the Southern Question" and offered more advice to the Republican Party on how to woo the South and reconstitute the Union. This editorial, more than any other in the 1880s, captured the paradox of the New South. In making the call to solve southern problems in the wake of Reconstruction, Godkin endeavored to reconcile his claims that the region was both foreign in nature and American in its manners and mores. "Southern whites are humans like the rest of us," he stated, and "Providence has not created in those parts a new and peculiar human being." Indeed, a "New Yorker" was often no different than a "South-Carolinian" or "Mississippian." But Godkin noted there were "real difficulties" that constituted a distinctive "Southern problem," and he urged Republicans to give "formal recognition" to the "White question." Poor whites jeopardized the development of a "peaceful" civilization, and without "the conversion of the Southern whites to the ways and ideas of what is called the industrial stage in social progress" there would be no solution to the region's stagnation. In fact, Godkin compared this "formidable task" to "pacify the South permanently" with the efforts of abolitionists to turn public opinion against slavery in the South some fifty years before. It was a curious analogy to make but underscored the continued northern interest in rehabilitating the South and setting it on the path toward industrialization.

Finally, "there is one other consideration which must not be overlooked," Godkin warned. "The South, in the structure of its society, in its manners and social traditions, differs nearly as much from the North as Ireland does, or Hungary, or Turkey." While the North did share many similarities with the South such as "religion, law, and language," the Nation's editor emphasized the region's alien and remote qualities that Republicans would be wise to consider in seeking a solution to the "Southern problem." Ironically, "viewing the land from afar, through a very thick mist of misinformation, prejudice, and passion" had contributed to a belief that the South was not so different from the North. Godkin compared northern visitors viewing problems on the ground to statesmen developing foreign policy in response to the actions of other countries. He acknowledged that southern intolerance of northern efforts to industrialize the South would certainly be fierce but insisted it could be overcome through "the high art of persuasion."[27] The Nation's assertion that the South was essentially a nation within a nation and afflicted with two central problems — the lack of industrial progress and the question of race (both white and black as these companion pieces demonstrated) — set the basic framework for the ensuing debates about the problems of the South.

In addition, an early group of liberal white southerners took a critical approach to their region, often in the face of much backlash from their more hot-tempered neighbors. George Washington Cable, who has been referred to as the "intellectual father" of southern liberals, published numerous works of fiction as well as opinion pieces in leading journals and magazines offering sharp commentary on southern problems. He is best known for his fictional accounts of Creole life in Louisiana, an investigation into the convict lease system, and the promotion of political rights for African Americans. Although Cable grew up in New Orleans and served in the Mississippi Calvary as a Confederate soldier, he ultimately became disenchanted with New South ideology and the fiction of the Lost Cause. "What we want — what we ought to have in view," he proclaimed, "is the No South!"[28] In an 1885 address given at the University of Alabama, and later published as "The Freedmen's Case in Equity" in *Century Magazine*, Cable argued that the most prominent social problem facing the American people was the problem of the "Negro" who had been treated unjustly in the post-Reconstruction period and deserved all of the political and civil rights accorded by law.[29] Cable also came to the defense of the "Silent South," a collection of liberal southerners who, he noted, were often too frightened to speak out against the reactionary forces in the region.[30]

Walter Hines Page, another liberal southerner, became a fervent critic of the Lost Cause and chastised his fellow white southerners for clinging to the dead traditions holding the South back from making progress. In 1881, he published "Study of an Old Southern Borough," which described his hometown of Cary, North Carolina, as a place with "little animation in man or beast" and where "no original arguments, or even phrases, are brought forth." What caused these typical southern communities to fall so far behind in the world was their inability "to go backward or forward."[31] Page makes an appearance in just about every chapter of this book due to his commitment to solving southern racial, educational, agricultural, and public health problems. He was regarded by his friend Charles W. Dabney as "a sort of missionary of the gospel of progress."[32] In the 1890s he served as the editor of two northern magazines, the *Forum* and the *Atlantic Monthly*, and then returned to New York to establish his own publishing house, Doubleday, Page, & Company, and his own magazine, the *World's Work*. Page played a prominent role as an intermediary between northern philanthropists and southern reformers struggling to resolve various social problems in the region. He served on the boards of several organizations including the Southern Education Board, the General Education Board, and the Rockefeller Sanitary Commission for the Eradication of Hookworm.[33] As Scott Romine notes, "His relationship to his native region would become that of its spokesman, interpreter, and admonisher."[34]

Thus, early critics began to raise doubts about the soundness of the New South creed and encouraged a new generation of southerners and northerners to question fallacies in the mythology of the New South. The New South ideologues often spoke as if the New South mirrored the North completely and was an entirely new creation. By the late 1880s even more voices had begun to question this unrelenting optimism. In 1888 a black clergyman and lawyer named D. August Straker published a book titled *The New South Investigated.* Straker acknowledged that "the South of 1886 [was] not the South of 1850 or 1863 or even 1870." He agreed that in some ways the New South marked a beginning and signaled an era of great change and progress; however, this did "not mean that the South in its new growth is perfect and without error, as some construe the new South to mean." Remnants of the Old South lingered and hindered the region's efforts to improve. Straker's friend, the Reverend J. C. Price, president of Livingstone College in Salisbury, North Carolina, pointed out that the region more aptly deserved the title of the "New Old South."[35] Ten years later Wallace Putman Reed stated more bluntly that the New South was "simply an invention of the optimists" and did not exist. In fact, what people called the New South was "only a very thin mask concealing the features of the Old South." He asserted that it was ridiculous to "indulge in any gush about the New South" because although the "masked figure may be very conspicuous at banquets and reunions," the Old South still lay "behind the mask, ready at a moment's notice to strike a blow with the iron hand."[36] The mounting level of criticism about the newness of the New South demonstrated that by the turn of the century the ideology of the New South creed had begun to wane, even if it had not entirely faded from view. Even those who made the case for continuity between the Old South and the New South did not necessarily view these persistent southern characteristics as beneficial.

The "Southern Problem" as the Problem of the Twentieth Century

As the New South creed began to lose steam, a prominent group of white southern and northern reformers began to proclaim loudly that the problem of the twentieth century was the problem of the South. Their understanding of the "southern problem" proved to be even more expansive than that of W. E. B. Du Bois, who in 1903 aptly noted that "the problem of the twentieth century is the problem of the color line."[37] A number of titles drew national attention to the defects of the region, including *The Ills of the South* (1894) by Charles H. Otken, a Mississippi Baptist preacher; *The Problems of the Present South* (1904) by Edgar Gardner Murphy; *Sectionalism Unmasked* (1907) by Henry Edwin

Tremain, a long-standing Republican and New Yorker who served as a general in the Union Army; *The Southern South* (1910) by Albert Bushnell Hart; *The Darker Phases of the South* (1924) by Frank Tannenbaum, an economist and professor of Latin American history at Columbia University; and *The Southern Oligarchy* (1924) by William H. Skaggs, an ex-Populist, three-time mayor of Talladega, Alabama, and resident of New York. Countless newspaper and magazine articles wrestled with the dilemma of the "southern problem." Southern reform organizations, such as the Southern Sociological Congress initiated by the governor of Tennessee in 1912, held large conferences between 1912 and 1920 that brought together "representative people from the entire South interested in social welfare and for the purpose of studying and improving the social, civic and economic conditions of the South."[38] The Southern Sociological Congress collaborated with northern philanthropists to "uplift" the region, relying on both scientific study and social reform.[39] Social organizations and clubs located in the North, made up of middle-class northerners and expatriate southerners, met regularly to discuss conspicuous southern problems and to consider funding investigations and journeys designed to target regional deficiencies. Despite the focus on sectional reconciliation, a general sense of discontent, confusion, and uncertainty lingered in the air.

Discussion of the existence of a general "southern problem" typically followed three lines of inquiry: the "race question" or "race problem," the problem of economic development, and the problem of illiteracy and lack of education in the South. These three strains of discourse also addressed questions about the nature of citizenship and the significance of cultivating a strong manhood in the South. Americans identified a whole variety of other southern problems, including violence, disease, rural poverty, political stagnation, and intellectual backwardness. Many critics identified poor whites as a distinctive southern problem, although they tended to view Appalachian poor whites as a separate group with more inherently redeemable qualities. Depending on one's race, regional identity, educational background and interests, or political affiliation, the use of the phrase the "southern problem" could refer to one or all of these issues. Almost everyone considered the "race problem" to be the archetypal southern problem. The phrase the "southern problem" was consequently elusive in meaning, but at the turn of the century most Americans recognized it; the expression evoked an image of a backward, stagnant, uncivilized region that was distinct from the rest of the United States.

The discourse on the problem had become quite commonplace in the Progressive Era. One New Yorker described this period as "the age of asking questions" when people were "unwilling to do or suffer anything without seeing a reason for it." He maintained that "all sorts of people, sociologists, and churchmen, philanthropists and dreamers, practical men and cranks" were trying to find out "why?" and "how?"[40] Americans talked about the "rural life problem," the "urban problem," the "farm problem," the "child problem," the "immigration problem," the "Philippine problem," the "Indian problem," the "African problem," the "labor problem," the "Far Eastern" problem, the "race problem," the "Mexican problem," the problem of Puerto Rico, the "pellagra problem," the "problem of the West," and general "twentieth century problems."[41] The "southern problem" (which was sometimes used interchangeably with the "race problem") consistently attracted the most attention in the nation's press and over the longest period of time. Walter Hines Page explained how periodical literature and national magazines were a "very useful piece of machinery to get ideas across to the country and the world." The commercialization of this industry, he declared, required ambitious young men who were "eager to solve the multitude of 'problems' that we are forever talking about."[42] The circulation of so many newspapers and magazines at the turn of the century ensured that discussions of the "southern problem" received a wide audience.[43]

While the heart of the publishing industry lay in the North, southern liberals tried their hand at publication too. John Spencer Bassett, a history professor at Trinity College who was almost run out of the South for declaring Booker T. Washington "the greatest man, save Robert E. Lee, born in the South in a hundred years," founded the *South Atlantic Quarterly* in 1902 to provide a space for candid discussions on the region.[44] Three years later, Edwin Mims and William G. Glasson assumed command of the journal and wrote in the opening editorial "that the best service that can be rendered the South today is the giving of opportunity for the writing of well-balanced constructive criticism, as it may be applied to all phases of life." As if to instill courage and a powerful sense of obligation in their future contributors, they added, "Many intelligent Southerners have hesitated to give free expression to their opinions about Southern problems because of their dislike of publishing in Northern magazines or papers that which may, perchance, wound the feelings of the people of their own section. There has been a natural sensitiveness about any appearance of criticism from the outside rather than from an inside and sympathetic standpoint. Hence the need for the development of Southern periodicals in which Southern men may speak frankly and honestly the thing they feel."[45] However, some southern liberals discovered they could not speak as freely as they wanted to unless they departed the region and settled in the North. After moving to New York in 1885, Walter Hines Page published many articles on the South in the *Outlook, Atlantic Monthly, Forum, Century Magazine*, and *Independent* and served as editor of three different journals. During these years the "southern problem" occupied much of Page's time. The 50 issues of the *Forum* printed under Page's direction as editor contained 13 articles on the South, the 21 issues of the *Atlantic Monthly* contained 8, and the 151 issues of his own magazine *World's Work* contained 82.[46] Here was a southern liberal not afraid to publish articles by persons critical of the New South (see fig. 1).

FIGURE 1. Walter Hines Page, 1855–1918. "The Pageant of America" Photograph Archive, vol. 7. Photography Collection, Miriam and Ira D. Wallach Division of Art, Prints, and Photographs, New York Public Library, Astor, Lenox, and Tilden Foundations.

In 1906 Walter Hines Page published a fictional series in the *Atlantic Monthly* titled "The Autobiography of a Southerner since the Civil War," which told the story of Nicholas Worth, the son of a slaveholding family headed by a father with Unionist sentiments. In 1909 the serial was published as a revised book titled *The Southerner*, and readers discovered that the anonymous author of the serial was none other than Walter Hines Page.[47] Some of the scenes in the novel mirrored Page's own experience, although not all. The tale of Nicholas Worth follows his early education at a military school, knack for oratory, attendance at Harvard University, return to North Carolina, brief interludes at teaching, efforts to reform education, and unsuccessful run for public office. Worth struggles to reconcile his feelings about the South's distinctive problems, which he begins to notice when he returns from Harvard. "I had forgotten the neglected homes visible from the cars," he recalls, "the cabins about which half-naked Negro children played and from which ragged men and women, drunk with idleness, stared at the train, the ill-kept railway stations where crowds of loafers stood with their hands in their pockets and spat at cracks in the platform, unkempt countrymen, heavy with dyspepsia and malaria, idle Negroes, and village loafers" and "the hopeless inertia of the white man who had been deadened by an old economic error." It was a world around which "the earth itself seemed to revolve slowly. It *was* another country from the country whence I had come." Over time, in the narrative, Worth grows disgusted with the region's intellectual stagnation, racist demagoguery, provincial clergymen, and allegiance to the "ghosts" of the past, as well as the "gallant and pious nonsense" put forth by the "Daughters of the Confederacy."[48]

Yet for all his criticism, Nicholas Worth feels compelled to rescue the South from its stultifying condition through frank conversation, public speaking, and social reform. In the original serial Worth and his wife enjoy a summer vacation in New England after attending his class reunion at Harvard University. He explains how the northerners he met displayed an "almost morbid curiosity" about the southern states and believed "'the South' was as remote from New England as Australia itself." "I discovered," he adds, "that I was invited to dinners with the expectation that I would talk about 'conditions in the South.'" Initially, the Harvard alumnus declines the invitations because "I shrank from having myself or my friends at the South regarded as 'a problem.' Doubtless we were a problem, but not for parade." He describes how he was "alternately amused and humiliated" at being thought of as a problem, yet changes his mind and elects to attend a dinner with a group of northern men who express a decided interest in learning more about the problems of the South. Worth discovers not only that these men desire earnestly to address the needs of the South but also that they are willing to extend their financial support to him so he and other southern reformers can institute a program of educational reform for poor blacks and the white "neglected, backward country population." Weeks later Worth returns to the South, and even though he is glad to be home in North Carolina, he confesses to the readers that he is left with "a keen longing for New England" and misses the "orderliness, thrift, frankness; a clean land, clean towns" and "open minds." He explains how whenever northerners "forgot, or were kind enough to seem to forget that I was a Southerner and, therefore, a problem, I felt intellectually at home." For a brief moment, Worth and his wife consider moving permanently to the North but realize that "in all truth, we were ourselves a part of the Problem. It enmeshed us. It was the background of our life. There was no escape from it." At this moment in the narrative, Worth discovers the importance of "duty" and devotes the remainder of his life to resolving the peculiar problems of the South.[49]

Walter Hines Page's vignette about Nicholas Worth's experience visiting the North would not have surprised the bourgeois readers who purchased the *Atlantic Monthly*. The South held a particular fascination for many middle-class northerners who viewed the region as an exotic locale, and indeed northern philanthropies and various social clubs and organizations in the North generated an interest in the problems of the South. The Rockefeller family's concern with reforming public education and eradicating hookworm also played a significant role in drawing national attention to various southern deficiencies (chapters 2 and 4 of this book focus on the influence of the Rockefellers in greater detail). In the Northeast, middle-class northerners and expatriate southerners held meetings and sponsored lectures to discuss aspects of the "southern problem." The Southern Club at Columbia University formed several committees to study educational conditions, politics, and law in the South.[50] Harvard University also had a Southern Club. Walter Hines Page, speaking as the guest of honor at a meeting of this Boston club, told his audience, "There are plenty of problems to solve, plenty of fields to roam, amid the plains and forests of Dixie. Why, the man that points out to the South the solution of the race problem will earn for himself a fame second only to that of Washington or Lincoln."[51]

New York City, in particular, proved to be the breeding ground for a number of exclusive societies and clubs interested in the welfare of the South. Robert C. Ogden, a wealthy businessman from New York City, a partner of the department store magnate John Wanamaker, and trustee at the Hampton Institute frequently sponsored meetings of the Armstrong Association, an organization described by one southern liberal as a society that "represents the wisest sentiment of the North in relation to the difficult problems of Southern life."[52] The Armstrong Association encouraged industrial training for poor blacks and poor whites with the hope of increasing the general prosperity of the South at large (Ogden's commitment to reforming southern education is explored in chapter 2). The Nineteenth Century Club met on a regular basis in New York City starting in the 1880s, and Walter Hines Page, who also was a member of the group, depicted it as "an organization of ultra fashionable fine ladies and gentlemen who assume, in their splendor of flesh and full-dress . . . that they have the brains and the culture of the town." The Nineteenth Century Club sponsored talks on such topics as the "race problem," education, and industrial development in the South as well as many contemporary issues and social problems including American imperialism.[53] Page also served as vice president of the Reform Club, another New York City–based organization. At one public dinner hosted by a New York businessman, *Century Magazine* reported "we hear[d], with shame and grief, of certain conditions, certain shocking events in some of the Southern states."[54] The existence of so many northern-based clubs and organizations interested in the South's problems enabled northerners to discover what made "the South" southern (sometimes from southerners themselves), and the process of identifying this southernness reinforced their own sense of difference and standing as northern middle-class men and women. In many instances, the fascination of these middle-class northerners with the rural South led to an infusion of northern capital earmarked for solving regional problems.

Beginning in the 1880s groups of white southerners founded their own fraternal organizations in northern cities although they manifested many conflicted feelings about their home region. The Southern Society in New York City was the largest and wealthiest, with three hundred initial members in 1886, although the city also had a North Carolina Society, Virginia Society, Georgia Society, and Delaware Society, among others. A turn-of-the-century Southern Society yearbook explains how the organization was formed with the objective to "promote friendly relations among Southern men resident or temporarily sojourning in New York City, and to cherish and perpetuate the memories and traditions of the Southern people."[55] While these organizations remained committed to sectional reconciliation, the New South creed, the romance of the plantation, and the Lost Cause, they still welcomed members interested in the distinctive problems of the New South and occasionally invited northern speakers such as President William H. Taft. These societies were not without their divisions and at times the paradox of the New South came to the forefront. In 1890 the *New York Times* described the "heated southern blood" and fired shots that some attributed to the recent resignation from the Southern Society of several prominent members over the group's decision to eulogize Jefferson Davis. While the society maintained that the "quarrel arose over a game of cards," it was difficult to ignore the resignation letter of the vice president of the organization, William P. St. John, who politely acknowledged his reverence for the former president of the Confederacy but also expressed his dissatisfaction with a certain "element" in the society who believed "all shades of political opinion" should be "entertained and welcomed."[56] As St. John told the *New York Times*, Davis "elected to become in the Northern mind the embodiment of the *great rebellion*," thus the society should not encourage any form of sectionalism. One wonders whether St. John would have considered supporting or promoting publicly George Washington Cable's "Silent South." Regardless, in the 1890s separate Confederate organizations in New York formed such groups as the Confederate Veteran Camp of New York, the United Confederate Veterans, and a chapter of the United Daughters of the Confederacy, and over time the Southern Society moved further away from the more militant stand and symbolism of these groups.[57]

As both northerners and transplanted southerners relied on regular social gatherings to explore the problems of the South, others made exploratory journeys to the region in search of answers. Chapter 2 shows how Robert C. Ogden financed a series of train excursions to the South carrying a diverse collection of northerners fascinated with southern educational problems, in particular those of poor whites. Albert Bushnell Hart undertook more than a dozen trips to the region including a thousand-mile journey by horseback and wagon in the winter of 1907–1908, riding from North Carolina all the way to Texas. As he told Oswald Garrison Villard, one of the cofounders of the

National Association for the Advancement of Colored People and editor of the *Nation*, Hart viewed himself as continuing in the tradition of Frederick Olmsted.[58] The Harvard professor published accounts of his journeys in the *Boston Transcript, Boston Herald, Independent, North American Review, Berea Quarterly,* and *Richmond Times-Dispatch*; gave public speeches on the "real South" at such places as the Lowell Institute in Boston, the Brooklyn Institute in New York City, and the Massachusetts Historical Society; and used his experiences to constitute the heart of his book *The Southern South*.[59] In one published article based on an earlier trip, Albert Bushnell Hart noted that "no Northern visitor crosses Mason and Dixon's line without realizing there is a Southern problem." He observed that any visitor who left behind the "manufactures and pleasure resorts" in the "Northern South" and headed to the "real Southern South" would discover that the population was diffused, resources were scare, commercial enterprise was lethargic, labor was difficult to find, and "above all, behind all, and through all" there was "an antagonism of [the] races" that hung over the whole community like a pall. Hart concluded that any northerner spending more than a couple of months in a southern community would become, like his fellow southerners, "infected with this uneasy sense of a destiny unfulfilled, of a civilization anxious for its own future."[60] Even if the problems could be identified, the solutions were often nebulous. In a companion piece outlining remedies for the "Southern problem," Hart remarked, "everybody down there is trying to find some way out but there is no more agreement on the solution of the difficulty than on its occasion."[61]

Although Albert Bushnell Hart was overtly critical of the South's lack of civilization, he often struggled with the paradox of the New South, oscillating between optimism and despondency in his writing. In another set of companion pieces for the *Richmond Times-Dispatch* the titles of the articles point to this tension: "The South's 'Backwardness'" and "The South's Progress."[62] At times he rejoiced in the region's industrial advancement and at other times he remained convinced of the intractable nature of the "race problem" and the ancillary poor white problem. Not surprisingly, the southern press responded in a hostile manner to Hart's assessment of the region, but as he told his liberal southern friend Edgar Gardner Murphy, "The truth is, I was not writing for the South, but for the North, where there seems to be much misinformation and misunderstanding of the question." He explained how he wished that a southern man and northern man would study the "southern problem" collectively, write independent reports, and arrive at similar conclusions because only then might their "reasonable impartiality" collectively sway negative public opinion about the region.[63] It is unlikely, however, that Murphy would have been interested in collaborating with the Harvard professor given the indignant letter the southern liberal sent to Hart while serving as secretary of the Southern Education Board. Murphy confessed that he was "frankly sorry" to hear that Hart planned to write a book on his travels and declared that Hart could not "begin to know the 'The Real South'; anymore than I can claim to know the 'Real North.'" After reading some of Hart's earlier articles, Murphy described his "sense of despair" and warned his contemporary of the dangers of "extemporaneous sociology" written "merely from the tourist point of view" rather than a deeper study written by a transplanted northerner living on southern soil.[64]

While Edgar Gardner Murphy chastised his friend and colleague Albert Bushnell Hart in the spirit of academic exchange, a chorus of other southern voices protested more caustically the wave of criticism emanating from the North. These voices suggest how ubiquitous the image of the Problem South had become, moving beyond intellectual circles and into the broader American popular and political culture. Less than a year after Hart's assessment of the "southern problem" in the *Independent*, Mrs. H. L. Harris, from Rockport, Georgia, wrote in the same magazine, "Perhaps nothing is more offensive to the Southern people than the impressions which Northern visitors often receive of the South. I do not know who is to blame . . . but I do know that it is very like laying a fuse across Mason and Dixon's line when some Yankee, gifted with the critical spirit and the missionary instinct, comes down here to see what is the matter with us and to propose a remedy which is utterly foreign to our tastes and to the emergencies of the situation."[65] Over the course of several years, Mrs. Harris published numerous articles complaining about the North's unfair treatment of the South. She reported that the South was "the object of more comment from every part of our country than any other section of it" and that the northerner's point of view, completely alien from the South, bred a "natural antagonism" in the southerner.[66] Like the character of Nicholas Worth, she resented being on parade for officious northerners. Echoing Mrs. Harris's sentiment, Governor James K. Vardaman of Mississippi complained that nothing had been done to "soften the asperity of Northern criticism" and the South was now "experiencing the recrudescence of malignity, hate, and envy that has a parallel only in the acts of reconstruction." He wondered if there was a "course of conduct left open to us to pursue that will stop the cant and hypocricy [sic] with which we have been nauseated for these many weary years of waiting for a welcome to the house of our fathers."[67] In Vardaman's mind, northern men and their criticism, such as Albert Bushnell Hart, were responsible for the impediments to national reconciliation, not the persistence of southern sectionalism.

The Problem South, of course, was more than just a contested discourse or set of images. The cultural iconography of reunion and the emphasis on southern industrial progress often stood in marked contrast to the actual conditions in some areas of the South. Holland Thompson noticed that the New South was a "puzzling region, full of contradictions and sharp contrasts. The population is predominantly rural, and yet industrialism is growing with marvelous rapidity. The people are religious — for there is more Puritanism surviving in the South than anywhere else — and yet instances of lawlessness are frequent. They are kindly, but occasional manifestations of cruelty shock the world. They believe in race purity, and yet we see the mulatto."[68] Again, it was not uncommon for New South ideologues to criticize occasionally the progress of the South or for critics to applaud the South's improvement and celebrate the region's possibilities. Many had difficulty reconciling the apparent inconsistencies in the region, and in some instances the two strains of thought overlapped. For example, as I will explore in chapter 5, the New South focus on the importance of cooperation between the races as a prelude to successful industrial development sometimes slid into commentary about brewing racial antagonism and the need to reduce racial tensions. Boosters often had trouble maintaining the falsehood of racial harmony. Social reformers and critics who spoke about tapping the South's most important undeveloped resource — poor whites — seemed to be mirroring the New South ideologues' optimistic proclamation to mine the region's resources and material wealth, even while the New South critics continued to highlight the backwardness of the southern white population. Thompson's region full of "contradictions and sharp contrasts" made it difficult to grasp the nature of the New South and left many writing contradictory statements and feeling perplexed about the progress of the region.

The Persistence of Sectionalism and Uneven Progress

Holland Thompson's identification of incongruities in the South in 1914 spoke to the long-standing American nationalist project to resolve the central paradox of the New South: the fact that persistent poverty and cultural backwardness went hand-in-hand with progress and the development of national ideals. In the 1880s and 1890s optimistic New South ideologues zealously preached the gospel of advancement. By the turn of the century Progressive reformers and the American public could not help but notice that the South had become a land of illiteracy, disease, and racial conflict. The attempt to reconcile these contradictory features of the region led many observers to describe the process of reincorporating the South into the nation-state as a process of "readjustment." They frequently couched their descriptions of the South in the discourse of civilization, with an emphasis on progress, evolutionary development, and Anglo-Saxon masculine ideals. This, of course, resonated with imperial imagery and language invoked to justify conquest abroad. The concept of southern readjustment permitted room for antithetical descriptions of the South since it incorporated the idea that the region could exist in a state of backwardness yet be improving simultaneously. From the vantage point of this universal framework, the American experience with the readjustment of the South mirrored the American or European experience with the readjustment of imperial territories. The tenets of sociocultural evolutionism could be used to describe the process by which all backward nations or regions became civilized or modern. Moreover, critics pointed to the rise of political demagogues, the celebration of the Lost Cause, and the region's tendency to overreact to northern scrutiny as evidence of persistent sectionalism even decades after the Civil War had ended. They highlighted the ways in which this sectionalism expressed by white southerners thwarted the process of national reconciliation and mirrored the hundreds-year-old tradition of sectional resistance in Europe.

During the nineteenth century, the United States and parts of Europe passed through a period of massive industrialization and technological advancement as they evolved into greater imperial world powers. According to Peter Bowler, the western world viewed this as an age of transition from medieval to modern values, and the ensuing shift not only generated a fascination with the past but also created considerable uncertainties about the future and what modern life would look like. Victorians' search for reassurance in an age of rapid and bewildering change influenced the methodologies of such fields as history, archaeology, anthropology, sociology, geology, biology, and paleontology. In response, Victorians invented various ideas about the process of progress, some linear and some cyclical, and the idea of evolution became a central theme in many of these disciplines. The problems that exponents of the philosophy of progress attempted to address were: What accounted for the discrepancy between various cultures and civilizations in the world? Why had the white race supposedly progressed further than the nonwhite races? Yet sociocultural evolutionists' belief in the linear movement toward some better state of being, and the accompanying conviction that civilized society was guided by liberal principles espousing equality for all human individuals, created a paradox. If society was progressing, how did one explain the persistent inequalities? One of the most troubling cultural conundrums the Victorian middle class struggled to resolve was the continued existence of savagery in a world of unprecedented progress.[69] The answer to the paradox lay in the remarkable metaphorical flexibility of sociocultural evolutionary theory. The theory could easily be adapted to explain inequalities of class, race, or gender and the disparities evident in the progress of civilization.[70] The paradox provided resolution with its focus on evolutionary movement, which included horizontal movement through time, toward a unified nation or people; and vertical movement, governed by a sense of hierarchy, since not all rungs of the evolutionary ladder were necessarily equal at any given moment. The concepts of status and progress embedded in sociocultural evolutionary thought allowed for a more elastic interpretation of the development of civilization. Yet the model left the door open for an exceedingly chauvinistic perspective toward anyone who did not appear to be civilized.

In fact, the idea of civilization that emerged during the Enlightenment was of central concern in western social and scientific thought. It defined a state that could be contrasted with barbarism or savagery. While philosophers, scientists, and political theorists had struggled to define the idea of civilization since the mid-eighteenth century, it did not become a familiar trope until the development of Victorian sociocultural evolutionism in the latter part of the nineteenth century. In the western intellectual tradition, a dialectical process taking place over the course of the nineteenth century generated ideas about the nature of progress, the origins of civilization, the relationship between civilization and savagery, and the significance of racial and cultural hierarchy. In the 1850s the formal discipline of anthropology experienced a major intellectual reorientation because of the impact of Darwin's *On the Origin of Species* (1859). Darwin's book left a lasting imprint on ideas about civilization. Anthropologists and others influenced by the idea of evolution began to rank peoples based on their intellectual and moral aptitudes and classifying them as either civilized or barbarous. Women, children, racial types (such as the "black savage" or the "Celtic Irishman"), laborers, criminals, the mentally unfit, and "deviants" were considered subordinate to those who dominated economic, political, and social life. On the evolutionary continuum everyone who ranked below elite white men supposedly existed in a perpetual condition of dependency and savagery.

Americans used the discourse of civilization not only to mark racial and cultural boundaries but also to mark regional boundaries. References to the South's lack of civilization in journalists' reports, reformers' assessments, medical discourse, and contemporary intellectual thought were ubiquitous.[71] The Southern Sociological Congress dedicated itself to solving "the Southern problem of civilization."[72] Many detractors complained that the New South (often intentionally) lacked a certain level of refinement and civilized life, an attribute that set it apart from the rest of the modern industrial nation. A northern woman traveling in the region reported that what caught her attention the most was southerners' "determined resistance to the inroads of civilization."[73] Even a transplanted foreigner living in the South for twelve years proclaimed that the region "as a section, does not seem fully to appreciate the importance of the inevitables in civilization — the fixed and unalterable laws of progress." He concluded that there exists "a disposition to plead exception from the operation of universal principles of growth which have proven their inevitableness everywhere else."[74]

Liberal critics of lynching and violence in the South pointed to the barbarism of southern whites as one example of the lack of civilization, which countered the more prominent and competing claims that black men, especially those who raped white women and deserved to be lynched, were uncivilized savages. Ida B. Wells, the well-known African American antilynching activist, is best known for her campaign to invert the discourse of civilization by suggesting it was southern white lynchers who were the real savages.[75] Walter

Hines Page came to similar conclusions in his article titled "The Last Hold of the Southern Bully" where he indicted white southerners for their savage support of lynching laws and criticized the white bully who threatened to pull the South back into barbarism. In the course of an eleven-page article, Page used the word "civilization" or "civilized" eighteen times. He observed that justice in the South had become "in civilized life the place that revenge held in savage life." Page was particularly critical of South Carolina, which he felt had "lost the true perspective of civilization" and was therefore antagonistic toward "the moral force of the nation."[76] In general most critics who commented on the lack of civilization in the South did not refer to anything as specific as the savage behavior exhibited during lynching. More often than not, the discourse of civilization was invoked to convey a broad representation of the South as a stagnant, backward region beset with a range of problems and resistant to any kind of progress.

As critics struggled to make sense of the South's lack of progress within the context of the optimistic New South creed, they consistently attributed the region's backwardness to slavery, a social condition thought to be the antithesis of progress. David Bryon Davis has shown how in the western intellectual tradition, conceptions of slavery and progress have always been juxtaposed with one another. Western thought widely regarded slavery as a liberal progressive force until the late eighteenth century when intellectuals and abolitionists began to view the institution of slavery as retrogressive, barbarous, and unchristian. Following this momentous ideological shift — from the notion of "'progressive' enslavement" toward the notion of "'progressive' emancipation" — slavery was deemed incompatible with civilization.[77] Later generations would declare that slave societies impeded modernization and industrial capitalism. In a sermon titled "The New South: Gratitude, Amendment, Hope," Atticus G. Haygood, the president of Emory College, told his southern audience that "our provincialism, our want of literature, our lack of educational facilities, and our manufactures, like our lack of population, is all explained by one fact and one word — slavery."[78] Concerned observers referred to slavery as "an insuperable obstacle to general industrial advance," described how the "blight of slavery" had left southerners two generations behind northerners, explained how "slavery gagged the South," and dubbed the institution the "great incubus" that had been thrown off.[79] Walter Hines Page noted wryly that slavery had "pickled all Southern life and left it just as it found it." Page, like many others, believed that slavery had kept the "social structure stationary" in the South longer than any other region of English-speaking people in the world and that virtually every "undemocratic trait" now evident in the southern people could be accounted for by slavery.[80] The greatest evil of the slave system, he concluded, was that it had forbidden "free inquiry and free discussion." It was this lack of a liberated intellectual life that precluded white southerners from questioning those traditions that continued to hold the South back from making progress.[81]

Broadly speaking, the southern problem of readjustment in the postbellum period was the problem of sectional readjustment to industrial democracy, the precise antithesis of slavery. In his book *The Problems of the Present South*, Edgar Gardner Murphy wrote that the industrial, educational, and political problems of the region were "phases of the essential movement toward a genuinely democratic order." Murphy stressed that the problems would never be "solved in any mathematical or final sense," only that the effort to resolve them would be part of the process of "southern readjustment." Either life would adjust to these problems or "their conflicting or complementary elements" would "find a working adjustment with one another," since there would occasionally be "recurrent periods of acute antagonism."[82] These periods of "antagonism" might temporarily slow down southern progress, but they were only part of the natural scheme of social development toward a higher state of civilization. In an article on national unity written for the *Arena*, Elmer Ellsworth Brown, a professor at the University of California, Berkeley, noted that a nation that "presents an unbroken front to the rest of the world" is one that holds its parts together. Brown believed that in order for successful modern states to achieve an outward appearance of solidarity they required fluidity among the parts. As he explained, a powerful nation was "strong in its capacity for unlimited internal readjustment of relations," not in its capacity to restrain change of any sort.[83] In the case of the South, the struggle to readjust to modern life was part of the process of forging a unified nation-state. Reformers' and intellectuals' faith in the interpretive model of readjustment, a process that included reconciling and balancing occasionally inimical parts or sections, allowed them to believe in the distinctiveness of southern problems while simultaneously viewing them as national concerns. Murphy agreed with the assertion that the "peculiar problems of the South" were "sectional in their form," however he did not see this assertion as inconsistent with the contention that every problem in every section of the country was important to the "Nation's life."[84]

However, as Edgar Gardner Murphy correctly observed, the paradox of the New South could exacerbate the sectional tensions many presumed had disappeared. The Problem South, or the poverty side of the paradox, was not the old plantation South romanticized in Lost Cause ideology and northern travel brochures or the opulent, industrially advanced South embodied in the New South creed. This South threatened to weaken the bonds of sectional reconciliation and retard the development of a national industrial democracy. Some self-proclaimed experts on the South who argued for the persistence of sectionalism into the early twentieth century attributed it to the legacy of slavery and the Civil War. Although they did not always agree on which region was at fault for nurturing old resentments, on one level the South made for an easy target given its lengthy history of sectional politics. In 1907 Henry Edwin Tremain published a book titled *Sectionalism Unmasked* in which he issued a scathing denunciation of the South's unrelenting sectionalism. "The South to-day demands, and is confidently expecting," he declared, "that the nation shall acquiesce in the South's sectionalized political life." The most pernicious aspect of this situation, Tremain argued, was the North's good-natured attempt to overlook the dangerous influence of southern sectionalism and in collaboration with the South to "obscure and veneer the issue with benevolence and commercialism." The larger problem manifested itself in multiple ways: the distortion of historical facts surrounding the Civil War (or "War of Rebellion"), the canonization of the Confederacy, the veneration of heroic manly valor on both sides of the battle, the South's institution of a segregated government, and the transformation of the region's black population into "a peasantry of disfranchised servitors."[85] Tremain's screed explicitly targeted the culture of reunion and in many ways echoed the arguments made by Albion Tourgée, another veteran of the Union Army. Tremain was promoted to brigadier general and served in South Carolina during the first year of Reconstruction, and perhaps the five years he spent in the South shaped his aversion to southern sectionalism and nurtured his decades-long commitment to the principles of the Republican Party.

Liberal white southerners dedicated to reform and equally skeptical of the overwrought sentiment issued by the culture of reunion were not as blunt as Tremain but they were more willing to censure the North for its own style of sectionalism. In an essay titled "The South: Backward and Sectional or Progressive and National?" Clarence H. Poe, editor of the magazine *Progressive*

Farmer, came to the defense of the region and argued, "It is an unfortunate fact that the very people who are saying most about 'Americanism' and 'American unity' are in many cases, the very people who are most often appealing to sectional feeling, and thereby—are they not?—tending to promote Northern distrust of the South." Poe felt compelled to answer the "oft-repeated statement" about southern backwardness recently being circulated in the "magazines and newspapers of other sections" and asserted that the South was the most "broadly national section of America."[86] Edgar Gardner Murphy was not one to defend the South's hypersensitivity to criticism but like Poe he suggested that condemnation of the region should be truly national in tone and substance and not a sectional criticism hiding behind the false guise of nationalism. "Too often we find," he observed, "that when our Northern journalism discusses wrongs at the North or at the West, it criticises [sic] the *wrongs*, but when it discusses wrongs at the South it criticises [sic] the *South*." Criticism of the region as a whole, rather than its specific problems, reflected "a Northern sectionalism as offensive as any sectionalism in our Southern states."[87] By pointing out the existence of sectional tendencies in the North, men like Poe and Murphy expanded the notion of sectionalism at the turn of the century. When reformers and intellectuals referred to lingering sectional friction, they spoke not only in terms of tension within the political arena but also about social, racial, and economic differences they believed highlighted the contrast between backwardness and progress.

In the first decade of the twentieth century, the meaning of sectionalism also drew the attention of prominent scholars in the national academic arena, many of whom presented their ideas in the public forum. The same year Henry Edwin Tremain published *Sectionalism Unmasked*, the preeminent American historian Frederick Jackson Turner delivered a paper at the meeting of the American Sociological Society in Madison, Wisconsin, titled "Is Sectionalism in America Dying Away?" Turner offered a new theoretical approach to the field of American history that stressed the significance of the section in understanding both the past and the present; his fascination with sectionalism persisted through the mid-1920s. Turner disagreed with Secretary of State Elihu Root's declaration that modern life was "crystallizing about national centers" at the expense of local power and influence and asserted that paradoxically nationalism had the potential to reinvigorate old sectional tendencies even in the face of the nation-state's move toward "national uniformity and national consciousness." Turner maintained that "capitalistic exploitation" emanating from the eastern section of the United States would ultimately trigger sectional resentment due to conflicting economic interests in other sections of the country.[88] Thus, ironically industrialization would not nationalize the American landscape but further divide it. Turner warned that in Europe the consolidation of the nation-state had actually failed to destroy sectionalism, and that it was unwise of Americans to assume that the same outcome would not occur in the United States.

A number of historians, such as Frederick Jackson Turner, acknowledged transnational linkages between the history of the United States and Europe, despite the burgeoning nation-centeredness of the American historical profession at the turn of the century. The belief in American exceptionalism was not a foregone conclusion in the profession's development. Transnational alternatives and frameworks coexisted with nationalist models for a brief period, at least until the onset of World War II.[89] In Turner's talk "Is Sectionalism in America Dying Away?" he linked the persistence of sectionalism to colonial designs and empire making through his comparative assessment of tensions in Europe and America. He described the United States as "imperial in area" and said that if one laid a map of the United States on top of a map of Europe one could clearly see that both areas were relatively equal in size and made up of "separate geographic provinces" that behaved as nations in their own right. Turner contended, "American history is in large measure still colonial history — the history of the exploration, conquest, colonization, and development of these physiographic provinces, and the beginnings of a process of adaptation of society to the section which it has occupied."[90] Turner's theoretical framework provided a historical scenario in which the United States, much like Europe, engaged in imperial domination over other nations (sections) within its contiguous boundaries as well as nations outside of its borders. As the historian noted in a much later piece, "Our sections constitute the American analogue of European nations."[91]

Turner's remarks intimated that the Northeast acted from a self-interested sectional stance by pursuing the colonization of regions, including one which had a long history of sectionalism itself, namely the South. While Turner's historical work is most associated with the American conquest of the West, he would have acknowledged that the process of colonization involved the South too, and that "capitalistic exploitation" both reflected and triggered residual sectionalism. Turner elided the conceptual boundaries of sectionalism and colonialism in his remarks and posited that both were less a product of continuity and stability and more a result of flux and discontinuity. Thus, in intellectual and academic circles in the late nineteenth and early twentieth centuries, ideas about section, nation, and empire could operate in tandem as compatible and frequently overlapping theoretical categories.

Consideration of the Problem South in a Colonial Context

The academic and social scientific communities' ability to juggle nation-centered frameworks with transnational perspectives was simply one example of a broader tendency to view the U.S. struggle with the South in a global context. The period in which the "southern problem" discourse reached its peak was at the height of great American expansion overseas. From the early 1890s to the end of World War I the United States acquired several colonies and protectorates that included the Philippines, Puerto Rico, the Hawaiian Islands, and Guam. In 1860 the United States did not have a single overseas colony; by 1920, 120,000 American troops occupied eight U.S. overseas territories with a combined population slightly more than that in the western third of the United States itself.[92] American imperialists adopted various models of governance including annexation, military occupation, economic domination, and colonial oversight. From the vantage point of this universal framework, the American experience with the readjustment of the South cannot be separated from the American or European experience with the readjustment of imperial territories. Commentators on the "southern problem" used the tenets of socio-cultural evolutionism to describe the process by which all backward nations or areas became civilized or modern. By the turn of the century, America's conceptual and geographical boundaries were quite protean, and it did not seem unusual to consider the South as another locale with populations in need of uplift. The following chapters in this book on public health, agricultural reform, poor whites, and the "race problem" explain in greater detail the ways in which a transnational understanding of rural backwardness both shaped and was influenced by the problem of the South. Paradoxically, observers viewed the region as simultaneously American yet un-American in nature, lending credence to W. J. Cash's assertion decades later that the South was thought to be "a nation within a nation."[93]

The question of integrating or appending new parts and peoples (backward colonial or regional spaces) into the developing whole (the progressive American nation-state) created scaffolding upon which to hang debates about the Problem South. Domestic and colonial projects entailed several designs: reeducation of the citizenry or colonized population, public health efforts to curb the threat disease posed to efficiency, the creation of a system of racial classifications and hierarchies designed to manage and control racial behavior, the extraction of raw materials for the national and international market, and the widespread improvement of farming practices. The transition of the South from an isolated semifeudal region to a part of the modern industrial democracy required state-sanctioned and philanthropic supervision of the South. Ann Stoler has suggested viewing nineteenth-century history "as made up, not of nation-building projects alone, but of compounded colonialisms and as shaped by multinational philanthropies, missionary movements, discourses of social welfare and reform, and traffics in people."[94] Individuals such as Walter Hines Page, Seaman A. Knapp, Clarence H. Poe, Kenyon Butterfield, Samuel Chapman Armstrong, Booker T. Washington, Charles W. Stiles, and Alfred Holt Stone, in conjunction with organizations such as the Rockefeller philanthropies, the Carnegie Corporation, and the U.S. Department of Agriculture, participated in a transnational circuit of ideologies and individuals. The paradox of the New South was that reform was simultaneously a "compounded colonialism" and a "nation building project." As late as 1915, the editors of the *New Republic* urged Americans to be magnanimous and patient with the southern state of Georgia, much like they would be with Haiti and "the more primitive Balkan states." They noted that Georgia had "self-government" but was "not yet fit for it" and that only a very small portion of its citizens had "risen to the normal civilization of the Western world." The remaining population was "primitive," "uneducated," and "burdened with a citizenship" they were ill-equipped to handle, thus Georgia ultimately required "the guidance of comparatively more advanced people."[95] As the editorial suggested, the rhetoric used to invoke compassion for this southern state's problems could easily be applied to any of the colonial possessions.

A significant number of Americans and Europeans frequently embarked on exploratory tours of "primitive" countries that combined visits to the U.S. South with the Caribbean and Latin America. One of the earliest examples is a travel diary written in 1864 by John Milton Mackie titled *From Cape Cod to Dixie and the Tropics*. While Mackie did not make his expedition during the height of American imperialism overseas, his inclination to link domestic and foreign spaces together points to the early onset of an imaginary geography characterized by fluid conceptual boundaries.[96] Travelers surveying domestic and distant landscapes likened southern topography and culture to exotic tropical locations and saw no inconsistency in touring the South and other tropical countries on one continuous trip. Mackie's journey connected "Dixie" with the "Tropics," including Cuba and the Bahamas. In the early twentieth century, William Archer, an Englishman who combined two locations — the South and the Caribbean islands — on a single whirlwind tour to study the "race problem," blissfully told his readers, "I see no reason why the fascinating ferment of the Southern States, in conjunction with the glorious beauty of the West Indies, should not attract the travelling Briton." Archer's interest in the South reflected imperial designs as he believed the South's racial situation might serve to illuminate the problems British imperialists faced in their own colonial empire.[97]

Other cultural geographers interested in studying the South developed parallel interests in foreign locales too. Just one year after Albert Bushnell Hart published *The Southern South* based on his seven-month exploration of the region, he published a second work titled *The Obvious Orient* (1911) in which he recounted his nine-month experience of "globe trotting" through Japan, China, and the Philippines. As Hart remarked in his lengthy monograph on the South, "Every year opens out some new unexplored field which must be taken into account if one is to hope for anything like a comprehensive view of the subject."[98] In each case of exploration, Hart presented a survey of an unexamined alien space from a fixed reference point: a view of the South as seen from the North and a view of the Orient as seen from the Pacific Northwest. Hart described the Orient as a place marked by "mystery, distance, romance, [and] myths" and the South as a place with "temperamental peculiarities" and a "peculiar life and standards."[99] Each place was mapped as distinctive, exotic, and either geographically or culturally remote. The titles of these travel accounts also reveal the author's intention to make the foreignness of these locales knowable. The South is qualified with the adjective "southern," high-lighting its southernness and rendering it recognizable. The Orient becomes "obvious," and thus it is easily understood. Hart's fascination with presenting a "comprehensive view" of allegedly uncharted territory cut a wide geographi-cal swath, linking domestic imperial tendencies with transoceanic imperial impulses.

The history of Reconstruction in the United States also led some experts on the South to consider that period as an example of early colonialism on domestic soil. The presence of military troops in the South and the govern-mental effort to transition the former slave population into useful labor-ers and citizens reflected imperial practices and overtones adopted decades later. White southerners interpreted this domination as northern oppres-sion and painted themselves as colonial victims of a northern empire run by "Negro rule." In reality, they engaged in just as much colonization of African Americans as any group they accused. What is significant, for the sake of this book's argument, is that although Reconstruction failed, later social reform-ers viewed it as a rehearsal for subsequent forms of federal and philanthropic intrusion into other countries. As Michael Salman shows in his work on the Philippines, national debates surrounding the Civil War and Reconstruction provided the context for future disagreement over the patterns of American colonial intervention in the Philippines, a country grappling with the legacy of its own system of slavery.[100] In a think piece meditating on the end of the Spanish-American War and what it meant to govern countries separate from the United States and populated with people of color, Walter Hines Page ex-plained how colonization was a new problem for Americans but certainly not for the British. He advocated using the "process of reconstruction of the local governments of the Southern States" as a blueprint for colonial rule since, "in principle," there were many similarities. Colonial administrators, he argued, should look to the South's experience with a long military occupation follow-ing the Civil War and the way in which the federal government determined that the states had established and tested a "competent local government."[101] While Page did not explicitly state in this essay that the South continued to suffer from similar troubles (in fact, he noted that the North and South had seemed to cohere into a unified Republic following the Spanish-American War), his later actions and rhetoric surrounding southern problems mir-rored many of the concerns of American colonial administrators, particularly his interest in public health and education in the first two decades of the twentieth century.

Since colonial administrators abroad and domestic reformers at home made intellectual connections between the situation in some of the overseas colonies and the South's experience during Reconstruction, it is hardly surprising that Americans began to reexamine the legacy of Reconstruction in the present-day South. Northern and southern intellectuals, philanthropists, and government experts began to question if the newly freed slaves had successfully made the transition into the body politic, if not as political citizens, then as members of the social and economic body politic. This marked a shift away from the political focus during Reconstruction to the social scientific, reform-minded focus of the early twentieth century. In addition, an increasingly conspicuous population of poor whites appeared to be suffering from the same social problems as poor blacks. Reformers questioned whether southern poor whites were truly fit to exercise the rights and obligations of a virile Anglo-Saxon class of citizenship and how their shortcomings might be rectified, if at all. Appreciable similarities between the economic and social status of poor whites and the southern black population led many to collectively view poor southern blacks, poor southern whites, and colonized people as those in need of uplift. Finally, Americans who either encountered or read about the poverty and apparent backwardness of locales outside of the United States asked what experiences in the southern states might provide instruction for colonial settings or if the lessons learned abroad might be applied to the retrogressive condition of the South. Perhaps the mission of civilization and the path of modernization followed the same trajectory regardless of the locale? The remaining chapters in this book explore more completely the conceptualization of southern problems within this global framework of uplift in the realm of public health, agriculture, education, and race relations.

The question of whether the South was backward and sectional or progressive and national dominated the discourse of the late nineteenth and early twentieth centuries and was a key component in the consolidation of liberalism in this period. Various intellectuals and reformers theorized endlessly about the "southern problem," and as later chapters in this book explore, they engaged in significant patterns of intervention in the region. The South was viewed as a significant problem, an eyesore on the American landscape that posed a threat to the ideals of progress, abundance, and modern civilization. Reformers and intellectuals wrote comprehensively on the region's faults, and their depictions of a backward, foreign-like region within the contiguous borders of the United States both mirrored and energized the missionary impulse of those people and institutions who would transform the South into a massive laboratory for social conversion. Interest in the deficiencies of the South reflected a growing faith in the value of social scientific solutions administered within a professional and middle-class context, accounted for by facts and recorded observations. Southern and northern liberals drew attention to regional deficiencies, often in collaboration with one another, and ensured that the image of the Problem South dominated the American imagination for decades.

The New South creed and its focus on progress and industrialization forced liberal commentators on the region to juggle the two sides of the paradox of the New South (that poverty and progress could co-exist). To reconcile this incongruity, social scientists and reformers began to focus on the *process* of southern development and described the South as existing in a state of conversion. The concept of moving toward a higher and better state of being enabled detractors to acknowledge, albeit uneasily, that the region was advancing despite its enduring defects. The more sanguine critics predicted a successful path of evolution in the region and justified slow or absent progress in the South as merely one stage of the transition toward a higher plane of development. The more skeptical critics harbored anxieties about the possibility of backward movement or degeneration along with increasing doubts about the South's ability to compete equally with the North. At times, both strains of criticism tried to reconcile the paradox of poverty and backwardness with almost mythical declarations of striking progress. This faith in the South's capacity to reach the standards of modernity reflected a desire to temper censure of the region with optimistic proclamations as well as a genuine belief in the viability of the evolutionary model. In general, intellectuals' and reformers' adherence to the doctrine of readjustment was part of the general discourse utilized to galvanize support for modernization. Yet the process of sectional reunion was a contradictory one. The essentialized nature attributed to the South often confounded any strategy of reform behind the reconciliation of North and South since it was difficult to embrace the belief that one could successfully induce change in the region with the belief in the enduring and immutable nature of southern problems.

Finally, the rhetoric of the "southern problem" underscored the distinctiveness of the South and was further invigorated by comparisons with foreign countries and the overseas colonies. The problem of southern civilization was part of the broader problem of the development of civilization around the globe. The fluidity of America's imagined geographical boundaries facilitated the tendency to regard the U.S. South as another locale in need of social and economic uplift. The attempt to incorporate the New South into the nation during the age of American imperialism and at the height of great jingoistic sentiment was no coincidence. Although observers knew the U.S. South to be American and harbored no doubt that the region would be reincorporated into the Union, unlike the overseas colonies, the language used to describe both overlapped in significant ways. As this book will demonstrate, efforts to educate and train the southern citizenry, restructure the public health system, rehabilitate agricultural life, and reconcile the "race problem" with the principles of democracy mirrored imperial impulses guiding the spread of American empire. Ironically, comparisons of the South to places outside of the United States wound up reinforcing southern distinctiveness, and in a curious way global expansion played a pivotal role in shaping the surge of regionalism at the turn of the century.

CHAPTER TWO

The Menace of the Diseased South

It is high time, anyhow, for the South to get over this morbid and babyish sensitiveness about the publication of every statistical fact that doesn't please our passing fancy. The true Southerner, the man we ought to honor and follow, is the man who looks an unpleasant fact squarely in the face and sets about getting a remedy. . . . Let us rather follow the doctor and the leader who loves the South with all his heart, but who loves her too well not to use the knife of criticism and reform upon the cancers upon her economic life and general well-being.

—CLARENCE H. POE

If society, like a machine, were no stronger than its weakest part, I should despair of both sections. But, knowing that society, sentient and responsible in every fibre, can mend and repair until the whole has the strength of the best, I despair of neither.

—HENRY GRADY

In May 1914 in Memphis, Tennessee, the Southern Sociological Congress gathered to address the social and economic problems of the South. James McCulloch, a clergyman and social reformer from Alabama, noted in the introductory remarks of the published conference proceedings that the state of affairs in the region was precarious at best, coming on the heels of Reconstruction, and that despite the "chivalrous spirit" at work for a "nobler civilization" in the New South, much still needed to be accomplished. "Readjustment has been so rapid that the march of progress is irregular," he continued. "The new civilization is lacking in symmetry. Many zones of danger and infection exist . . . the world has disturbed the South by talking over-much about its danger zones." The development of a diseased South in the post-Reconstruction period, McCulloch concluded, had inspired "the best intelligence and leadership" in the region to meet annually to resolve an array of problems that were distinctive to the South. On the one hand, McCulloch and his colleagues were sensitive to outsiders' criticism of the region and were hesitant to address publicly the full extent of the ills plaguing the postwar South. Many of them often preached an optimistic New South gospel of progress in public and were more critical behind closed doors. On the other hand, they acknowledged that the South had serious problems that needed to be resolved, especially if the civilization of the New South were to ever match the former greatness of the civilization of the Old South. Therefore, the urgency of the task required a certain level of open discussion about the region's problems, particularly since this was a "crusade of national health and righteousness."[1] In short, regional health and fortitude were essential to the progress of national civilization. An infected region not only impeded the healthy development of the New South but also retarded the economic and social progress of the national body.

Medical historian Charles E. Rosenberg has theorized that disease does not exist until we have collectively decided that it does, "by perceiving, naming, and responding to it." It is both a material reality and a "repertoire of verbal constructs" used to explain or justify medical authority and comment on social life.[2] This proposition is hardly a new theoretical idea in southern history. In fact, one scholar in the field has suggested that the choice lies "between seeing the South itself as an idea, used to organize and comprehend disparate facts of social reality, or viewing the South as a solid and integrated social reality about which there have been disparate ideas."[3] Disease in the South was both a material reality and an analytical tool; or, as Rosenberg would say, it could both frame and be framed. Progressive reformers, such as McCulloch and his colleagues, supported public health efforts to eradicate real diseases in the South. These reformers also used disease as a metaphor and frame to understand social conditions in the South and the economic relationship of the region to the rest of the nation in the late nineteenth and early twentieth centuries. During this period new scientific understandings of disease not only defined what was peculiarly southern but also explained how illness affected those who were not diseased. Reformers' focus on healthy bodies as well as sick bodies drew increased attention to what was different or abnormal, thereby reinforcing regional distinctiveness.

While some scholars have explored how particular diseases like pellagra and hookworm helped fuel notions of southern distinctiveness, they rarely move beyond the tautological assertion that these particular diseases were peculiar to the South and therefore made the region distinctive. By examining the conceptual framework physicians and scientists used in their discussions of the South, we can begin to understand how and why people used the rhetoric of disease and metaphors of contagion as a means of framing ideas about the precarious relationship of regions during a period of intense nation building, massive corporate restructuring, and rapid industrialization.[4] The proliferation of metaphors of disease and infection as well as active efforts on the part of public health reformers to eradicate illness in the South constituted part of the process of sectional reunion and nation-state construction in the post–Civil War era. Observers of the presumed degraded South invoked medical imagery to invest legitimacy in the nation as the authoritative healer. The South was constructed as the ailing patient (or region) and the North was inscribed as the all-knowing physician (or nation).[5] The state-building process — the attempt to draw the periphery into the core — drew on images of regional dysfunction and sickness to legitimate the process of national reunification.[6]

The image of the diseased South had some basis in reality. The lack of rural sanitation and the existence of distinctive diseases in the region inspired a generation of public health reformers to clean up the South. National philanthropic organizations dedicated to this task worked in conjunction with local state boards of health. Strong ties between corporate capitalism and philanthropic foundations, led by individuals such as Andrew Carnegie and John D. Rockefeller Jr., ensured that the health of America's workforce would become an issue of central importance in the organizations' agendas. Growing attention to the connection between disease and the social environment reflected an uneasy feeling that the economy in the region was rapidly deteriorating and not keeping up with the industrial economy in the North. Rather than relying on northern finance and technology alone, making human bodies in the New South healthy was the key to overcoming southern backwardness and poverty and consolidating the power of the nation-state. Moreover, several dramatic conceptual shifts and advances in science and medicine during this period provided Progressive reformers a vocabulary for talking about the South and explain the prevalence of metaphors of disease in social and economic commentary on the region. Both place and person could be sick in the new medical age. At the turn of the century, several developments, including the institutionalization and professionalization of the public health field; scientific research in parasitology, bacteriology, and medical entomology; and a sudden interest in the new germ theory of disease, all drew attention to the links between disease, place, and the state of civilization.[7]

Yet, these paradigmatic shifts in science and medicine, as well as the interest in producing a healthy labor force in the South, cannot be separated from global concerns. By the late nineteenth century, the international rise of tropical medicine as a scientific specialty encouraged scientists and reformers to make comparisons between the U.S. South and the tropics, since tropical diseases such as hookworm, malaria, pellagra, and yellow fever could be found in both places.[8] American and European scientists worried about the effect of disease on racial degeneration and the decline of civilization in the tropics and the U.S. South. Western imperialism brought Americans and Europeans into contact with people of color and raised questions about the health of the new colonial possessions, including the potential threat posed to white colonists by diseased "natives." At a time when the United States was engaged in economic and cultural imperialism abroad, it became crucial to establish and project an efficient national economy and culture whose parts functioned as a healthy and vigorous whole. The containment of tropical pathologies at home guaranteed healthy bodies fit for imperialist expeditions into the tropics as well as efficient disciplined workers who contributed to the nation's wealth and resources. A backward and diseased region had the capacity to weaken the American imperial prerogative abroad.

Thus, Progressive reformers' treatment of the South as a distinctive place in the United States was not simply reinforced by comparisons between the region and the rest of the country. The identification of the region as a diseased space in a healthy nation also was part of a larger view of the diseased tropics in the world viewed from the industrialized northern hemisphere. Comparisons between the U.S. South and the tropics (viewed as the Other) helped to set the region apart from the rest of the nation. Many of the physicians and scientists who identified similarities between the subtropical South and tropical regions abroad had worked outside the United States in the tropics before undertaking work in the U.S. South. The story of disease in the South is as much about the perceived distinctiveness of the region in the United States as about the comparison of the South to the tropics during the height of western imperialism and within an even wider chronological and global context.

Public Health Reform in the South

Domestically, in the late nineteenth and early twentieth centuries, a number of organizations such as the Rockefeller philanthropies, the Smithsonian Institution, the U.S. Public Health Service, and the U.S. Department of Agriculture engaged in research, philanthropy, and federal intervention in the South, activities that reflected a new understanding of the geography of disease. American philanthropic foundations had a profound social and financial influence on medical science from 1900 to 1930. They not only supported a variety of public health efforts to eradicate disease but also funneled significant amounts of money into scientific research and the development of prominent medical schools. These foundations linked the interests of medical science and corporate capitalism together.[9] By the first decade of the twentieth century, the medical and scientific community had identified several diseases that appeared to be largely confined to the southern regions of the United States. Newly discovered maladies such as hookworm and pellagra, along with more familiar diseases such as malaria and yellow fever, provided clear evidence that the South suffered from a host of distinctive bodily pathologies. The Rockefellers were some of the first philanthropists to address the distinctive diseases of the South. In 1909, the Rockefeller Sanitary Commission for the Eradication of Hookworm (RSC) began a five-year effort to treat hookworm in the region. Acknowledging that work still needed to be done in the South after disbanding the commission, the Rockefeller family founded the International Health Commission (renamed the International Health Board in 1916) and also established the broader Rockefeller Foundation. The commission appropriated the activities of the RSC, added a focus on the prevalence of malaria in the South, engaged in wide-scale public health education, and initiated a philanthropic effort to eradicate similar diseases abroad in places such as Mexico, Brazil, and the Caribbean.[10] The work of scientific philanthropic organizations in conjunction with state boards of health in the South helped publicize on a national level the existence of geographically specific diseases.

In 1914, the year the Rockefeller Sanitary Commission concluded its initial effort to eradicate hookworm and the Southern Sociological Congress met to discuss the problems of an "infected" South, public health reformers turned their attention to rural public health education as a result of the work that had previously been done in the region. A small group of public health leaders met with the General Education Board funded by Rockefeller money to work out the details for the first independent school of public health at Johns Hopkins University. Although local urban public health efforts had begun as early as the late eighteenth century and the first state boards of health appeared in the 1870s and 1890s, the institutionalization and professionalization of the field was largely a product of early twentieth-century efforts to eradicate hookworm disease in the South.[11] During the steady professionalization of the public health field in the second and third decades of the twentieth century, reformers continued to manifest a decidedly regional interest in the South. In 1911, Dr. Allen W. Freeman, assistant health commissioner in Virginia, noted, "we are witnessing at the present time a spectacle unique in the history of the United States" because "from Virginia to Texas we find there is a common menace, a common need, and a common problem."[12] Public health education in the rural South took a variety of forms, including county fair exhibits, community lectures and demonstrations, free dispensaries, motion pictures, moving train exhibits, state board of health bulletins, public health primers, and newspaper articles warning southerners of the dangers of disease and extolling the values of proper sanitary practices. The greatest agency for rural public health education was the public school system, and reformers encouraged teachers to offer classes on sanitary subjects, personal hygiene, and disease transmission.[13] Others argued that sanitary improvement of the rural home was the most vital need, since southerners had allowed their dwellings to fall into a state of "filth and ruin." Teaching the farmer to keep his home clean would help "lay the foundation for a stronger manhood and womanhood, a more hardy race, a greater state, and a mightier nation."[14]

The increased attention to public health education was partly due to a late nineteenth-century conceptual shift in how ordinary Americans perceived the nature of disease.[15] The miasma theory, which stated that disease spread without any known connection to the infective substance but rather through atmospheric infection, gave way to the germ theory, which held that small living microorganisms hidden from the naked eye existed on such things as food, toothbrushes, latrines, and drinking cups. The new theory of disease transmission stressed the potential danger in passing daily household items from person to person.[16] Casual contact with others could prove deadly, and notions of contagiousness suddenly took on new meaning. The germ theory also laid claim to the authority of the scientific world, because medical officials with microscopes and laboratories were the only ones who could visually confirm the existence of these infectious microbes. This new way of conceptualizing disease imposed a far more rigid taxonomic order on clusters of symptoms, since the germ of the disease itself could be easily demarcated and categorized. As a result, the tendency toward classification lent itself to understanding illness in relationship to hierarchies of race, class, and gender.[17] An emphasis on these hierarchies in the new world of germs, as well as the germs' contagious nature, encouraged the medical community to make sharp distinctions between carriers of disease who threatened healthy individuals and the victims who were infected. In addition, the taxonomic classification of germs added another spatial dimension to discussions of illness since particular germs could be identified as indigenous to certain locales.

Visiting northern philanthropists and local southern public health reformers noted that the rural South was host to an astonishing array of "germs." They found southerners suffering from typhoid fever, yellow fever, malaria, hookworm, roundworm, pellagra, smallpox, dysentery, tuberculosis, cholera, venereal disease, diphtheria, scarlet fever, measles, mumps, chicken pox, whooping cough, infected teeth and tonsils, and pneumonia. Children, especially, were examined for "all infectious and contagious diseases and defects of eye, ear, nose, throat, lungs, teeth and other physical defects."[18] While only certain illnesses, such as malaria, hookworm, and pellagra, appeared to be confined to the South, the constellation of so many universal infectious diseases in the region also drew attention to the extensive nature of the public health problems. One public health pamphlet erroneously reported that the hookworm parasite (not usually a fatal illness) acted as a magnet in the body, "inviting disease and death from dangerous germs."[19] Many physicians attributed an assortment of infectious diseases to this distinctly southern illness, which could be treated quite easily with thymol (a natural biocide that loosened the worms from the intestines). The problem, of course, was that the hookworm parasites thrived near privies where sanitation was minimal and would always pose a risk if the larger environment was not kept clean continually.

Lack of basic sanitation in the rural South (and some urban areas) was virtually ubiquitous and posed a serious hindrance to the establishment of quality public health care and disease control. The public health field's educational hub was located in the South at Johns Hopkins University, which proved to be quite auspicious, since the region had a reputation for crude sanitation measures and state public health departments were in an embryonic state. Some rural communities instituted "clean-up" days to try to eliminate the large amount of trash, weeds, and filth in homes and on the streets.[20] The county and city health officer of Montgomery, Alabama, commented that "all these things are very unsightly and it is a well known fact that people who are careless about keeping their premises clean are apt to take poor care of themselves."[21] The Public Health Department in Lee County, Mississippi, oversaw the construction of road signs placed at every dangerous curve and every milepost. Reformers and citizens drafted more than two hundred different slogans for the signs, such as "You Are Not Germ Proof, Wake Up," "Get the Habit of Clean Living," "Shun the Perils of Uncleanliness," "Pollute Not the Soil," "Keep the Backyard Clean," and "Good Roads, Good Health, Good Citizenship."[22]

At times the level of filth and community indifference was so appalling it startled those sanitary engineers working in the region. The director of the Public Health Department in Tennessee traveled to Kingsport to make an inspection of an area owned by a local corporation and made this report on his findings:

The work was begun with fear and trembling and with a feeling that any effort we could make would fall short. . . . People were crowding into the place on every train; large numbers of negro laborers were housed in shacks and tents in swampy places; houses were overcrowded, as many as eight or ten persons sleeping in rooms originally intended for occupancy by one or two persons; what privies there were were overflowing with filth, and soil pollution was evident all over the place where any dry ground could be found large enough in extent for a person to tarry long enough to relieve himself; flies were buzzing by the millions; the whole territory around the place was covered with a rank growth of weeds, grass, and bushes; garbage and refuse material were piled about and thrown around in amazing profusion; restaurants and eating booths were serving food which swarmed with flies, being exposed on counters and tables which, many times, were less than twenty feet from an open privy from which the contents flowed like volcanic lava . . . people came and went—all sorts of people from all sorts of places, but principally those of an irresponsible class . . . there were very few wells and practically all of these were soon discovered to be very badly contaminated; more than eighty cases of disentery [sic] appeared in a single morning . . . the state law was absolutely inadequate and the county Board of Health absolutely indifferent; money was scarce and the outlook well-nigh hopeless.[23]

In New Orleans, a local newspaper reported on a city district, near Canal Street and Tulane Avenue, that had become a massive garbage dump and described it as a "loathsome spot," a "disease-breeding ulcer," and a "festering mass of law-violating putrescence."[24] Local citizens, fearful that the wind would carry "germs and disease-breeding flies" from this dump (and others) to the residential sections of the city, worked to sanitize the area and get rid of the "dead animals, garbage, flies, vultures, human scavengers, dogs, and stray goats."[25]

The absence of privies in many homes and schools in the rural South constituted the most offensive breach of cleanliness in the minds of public health reformers.[26] In some counties in Mississippi the percentage of homes without proper sanitary privies was as high as 94 percent.[27] Southerners lacking indoor toilets or outhouses often defecated on the ground, and the resulting "soil pollution" was the principal means of hookworm transmission; the parasite lived in human feces and was acquired through the soles of the feet. Elementary privies like the "umbrella privies," which were holes in the ground over which there was a box with no bottom, and privies situated over rivers, which washed away the waste, posed a grave danger to human health. Photographs in the Rockefeller Foundation collection show freestanding piles of corncobs used as substitutes for toilet paper. Some farmers fertilized their fields with human excrement.[28] Public health reformers often described southerners' sanitary practices as animal-like and argued that even cattle and hogs made the effort to stay away from their own excrement. A doctor in the U.S. Public Heath Service noted that since "we house-break our pet cats and dogs," it did not "seem too much to expect of human intelligence" that people could be trained to become "yard-broke" and give up their practice of defecating on the ground in such a "dangerous and disgusting manner" so close to their water supplies and kitchens.[29] Charles Wardell Stiles, the scientist credited with discovering hookworm, caused quite a bit of consternation in a few southern communities by encouraging the local public health officers to send out letters informing parents that their children were eating human feces.[30] The suggestion that white people might even be ingesting the excrement of blacks precipitated tremendous alarm and aversion.[31]

Many victims of hookworm were known as "clay-eaters" because of the parasite's occasional tendency to precipitate bizarre eating habits (such as dirt), although in reality it was pellagra that precipitated this conduct. These practices only reinforced the notion that southerners were a backward class of uncivilized people who were inclined to eat soil and human feces. Both official reports from the RSC and articles in popular magazines published sensational accounts of poor white southerners' inclination to ingest strange objects because of hookworm infection. *McClure's Magazine* reported that "pebbles, sand, clay, mud, chalk, slate-pencils, shells, rotten wood, salt, raw cotton, cloth, paper, tobacco-pipes or pipe stems, mice, and young rats all have their devotees. Dr. Stiles saw one person eating live mice; another — a blind boy — had eaten up three coats, thread by thread, in a year."[32] Annual publications of the RSC regularly included photographs documenting the peculiar habits and behavior of hookworm victims, such as an account of a boy named "Chalky" whose pale white face did not keep him from using "chewing tobacco, profane language, and snuff."[33] Such accounts of "pure Anglo-Saxon stock" behaving in an unhygienic, animal-like manner usually attributed to nonwhite races shocked the American public and reinforced stereotypes that somehow the white race in the South was degenerating rapidly (see fig. 2).[34]

The sudden interest in the proliferation of deadly germs spawned a generation of middle-class reformers bent on educating Americans, and not just southerners, in daily habits of cleanliness. In 1910 Stiles gave a speech at the Child Conference for Research and Welfare in which he informed his audience, "After an experience of seven years residence and travel among other civilized nationalities which also claim to be civilized, I am unable to escape the conclusion that, taken as a nation, we Americans are dirtier than any of the other civilized nations." Stiles was probably exaggerating for effect. Yet, he believed that public health education in the nation's primary schools constituted the best antidote to "America's filthy habits."[35] Across the nation Progressive reformers worked diligently to restructure the public health departments in municipal and state governments. The war against germs had begun, and military

FIGURE 2. Typescript below the photograph reads "A 29 YEAR OLD RUNT. Probably hopeless. A neglected opportunity to make a man." Courtesy of Rockefeller Archive Center.

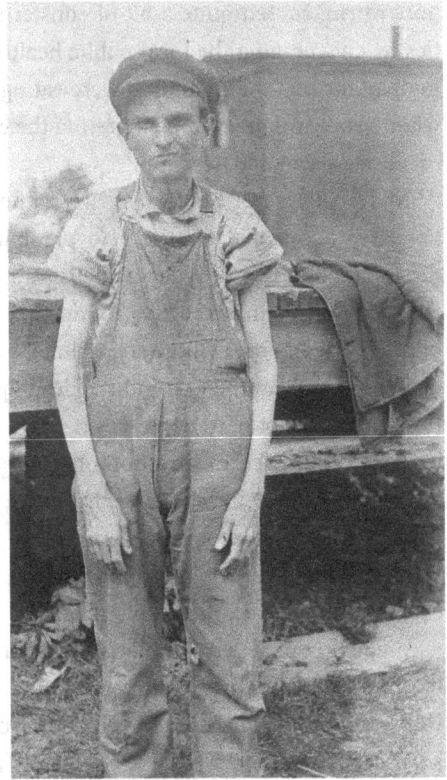

metaphors of disease control were ubiquitous.[36] Prevention of disease through the adoption of a strict sanitary regime was the highest priority. Curing disease was merely secondary.

Sickness in the Body and the Body Politic

Changes in scientific understandings of disease transmission gave rise to a new professional class of doctors, whose duty to the public shifted from a focus on treating the individual to an emphasis on serving the community as a whole. Medicine's growing attention to the training of select bodies of specialists with legitimate credentials reflected a broader trend of professionalization occurring in an array of disciplines and fields at the end of the nineteenth century.[37] Using the microscope and the laboratory, these medical officials asserted that only they were qualified to make diagnoses and to help insulate the community from the spread of potentially deadly germs and parasites. Charles E. Rosenberg notes that when the boundaries of medical knowledge expanded in the nineteenth century, a small minority of progressive physicians viewed this as advancement toward a "more rational and enlightened society." Growing secularism in this period encouraged these new doctors to put their faith in science, not theology, as the mediator of social morals. Thus the physician, not the priest or judge, became "the appropriate guardian of the rights of society and the individual."[38] In 1922 the president of the Rockefeller Foundation, George E. Vincent, noted that the physician and the public health officer should understand men as well as microbes and "be a politician in the older and better sense of the word."[39] The modern physician's new role as a civic diagnostician reinforced the connection between place and disease, since disease itself could be located within the individual body as well as demarcated in geographical space. The implication was that disease infected a part of the body as it did a part of the landscape. The South became one of the principal experimental laboratories for these new physicians and scientists intent on identifying such previously unknown dangers as germs, parasites, and common insects carrying disease. The South made for a rather convenient and relatively identifiable geographic laboratory because of its high rate of diseases, many of which were not found in other parts of the United States; its characteristic climate (often referred to as subtropical); and its general lack of rural sanitation, even on the most rudimentary level.[40]

The assertion that it was the responsibility of the physician to diagnose the ailing body politic as well as the diseased citizen led to scientific reports and lectures that described locations or communities as having anthropomorphic characteristics. Both individuals and their locations could be sick in this new medical age. In 1913 Dr. George Thomas Palmer presented a paper before the sociological section of the American Public Health Association titled "The Diagnosis of the Sick City." The speech largely focused on the specific sanitary deficiencies and diseases found in an unidentified city he chose to call Springfield. Palmer argued that a survey was more than just a "great blueprint of the community as a going institution." He maintained that a survey could accurately be compared to a doctor's case record and that only a careful recording of the symptoms would lead to a proper diagnosis and an effective line of treatment.[41] His inclination to move beyond a merely descriptive account of diseased individuals and to act as a "municipal diagnostician" demonstrated a new way of thinking about disease and geography. In public health discourse, conceptualizing the place as patient — rather than the citizen as patient in a particular locale — meant that scientific and medical professionals would begin to make more connections between individual illness and societal infirmity. The idea of the sick city implied that larger territorial areas such as states, regions, and nations might be afflicted with illness too. One newspaper in Alabama embraced this broader perspective when it noted, "Six-hundred thousand American lives are ruthlessly sacrificed every year because it seems we cannot learn that a nation can be sick just as a man can. For America is sick and sick with serious diseases . . . a hundred thousand shiver and sweat because the nation has chills and fever."[42]

Public health reformers, social scientists, and physicians often saw both man and society as a social organism and compared the role of the social scientist to the role of the physician. A physician speaking in front of the American Academy of Political and Social Sciences in 1911 stated, "Many of the problems that demand solution at the hands of the sociologist concern the parasites that infest the body politic, impairing its efficiency. The physician, on the other hand, particularly he who is engaged in the solution of the problems of sanitation, is concerned to a very large extent with the study of the parasites that infest the physical body, producing sickness and death."[43] Partly derived from Comtean positivism and the philosophy of Herbert Spencer, the analogy of the social organism could be employed to link the well-being of the individual to the well-being of the nation-state. Dr. Lewellys F. Barker, the president of the Southern Medical Association, made few distinctions between man as social organism and society as social organism. As he remarked in a presidential address in 1919, "This complex whole of human society is made up of parts so interdependent that what happens to one part, or what one part does, influences the rest. This idea, known as the 'organic' conception of society, can be grasped more easily by physicians, perhaps, than by most men, for as students of medicine they have become acquainted with the structures and functions of living organisms."[44]

The analogy of the social organism and an understanding of the relationship between parts and wholes operated on several levels. First, it was clear that an illness in one part of a patient's body ultimately affected the constitution of the entire body. Second, Barker believed that an increase in ill citizens might eventually lead to an ill community. He argued that an unhealthy individual was unable to perform social tasks efficiently and could often become a "burden upon society and a menace to its welfare."[45] Sick people had the capacity to strain the local economy if they were not laboring at full capacity or if they were relying upon social welfare to survive. Barker hoped that municipal and national infrastructures would be developed to allow for "control by the whole" to "insure the physical and mental well being of its units."[46] Finally, given this framework, it was clear that a sick community might potentially infect the larger geographic area of which it was a part, since the parts functioned as components of the organic whole. General illness on a regional level had the potential to sap the vitality of the nation. This organic conception of society, which emphasized the inextricable connection between part and whole, encouraged new ways of thinking about the South as diseased and dangerous. In 1909 George Washington Cable remarked, "This country of ours is a giant with one arm in a sling. That arm is the South." In relying on this metaphor to stress the threat the South posed to the nation's health, he concluded by suggesting that the most important question was "how to establish a full share of our national vigor, freedom, enlightenment, and wealth in this crippled, bleeding, and aching arm."[47]

As Michel Foucault has noted, medical knowledge in the nineteenth century shifted toward a new understanding of illness with a focus on the study of the "non-sick" man rather than continuing to confine itself to a "body of techniques for curing ills." Medicine, backed by the power of the nation-state, now analyzed the normal functioning and structure of an organism, searched for deviation, and worked to restore the natural equilibrium. Armed with knowledge of the "normative," medicine could dictate the standards by which man's body and society should function; or in Foucault's words, medicine became linked to "the destinies of states."[48] The act of defining disease in the South reflected both local and national concerns, since the ill part invariably threatened the well-being of the whole; thus, the "southern problem" could be simultaneously identified as a distinctive problem and as an American problem.

The metaphor of illness in this new medical age turned out to be highly malleable and could be used to explain the condition of the economy, the state of social or racial relations, or the general function of society. In fact, the metaphor of the sick body politic (or pieces of the body politic) was not peculiar to the American medical and social scientific lexicons. The international use of this metaphor often linked sickness with a nationalist agenda. During the late nineteenth and early twentieth centuries, the trope of the sick national body appeared regularly in Brazilian social scientific thought and Japanese medical science.[49] In Italy medical imagery was used to describe the country's own diseased South and legitimate the process of national reunification.[50] Like the Italian case, American reformers and scientists identified a sick region as the source of illness in the nation-state. In the case of the U.S. South, disease as social diagnosis helped reinforce regional identity and economic distinctiveness, since there was often little distinction made between the physical body and the social body. In curing the material and metaphorical ills of the South, the United States could lay the groundwork for the rise of a robust national industrial democracy.

Thus nationalist efforts to reunite the North and the South in the post–Civil War era were hampered by a belief in the differences between a diseased agricultural South and a healthy industrialized North. Scientifically constructed knowledge about disease, and in particular regionally specific illnesses, framed apprehension about the fate of the political economy in the New South and created a compulsion to pull it in line with the modern capitalist state. Further, the language of public health reform and the attempt to cure the sick South ultimately contributed to the nationalist agenda of reconciliation since a healthy part ensured a healthy whole.

The Economy of Disease

An analysis of medical and popular discussions of hookworm and, to a greater extent, malaria cannot be separated from the history of the South as a colonial economy. In the postwar period, the region developed a somewhat isolated labor market due to the economic downturns in the 1870s and declining cotton prices. Wages were lower in the South than anywhere else in the nation. The South's distinctive demography (lack of immigration) and an economy dominated by a single agricultural commodity (cotton) also ensured a separate economic identity. Southerners bought almost all of their manufactured goods outside of the region. The infusion of outside capital into the region did not follow patterns found elsewhere, because the capital was not usually accompanied by flows of people, such as bankers, laborers, farmers, and businessmen. This capital never lost its outside identity since investors often did not physically follow their capital and integrate themselves into southern communities.[51] All of these dynamics shaped the South's semicolonial economic status. Northerners, and even complicit southerners, had much to gain from cheap labor in the region. Therefore, national interest in an efficient, healthy, productive southern workforce reflected a broader colonial effort to dominate economically the South. The profits derived from low-cost labor were immaterial if labor could not perform.

The scientific and medical communities' assertion that hookworm, malaria, and pellagra were rural diseases reinforced the belief in distinctions between the diseased agricultural South with a faltering economy and a healthy industrialized North. Doctors believed "country diseases" to be more insidious than "urban killing diseases" such as tuberculosis, fever, and pneumonia because although "country diseases" never led to death, they slowly drained a community of its economic vitality.[52] Moreover, a report regarding appropriations for rural health work in North Carolina stated that "rural people are less health conscious than town people" by nature and often failed to seek medical attention when necessary.[53] The Rockefeller philanthropies informed local public health workers that the importance of the rural population could not be overestimated because it represented the foundation upon which cities and industries were erected; essentially, it fed and clothed the nation-state. These organizations concluded that public health conditions within the rural population were of "striking importance in their relationship to the economics of disease."[54] At this time, according to the U.S. Census, a "rural" community did not exceed twenty-five hundred people.[55] In the postwar period the South urbanized quite rapidly, yet taken as a whole, the South was largely rural.

The identification of distinctly rural diseases served to reinforce the connections between disease and geography and made it easier for those reformers working on other rural problems to frame their efforts in terms of sickness and health or pathology and normalcy.[56] In an attempt to get southerners to pay more attention to disease, public health reformers made analogies between the farmers' interest in his animals and crops and the significance of treating family members for hookworm and malaria. As part of the state's rural public health education, F. W. Dershimer, a physician in the Alabama State Board of Health, published a number of stories in the local newspaper about a fictional farmer named Barney Boggs and his interactions with the local health officer. Barney was not the brightest farmer, but he was always eager to learn. In one tale, Barney explains to the public health officer how his thoroughbred pigs produce more pork because of the additional care he gives them. The extra cost, he says, is a good investment. The visiting officer then asks Barney whether he wants to treat his children as well as he does his pigs and cattle, since investment in his children will reduce future "defects."[57] A paper in Kentucky noted that a farmer takes care not to "'runt' his pigs" by failing to feed them yet "brings up anemic children" who are underfed and neglected.[58] The *Southern Medical Journal* took a more contemptuous stance when it declared, "The estimated value set upon the life of a human being borders upon mockery and becomes paradoxical when compared with the merits of the existence of a single cow, hog, or sheep."[59] Public health reformers aimed to teach southerners that attention to disease in the rural community was as much a part of improving agricultural life as fertilizing crops, feeding hogs better food, and dipping cattle for diseased ticks. Dershimer also told Barney that "the fields of the business man are the people of the country."[60] The Federal Bureau of Animal Industry encouraged some southern communities to institute quarantines to prevent the spread of the North American fever tick that had been infecting southern cattle. The bureau made the comparison between the transmission of Texas fever by tick to southern cattle and the transmission of malaria and yellow fever by mosquitoes to man. The quarantine forbade the shipment of southern cattle to northern markets. In fact, all cattle had to be shipped in special cars and labeled "Southern Cattle" regardless of its point of origin. One newspaper speculated that as a result, even southern cattle that were healthier than northern cattle and had been raised outside of quarantined areas suffered the stigma and financial loss brought by the label.[61]

Local physicians and visiting northern philanthropists tried to stress the broader relationship between rural diseases and general poverty in the New South. Dr. Lewellys F. Barker insisted that all physicians consider the "economic problem" when treating diseases in the South. The infusion of northern capital into the region, the growth of manufacturing, the extension of the railroad system, and the diversification of agriculture had contributed to the advancement of the South, but disease threatened to retard this progress since it weakened the southern labor force and ultimately caused a loss of economic production.[62] Physicians and social reformers noted that illness also led to depreciation in land values and frightened away potential investors.

Some northern farmers wrote to southern health boards asking whether the localities they were interested in had high rates of hookworm and malaria, and they chose to avoid areas lacking a public health board. One newspaper reported that, at one point, land sold for an average of ten dollars an acre in the Mississippi Delta because of the number of people suffering from malaria. Once the inhabitants of the section instituted antimosquito work and eradicated the disease, the land value increased an astonishing 2,400 percent and then sold for $240 an acre.[63] Most state health boards welcomed the assistance of the Rockefeller philanthropies, although they worried about the details published in the organization's annual public reports. The director of the Alabama State Board of Health cautioned Wickliffe Rose, the secretary of the RSC, against listing mortality and disease statistics for fear of frightening potential investors and people looking to immigrate to the area.[64] The Tennessee Department of Public Health harbored these anxieties too.[65] South Carolina sanitary engineers reported that portions of the state had a bad reputation with reference to malaria and sometimes white settlers avoided them for fear of setting down roots in a stagnant community.[66]

Even more specifically, reformers and philanthropists argued that malaria and hookworm retarded industrial development in the region. J. A. LePrince, a sanitary engineer from the U.S. Public Health Service, stated that malaria was the businessman's problem and influenced urban progress even though it was a rural disease.[67] Disease could set in motion a destructive chain of events. The Yazoo County Health Department in Mississippi issued a circular titled "How Does Malaria Affect Your Business?" which argued that since agriculture was the foundation of commercial welfare, and the "farmer set the commercial pace of the county with an abundant or short crop," his prosperity could not be divorced from that of the merchant. Malaria led to less efficient labor, greater expenses due to medical care, and a loss of production that ultimately drained the resources of the merchants and the banks, and finally it ruined the credit of the community.[68] Reminiscent of the organic conception of society articulated by the president of the Southern Medical Association, the Yazoo County Health Department stressed the danger one diseased part posed to the health and well-being of the whole. More than the health of an individual body was at stake.

The scientific and medical communities noted that slow economic growth in the region began with the loss of efficient labor caused by disease. Even as late as 1920 the *American Journal of Public Health* argued that malaria was the South's greatest problem and that control of the disease was essential to industrial progress. In short, the problem was that "human efficiency and malaria [could] not occur together."[69] W. E. Hinds, the state entomologist of Alabama, estimated that two million people in the South annually suffered from malaria; estimating the value of their lost labor at $100 each, he stated that $200 million worth of productive labor was lost each year.[70] Some people estimated that hookworm decreased the earning capacity of southerners from 50 to 65 percent since it left its sufferers chronically lethargic and disinterested in work.[71] A public health handbill circulated in Louisiana likened the loss of productive power in the rural South to a factory compelled to reduce its workforce or a store required to close an extra day each week while its competitors were open full-time.[72]

Countless stories published by the Rockefeller organizations, conveyed by fieldworkers or reprinted in southern newspapers, reported miraculous recoveries from hookworm, and these accounts always pointed to the increase in earnings and efficiency following the treatment. Previously these families had been living off of charity.[73] One narrative told the story of an illiterate white family living in a "tumbledown shack" in complete "misery." The father worked at half capacity; the mother and the children could not work at all. After treatment, the eldest son became a "sturdy healthy boy" who used his "muscle and energy to bring the family into a prosperity never known before." The family moved to a freshly painted, neat, two-story house and the children began to attend the local school. The story was accompanied by a set of before and after photographs depicting the journey from "squalor and wretchedness" to "the new cheerfulness of clean and industrious living."[74] Other stories reported that after being cured, families were able to produce more cotton and rent their own farms. In the Mississippi Delta, where the rate of malaria could be as high as 75 percent, reformers encouraged plantation owners to administer quinine to their tenants and sharecroppers, because more efficient labor would mean greater crops. William Dockery, in Sunflower County, Mississippi, enthusiastically distributed free quinine to his tenants and anyone else who patronized his store. On one of his largest plantations, containing 250 families of about 1,000 people occupying 5,000 acres of land, he noticed an immediate difference in the "efficiency, contentment, and appearance of the negroes" after administration of the drug.[75]

The emphasis on the relationship between disease and the earning capacity of southerners drew attention to the value, health, and character of the physical body itself. Louis L. Dublin, an agent of the Metropolitan Life Insurance Company, writing on the relationship between economics and world health, stated, "It is a habit with us Americans to emphasize the importance of national wealth but always in terms of property, machinery, and of manufactured products. We quite forget that human life exceeds in value all such goods by a very large margin. Human capital is the nation's greatest asset."[76] Wealth in the South could be measured in terms of healthy bodies, not just in terms of technology, financial investments, or crops produced. The president of the University of South Carolina, Samuel C. Mitchell, remarked, "I often tell them in South Carolina that our first need is a million and half healthy human animals."[77] The focus on healthy bodies as "human capital" highlighted the problems with the sluggish southern economy and the enfeebled southern body and reinforced the notion that a diseased region would lead to economic decline for the nation as a whole. Reformers also compared healthy bodies to machines. A public health official affiliated with the U.S. Public Health Service described the handicaps malaria placed on children during the years "when the body should be developing into a sturdy, dependable machine."[78]

Descriptions of diseased bodies in the South consistently emphasized the themes of degeneration and emasculation. In 1913 the *Atlanta Journal-Record of Medicine* described the effects of hookworm this way: "In such cases we find the victim's normal color replaced by a pale, sallow complexion; the eyes are listless, the pupils not very responsive to light; often they present a blank stare, fish-like in character. The hair is dry and scant, especially in the armpits. . . . The chest is flat, and the shoulder blades standing out prominently, suggesting 'angel wings.' When the disease occurs during the growing period there is a marked retardation in development."[79] One doctor in Kentucky described a hookworm victim as a "pale, flabby, useless hulk of flesh."[80] Photographs and written descriptions pointed to the stunted growth of southerners infected with the parasite. In a letter to Wickliffe Rose, Charles W. Stiles spoke of several cases of children who were thirteen and fourteen years old but who looked as if they had not developed beyond the age of seven or eight. He noted there was absolutely no sign of puberty (see fig. 3).[81] A handbill announcing free treatment circulated by the Rockefeller Foundation warned that hookworm stunted the child's growth "depriving him of a robust, vigorous, manly body."[82]

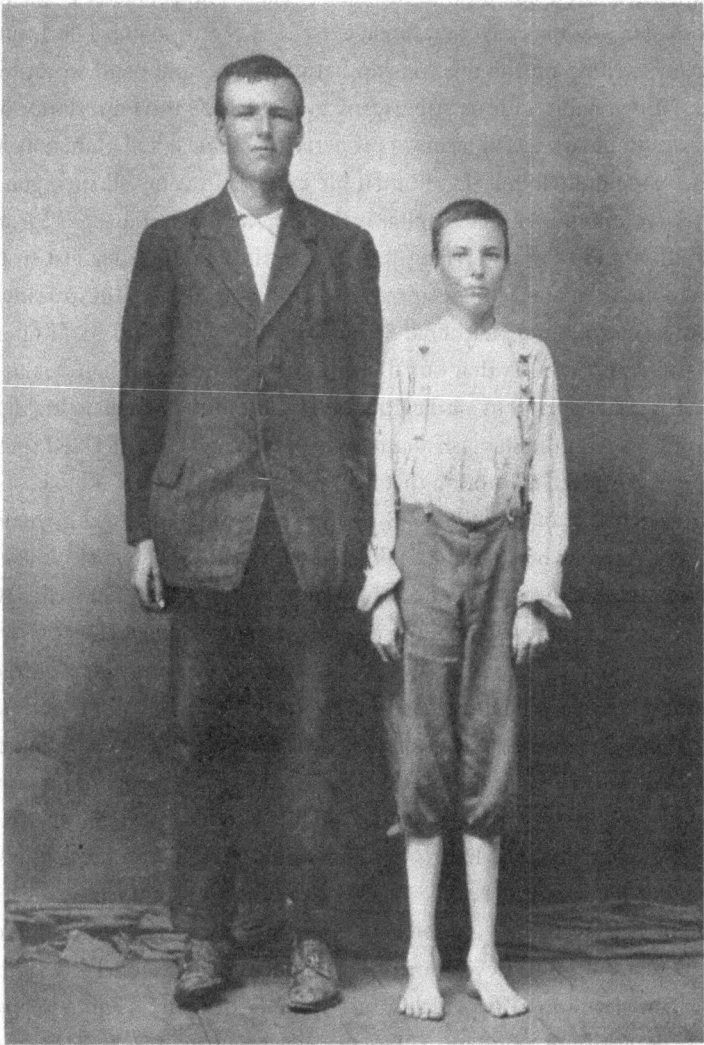

FIG. 2.—Showing dwarfing effect of the disease. These boys are brothers. Jones County, Miss. No. 1, age 17, weight 156 pounds; light infection. No. 2, age 18, weight 74 pounds; heavy infection.

FIGURE 3. Rockefeller Sanitary Commission for the Eradication of Hookworm Disease. *Second Annual Report*. Washington, D.C.: Offices of the Commission, 1911.

A doctor in Mississippi verified this assertion in his field report when he described a former patient's miraculous recovery. "I know him now — a great big, fine looking, robust, prosperous, energetic and influential citizen . . . a finer specimen of physical manhood cannot be found in Mississippi."[83] In short, the disease had rendered the South a region populated by economically impotent citizens.

Moreover, Americans viewed a virile masculine body not only as the key to economic productivity but also as a prerequisite for success in politics and imperialist ventures. The call to take up the "strenuous life," best embodied in President Theodore Roosevelt's Rough Riders, linked nationalism, racial imperialism, and manhood. National unity required a virile American manhood ready for military ventures abroad and a vigorous life at home.[84] The pale, underdeveloped, feeble bodies in the South stood in stark contrast to these national ideals. Later on, the Rockefeller Foundation received word on the prevalence of hookworm in southern recruitments for the U.S. Army during World War I; it was discovered that the men displayed a high level of apathy and indifference, hardly qualities valued by the American military. A doctor writing to the surgeon general of the U.S. Army complained that southern recruits showed a "poorer degree of physical development" and that "weight, chest development, and general physique" were undersized compared to northern recruits.[85] In one unit hookworm infection was as high as 78 percent, and officials deemed one out of three men in North Carolina as unfit for military service.[86] The emasculated bodies of southern men were not primed for combat or colonial exploration in the tropics. The Life Extension Institute, a philanthropic organization dedicated to public health service, reminded Americans that life destroyed at home by disease was no more needless than life destroyed in war and argued that World War I brought about an "urgent need of up-building American vitality . . . where modern methods of warfare have made the most extraordinary demands upon the strength and endurance of both soldiers and non-combatants."[87] Southern men's lack of manliness weakened the home front too, since it was clear that puny underdeveloped men suffering from an array of diseases could not be efficient laborers or useful citizens. General economic fortitude and the capacity of the southern manufacturing industries to mobilize for war were conspicuously absent in the South. "Our national health is physically our greatest national asset," President Roosevelt announced to the Committee of One Hundred of the American Association for the Advancement of Science. "To prevent possible deterioration of the American stock should be a national ambition. We cannot too strongly insist on the necessity of proper ideals for the family, for simple living and for those habits and tastes which produce vigor and make men capable of strenuous service to their country."[88]

The Danger of Tropical Diseases

At the turn of the century, most Americans believed the United States was a model of democracy in Western civilization, the leader of technological and scientific progress, and the guarantor of laissez-faire individualism. All of these things, coupled with a belief in the superiority of the Anglo-Saxon race, engendered a faith in the legitimacy and viability of American supremacy in the world. Any domestic weakness, envisioned or genuine, undermined American ideals of progress and civilization. The South figured prominently in this picture. A dependent labor force that was crippled by chronic illness and incapable of productive labor in a region that produced the majority of the world's cotton supply threatened the economic supremacy and cultural authority of the American nation. The region also contained 90 percent of the entire U.S. population of black Americans, which reinforced the colonial belief that people of color and disease went hand-in-hand, whether in the tropics or the U.S. South. By the second decade of the twentieth century, as a result of the public work accomplished in the southern states, the Rockefeller Foundation was established (in 1913), broadened its geographical reach, and sought to eradicate disease in such places as the Caribbean, South America, and British colonies in the Far East. In fact, the domestic and global focus on disease existed in symbiotic relation. Public health work done in the tropics encouraged new ways of thinking about the place of the South in the nation, and efforts to eradicate disease in the South encouraged reformers and philanthropists to expand their activities in additional tropical places.

The need for healthy bodies in military combat and in imperialist expeditions to the tropics generated an interest in a scientific field designed to facilitate these goals. The theoretical connections made between medicine and place during the rise of the modern nation-state in the late nineteenth and early twentieth centuries was energized by the emergence of tropical medicine as a scientific specialty. While physicians recognized and treated diseases in the tropics throughout the nineteenth century, a series of closely related developments in the last two decades of the century contributed to the identification of specific tropical diseases that warranted treatment by a separate medical discipline.[89] In the earliest attempts to colonize the tropics, Europeans noted the existence of certain diseases that appeared to be indigenous to the warm damp climates. The development of medical geography and the topographical survey demonstrated a belief in the influence of the physical environment on disease, including climate, vegetation, and physical topography. Physicians of colonial medicine adopted the use of detailed "medico-topographical surveys" in these tropical regions and contributed to a new body of knowledge that helped define these areas as exotic, alien spaces. The invention of tropicality — a space defined as the tropics — emphasized the danger of the place and the miasmatic theory of contagion.[90] Foucault has described the development of this kind of perception in the nineteenth century as a "historical and geographical consciousness of disease."[91] The need to know, to look, to catalog, and to map the place (and ultimately the body) would make it possible for western colonizers to survive the dangers of the tropics.

Many Europeans adopted the belief that human beings, like plants and animals, did not adapt very easily, if at all, to unfamiliar climates. In the late nineteenth century, the germ theory of disease and research done in parasitology changed the conceptual framework for understanding the tropics by positing that microbes and parasites, not the climate, were responsible for tropical diseases. The developing power of the microscope and laboratory in the study of tropical diseases now meant that explanations for the etiology of illness were exclusively scientific and could not be based on loose observations and impressions of the environment. The new tropical medicine argued that the direct causes of disease in the tropics were germs and parasites and that a reliance on scientific solutions like sanitation and public health would enable human beings to survive in unfamiliar topographies and environments. Various schools of tropical medicine dedicated to this philosophy emerged in the early twentieth century, including one in London in 1899 and others at Harvard University and Tulane University roughly a decade later. By that time, the study of diseases in the tropics rooted in the on-site topographical survey was shifting toward the study of tropical diseases in scientific surroundings far removed from the tropics.

While revolutions in the scientific world contributed to the development of tropical medicine as a separate discipline in the late nineteenth century, imperial expansion and the possibility of settlement had always fueled the interest in the connection between disease and the tropics. As far back as the fifteenth century, Portuguese exploiters of equatorial Africa knew the climate was unhealthy, and Europeans, on average, lasted only a year or two. In the early part of the nineteenth century, the French conquest of Algeria and the British interest in India, the West Indies, and Africa brought Europeans into contact with the tropics and raised familiar questions about the ability of the white man to survive in foreign environments.[92] Discussions of European settlement in the southern states of Louisiana, Mississippi, Alabama, and Georgia also manifested a concern with health and climate.[93] The study of diseases in the tropics initially fell under the purview of the military, and medicine played a pivotal role in negotiating the relationship between the colonized and the colonizers because scientific knowledge constituted a powerful medium of authority and control.[94] The supremacy of military control also depended upon the ability of the colonizers to survive in foreign environments. Moreover, the successful extraction of labor from indigenous peoples and the economic viability of the new colonial possessions depended upon the health of individual bodies. The *American Journal of Sociology* remarked that "civilized man, by introducing his mental and moral equipment into the social and economic situation of the tropics, will mold the helpless, shiftless native into a producing machine . . . the striking thing about this method of attack of the problem is the fact that no inexhaustible supply of capital is required."[95] Like the U.S. South, the key to extracting efficient labor from the "natives" was to turn the body into a healthy producing machine rather than relying solely upon an infusion of capital, technology, and military might.

By the late nineteenth century several developments, including further British exploration of Africa; the U.S. acquisition of the Philippines, Puerto Rico, the Hawaiian Islands, and Guam; and the American presence in Cuba during the Spanish-American War, guaranteed that the political and economic imperatives of western imperialism would continue to influence the field of tropical medicine as it developed into a scientific specialty. A popular medical text by Patrick Manson titled *Tropical Diseases: A Manual of the Diseases of the Warm Climates* (1898), published at the height of western imperialism, offered doctors a new tool for interpreting foreign environments and cataloging disease. European and American exploration of new regions across the globe linked the acquisition of geographical knowledge of the globe with imperialism. The presence of disease in these newly discovered spaces irrevocably connected the subject of health with global expansion. The American and European acquisition of so many new territories in the southern and eastern hemispheres by the turn of the century illustrated how closely associated the various regions of the world had become. Although writing several decades later, Dr. Earl Baldwin McKinley of George Washington University identified the key repercussion of global expansion in his work *The Geography of Disease* (1935) where he stated that "with the constant shifting of world centers more closely to one another because of more rapid transportation and greater facilities in communication it behooves all of us to be concerned with these problems of tropical diseases."[96]

Yet, the new scientific paradigm of tropical medicine was somewhat unstable, since the older notion of miasmatic infection and the tendency to stress the significance of climate lingered well into the twentieth century. Old ideas about the connections between disease, climate, and topography existed uneasily with new ideas about the scientific reasons for specific tropical diseases. Even when the scientific and popular communities came to accept germ theory, the notion of place as intrinsic to the question of disease remained a central component of this new knowledge. While the new medical discipline emphasized the power of science in conquering germs and parasites responsible for tropical maladies, the paradigm still reinforced notions of diseased geographical spaces, since certain microbes were believed to be specific to the tropics. Most now believed that climate was unlikely to be the direct cause of illness, but it could certainly provide a milieu conducive to the cultivation of distinctive germs and parasites. In some cases, the framework of climactic determinism stubbornly held on. Moreover, in the late nineteenth century the discovery of the malarial parasite and the hookworm parasite helped draw continued attention to the indirect role topography played in disease transmission. Hookworms survived best in sandy soils, and the mosquitoes that carried malaria were far more prevalent in warm humid climates. Thus, colonial administrators and public health reformers continued to map these locales as degenerative spaces, and they generated a tremendous quantity of statistical material, charts, topographical maps, narrative commentary, and official reports. The staggering amount of paperwork lent authority to the architects of disease control and legitimized the imperial power of the modern nation-state in its quest to grapple with the impact of tropical and subtropical climates.

Depictions of the tropics typically drew upon a complex of themes such as climate, race, landscape, and disease. The discourse on tropical spaces often was unstable and marked by representational duality. As David Arnold notes, "The symbolism of the tropics was deeply ambivalent, for a landscape of seeming natural abundance and great fertility was also paradoxically a landscape of poverty and disease."[97] In his 1929 book *The Romance and Rise of the American Tropics*, Samuel Crowther stated quite precisely, "The curse of the tropics is poverty—a startling poverty existing amid splendour."[98] This paradox raised questions about how easily the tropical region could be subordinated and made productive for imperial powers. In short, the question being asked was: Could civilization overcome the perils of the tropics? The tendency to paint the tropics as both pathological and paradisiacal also generated what one geographer has called a "moral climatology."[99] In mapping the tropical world, colonizers repeatedly offered moral judgments on tropical lands and peoples, even while programs of colonization were often undertaken under the guise of scientific objectivity. The use of moralistic idioms contributed to the construction of the tropics as the Other, a geographical entity often deemed inferior to the temperate regions of the world. A binary understanding of the world in terms of who belonged and who did not was a central component of the ideology of imperialism. The Other could take the form of person or place.[100]

The U.S. South also was figured as the tropical Other, as a diseased and degenerative space, a land and people ravaged by what one writer in the *North American Review* called "tropical poverty."[101] Certainly southern tropicality was imbued with a host of contradictory meanings, cast in both a negative and a positive light. The region was simultaneously viewed as alluring and perilous, exotic yet familiarly American. As early as the sixteenth and seventeenth centuries, colonists considering transplantation to Virginia and the West Indies harbored anxieties about the dangers hot climates posed to English constitutions. In the early nineteenth century, discussions of European settlement in the southern states of Louisiana, Mississippi, Alabama, and Georgia also manifested a concern with health and climate.[102] Northern travelers to the Deep South often commented on the dangerous, dank, and primitive characteristics of the landscape. In his travel diary titled *From Cape Cod to Dixie and the Tropics*, John Milton Mackie described the "primeval aspect of things" and marveled at the fecundity of the vegetation. In Louisiana he noticed that "it [wa]s the beauty of the garden and the desolation of the waste combined" that drew his attention to the local scenery. Yet while Mackie was enthralled with the paradoxical combination of spectacular beauty and decay in the South, he was glad to leave behind what he called the "pet nursery of fever and pestilence" and return to a more acceptable environment.[103] Some Americans viewed the region as a tropical Eden, a therapeutic escape from the alienation engendered by the rise of corporate capitalism in the North.[104] In the late nineteenth and early twentieth centuries a spate of promotional books and pamphlets focusing on the salubrious climate, the Edenic landscape, and the availability of exotic fruits and vegetables welcomed tourists and real estate developers to the region. Florida, in particular, was often portrayed as a bountiful tropical paradise.[105] Yet underneath the allure of southern tropicality there lurked a dark side, a dangerous and pestilential character that needed to be tamed. As Rebecca McIntyre explains, even the travel promoters often found themselves inexplicably drawn to the "medieval, melancholy, and slightly grotesque" features of the region.[106]

As the scientific and medical communities began to focus on the connections between insects, climate, and disease, many physicians and reformers began to associate the South with tropical pathology. The U.S. acquisition of the overseas colonies raised questions about the nature of infectious diseases thought to have entered North America in the bodies of American soldiers, missionaries, businessmen, sailors, or diplomats who had been traveling abroad. One doctor noted that southern ports in particular were potential hotbeds for diseases indigenous to the damp hot climate of tropical regions.[107] Relying on a military metaphor, the *Southern Medical Journal* declared that as a result "it falls to the lot of southern physicians to act as outpost sentinels, guarding the land from being unconsciously invaded by devastating diseases."[108] The opening editorial of the first issue of the *American Journal of Tropical Medicine* in 1913 warned that formerly "exotic" diseases such as yellow fever, hookworm, pellagra, and malaria had planted themselves in some sections of the United States.[109] The existence of tropical diseases in the South meant that one did not need to travel abroad to discover an "exotic" disease or to experience the enervating effects of a tropical climate. One person writing to the Rockefeller Foundation worried that, since the number of people emigrating to the South to escape the frigid weather of the North was rapidly increasing, tropical diseases not only threatened southerners but endangered northerners too.[110] Tropical diseases in America's own backyard also continued to highlight the dangers that imperialists still faced abroad because the existence of tropical pathologies at home generated doubts about whether they had been successfully contained around the globe.

The spectacle of tropical geographies was accessible to the public most readily in the art of world expositions and exhibits and national coverage. The exposition proved to be the best cultural model for imperial propagandists to showcase both the potential merits and the exotic features of the new colonial possessions.[111] The display of tropical otherness included both the U.S. South and foreign locales. In 1915 the Rockefeller Foundation presented an exhibit on hookworm disease at the Panama-Pacific International Exposition in San Francisco, California, to raise public awareness about infection in the southern states through the use of models, life-sized photographs of diseased bodies, and live demonstrations of microscopic examinations of fecal matter. The exhibit included a colored map of the world showing places where hookworm could be found and the various tropical regions targeted by the International Health Board for public health reform. Juxtaposed next to the illustrated charts on the results of the campaign in the U.S. South, the world map reinforced the connection between the social and corporeal deficiencies of the tropical South and distant tropical countries.[112] Walter Hines Page published an article in his widely distributed magazine *World's Work* titled "The Hookworm in Civilization," which made comparisons between the "disease belts" of the world and described the way public health work in the U.S. South seemed likely to lead to "the reclamation of other tropical peoples." The subtitle of the piece, touching on several key points, read, "The work of the Rockefeller Sanitary Commission in the southern states making men of anaemics [sic] and adding incalculable wealth as well as health to our national assets—the way toward the reclamation of all tropical peoples and the utilization of their lands—the prodigious part that this parasite has played in the history of all warm countries." The "reclamation of tropical peoples" in the U.S. South, the Caribbean, South America, Latin America, and eastern countries were intimately related, linking together the southern states, Puerto Rico, Columbia, Venezuela, British Guiana, Dutch Guiana, and Ceylon (which later became Sri Lanka).[113]

Those writing and talking about disease in the U.S. South did not always make the distinction between imported tropical diseases and diseases understood to be native to the region. The tendency to blur the line between the two possible modes of origin in scientific and popular discourse contributed to an image of the tropical South as a place that had long harbored unusual and potentially life-threatening illnesses. The idea that diseases have histories and are not timeless entities often became lost in discussions of tropical areas. In 1915, Ellsworth Huntington, a professor at Yale University and proponent of environmental determinism, argued in his work *Civilization and Climate* that the South suffered from certain "climatic handicaps" and that the "depressed climate" in the region accounted for the failure of the South to develop a civilization along the lines of the North. Huntington explained how many southerners suffering from hookworm and malaria had "ceased to be careful about food and sanitation" and did "not feel the eager zest for work which is so notable in parts of the world where the climatic stimulus is at a maximum."[114] To observers at the turn of the century, southerners' apparent ignorance of rudimentary health measures, as well as their disease, dirtiness, and lassitude, looked remarkably similar to the lack of basic public hygiene found in the nonwhite peoples living in the American colonial possessions. The lack of privies in the South coupled with accusations that southerners were essentially eating and living in their own feces was reminiscent of a similar situation: American colonialists in the Philippines accused native Filipinos of purposefully polluting the soil with their own excrement and maintained that the incidence of "filth diseases" was extremely high because of the tropical environment and lack of personal sanitation.[115]

Topographical and cultural comparisons between the U.S. South and places such as the Philippines, Cuba, and Puerto Rico were not surprising given that many of the doctors and public health officials who wound up working in the U.S. South in the early twentieth century had previously been stationed in some of these tropical countries. Lewellys Barker had received his training in tropical diseases in the Philippines as a young student from Johns Hopkins, and Charles W. Stiles taught army regulations at the Army Medical School, with a special emphasis on military hygiene, sanitation, and tropical diseases. Inspired by an army surgeon's work in Puerto Rico, Stiles began his search for the hookworm parasite in the U.S. South because he believed it might explain the indolence and anemic appearance of poor whites. Likewise, the International Health Board maintained that public health work in the U.S. South was valuable because it served as a training school for men "given responsible posts in foreign countries."[116] In his book on the Rockefeller

Foundation's public health work in the Caribbean, Steven Palmer explains that in fact the effort to eliminate hookworm was a global crusade with roots in the nineteenth century, including efforts by Europeans and Americans to eradicate the parasite in Latin America, Central America, the British Caribbean, and Puerto Rico, long before the Rockefeller family initiated its work in the southern states.[117] Thus the transnational back-and-forth movement of knowledge on hookworm over decades captured the U.S. South in a long-standing global web of health reform.

Race and Disease

Scientific inquiry into tropical pathology could not be divorced from conceptions of race, since one of the objectives of tropical medicine was to explain the various interactions between racial constitutions and regional environments. During the nineteenth century many physicians, zoologists, anthropologists, and geographers turned to the study of "acclimatization," which often focused on the tropics, and in part investigated the connection between race and climate.[118] The tension between race and place was obvious. Could the energy, initiative, and progressive drive believed to be intrinsic to the white race overcome the debilitating effects of the tropical climate? The tropical environment was not a suitable place for the white man, yet the imperatives of imperialism at the turn of the century dictated that Anglo-Saxons must learn to adjust to new locales. Furthermore, scientists and others wondered if the environmental element could be managed and subdued, and whether the contact with a different race would still retard the advancement of the Anglo-Saxon race. The prevalence of diseases particular to the tropics only complicated matters and pointed more directly to the need for a solution cloaked in scientific garb. Medical and social theory presumed that racial identity influenced the expression of disease. This explained why the white man traveling in foreign environments might be more susceptible to certain illnesses and why the black man might display an inherent immunity to certain pathogens that could threaten the vitality of the Anglo-Saxon race.[119] Of course, the logic of this medical reasoning muddled the popular belief in the superiority of the white race because in a curious contradiction it suggested that a nonwhite race might show evidence of a particularly strong constitution yet still be living in a state of degradation and backwardness. The new tropical medicine of the late nineteenth century provided answers to these medical conundrums by demonstrating how attention to public health and sanitation could guarantee the survival of white civilization. Ten years before the first school of tropical medicine was founded in England, Truxtun Beale, a foreign diplomat to Persia and later Greece, wrote about the survival of the white race in the tropics and asserted boldly that "science will eventually harmonize our life with tropical environments" and that as nations advanced toward civilization they would increasingly become more independent of the environment.[120]

In spite of some rather broad, optimistic proclamations about the ability of science to conquer disease and reverse the decline of civilization, anxieties about the dangers of race-specific expressions of disease lingered in the popular and medical imagination. Colonial doctors working in the tropics initially pointed to the nonwhite races' apparent immunity to certain illnesses while simultaneously implicating them in spreading those diseases. These accusations were largely based on anecdotes, and further experience in the tropics demonstrated that the local inhabitants were not necessarily immune from local diseases.[121] Yet the assumption that nonwhite races were likely simultaneously to be free of the symptoms of disease and carriers of disease persisted because of the American and European belief in the supremacy of the Anglo-Saxon race. In a popular national magazine Dr. Charles T. Nesbitt of North Carolina argued that the "most serious problem that Americans face when any large numbers of an alien race enter this country is the menace to the health of the people of the entire nation."[122]

In the South, the significant presence of black Americans—almost 90 percent of the total black population in the United States through the first decade of the twentieth century—reinforced the idea that the region was disease ridden. White southerners were often quick to point out the health problems of blacks, particularly the menace of tuberculosis, in order to divert attention away from the nationally advertised problems of diseased poor whites.[123] The "negro health problem" received a substantial amount of attention from public health reformers and physicians who argued that the black race had deteriorated significantly since emancipation and had begun "to practice all the vicious habits known to civilization," thereby spreading infectious diseases through intimate contact with whites.[124] Physicians also attributed the origins of some diseases to the black race. Surgeon L. D. Fricks, writing on behalf of the Rockefeller Foundation's International Health Board, stated that malaria was an "exotic" in the true sense of the word, since it had been brought to the United States from Africa.[125] The medical community repeatedly claimed that Africans arriving on the slave ships in the United States had transported hookworm as well.[126] In an article in *McClure's Magazine* titled "The Vampire of the South," Marion Hamilton Carter declared "the price of slavery" was an "imported disease" and that "its 'import tax' [had] been literally paid in blood — pure Anglo-Saxon blood."[127] Ironically, despite the attempts to link blacks with a range of infectious diseases, hookworm appeared to be predominantly a poor white illness. Moreover, black and white southerners suffered from malaria in equal numbers.

The medical paradox regarding the white race's tendency to succumb to tropical diseases despite its supposed racial superiority was especially apparent in the U.S. South, because a large proportion of the poor white population suffered from hookworm and pellagra. An increasingly conspicuous population of diseased poor whites drew attention to one variation of the inherent tension between race and place. Ellsworth Huntington explicitly stated in his work *Civilization and Climate* that certain tropical diseases native to the southern climate had exacerbated the penchant for laziness that had caused white southerners to "fall below the level of their race" and become "'Poor Whites' or 'Crackers.'" Disease created a weak labor force and led to an increase in rundown farms. Huntington also noted that these people increased in number as one moved "from a more to a less favorable climate." This was evidence, he concluded, that the average southern white person was degenerating and sinking "dangerously near the level" of the average southern black individual.[128] Marion Hamilton Carter simply called poor whites suffering from hookworm "a great abnormal race of the South."[129] Wickliffe Rose observed the degeneracy of the white race during a trip to Richmond County, Virginia, in 1911. He reported that the poor whites in this community called "Forkemites" were known for their extreme poverty, lack of thrift, "dense illiteracy," and "low moral tone" and subsequently had begun to take on the appearance of a "distinct race."[130] In a report made to Rose from Kentucky two years later, a doctor reported on his treatment of some "aboriginal Anglo-Saxons" and stated that he was "reliably informed that in many places they are still speaking sanscrit [sic]."[131]

By the mid-nineteenth century in the United States, Latin America, and Europe, theories of degeneration began to appear in works by physicians, biologists, social scientists, psychiatrists, anthropologists, historians, and political theorists. Degeneration was an all-inclusive, dynamic, malleable term that conveyed a sense that, somehow, the past was superior and the present was declining or moving backward from a more perfect form.[132] Racial degeneration particularly interested biologists, anthropologists, and sociologists. The theory of degeneration utilized the language of racial imperialism by invoking such words as "savagery," "barbarism," "retrogression," "moral weakness," and "decay." The images and metaphors of racial degeneration lingered in social scientific and medical discourse into the early twentieth century despite persistent challenges to the belief that changes in the environment would lead to degeneration and the rise of separate racial types. As Saul Dubow explains, "Indeed, the capacity of the degenerationist paradigm to incorporate opposing arguments within its explanatory framework was an important element of its hold on the public imagination."[133] Racial biology drew scientific borders between distinct groups, and degeneration theory provided a convenient way to explain what happened when certain racial groups transgressed those social boundaries. Since movement out of particular environments or social roles constituted a kind of degeneration, the white race's colonization of tropical climates as well as the movement of nonwhite people or recently freed slaves into white spaces meant that debates about the erosion of racial types within certain limits would continue. American and European scientists discussed whether the "tropicalized" white race was a degenerate type and they developed a set of negative ideas about "miscegenation," which they believed led to biological race degeneration.[134] The Lamarckian idea that acquired characteristics could be inherited also was a central tenet of degeneration theory.[135]

In the South, a white race moving backward toward a state of barbarism rather than forward toward a state of civilization muted the distinction between black and white, civilized and savage. In an era in which the social separation of the races had become codified into law, as well as a universal de facto practice, the possible existence of a degenerate white race created tremendous anxiety about the potential violation of these boundaries. Disease threatened the social foundation of the South — segregation — since it played a critical role in this process of racial de-evolution. The Lamarckian model of inheritance, which was an integral part of degeneration theory, corresponded with public health efforts to alter the environment through the adoption of new sanitary practices and preventative health measures. A strict sanitary regime, an attempt to order and rearrange the environment, was the key to slowing down, if not stopping, the decline of civilization. Evidence of Anglo-Saxon regression in the South challenged the national consensus on white racial superiority that underlay much of modern American identity at the turn of the century.[136] Just when the American imperialist project abroad was contributing to the construction and celebration of a white national identity through the dominance of the nonwhite races in the tropical world, the distinctive problems of the diseased tropical South, magnified by the new interest in tropical medicine, including the pathology of the poor white, threatened to weaken this ideology from within. Thus, mastering disease in the U.S. South and abroad was a crucial step toward saving white civilization.

The relationship of disease to civilization and barbarism was clear because it interfered with the normal progression of man and society. The *American Journal of Tropical Diseases and Preventive Medicine* speculated that hookworm had existed in the world for thousands of years and wondered at "what stage of advancement and civilization" man would have reached by the early twentieth century if the parasite had not "interfered with the mental and physical development of every generation during the development and learning period of life."[137] Ronald Ross, the physician who made the discovery that mosquitoes were responsible for the dissemination of malaria, described the disease as "the principal and gigantic ally of Barbarism" and warned that "no wild deserts, no savage races, no geographical difficulties have proved so inimical to civilization [sic] as this disease."[138] In short, the prosperity and fortitude of the modern liberal state and civilization depended upon the mastery of the mosquito, the malarial parasite, hookworm, and the human body. The rural South, without public health reform, stood in the way of progress, civilization, and productivity.[139] Finally, even if the parasites did not lead to loss of labor and production through actual disease, the mosquitoes themselves often interfered with the region's agricultural progress. The *Louisiana Times Democrat* reported that in Abbeville the insects were "so numerous and bloodthirsty" that one could not travel on the country roads by "reason of the clouds of mosquitoes which rise and literally cover driver and team." Fieldwork was entirely out of the question, the local paper added, until the pests had left the area, which turned out to be some nine days later.[140]

Trenchant criticism of the South's diseased citizens and lack of civilization often provoked hostile reactions from the region's inhabitants. In an address before the Alabama Methodist Conference, Bishop Warren Candler of Georgia, the former president of Emory College and an influential religious leader, severely chastised northern philanthropists for harboring a disingenuous tendency to characterize white southerners as primitive, uneducated simpletons. As a leading critic of hookworm reform in the South, he warned, "The northerners are coming south to teach the southern barbarians new and strange theories. I want to say to them now and to John D. Rockefeller especially that we do not want any of their ideas, any of their theories, any of their advanced civilization, any of their suggestions and not a greasy penny of their money. We will remain in our barbarity and we will enforce our laws and inculcate our ideas without any impertinent suggestions from them."[141] Candler published a scathing article denying the prevalence of hookworm in the South and criticized the popular germ theory of disease.[142] Since the germ theory of disease had shifted focus to an understanding of the strict taxonomic ordering of illness, it resonated with ideas of hierarchy in discussions of progress and civilization. Candler and others resented the implication that the lack of public hygiene and the pervasiveness of disease in the South were peculiarly southern and evidence of a low place on the continuum of social evolution. What Candler could not have known is that the RSC's survey of six hundred counties across the South and its deworming treatment of four hundred thousand patients led to a drop of infection by 50 percent, greater economic productivity, and higher school attendance.[143]

In fact, Candler was closer to the truth than he realized when he implied that the lack of public sanitation and the pervasiveness of disease in the South were not peculiarly southern. It was not that the South was more like the rest of the United States. Rather, in some ways the South was similar to other countries around the globe. Ironically, regional distinctiveness was reinforced by comparisons between the tropical South and the tropics. Imperial anxieties about climate, racial degeneration, and disease in the tropics encouraged Americans to locate the tropical pathology of the South in a transnational framework. Civilizing missions at home, or patterns of domestic imperialism, reinforced the power of imperialism abroad. The focus on healthy, efficient bodies prepared to face the dangers of the tropics and contribute to the nation's economic supremacy in the world was crucial to the spread of American ideals of progress, Anglo-Saxon superiority, and civilization. In addition, the emphasis

on preventing defects in the body and curing sickness was a far more successful strategy for building up a colonial economy than relying on the infusion of
outside capital and expensive technology. The dangers involved in jumpstart-
ing a colonial economy with external resources or new technology aimed at
improving production included the possibility of creating a situation of perpetual dependency on outside help. The desire to cultivate efficient, machine-
like bodies through the eradication of disease would stimulate productive labor in the new colonial possessions as well as in the New South and generate
more wealth for the nation.

The politics of disease at the turn of the century, embedded in the language of medical science, cannot be divorced from our understanding of the
development of the New South. Metaphors of illness and infection as well
as attempts to eradicate distinctive diseases in the region reflected a growing concern about the rural problems of the South and called into question
the previous optimism of New South ideologues that predicted a smooth and
rapid transition to modern industrial life. The broader implication of industrial development in the region — namely, the effect of the southern economy
on the national economy — was implicit in these discussions on southern illness. Both the individual body and the specific geographic locality could be
sick in this new medical age. The collective image of a diseased people, diseased land, and diseased crop only served to remind the federal government
and northern philanthropists that regional pathology could endanger the well-
being of the larger nation. By linking the discourse of disease to the function
of the national economy, the medical and scientific communities provided a
very powerful argument for federal and commercial intervention in the South.
By the early twentieth century, the U.S. South generated at least 50 percent
of the world's cotton supply, and disease-carrying bugs, worms, and parasites
had the capacity to weaken this stronghold by reducing production and creating a chronically dependent labor force incapable of efficient labor. Interest in
the diseased South was also a domestic reflection of the ideology of American
imperialism and economic expansion at the turn of the century. Efforts to control and contain tropical pathologies abroad as part of the American imperialist project justified the taming of dangerous tropical pathologies at home.
Progressive reform efforts to reduce illness in the rural South with the help of
modern science could ensure the continued economic health of the nation-
state and solidify its power as an international leader in the world.

CHAPTER THREE
The White Plague of Cotton

For more than a century, this greatest of economic assets has been also our greatest social humiliation . . . although adding a billion dollars annually to the wealth of the world, the cotton farmers themselves are the most impoverished and backward of any large group of producers in America.

— CHARLES S. JOHNSON, EDWIN R. EMBREE, and W. W. ALEXANDER

So it is not illogical that the illness of King Cotton should be regarded as distinctive in character and largely unrelated to the health conditions of our economic activity as a whole. To be sure there will be for him no funeral; but is he destined to be the victim of a chronic invalidism?

— CLAUDIUS T. MURCHISON

Nowhere is the paradox of progress and poverty in the New South more apparent than in the region's reliance on and devotion to cotton. Writing in the *Independent*, G. L. Fossick proclaimed, "Cotton is the South's blessing or its curse; at once its hope and its greatest problem."[1] At the turn of the century, the South produced roughly 50 percent of the world's cotton supply, and optimistic champions of southern progress and material prosperity foresaw a golden future in the continued cultivation of the crop. Some self-proclaimed experts estimated the South could produce as much as 75 percent of the world's cotton supply. Although other industries such as mining and timber promised to bring great wealth to the region, investors, boosters, and New South proponents paradoxically turned to the commodity most associated with southern rural life and argued that the continued production of cotton would facilitate the economic integration of the region into the modern industrial state. The southern cotton mill industry had made great strides in its competition with New England mills. Optimists celebrated the South's contribution to worldwide prosperity and the key role the region played in bolstering national abundance and progress. Yet cotton was an agricultural product subject to the vagaries of weather, soil exhaustion, disease, and insect devastation, and it did not always bring the same price per pound from year to year. Overproduction of the crop during any given year might satisfy the international market's demand, furnish raw supplies for burgeoning manufacturers, and guarantee low prices for consumers, but it drove the market price of raw cotton so low that producers often could not recover the cost of production and make a profit. In addition, the cotton exchanges in New York, New Orleans, and Liverpool were wildly speculative and fluctuating prices made it almost impossible to predict future profits. Often these exchanges appeared to act independently of and not in response to actual agricultural conditions. Finally, the region's devotion to cotton led to dependence on a system of tenancy that contained the fundamental seeds of poverty and debt.

The struggle to reconcile King Cotton's image of grandeur and promise with the reality of material and social decline in the New South reflected a much larger problem. How easily could the South be incorporated into the national fold economically and what, if anything, did it have to offer in the wake of the Civil War? The cotton plant became the symbolic flashpoint for national debates about the economic repercussions of the Civil War, the place of agricultural pursuits in a rapidly industrializing nation, and the South's long-standing battle with poverty and destitution. Indeed, the region provided a reform template for how to convert a backward locality into a progressive element of the greater productive society.

The problem of reconciling regional agricultural backwardness with national industrial progress challenged the fiction of sectional reconciliation, which celebrated harmony between the races, the great industrial strides being made by the South, and the economic unanimity among sections. As early as the 1890s, with the arrival of the boll weevil and the ideological surge in Populist Party principles, federal experts, northern philanthropists, and liberal reformers began to focus on rural problems as the root cause of southern backwardness and stressed the importance of regional rehabilitation to liberal nation-building. By the turn of the century, efforts at reuniting North and South involved the transformative initiatives of the U.S. Department of Agriculture (USDA), which pushed for intervention in the South in an attempt to resolve the problem of one-crop agriculture, eradicate the encroaching boll weevil, revitalize country life, facilitate the adjustment of rural people to the modern industrial world, and ensure the continued affluence of the nation as a whole. Federal experts and northern and southern reformers turned to social science as a tool for rural uplift even while they sometimes romanticized the very rural life they were working to transform. Many tried to resolve what they identified as the paradox of poverty and progress, since there was evidence that cotton simultaneously generated great wealth and caused regional destitution. Much like contemporary historiographical debates, deliberations at the turn of the century revolved around the idea of the New South's shifting economic landscape, its lingering distinctiveness, and its relationship to the function of the larger national and international economies. These reformers discussed whether the economic constitution of the postbellum South was largely agrarian or more industrial in nature and questioned how easily the region could be aligned with the nation's capitalist ethos.[2]

In addition, the paradoxical nature of the cotton plant was reconfigured on a global scale. Many businessmen and social commentators viewed cotton as the great civilizer and the centerpiece of international commerce. Cotton linked the financial centers of the world and clothed so-called savage people. The export of raw cotton guaranteed that the South occupied a crucial position in the preservation of American dominance in the world market. Yet within the context of turn-of-the-century Western imperialism and transatlantic Progressive reform, the region appeared to be distinctively vital to the United States yet simultaneously analogous to foreign locales, in particular the overseas colonies. It was an "imperial crop," according to Henry Reed, editor of the Atlanta *Cotton Journal*, with power to bring great wealth and economic authority to the United States, yet it engendered a level of backwardness and poverty in the South that left the region looking very much like a rural colony.[3] The federal government's effort to reconstruct the cotton economy and the discourse surrounding backward rural economies mimicked the strategies of reform in such places as the Philippines, Puerto Rico, and Hawaii. Several agricultural reformers and spokesmen for southern agriculture such as Seaman A. Knapp, Clarence H. Poe, and Kenyon L. Butterfield consulted with European experts, traveled to European and Asian countries in search of guidance, and tried their hand at reform in American colonies and protectorates.

The idea of the South as a colonial economy is certainly not a new concept in the economic history of the South. C. Vann Woodward and Gavin Wright have argued that the dominance of a single agricultural commodity, the reliance on northern capital in the South, the nation's extraction of raw materials, and the region's isolated labor market and low wages made the South a colonial economy for many years.[4] While there is continued debate over the extent of northern investment in the region, there is no doubt that the South was predominantly rural, that it was not as industrial as the Northeast, and that cotton was a raw material and a prime national export. What matters, however, is that the imaginative view of the southern cotton economy as a colonial space may not have always reflected the reality of the situation but the impression was just as powerful all the same. Commentators at the time paradoxically viewed the South as a colonial economy to be utilized for its important resources even while they considered it a part of the United States that, if it had not already been fully integrated, would certainly reach that point in the near future. Thus the southern economy was regionally distinctive, nationally integral, and globally significant all at the same time.

The Centrality of Cotton

Nothing drew attention to the regional distinctiveness of the South quite like the continued dominance of King Cotton. In both the antebellum and postbellum periods cotton often symbolized all that was characteristic of the South. Following the Civil War, the continued production of cotton contributed to a sense of continuity between the Old and the New South. The relative lack of change in the agricultural methods used to grow cotton reinforced the image of the region as timeless and distinctive. Rupert Vance, a scholar affiliated with the Institute for Research in Social Science at the University of North Carolina in the 1920s, conceded, "Without accepting geographic determinism, one must admit that much that is distinctive of southern culture, its plantation system, its sectionalism, its agricultural life, its rural practices, has developed as a kind of complex around the cotton plant." Using the cotton plant as a template for a social geography of the South, Vance demonstrated how specific racial groups corresponded to the production of particular types of crops and how the effect of one crop on the economy had the capacity to shape a region's political ideology and accompanying civilization. By the early twentieth century the familiar phrase "cotton culture" referred to not only the basic agricultural methods employed in the cultivation of a good crop but also how society organized itself around the plant. One journalist noted succinctly, "In the Belt — Black, Cotton, or Bible, as you prefer — cotton is Religion, Politics, Law, Economics, and Art."[5]

Many noted that southerners seemed obsessively preoccupied with cotton, unlike their attitudes toward any other crop. Charles William Burkett, professor of agriculture at North Carolina College of Agriculture and Mechanic Arts, coauthored a book with Clarence H. Poe on the cultivation, marketing, and manufacture of cotton. The two authors argued that the plant shaped the lives of all white and black southern men from the time they were old enough to recognize the plant. In a chapter titled "Cotton: What It Means and Will Mean to the Southern States" they crooned, "Cotton! To every boy born and bred in the Southern States it is a magical word from the time he is big enough to roll in its billowy heaps in the 'cotton house' or go out into the June cotton field to find the first white bloom for his father, or ride to the gin on the big two-horse wagon-bed which the hands have packed with the snowy fleece new-gathered from the autumn fields. White or black, if his father is not of unusual wealth, he early learns to labor with his own hands in making the crop; and the entire process of cultivation is familiar to him."[6] Burkett and Poe explained how every southern man knew from the time he was young that cotton was "his inheritance and a part of his life" that he could never escape from. The authors argued that whatever else the rest of the world thought about cotton, "in 'Dixie' cotton is King."[7] Cotton dominated the market, the topic of conversation, and the culture as a whole. Earley Vernon Wilcox, a former special agent in charge of a USDA agricultural experiment station in Hawaii, also noted the centrality of cotton to southern life. "And what does cotton mean to the cotton states?" he asked. "It means life, health, happiness, and prosperity to them. In fact, nothing else matters much. If cotton is all right, all's well in the Cotton Belt. And if cotton is sick, the whole South is sick."[8]

Although the South produced other crops, cotton was irrevocably linked to the region in the national imagination too. One could not think about the South without thinking about cotton. The South was cotton and cotton was the South. The directors of such classic American films as *The Birth of a Nation* (1915) and *Gone with the Wind* (1939) opened their movies with scenes of slaves tilling cotton in the southern fields. The sentimental plantation school of fiction popular in the late nineteenth and early twentieth centuries in both the North and the South typically featured cotton plantations in the story lines.

Tourist brochures and postcards highlighted the importance of cotton to the development of the "Sunny South," and the plant emerged as a nostalgic and somewhat saccharine symbol of Dixie. Claudius T. Murchison, a professor of economics at the University of North Carolina, noted how visitors to the South with a "romantic disposition" would typically end their travel accounts with pictures of "the cotton fields where tuneful darkies gather the fluffy staple from the arms of smiling Pan."[9] Indeed, "cotton culture" could not be separated from racial associations. Regional images of the cotton-growing South fueled the mythology of the happy-go-lucky African American cotton picker in spite of the fact that many poor white farmers toiled relentlessly to grow the crop too. Grace Elizabeth Hale has demonstrated how tourist publications, souvenir objects, and national advertisements never made white bodies commodities in their cultural construction of southernness but always used racialized representations, linking black figures to southern brands and images.[10]

Those who celebrated the distinctive qualities that cotton brought to southern culture also viewed the crop as indispensable to the nation's overall financial and social well-being. While regionally specific, the crop remained indispensable to national prosperity. T. S. Miller Sr. observed that the national fixation with cotton was not extraordinary and that it was only "natural that we should wish to know something of the origin and history of the plant that wraps the human race, moves the wheels of commerce and controls the finances of the nation."[11] Since the South produced more than half of the world's cotton by the turn of the century, many believed the region not only played an integral part in the expansion of wealth in the United States but also constituted the core of the national economy. Harvey Jordan, president of the Southern Cotton Association in Atlanta, Georgia, explained how the export of raw cotton from southern ports to international mills helped stabilize the balance of trade between the United States and other nations. Indeed, Jordan maintained that the gold received in exchange for the export of raw cotton represented "the great bulwark of safety to the financial institutions of the American nation." Thus, the United States had a vital interest in sustaining the continued health of the cotton-growing South.[12] Cotton seemed as good as cash in hand, and commentators often likened it to precious metals. The *New York Times* referred to cotton as "new wealth," "gold," "sunshine," and "actual money."[13] In short, it served as legal tender. Cotton was one of the few products that southern farmers could not eat, and merchants demanded that debt-ridden tenants grow the crop in order to pay back the credit with interest that merchants had extended for the purchase of foodstuffs and farming supplies.

In the 1880s and 1890s the South hosted a series of expositions that celebrated the region's industrial and agricultural potential while embracing the philosophy of progress. The International Cotton Exposition in Atlanta in 1881 and the Cotton States and International Exposition in Atlanta in 1895 were the most striking examples of southern boosterism. The organizers of the 1895 exposition believed that the World's Columbian Exposition in Chicago in 1893 had failed to represent adequately the South's potential, and thus they felt compelled to remind the world of southern possibilities and promise. The intention of the Atlanta exposition was to foster existing trade relations between the South and Mexico, Central America, and South America as well as to promote commercial exchange between the South and chief European ports. The Department of Publicity and Promotion for the exposition declared the southern cotton-producing states the "most fertile and productive in the world."[14] The *Official Guide to the Cotton States and International Exposition* explained how one of the purposes of the fair was to develop "the opportunity for a new conquest" in the cotton market, outstripping the British control of the monopoly.[15] The organizers and sponsors of the Atlanta exposition used the venue to launch a massive propaganda campaign for southern progress and potential and provide a display for international products and raw materials designed to rouse enterprising American businessmen. This fair was not to be a showcase of southern rural deficiencies or a plea for regional reform but a celebration of the global potential of the South. One official from the U.S. Department of the Interior captured the true intent of a successful fair when he returned from the Atlanta exposition and declared, "An exposition is hardly a proper place for serious study. People attend it to receive impressions, not to pursue profound investigations."[16] The impression Atlanta exposition organizers hoped to convey was that of New South progress in the wake of the Civil War, southern power and dominance over the world cotton market, and the supremacy of the white crop to bring civilization to distant countries. Earlier titles for the exposition included the "Cotton States and Subtropical Exposition" as well as the "Cotton States and Pan-American Exposition."[17]

In the years following the Atlanta Cotton States and International Exposition, optimistic boosters continued to stress the importance of the cotton plant to the process of industrialization and agricultural progress in the New South as well as its ability to generate national and global wealth. From 1904 to 1906, when the price of cotton was higher than it had been in the 1890s, the *World's Work Magazine* published a series of articles that celebrated the immense possibilities of cotton and sustained the legacy of boosterism. In one such article titled "The Rich Kingdom of Cotton," Clarence H. Poe called cotton the "life-blood of commerce" and argued that the crop would help the "vanquished people" of the South rise to great positions of wealth and glory like they held before the Civil War.[18] Poe saw no limits for the South; production of the crop would not only restore the region to its rightful place in the nation but also play an integral role in a healthy international economy. In a book titled *Cotton as a World Power*, James A. B. Scherer praised the crop as the "world's Golden Fleece" and explained how "the nations are bound together in its globe-engirdling web; so when the modern economist concerns himself with the interdependence of nations he naturally looks to cotton for his most effective illustration."[19] In point of fact, by the turn of the century, the South was merely part of what Sven Beckert has described as the "global empire of cotton" that emerged out of the wreckage of the Civil War. Cotton production skyrocketed in Egypt, Brazil, India, West Africa, and Central Asia. As Beckert explains, "New forms of labor, the growing encasement of capital and capitalists within imperial nation states, and the rapid spatial expansion of capitalist social relations were the building blocks of a new political economy that dominated global affairs until the 'Great War' a half a century later."[20]

From a global perspective, the compulsion to reform economic backwardness in the South reflected a much greater design than mere rehabilitation of an isolated regional economy. In part, boosters aimed to restore the primacy of the South in the global cotton economy. In addition, the South figured prominently in the picture at the height of American imperialism. The power of imperialism depended upon two things: the capacity to project an image of authority, legitimacy, and racial superiority and the ability to dominate international markets and to finance viable colonial administrations. Any imagined or extant weaknesses in the American body politic or economy undermined imperial progress and the ideal of western civilization. The South's financial well-being proved to be crucial to the projection of American power abroad. If the region failed to keep pace with the international demand for cotton then it threatened the material prosperity and civilizing influence of the United States.

Many harbored anxieties that other imperial powers, such as England, had undermined the South's monopoly by exploring the possibilities of cultivating cotton in their colonial possessions. Others feared that the overproduction of cotton had depressed the regional and national economies so acutely that the only solution was to seek out foreign markets for either textiles or raw materials. Regardless of the source of danger, those who made the case for cotton as an agent of commerce and civilization linked regional prosperity to national imperial prowess and economic supremacy. Efforts to maintain the South's dominance in the cotton market could be construed not only as a national patriotic duty but also as support for the legitimacy and importance of American imperialism and global capitalism.

In fact, Americans and Europeans viewed cotton, itself, as an agent of civilization. Almost every commentator writing on the significance of cotton addressed one of the unique characteristics of this agricultural product: its ability to clothe and thereby civilize the world. James L. Watkins, a cotton statistician in the USDA, projected "that of the world's population of 1,500,000,000, about 500,000,000 regularly wear clothes, about 750,000,000 are partially clothed, and 250,000,000 habitually go almost naked." He speculated that the cotton industry would continue to expand until everyone on earth was clothed.[21] The world displayed an inexhaustible requirement for clothing, which represented civilized living, and the South was primed to meet this critical need. Watkins walked his fellow reformers through the path to civilization and the role that cotton played. He noted that once "man" attained clothing and acquired a "fondness for dress" he then sought "other comforts of life." This engendered a desire to learn a trade and own property. As a result of owning property man then developed the habits of thrift and industry. Subsequently, to protect property, men enacted laws, established order, and civilization followed. In short, Watkins described cotton as "a great civilizer" and underscored the South's moral responsibility to grow more of the crop so that millions of people around the globe could "hide their nakedness" and adopt the accoutrements of civilized life.[22] In his account, one single plant held the key to modern social and economic development. Likewise, in a promotional pamphlet designed to explain the transformation of cotton from "plant to product," a textile manufacturer in Massachusetts speculated that when man emerged from barbarism one of the first things he probably learned was the usefulness of cotton.[23]

Of course, ideas about racial hierarchy and savagery could not be divorced from the connections between cotton, clothing, and civilization. As Gail Bederman has argued, the Progressive Era discourse of civilization in the western intellectual tradition was rooted in ideas about the nature of savagery in relationship to civilization, racial hierarchy, and the superiority of the Anglo-Saxon race.[24] Edna Henry Lee Turpin, a fiction writer and social commentator, argued in her book *Cotton* that when men began to rise from savagery they turned to certain plants such as cotton. Even as late as 1924, she explained, cotton was used in "New York and London and all other great centers of civilization, as well as in African huts and South American jungles." In Turpin's and others' accounts, all races depended on cotton as a potentially civilizing force, and the plant proved to be the great equalizer since cotton aided in the process of evolution toward a higher society. Turpin highlighted the importance of this southern crop to the civilizing force of Anglo-Saxon civilization by including sketches in her book of two children with captions reading "savage child" and "civilized child." The first picture depicts a young nonwhite boy, standing defiantly on a rock, dressed only in feathers around his waist, a lavish ornamental necklace, and a ring through his mouth. The second picture shows a very young white girl wearing a white cotton dress, long cotton socks, and a bow in her hair (see fig. 4).[25] These companion images linked nakedness and savagery with the absence of cotton. In his book *Cotton as a World Power*, James Scherer declared, "Cotton cloth paves the way for Christianity in the jungles of the Dark Continent" because "to the savages of the Congo cotton cloth is more precious than ivory or gold." He explained how one could follow "the course of empire ever westward . . . the power of cotton evolving with the evolution of the power of man."[26]

In the late nineteenth and early twentieth centuries American manufacturers, politicians, and businessmen touted the advantages of worldwide markets for American exports, and these efforts rested on the conflation of ideas about imperialism, material prosperity, and racial evolution. A race's capacity for progress depended on its ability to adjust to and adopt the accoutrements of modern life. James Bryce, an Englishman, theorized that "race-contact" around the globe, presumably owing to imperialism, had increased because of "the desire of civilized producers of goods to secure savage and semi-civilized consumers."[27] Introducing backward peoples to American goods, including cotton clothing, not only contributed to the spread of civilization but also

SAVAGE CHILD   CIVILIZED CHILD

FIGURE 4. "Savage Child" and "Civilized Child." Edna Turpin, *Cotton*.
New York: American Book Company, 1924.

benefited American capitalism. Economists frequently emphasized the dangers of "overproduction" during this period and explained how the nation's economic health required a commercial outlet for its surplus. China and other countries in the East received considerable attention, and American foreign policymakers articulated a new policy known as the "Open Door," which aimed to augment American access to eastern markets.[28] One newspaper in Louisiana reported on the importance of developing Asian markets because if every person in China purchased a cotton shirt, southern farmers would be able to dictate the price of cotton on the market.[29] Cotton figured into discussions on the significance of eastern markets for two reasons: first, economists ruminated extensively on the overproduction of the crop, and second, raw cotton was one of the United States' chief agricultural exports.[30] In short, cotton itself was the prime agent of imperialism, circling the globe and pushing onward toward remote frontiers.

Paradoxically, even while cotton was considered a civilizing force, the crop evoked images of exotic, more primitive locales. Histories of the cotton plant typically emphasized its eastern origins, including India and China. Writers noted that even though a small region in the southern part of the United States produced most of the world's cotton, the plant had originally made its way to the South from the "Orient."[31] Scientific experts and social commentators also considered cotton indigenous to tropical countries. Two men writing on the Knapp method of growing cotton explained how cotton was subject to more disease and insects than any other southern crop because it was a tropical plant that had been "forced to adapt itself to more or less artificial conditions" in semitropical locales such as the South.[32] Thus, cotton was simultaneously alien and regionally specific. In 1890 Edward Atkinson published a long paper on the future of cotton manufacturing in the United States that he presented at a meeting of the New England Cotton Manufacturers' Association. He talked about the increase in the number of spindles in the South and reassured his northern audience that the South did not pose a threat to northern manufacturing. Although he only briefly addressed the possibility of foreign competition in the cultivation of raw cotton, including China, Atkinson included six elaborate pictures of "prehistoric" Chinese men and women cultivating, ginning, baling, spinning, and weaving cotton.[33] This curious juxtaposition of a discussion on "cotton culture" and textile mills in the South with pictures exoticizing ancient Chinese laborers seems unusual at first glance. Yet, the combination of these images mirrored a growing tendency to associate the South with foreign locales. The South as agricultural Other could not be reinforced any more definitively than through a comparison between the South and the actual Orient.

In 1910–1911 Clarence H. Poe traveled to Japan, China, Korea, India, and the Philippines with the explicit design of studying the countries' social and economic conditions for what they might teach southern farmers. Poe arrived with letters of introduction in hand from Walter Hines Page, Theodore Roosevelt, William Jennings Bryan, James Bryce, and Seaman A. Knapp. As a representative of southern agriculture and editor of the *Progressive Farmer*, he met with key Chinese leaders, Japanese education officials, American colonial administrators in the Philippines, and British imperialists. Poe saw many similarities between what he called the "Old South" and "Old Japan" where "agriculture was held in highest esteem" and those who labored with their hands rather than produced wealth from others' work were accorded great honor. Curiously, "Asia's greatest lesson for America" was its allegiance to an Asian version of preindustrial republicanism including a commitment to the commonwealth over the individual, "the essential immorality of waste" in war and farming, and "cooperative credit societies." Poe acknowledged that he was challenging the traditional idea of Asians as effeminate, luxurious, and self-indulgent and instead praised their attentiveness to "conservation," literacy, and agricultural industrial training. He also noted "brown Japanese 'heathen'" passed compulsory education laws and had lower illiteracy rates than whites in the South. Yet Poe's argument was replete with racial contradictions, especially when he explained how the Orient's lesson of conservation spoke to the significance of white "racial strength and power," much like the theories of Herbert Spencer and Theodore Roosevelt's celebration of high birthrates among whites. Paradoxically, Poe advocated the future development of an Anglo-Saxon American agrarian commonwealth while using the progress of "brown races" as evidence of the importance of educational sophistication, the conservation of agricultural resources, and racialized physical prowess. Regardless, the editor of the *Progressive Farmer* made it clear not only that Americans should look to Europe for guidance about agricultural reform but also that a "comparative view of the world" must involve Asian countries.[34]

The global interest in farming and rural life also was evident in federal experts' and economists' attention to the new field of "tropical agriculture," a phrase that invoked notions of imperialism and hinted at the commercial benefits to be derived from the extraction of raw materials from American or European colonies. As one writer in the *Scientific American* wrote in 1900, "Part of the 'white man's burden'" was to "revolutionize agriculture" in the tropics.[35] Almost two decades later, Earley Vernon Wilcox, who held many agricultural posts at the USDA, published a handbook titled *Tropical Agriculture* (1916) that announced the long-standing interest in "the commercial importance and opportunities of the tropics." Wilcox, who had based some of his work on his experience as head of the Hawaii Agricultural Experiment Station and visits to Florida, California, and Cuba, focused predominantly on the traditional understanding of the tropics but included material on the cultivation of sugar in Louisiana and cotton in the South.[36] Orator F. Cook, a botanist in charge of investigations in tropical agriculture in the Bureau of Plant Industry at the USDA (and a eugenicist as well), stated there was no reason why the United States should not engage in the "pioneering and missionary instincts" that other European countries had initiated in the tropics over the course of the past few centuries.[37]

Cotton was considered a tropical plant by nature and the Bureau of Plant Industry's interest in using agricultural reform as a tool of colonization resonated with the interest of businessmen, economists, and experts writing on and interested in cotton in the semitropical South. The USDA added established agricultural experiment stations in Hawaii, Guam, Puerto Rico, and the Philippines whose purpose, like those stations in the United States, was to yield educational information on such topics as proper soil cultivation, selective seed use, crop diversification, and the diseases of plants and animals. A transnational circuit of agricultural reformers affiliated with the USDA, including some with experience working in the South, moved between the United States and the American territories exchanging information on agricultural problems and touting the possibilities of commercial enrichment. William C. Stubbs, the director of three agricultural experiment stations in Louisiana, traveled to Hawaii to offer advice on sugar cane and subsequently reported in his investigation to Congress that the islands should be encouraged to maximize their production by also focusing on coffee, stock raising, dairy production, and the cultivation of certain fruits and vegetables. Seaman A. Knapp, who introduced the cultivation of rice in Louisiana through the development of several demonstration farms, was sent to Puerto Rico in 1900 to assess its need for an experiment station in San Juan.

At a meeting of the Southern Commercial Congress, an economic organization established in 1908 by reform-minded developers, the papers on the 1909 program reflected the connection between the southern economy, empire, and the quest for foreign markets. Some of the titles listed were "Colonization Opportunity in the Southern States," "Neglected Agricultural Opportunities in the South," "Opportunity for Southern Trade in South American Republics," "Opportunity for Southern Propaganda in the British Isles and Europe," and "The Port Opportunities of the South."[38] These topics suggest that agricultural reformers and industrial boosters viewed the South as both an economy that might yield raw goods similar to those being extracted in the overseas colonies and a significant player in the economic colonization of foreign countries. At issue was nothing less than a global understanding of the significance of cotton and other tropical crops in the mastery of empire.

The Reality of One-Crop Agriculture and the Market

Economists and reformers who advocated reliance on southern cotton as an agent of civilization, a regulator of international trade, and a commercial boon to the nation sometimes had trouble accepting evidence that suggested otherwise. Eugene Clyde Brooks pointed to the crux of the matter by asking how the South could "meet the demands of the world for raw cotton and at the same time remain economically independent?"[39] Agricultural practices that benefited national interests did not always guarantee regional prosperity. Even as early as 1881, Henry Grady, a prominent southern booster, observed that the South found itself "confronted with a new problem" as equally important as slavery, secession, and Reconstruction. Grady described how the cotton grower in the postbellum period, unlike his slaveholding ancestors, was "impoverished, unsettled, and thrown upon free labor, working feverishly with untried conditions . . . and too impatient to wait upon his own experience." He concluded that whether cotton cultivation "shall bring the South to independence or to beggary, are matters yet to be settled." The problem of cotton was a paradoxical quandary that reflected competing discourses about progress and poverty. M. D. C. Crawford simply described the role that cotton played in the history of civilization as "a history in paradoxes."[40]

That cotton embodied the dual symbolism of poverty and progress allowed it to serve as the perfect icon for deliberations over the incongruities inherent in the southern economy. Cotton was unmistakably rural in nature because it was an agricultural crop cultivated by a southern "peasant" class. Yet, since cotton sustained the burgeoning manufacturing industries within the South itself as well as in New England and England, it also fueled regional, national, and international commercial growth. Cotton could not be consumed and it was a preeminent cash crop. In short, the plant possessed both rural and industrial/commercial connotations. It linked the fields with industry and the countryside with the town. Ambivalence about the coexistence of rural poverty and industrial advances in the New South (and the nation at large) framed the debate about the place of cotton in both the marketplace and social life. The increasing interest in the economic and social problems of the South reinforced the bifurcation between an industrial worldview and an agrarian way of life. Moreover, the national fascination with the "agrarian myth" — a celebration of the yeomen farmer, who operated a small, independent, self-producing farm, as the ideal man and ideal citizen — shaped the response to seemingly calamitous agricultural problems in the South and the need for swift resolution for the sake of the nation's economic well-being.[41] Commentators repeatedly juxtaposed the national ideal of the virtuous independent farmer with the image of the indigent, thriftless, anemic cotton grower. Usually commentators portrayed this cotton grower as a degenerative poor white. Despite the fact that southern farmers grew other crops, agriculture in the South increasingly came to be associated with the production of a single crop.

Beginning in the 1890s a spate of articles, social scientific studies, books, and government investigations tried to reconcile the problem Grady had identified. All these publications questioned the boosters' faith in the supremacy of cotton. Economic depression in the last decade of the nineteenth century hit southern farmers exceptionally hard, and the plight of the cotton grower looked especially bleak. Many failed to produce their own foodstuffs and had to purchase supplies on credit from merchants by mortgaging their future crops. Exorbitant interest rates coupled with declining cotton prices led to heavy indebtedness and loss of land. Political agitation in the farmer class reached a zenith with the development of the Populist Party. Although the Populists ultimately failed to get many of their proposals codified into law, their campaign drew national attention to the economic problems of farmers. Criticism of the tenancy system and skepticism about the ability of cotton growers to generate new wealth for the New South found expression in the investigations and writings of students of agriculture, the federal government, and local cotton planters. In 1894 Charles H. Otken published a book titled *The Ills of the South*, which exposed the evils of the credit system and the "lien law machine" in the southern states. Otken described how conditions in the region at the end of the Civil War had fostered the development of a "vast credit system," bringing only "poverty and bankruptcy to thousands of families." He derided the system as "vindictive" and explained how it had "crushed out all independence and reduced its victims to a coarse species of servile slavery."[42] A decade later, Professor D. D. Wallace of Woford College in South Carolina described the crop lien as the "vampire lien system" that had ushered men into "a system of indolence," ruined "their credit and self respect," and allowed "earth butchers" to manage land that led to the destruction of natural resources.[43] The oppression of the crop lien system had produced a large class of tenant farmers powerless to extricate themselves from a tightening cycle of debt and unable to achieve independent owner-ship, an achievement long cherished in the American political and economic imagination.

In 1895, the same year Atlanta sponsored the Cotton States and International Exposition, the U.S. Senate held hearings to determine the cause of the cotton growers' wretched financial condition and came to many of the same con-clusions as Otken and Wallace. During the summer of 1893, the Committee on Agriculture and Forestry mailed a circular with a series of questions to members of several cotton exchanges, a number of cotton farmers, business-men, and cotton factors and also conducted interviews in St. Louis, Memphis, and New Orleans. The agency then published the resulting public testimony and written replies in a five-hundred-page report. The boosterism of the cot-ton exposition in Atlanta stood in stark contrast to the sense of despair in the Senate testimony and accounts, and this discrepancy embodied the paradox of the New South. Based on the material the committee had collected, it con-cluded that cotton growers had no chance "to better their condition or to live with comfort" because of the low price of cotton on the market. In short, the cost of production exceeded the value of the cotton raised. Moreover, a large percentage of farmers were insolvent and very few had managed to acquire their own property. The committee disagreed with the theory of overproduc-tion as the cause of the cotton growers' chronic difficulties and instead ex-plained how the demonetization of silver and the tariff were the main culprits. Letters from prominent cotton growers across the South described farmers as "worse off to-day than ever before," "involved in a hopeless vortex of low prices and usurious interest," and suffering from "depression and great finan-cial distress." Honorable John E. Gwin of McNairy County, Tennessee, told the committee that southern cotton growers were in dire need of relief and could not stand the situation much longer. If Congress failed "to stop such injurious effects upon the farmers' products" then the region would soon be overrun by "tramps."[44]

In addition, the Committee on Agriculture and Forestry deemed the fu-tures market a significant part of the problem. The rise of cotton exchanges in the 1870s pushed the cotton market in a new direction. The decline of the cot-ton factorage system and the changes in buying and selling practices led to the rise of cotton exchanges designed to centralize the process and establish uniform rules and standards.[45] In 1871 businessmen incorporated both the New York Cotton Exchange and the New Orleans Cotton Exchange a year after the Liverpool Exchange in England had been formed. A key part of the cotton exchange structure included the futures system, which involved the buying and selling of contracts for cotton for delivery at a future date.[46] The committee estimated that in New York alone, the cotton exchange dealt with less than half a million bales of actual cotton and more than sixty million bales of "fictional" cotton.[47] Both the committee and a large number of social critics and cotton growers accused the northern-based futures system of reducing the South to a state of extreme degradation and poverty. They pointed out how the system artificially tampered with the legitimate and natural operation of the market. The committee denounced the system as a sham and argued that this kind of intentional manipulation of the market had spawned "an oligarchy of wealth" that held the people of the South in a state of subjugation.[48] M. D. C. Crawford described the whole speculative enterprise as a "vicious form of gambling."[49] W. W. Carter, a cotton dealer from St. Louis, Missouri, argued the system's "moral effects are more disastrous and far-reaching than any other gambling device known to and tolerated in civilization" since it tempted people who could not afford to speculate.[50] Small tenant farmers did not have the capital to engage in speculation or purchase "insurance" and found themselves the victims of an unstable market on which fluctuating amounts and varying qualities of cotton were being sold.

Others offered more explicit accusations about who was to blame for the wretched condition of southern farmers. Silas Wade Hampton of Memphis, Tennessee, testified the "future scheme in New York" had created a "strong, powerful financial syndicate" injurious to the South. "It is the most perfect piece of machinery ever manipulated," he remarked, "the shrewdest set of fellows that ever walked on ground, ready to take advantage of every possible piece of news or every scheme to carry their ends." He did not feel optimistic about the South's future wealth and said the likelihood of southern prosperity was no more possible than him "flying to the moon."[51] Hampton's image of the southern economy dominated by the New York Cotton Exchange certainly resonated with the southern mythology of northern oppression of the South. Yet the crop lien system, the dominant northern futures market, and the overproduction of cotton coupled with the low price per pound hardly seemed apocalyptic until a tiny black insect known as the boll weevil made its way across the border between Texas and Mexico in 1894.

The Boll Weevil Evil

On the surface, the threat of the boll weevil to the prosperity of cotton-growing regions in the South appeared to be beyond the control of the farmers, merchants, and speculators. Over the course of the next several decades, the weevil steadily pushed its way across the South, wreaking havoc on the cotton plant and costing farmers millions of dollars. By 1916 the boll weevil had made its way as far as Georgia. Ironically, despite the frenzy generated by the arrival of the boll weevil, cotton production and demand increased between 1900 and 1920.[52] But the encroaching insect precipitated federal intervention in the region that slowly transformed the South into a laboratory for agricultural reform. Widespread devastation gave rise to an extensive debate about the merits of single crop agriculture, the value of diversification, and the practices of scientific farming. Farmers, cotton merchants, politicians, government officials, agricultural college teachers, experiment station workers, and businessmen periodically met on the local and state levels to discuss the threat of the boll weevil to the cotton belt. Some met informally and others held congresses and commissions. In 1902 a group of leading citizens met in Dallas and formed the Texas Boll Weevil Convention. This organization established subcommittees in each county of the state and continued its activities for the next few years. In 1904 the National Boll Weevil and Cotton Convention held its second meeting in Shreveport, Louisiana, and drew the largest crowd yet, including federal and state government experts. The attendance of so many people outside of the infested states of Texas and Louisiana indicated a mounting recognition of the weevil's potential impact on other regions in the South as well as the nation as a whole.[53] The National Cotton Association based in Shreveport, Louisiana, adopted mottos such as "Cotton is the nation's greatest crop. It is the world's greatest need," and "The States producing cotton and the Nations using the staple must awake to the menace."[54]

Federal interest in southern agriculture began with the arrival of the weevil and lasted well into the first few decades of the twentieth century. In 1895, the Division of Entomology headed by Leland O. Howard (which became the Bureau of Entomology in 1904) sent entomologists into the South to study the life cycle of the boll weevil, discover the means of eradication, and research agricultural methods designed to outwit the insect, such as early planting. Howard led the campaign to warn the public and Congress of the dangers insects posed to human health and the nation's economy. The Bureau of Plant Industry, headed by B. T. Galloway, also played a significant role in the federal government's efforts to reform southern agriculture. In 1901 the U.S. Congress allocated special appropriations to expand the investigation of the cotton boll weevil in the South. Leland O. Howard chose entomologist Walter D. Hunter to head the division of the bureau known as the South Field Crop Insect Investigations (SFCII). While the SFCII initiated research into other southern pests, the boll weevil received prime consideration. Between 1901 and 1903 Congress offered $10,000, $20,000, and $30,000, successively. In 1904 federal appropriations jumped to $250,000, partly due to the publicity generated by the Shreveport Convention as well as testimony offered by delegates from various associations in Texas and Louisiana to the House of Representatives Committee on Agriculture. Secretary of Agriculture James Wilson was permitted discretionary use of this "cotton-investigation fund."[55] The government appointed Seaman A. Knapp as Special Agent for the Promotion of Agriculture in the South in 1902 and offered him $40,000 of this appropriation to initiate farmers' cooperative demonstration work. In 1905 the Rockefeller family also lent its financial support to the farm demonstration program in the South through the auspices of the General Education Board, thus connecting the federal government with northern philanthropies.

The spread of the boll weevil in the South generated considerable panic on both local and national levels. Colonel Hiram Hawkins of Louisiana described the insect as a "small, harmless-looking little cuss in appearance" yet explained how it was "the great sword-fish javelin in front that gives him entrance way and makes him a screaming terror in the cotton fields." Hawkins observed that the boll weevil had both a psychological and material effect on the human population. This "infernal, slim-shanked sharp-nosed cuss from the land of Montezuma," he reported, "not only flourished in cotton fields but had nestled its way into "men's minds, also in stores, also in boards of trade and commercial exchanges and in banks."[56] Others referred to the damage wrought by the boll weevil as "a very grave problem," an "alarming state of affairs," and "a destruction more fearful than wars and pestilences."[57] Another described the insect as "the most formidable enemy to agriculture ever known."[58] Even as late as 1923 the sense of alarm and anxiety had not dissipated. Repeating a warning that had been sounded before, President Warren G. Harding, at the National Boll Weevil Menace Convention, cautioned, "The ravages of the Boll Weevil have long since passed a point where they may be regarded as constituting a local and State or a merely sectional threat. The Menace is now recognized as involving our National prosperity and is threatening the whole world with such a shortage of textile fibres [sic] that it will constitute a universal calamity."[59] Agricultural experts, politicians, and businessmen alluded to the domino effect of the boll weevil's destruction on national and international commerce. The destruction of cotton would lead to the decline of New England cotton mills, the slowdown of factories in the Midwest that utilized supplies from the cotton mills, the dissolution of business among the cotton dealers and merchants, and the subsequent decline in cotton exports that would adversely alter the United States' international balance of trade. Agricultural disaster in the South meant immediate national and global catastrophe.

Federal entomologists, agricultural experts, and newspaper editors writing on the boll weevil frequently resorted to the use of military imagery and metaphors of war when making the case for the insect's prospective damage. The field of entomology had a long history of using military metaphors in its reports, and the Bureau of Entomology often referred to its research as "scientific warfare."[60] Moreover, those writing on the bugs imbued them with anthropomorphic qualities, and entomologists and others compared the migration of "races of insects" to the migration of people.[61] Advertisements for insecticides often played up images of combat and martial conduct in their sales pitches. One company's logo for an insecticide read "HAMMOND'S SLUG-SHOT KILLS INSECTS, SAVES FOLIAGE" and included an illustration of a devil slaying a large beetle in a bloody fashion with a long sword.[62] Frequently, people linked the actual movement of the boll weevil to an oncoming army. Doctor J. A. B. Lovett, president of the Alabama Central Agricultural College in Blount County, Alabama, associated the insect with the Union Army and warned his community that the boll weevil promised to inflict "greater devastation than the army of Sherman, in marching to the sea."[63] Another newspaper included an article with illustrations of large boll weevils carrying rifles, manning cannons, and setting up military camp. The caption under a photograph of Walter D. Hunter from the Bureau of Entomology described him as the opposing army's "commander-in-chief in the field." This paper also framed the warfare as a conflict between the "Mexican destroyer" and "Uncle Sam," which called to mind battles against foreign armies and pleas for American patriotism.[64] The reliance on military metaphors such as these legitimized federal intervention in the South by calling on the power of the nation-state to defeat the assault of invading enemies. These images also resonated with feelings of national might so evident in American imperialist ventures overseas.

In addition, images of invading armies of insects could be easily likened to invading armies of germs, and those worried about the agricultural future of the South often framed the invasion of the boll weevil in terms of contagion and disease. This is not surprising given the fact that the field of entomology had a broad reach, including research into insects as disseminators of disease to humans and insects as dangers to crops and animals. The Bureau of Entomology frequently collaborated with federal and state boards of health, and since the South suffered from an array of illnesses caused by parasites and insects (such as hookworm, malaria, and yellow fever), it made sense to frame the movement and destruction of the boll weevil within the context of public health and medical concerns. Newspapers and farm demonstration agents sometimes called the insect the "weevil germ," "the boll weevil parasite," or "the traveling scourge"; described its movement as plague-like; and frequently referred to areas as infected rather than infested.[65] Just as the mosquito or hookworm disseminated disease to the human body, the weevil brought disease to the crops and land. Rumors spread that unknown individuals were depositing the boll weevil in the cotton fields of Georgia and South Carolina; one northern newspaper likened the action to a doctor who would purposely infect his patients with the bacilli of contagious diseases to promote his own selfish ends.[66] Farm demonstration agents encouraged southern farmers to engage in "clean farming" as a means of protecting the body agricultural, much like those public health reformers who advocated proper hygiene and cleanliness as preventative measures against infection in the human body.[67] By resorting to the use of an analogy between infected people and infected soil, government experts and advocates of agricultural reform succeeded in painting a picture of a southern landscape threatened by an onslaught of bugs, worms, and parasites. In conjunction with public health warnings about the role of soil pollution in spreading hookworm as a result of the lack of privies in the region, the USDA's attention to a dirty, infected land contributed to this national discourse on the diseased and contagious nature of the South.

The new germ theory of disease gaining prevalence in the field of medicine also shaped some of the solutions to the weevil problem. Scientists working with the USDA studied the possibility of inoculating crops or soil and introducing weevils carrying parasites or germs that would eradicate the insect from within its own ranks.[68] One entomologist even concluded that the weevil was more susceptible to diseases by infection than warm-blooded animals.[69] Fear of the encroaching weevil led some communities to institute quarantines much like the ones used to curb yellow fever several decades earlier. The Bureau of Plant Industry banned the importation of southern cottonseed into uninfested areas, even as far away as California.[70] Annual agricultural yearbooks published by the USDA contained scores of articles addressing issues like the diseases of cotton, the relation of nutrition to the health of plants, the treatment of plant diseases, insects as carriers and spreaders of disease, and control of contagious diseases among animals. W. B. Mercier and H. E. Savely, two field agents and agriculturalists for the USDA, maintained that the cotton plant was "subject to more diseases and insect enemies than any of the farm crops of the South."[71]

The metaphor of disease used to describe the roving nature and voracious appetite of the boll weevil also was applied to the disruption of labor generated by the insect's presence. White critics accused black laborers of spreading the weevil through their belongings and infecting new districts as they moved in search of better jobs. There were no reports of white laborers spreading the insect. The Louisiana Crop Pest Commission, anxious to stave off the inevitable arrival of the boll weevil, advocated quarantines against the infested districts in Texas. Not only were cottonseed and baled or loose cotton from infested areas prohibited from entering the state, but laborers and others traveling with household goods were subject to inspection. Shipments of household goods had to include an affidavit stating that shippers had not packed the cargo with any cotton products.[72] The state of Louisiana established patrols along the border of Louisiana and Texas whose duties included examining the cotton fields on the perimeter for signs of "infection" and inspecting black laborers traveling through the area.[73] Glenn W. Herrick, a state entomologist in Mississippi, described how Louisiana planters had imported laborers from weevil-infested districts who brought the insect with them in their "cotton picking sacks." He advised that no laborers from Texas be introduced to other states and that if planters had no alternative but to hire these migrant laborers then these workers must leave behind all household items, clothing, and sacks. Herrick cited one man's humorous remark: "'It might be well to dip the laborers.'"[74] Indeed the imagery of dipping black laborers to prevent the spread of the boll weevil plague corresponded with the practice of dipping cattle to prevent the spread of Texas fever carried by ticks. This comparison not only reinforced the metaphor of contagious disease but also devalued black workers by associating them with animals.

Planters had no trouble connecting the exodus of black labor to the ravages of the boll weevil, and the anxiety about a labor shortage only served to underscore the need to find a swift and effective solution. Without labor, the South could not harvest cotton for the national and international markets. A labor shortage also endangered regional prosperity. Planters in the Delta lamented the fact that labor agents targeted areas damaged by the boll weevil and used "exaggerated and misrepresented conditions" to paint a picture in "too glowing colors" of areas not infested by the insect.[75] One paper described how the immigration of laborers had "grown from a rivulet to a river" and that this development had generated considerable apprehension among planters, bankers, and merchants because a "country stripped of its agricultural labor, and its output thus destroyed, [would] very soon plunge into bankruptcy and business chaos."[76] Apparently labor agents and the planters who had contracted them had relatively little fear, or were willing to take the risk, that recruited labor from the Delta would arrive with boll weevils in tow.

However, not all considered the disruption of black labor an adverse event and instead some viewed the arrival of the insect as a fortuitous moment. The *Chicago Post* proclaimed that by "breaking up the blackest of the black belts in the South" the boll weevil had indirectly provided a solution to the "negro problem."[77] W. T. Hefley was even blunter in a letter to the editor of the *Fort Worth Texas Register*. He declared, "The greatest race question this world has ever known was settled by the Lord with plagues of lice, frogs, locusts, etc., when Pharaoh refused to let his people go. . . . I now prophesy that Jehovah will settle the race question in the Southland with the boll weevil, considered by some to be the greatest plague of modern time." Since black workers principally raised and picked all of the cotton, Hefley argued, the loss of labor due to the arrival of the weevil would lead to diversification because there would be no one left to pick the crop. Less cotton on the market would mean higher prices for those areas that continued to harvest the plant. Hefley concluded by saying that most farmers and leading men would agree that the boll weevil was actually the "greatest blessing."[78] White southerners who supported Hefley's views believed the boll weevil would lead ultimately to variegation in agriculture, the substitution of white labor, and the end of the "race problem."[79]

Government experts and progressive leaders also had no difficulty viewing the devastation wrought by the weevil as a "blessing in disguise" but they did not typically address the question of race. They believed the incursion of the weevil was the South's greatest salvation since it would encourage diversified farming and ultimately purge the South of the crop lien system that kept the region in the tenacious grip of poverty. Both northerners and southerners claimed the weevil had revolutionized social and economic conditions in the South even more than the Civil War. As a result, farmers were beginning to abandon outdated methods that had kept them mired in a provincial way of life.[80] By invoking the image of the Civil War, advocates of agricultural reform implied that the devastation of the boll weevil was not merely a sectional issue but of national concern too. The South may have failed to win the Civil War but the region could now wage war on the weevil and win a second battle of tremendous import. In short, the revolutionary impact of the boll weevil provided the South a new opportunity to change its traditional ways and economically reunite the nation.

The blessing in disguise rhetoric was a powerful one and it regularly appeared in many newspapers, agent reports, farmers' bulletins, and agricultural yearbooks. Optimistic champions of diversification questioned the value of hysteria and panic in response to the boll weevil. An editorial in the *Dallas News* promised, "A little less of the calamity howl and a little more 'backbone' and hard work" would do wonders in surviving the onslaught of the boll weevil.[81] Relying on the power of a medical metaphor, the *Natchez Democrat* in Mississippi explained that the boll weevil, adapting "his proboscis as a surgeon's knife, has performed an heroic operation on our body agricultural, which will result in the immediate eradication of the disease long known as the 'one crop system,' and the wounds swathed in the antiseptic bandages of 'diversified farming' will soon heal causing the still old body to take on new life and renewed energy." The weevil proved to be a blessing in disguise because, ironically, it pushed southern farmers to embrace northern values such as thrift and industry as a means of overcoming the ailing southern cotton economy. The paper proclaimed that "the strains of 'Dixie' would in time be as sweet as the more familiar air of 'Yankee Doodle.'"[82] The effort to see some value in the onslaught of the boll weevil reflected the USDA and country life reformers' desire to defend mounting social and financial investment in the South's cotton growers. Unlike the boosters of the 1880s who were inclined to evade acknowledgement of any problems with southern agriculture, the reformers and government experts who arrived later deliberately exposed the persistent agricultural troubles in the region. They placed their hope in scientific solutions and promoted the instruction of new ways of farming in the region.

Rural Sociology and the Farm Demonstration Movement

One solution to the problem of debt, soil depletion, the boll weevil, and the overproduction of cotton in the South included encouraging cotton growers to adopt new ways of farming. For several decades, land-grant agricultural colleges had already been at work on various agricultural problems in the United States and abroad, and the idea of training farmers was not a new one. As early as the 1870s various experiment stations and government model farms had been established in the United States and the overseas colonies, and a number of agricultural journals and farmers' institutes began to preach the virtues of a new form of education that emphasized scientific and practical knowledge. By the early twentieth century, the widespread concern about the condition of southern cotton farmers reflected a broader crisis that some simply referred to as the "farm problem." Historians, sociologists, political scientists, and economists turned to social science for answers to the growing problems of the nation's agricultural class. This developing interest in rural sociology signified a shift away from a strictly economic perspective to an approach that viewed the farmer from a sociocultural standpoint and the countryside as an enormous practical laboratory for change.[83] Hugh MacRae, a wealthy businessman from Wilmington, North Carolina, who recruited European immigrants from Italy, Holland, Denmark, Germany, and Poland to work on farm colonies in the state, declared there was "no field today richer in opportunity for the scientist and for the sociologist, than that which relates to agriculture." He believed the countryside would "be a great laboratory in which our national problems are first analyzed" and then resolved with new policies and programs.[84] The desire of social scientists and agricultural reformers to survey agricultural areas created a topography of the people and landscape that resonated with the efforts of public health reformers to map diseases in the southern environment.

Supporters of what is commonly referred to as the country life movement were predominantly middle-class urban and rural professionals such as editors of prominent farm journals, officials in the USDA, academics at land grant colleges and agricultural institutions, and social reformers interested in education, public health, and religious betterment. They had an abundant faith in the efficacy of education, the importance of efficiency, and the value of scientific practices and solutions. The goal of this kind of social engineering was to reshape the countryside along the lines of modernity. As Kenyon L. Butterfield explained, "The farm problem thus connects itself with the whole question of democratic civilization."[85] By making rural areas more attractive, efficient, and profitable, one could reduce out-migration, educate progressive citizens eager to work the land, and contribute to the nation's material wealth and political stability. Country life advocates aimed to facilitate the adjustment of rural peoples to the modern industrial world while at the same time encouraging farmers to retain all that was best about country life. This reform impulse also harbored a predisposition to glorify rural life in a sentimental, romantic fashion even while it leveled criticism of the farmers' deficiencies.[86]

The sociological interest in American rural life drew extensive national attention with President Theodore Roosevelt's creation of the Commission on Country Life in 1908. Roosevelt appointed several prominent men to collect and assemble data on the condition of America's farmers, including Henry Wallace, editor of *Wallace's Farmer*; Liberty Hyde Bailey, dean of Cornell University's College of Agriculture; Kenyon L. Butterfield; and Walter Hines Page. Working in conjunction with the USDA, the commission distributed questionnaires to over 550,000 people and held thirty public hearings attended by farmers and their families from forty states. Roughly 120,000 people responded to the circulars, which asked basic questions about the general condition of farming in their communities. In the commission's official report, Roosevelt wrote a personal message to the Senate and the House of Representatives. The object of the commission, according to Roosevelt, was "not to help the farmer raise better crops, but to call his attention to the opportunities for better business and better living on the farm." Roosevelt stated that people had paid far too little attention to the "problems of farm life," and the national neglect of rural life had not only held back the countryside but "also lowered the efficiency of the whole nation."[87] The report issued by the Commission on Country Life concluded that farmers had not yet readjusted to recent revolutions in the American economy and as a result the development of "contemporary civilization" was asymmetrical and unequal. The commission's objective was to initiate a process of rural uplift, revitalize social and moral life in the community, and reduce the sense of isolation experienced by the farmer and his family. The report stressed the need for rural free delivery of mail; improved sanitary conditions; better schools; the development of good roads; and autonomy in the face of monopolistic interests, temperance, and environmental renewal.

Although sociologists and rural experts interested in solving the "farm problem" did not necessarily distinguish between regions when talking collectively about reforming the farmer class, all believed the South posed the most complex of problems. Seaman A. Knapp's appointment as Special Agent for the Promotion of Agriculture in the South by the USDA at the turn of the century demonstrated the federal government's particular commitment to the region (see fig. 5). The agricultural reformer came to be known as the "Missionary Bishop of Agriculture" and "the apostle of agriculture in the Southern States."[88] Knapp held a slightly more optimistic view of the South's potential than some of the more vociferous critics anxious about the arrival of the boll weevil, the futures cotton market, and the crop lien. He once told the chancellor of the University of Georgia "'that the South was destined to become a great agricultural country and that the Southern people would be conservators of the best American traditions.'"[89] Knapp grew up in New York state and had a lengthy career that included serving as the superintendent of a state school for the blind, editor of the *Farmer's Journal*, chair of practical and experimental agriculture at Iowa State Agricultural College, and president of the Rice Grower's Association. Beginning in the early 1880s Knapp spent many years lobbying Congress for federal aid to support his agricultural vision. His tireless promotion resulted in the passage of the Hatch Act in 1887, which established a network of experiment stations at agricultural colleges throughout the country. In 1885 Knapp moved to Louisiana after being hired by an entrepreneur to map out a large-scale, profit-driven agricultural community in a previously unsettled area close to the size of Connecticut where he developed successfully a profitable system of rice cultivation. This system made the state of Louisiana the leading rice-producing state by the end of the decade. The arrival of the

FIGURE 5. Seaman Asahel Knapp, 1833–1911. Iowa State University Library, Special Collections Department.

boll weevil in the 1890s shifted Knapp's focus and he turned to his crusade for farm demonstration work throughout the South until his death in 1911. Knapp's efforts, which included publicized instruction in proper cotton cultivation; his collaboration with the Rockefeller's General Education Board; his participation in a national lecture circuit, particularly in New York City; and his federally supported supervision of several hundred demonstration agents and thousands of participating farmers in twelve southern states, underscored the nation's dedication to solving southern problems.

Like many other reformers interested in the problem of the South, Seaman A. Knapp was influenced by global patterns of reform and explored the question of what farming practices outside of the United States might have to offer Americans. In 1898 the USDA sent Knapp to Japan, China, India, and the Philippines in search of new rice seeds and plant breeds and to explore Asian styles of farming. As an ambassador of the USDA, he made multiple trips to "the Orient" and published a long bulletin for the Bureau of Plant Industry titled *Recent Foreign Explorations, as Bearing on the Agricultural Development of the Southern States.*[90] On one visit Knapp found himself in the midst of the Philippine War and was arrested by Emilio Aguinaldo's troops until, as a fellow agent recounted, "he convinced the minions of the Malay chief that he was the representative of the great white father and engaged in the peaceful pursuit of agriculture."[91] In 1900 Knapp conducted an official investigation of Puerto Rico, which involved over 350 miles of travel in rural districts, to determine the agricultural resources and rural possibilities including agricultural experiment stations on the island. He also traveled to Hawaii and the Philippines on a special mission for Theodore Roosevelt, who had commissioned Knapp to assess the islanders' state of mind on the recent annexations. When Knapp returned to the United States in 1902 to assume the role of Special Agent for the Promotion of Agriculture in the South, he arrived in the region with a vision of cooperative farming strongly influenced by a transnational agricultural reform circuit. Knapp's global understanding of agriculture proved to have a far-reaching effect on the development of rural life in the South, and as farm demonstration agent Oscar B. Martin noted, Knapp's trips to Asia "must have given him points of contrast as well as comparison, when it came to analysis of conditions and the planning of methods for the great movement in our American civilization."[92] In fact, Knapp's visit predated the trip made by Clarence H. Poe but both agricultural reformers viewed Asia as a learning tool.

In the beginning, federal funds for the farm demonstration movement were exceedingly limited, but as the need for southern-directed assistance became clearer, the funds expanded rapidly and the number of demonstration farms exploded. In 1903 Knapp created his famous demonstration technique in Terrell, Texas, where he went directly to the farmer with a hands-on approach. The process involved allowing an executive committee of progressive farmers and respected businessmen in the community to choose a suitable small farm and promise to cover any losses the farmer might sustain after he agreed to plant and cultivate according to government instructions. Any profits derived from the new agricultural methods would belong to the farmer. Knapp and others viewed the chosen demonstration farm as a powerful piece of propaganda and an important educational tool in the community. Agricultural reformers predicted that the accomplishments of these demonstration farms would inspire a new generation of farmers to adopt innovative agricultural techniques designed to eradicate rural poverty in the South. Moreover, the boll weevil crisis underscored the need to extend the demonstration program to weevil-infested farms, and in 1904 the federal government distributed a portion of the federal appropriations granted for the boll weevil catastrophe in the South to Knapp and his agents. Knapp used this money to organize and expand the Farmers' Cooperative Cotton Demonstration Work, which had initially focused on Texas and Louisiana. He assigned local men as special agents of the USDA to supervise and arouse interest in the cotton demonstration farms, and by 1909 there were 13,471 demonstration farms, 34,176 cooperative participating farmers, and 367 field agents across the South.[93] Two years after Knapp began his demonstration work, the Rockefeller's General Education Board also stepped in and initiated farm demonstrations in areas outside of the weevil-infected areas, including Mississippi in 1906, Alabama and Virginia in 1907, and eventually every other southern state by 1909.[94] Frederick T. Gates, John D. Rockefeller Jr.'s chief philanthropic assistant, chairman of the General Education Board, and later secretary of the Rockefeller Foundation, developed an interest in southern agricultural reform after taking one of Robert C. Ogden's train trips through the South. The Rockefeller family was very careful to make it clear that the organization was supplementing the activities of the federal government and not explicitly mingling funds. In addition, the Bureau of Entomology continued to establish its own "field experiments" to demonstrate how cotton might be grown profitably in spite of the boll weevil. Ultimately, this intensive focus on the South in the early twentieth century encouraged Congress to pass the Smith-Lever Act in 1914, which merged and centralized the farm demonstration program under one governmental agency in the hope of extending Knapp's methods to every county in the United States.

Although Seaman A. Knapp was overly sanguine about the prospects of southern prosperity, he understood that rural conditions in the South had not kept pace with the progress of urban life and required uplift. In a speech given at the Conference for Education in the South in Louisville, Kentucky, Knapp described how conditions in the South were not any different than a generation before, explaining "the houses are a little more dilapidated, the fences give evidence of decay" and identifying features like the "same old mule" with the outdated plow, "the same old bushes" and "the same old weeds." It was as if nothing had spoiled "the serenity of Rip Van Winkle." Southern rural blight and "the general lowering of the civilization of the country," Knapp concluded, could be attributed to the movement of "the most intelligent and progressive classes to the city" and the persistent ignorance and apathy of those left be-hind.[95] In another lecture before the State Teachers Association in Chick Springs, South Carolina, he warned the audience that "we are rapidly becom-ing a nation of idlers." "There is no sufficient reason why every American fam-ily," he declared, "should not own a good home and have a snug sum laid by for a rainy day, except our laziness, our lack of thrift or possible sickness, and nine-tenths of all sickness is due to mal-nutrition, which is another name for ignorance." As if to highlight the gravity of the situation, Knapp drew on his global experience and informed the teachers that white southerners had more in common with "the Filipino, the Malay, and the Hindoo" since as a collec-tive group they lacked frugality and common sense. In contrast, he concluded, the Chinese and Japanese were the most industrious and prudent of all, and it would behoove those teachers concerned with improving rural conditions in the South to instruct their students to follow the agricultural success of China and Japan lest the entire nation "drift to wreckage."[96]

The principal educational technique that Knapp used for demonstration was the "cultural method" or the "cultural remedy," which stressed efficiency, hard work, and learning by instruction in the fields. Cotton was known as the "lazy man's crop" and the application of the cultural method was designed to minimize indolent farming.[97] The plan included the removal and burning of old cotton stalks from the fields in the fall to eradicate lingering weevils, deep fall plowing to clear the fields, early spring planting with quick matur-ing varieties of cottonseed, the use of fertilizers, harvest of the crop as late as possible to ensure high yields, and the diversification of crops to transition from one-crop agriculture. This method differed slightly from the Bureau of Entomology's primary focus on the extermination of the weevil with poisons or natural predators such as ants. With the right dedication and application of the "cultural remedy" the farmer could avoid the type of southern cotton crop that entomologists and demonstration agents described as "poor," "per-manently stunted," and "very small and backward."[98] Ironically, the adjec-tives used to describe unhealthy cotton sounded very much like those used to describe languid hookworm victims. In the same fashion as public health workers, demonstration agents distributed thousands of leaflets, farmers' bulletins, and special articles on an array of topics including plowing tech-niques, the selection of seed, the application of commercial fertilizers, and raising livestock, all of which underscored the importance of industry and overcoming idleness. Agents showed instructional motion pictures and took photographs of successful farmers and made them into slides to aid their propaganda campaign. In an article on the merits of planting early, the *Atlanta Journal* included an illustration of a snoring farmer in bed with a clock on the wall reading 1:30 p.m. while, outside the sleeping farmer's door, a neighbor assiduously worked the fields in the heat of day.[99] As Knapp summarized, "It would be a crime not to send the gospel of maximum production to the rural toiler."[100]

Although the campaign to educate farmers involved written and spoken propaganda, the heart of the movement revolved around the application of scientific principles that could only be learned by demonstration in the actual cotton field. As the *Washington Herald* declared, Knapp's demonstration model enabled "the farmers of neighborhoods to read in the living pages of the field the message that they were slow to believe from the printed pages of bulletins."[101] The applied nature of farm demonstration inherently drew upon the concept of discovery through experimentation and therefore social scientists labeled hands-on farming as "scientific." In short, the goal of the movement was to instruct the farmer on how to become his own scientist in the field. Reporting in a USDA agricultural yearbook, Knapp noted that chemists and physicists required "their students to work out their problems in the laboratory" and so it seemed that farmers could be taught to "work out their problems in the soil and obtain the answer in the crib." Literally, the soil would serve as the farmers' laboratory.[102] Some southerners still viewed Knapp's work as "book farming," despite his protestation otherwise, and were suspicious of anything designated as scientific, while others remained hostile to new ways of farming advocated by what they perceived to be overly educated outsiders. But Knapp and his agents claimed they were teaching a practical knowledge rooted in sound judgment and systematic principles, and at times the metaphor of the laboratory gave way to that of the factory. In a nod to the precepts of scientific management advocated by Frederick W. Taylor, Knapp explained how "the farm must be managed with the exactness of detail that has made the factory a success" and the home "should be a model of economic labor-saving devices, of adjustments to increase convenience and promote thrift."[103] The mechanization of agriculture, either through the use of real machinery or the development of the farmer's body as a machine, guaranteed that the South could adopt more northern-like modes of labor.

One key aspect of scientific farming as applied to one-crop agriculture in-cluded the practice of diversification. The idea of diversification was hardly a new one. As early as the 1830s southern politicians contemplated the nature of southern economic dependency and questioned whether the overwhelming attachment to staple crop agriculture benefited the South.[104] Yet in the early twentieth century the battle cry for diversification took on renewed life and dominated the discourse of social scientific agriculture for several decades. Diversified farming involved a reduction in planting cotton, the cultivation of crops other than a single staple plant, and the rotation of an array of crops, all with the intention of increasing southern prosperity by encouraging sub-sistence farming. Theoretically diversification would free the southern farmer from dependence on northern and western foodstuffs and increase the earning capacity of farmers who would no longer need to borrow against their crop to purchase food and clothing. The decrease in the amount of cotton produced in the South would also solve the problem of overproduction and raise the price of cotton on the market. Ironically, Knapp's emphasis on diversification ran counter to the ideology of the boosters who preached that increased pro-duction of cotton was the key to national prosperity in the face of increasing global cotton production. The work of the demonstration movement on the ground, and its almost religious support of diversified farming, laid bare one half of the paradox of the New South. If one-crop agriculture and the attend-ing crop lien was the root of southern poverty, then solving regional problems with diversification would weaken national economic and cultural claims that the nation's salvation lay with more production of cotton. In part, the convic-tion that the South would maintain a central role in the global empire of cot-ton and generate immense national wealth was nothing more than a fiction. Knapp's focus on predominantly increasing regional prosperity made the ques-tion of national prosperity almost a secondary one.

In addition, Knapp and his agents believed that scientific agriculture would not only make farming more profitable but also make country life more ap-pealing aesthetically. Knapp explained how between 1861 and 1890 the South suffered from a great agricultural disaster and that nothing of value had re-placed the ruins of the "old civilization." Wartime destruction, emancipa-tion, the extension of the ballot to former slaves, and the rising number of black landowners and renters had stimulated a "lowering of country life" that had driven out the "better classes." As a result, nonresident ownership had increased bringing with it "a more careless tillage, immense waste of fertility by erosion, and a general deterioration in the character of farm improvements and equipment."[105] Knapp's farm demonstration program encouraged farmers to work toward building a more attractive rural life marked by the accoutrements of modern civilization. Only then could farmers stem the tide of young people leaving the countryside. One newspaper in Mississippi advocated scientific farming and diversification so that "each farmer may have a bank account, every boy a horse and carriage of his own" and the girl "a piano and a parlor in which to put it." The paper also declared, "We want the south to become noted for her splendid homes, her fine horses, her comfortable barns and sheds . . . her fences and fields so cared for that every passerby will note the attractive and prosperous conditions of the new southland."[106] Like the public health reformers who taught farmers the virtues of sanitary practices and the significance of a better physical appearance, so the demonstration agents preached the value of an attractive home and land. They reinforced the notion of "clean farming" as a means of improving the value of and respect for the land on which the farmers worked.[107] John Lee Coulter, an agricultural expert at the University of Minnesota, explained how a prosperous agricultural class would lead to "better roads, better churches, better schools, rural telephones, better sanitation, better education, and *better living*."[108] Efforts to reshape the lives of farmers constituted simply one solution to the broader "southern problem" plaguing the nation. Encouraging southern farmers to aspire to a more civilized life was at its core an effort to transform the South along the lines of the North and facilitate the uplift of a backward population to embrace American ideals.

The farm demonstration movement's focus on southern farmers coincided with the wave of educational reform directed at poor whites in the first decade of the twentieth century; however, what made it dissimilar was its concentration strictly on adults rather than on children or adolescents. Educational reformers often questioned Knapp about his opinion on secondary education and industrial training schools, and while he supported those forms of rehabilitation he remained convinced that the only true answer to the broader problem of the South was practical instruction in the setting of the farm and the home. In a letter written to Walter Hines Page he insisted that adult education was the most pressing and valuable issue at hand because it was an "investment at once for human betterment," set the standards for the farmers' children, and provided a template for future generations.[109] As Knapp him-self explained, "The world's most important school is the home and the small farm."[110] Over time the movement shifted away from strictly addressing the role of men in the field and began to address the need for female instruction in the household. Not until World War I, following the passage of the Smith-Lever Act, did the federal government hire female county agents and concentrate on home demonstration work. Knapp viewed women and mothers, in particular, as central to the mission of enabling the South to move forward on the path toward progress and "civilization." If one could liberate women from "the burden of housekeeping" and "the slavery of cooking" through the lessons of scientific management, they could turn their labor elsewhere and furnish income through the garden, poultry, and dairy.[111] A contented housewife would also raise patriotic, virtuous citizens in the republican tradition.

Thus, in a larger sense, the rural uplift of the South inevitably made for better national democratic citizens as well as contributed to the economic welfare of the nation. Knapp's farm demonstration movement was a nation-building project designed to facilitate reunion between the sections.[112] In an article titled "Raising a Crop of Men," Everett W. Smith described the demonstration agents as a "band of enthusiasts with a spirit very similar to that which animates the religious evangelist." They preached the benefits of the "cultural method" and diversified farming and successfully transformed "debt-ridden tenant farmers whose condition has been little better than that of slaves" into worthy American citizens.[113] Just as the farmer's task was to raise a first-rate crop of cotton, so the job of the demonstration agent was to raise a crop of good farmers. Knapp celebrated education on the small farm as the key to the development of manhood and citizenship, and he equated rural pride with civic pride in the republic.[114] More important, he argued that it was the nation's patriotic duty to carry on these reforms in the South.[115] Teaching the farmer to cultivate his small farm with the techniques of scientific agriculture would initiate the flowering of democracy in the New South. The advancement of democratic principles in the southern states would ultimately erase sectional tendencies and support nationalizing forces in the United States at the turn of the century.

However, the goal of supporting nationalism and creating an efficient, contented farm population capable of keeping pace with the development of modern civilization was riddled with contradictions and underscored the paradox of the New South. On the one hand, rural sociologists and reformers celebrated the "agrarian myth" and displayed nostalgia for the independent, self-reliant farmer. Many venerated farming as a traditional way of life. This romanticized vision of the simple self-sufficient farmer offered a soothing antidote to the traumas of industrialization and urbanization. Yet, the impulse to apply scientific methods to rural problems and create farmers who were better "scientists" and businessmen seemed to run against the celebration of a traditional rural way of life. Teaching the farmer to produce more at less cost entailed instruction in commercial skills and habits. John Lee Coulter praised the Farmers' Demonstration Work for training the farmer in "modern business methods" more than any other association in the history of the South.[116] Instruction in crop diversification to improve farmers' lives by reducing the surplus, raising prices, and allowing for subsistence undercut the optimistic rhetoric championing the continued production of the "fleece of gold." In many ways Knapp and his demonstration agents desired to remake the southern cotton grower in the image of the thrifty Yankee citizen. The broader goal of southern readjustment involved reshaping the South in the likeness of the North. The dilemma then was how to accomplish this feat while retaining what was best in southern traditional life. Could the South hold onto its distinctiveness even after it had been successfully incorporated into the economic and social fabric of the Union? Could the paradox of the South ever be resolved, integrating the region into the nation and resolving its backwardness for the benefit of national prosperity, yet still maintaining characteristically southern features?

The particular nature of the cotton tenancy system, the growth of a large poor white population, the arrival of the boll weevil, and federal criticism of the futures market, together with the constant fluctuation in the price of cotton, existed uneasily with the expectation that King Cotton would deliver the South from poverty and help maintain the superiority of the United States in the world market. The key to deriving great wealth from "cotton culture" contained an inherent paradox. On the one hand, federal reformers working on the local level to improve agricultural conditions and reduce poverty in the South preached the doctrine of diversification. They argued that diversifying crops would prevent the overproduction of cotton, help extricate the farmer from debt, and keep the price of cotton from declining too precipitously. Curbing the gambling on fictitious crops on the various cotton exchanges would also help stabilize the price of cotton. On the other hand, those northern investors, manufacturers, and New South ideologues who celebrated the magnificence of the cotton plant insisted that one could never produce enough cotton. They postulated that if farmers limited their production of the crop, the United States would lose its monopoly on the world market and subsequently cease to be one of the most powerful and wealthy nations in the world. The essential dilemma was that one could not maintain economic health in the South unless farmers stopped growing cotton in order to disentangle themselves from debt, and one could not maintain national and global economic supremacy unless southern farmers continued to produce steadily as much cotton as possible. The paradox of the New South was that cotton had the capacity simultaneously to generate great poverty and great wealth.

The escalating public attention given to the problem of the South and the inclination of the majority of Americans to view the South as a stagnant, backward region by the early twentieth century only exacerbated anxieties about the region's inability to keep pace economically with the rest of the nation. Agricultural backwardness was a prominent component of the "southern problem" and it threatened continually to thwart efforts to reconcile North and South. Nothing highlighted southern distinctiveness more than rural poverty. By the turn of the century, the nature of the South's backwardness and the continued focus on economic reconciliation reached the point where it influenced state policymaking. Ultimately, agricultural reformers, social scientific experts, and national politicians decided that federal and philanthropic intervention was the answer to the paradox of poverty and progress. Public debate and federal policy making proved to be the building blocks of nationhood, and labeling a region backward and in need of economic reform helped generate support for modernization. Moreover, the intense scrutiny given to poor white cotton growers only reinforced the nation-state's commitment to the ideal citizen, a person who was intelligent, self-disciplined, efficient, and brimming with civic pride. In short, the problem of the cotton grower in the South was central to strong-state liberalism and raised questions about how or if the federal government should intervene and regulate the market. What, if anything, did the federal government owe the impoverished cotton farmer? If the government failed to intercede, would social conditions in the South undercut the nation's economic well-being? These questions were not addressed until the early twentieth century when the U.S. Department of Agriculture, in conjunction with the Rockefeller family, decided to embark on a massive program of federal intervention that essentially transformed the South into a regional laboratory for agricultural reform. These questions would only grow more relevant as the United States entered the Great Depression.

Finally, given the global context of agricultural reform it was even more vital that southern and northern reformers resolve the problem of economic backwardness and nationalize the South. At the turn of the century, participants in the debate over the significance of cotton to social and economic life repeatedly described the crop as essential to American global dominance over the market. What made the cotton plant unique was its regional specificity and simultaneous global value — it was a signifier of region and an agent of international commerce. But paradoxically, many commentators also viewed the South as a colonial economy even while they assumed the southern economy could be successfully integrated into the national and international economies on equal footing. Men such as Seaman A. Knapp and Clarence H. Poe observed that white and black cotton growers appeared similar to if not more abject than that of other agricultural workers around the world in such places as Japan, China, the Philippines, Puerto Rico, Guam, and Hawaii. The effort to uplift the southern population, particularly poor whites, was in many ways a domestic civilizing mission. A transnational rhetoric and exchange of ideas revolved around harnessing the power of a backward rural economy and educating its citizens to exercise their economic and civic duties. The farm demonstration models in the South had roots in both the United States and other countries. Ironically, over time the popularity of agricultural science and the establishment of demonstration farms (all programs that were very colonial in nature) grew in direct proportion to the decline in imperial ventures abroad. Yet the United States was no less imperial in nature; it had simply refocused its attention to domestic colonial projects at home.

In 1938, the National Emergency Council issued the *Report on Economic Conditions in the South* in which Franklin D. Roosevelt declared the South "the Nation's No. 1 economic problem." The report concluded that the poorest belt of the southern states "was a belt of sickness, misery, and unnecessary death," and in words that would not have been surprising to the previous generation declared, "the paradox of the South is that while it is blessed by Nature with immense wealth, its people as a whole are the poorest in the country." The council also underscored the colonial nature of the southern economy when it proclaimed, "Lacking industries of its own, the South has been forced to trade the richness of its soil, its minerals and forests, and the labor of its people for goods manufactured elsewhere."[117] Even in the years shortly before World War II, it looked as if the massive effort to reform and rejuvenate the social and economic status of the cotton grower had failed. The southern agricultural conditions that Roosevelt agonized over in 1938 were an outgrowth of the agricultural conditions Seaman A. Knapp had discovered. Although the Great Depression touched all regions of the United States, the South still embodied many distinctive rural features that continued to set it apart from the rest of the nation. The plight of the rural cotton farmer drew attention throughout the 1930s until the system of cotton tenancy collapsed as a result of the inevitable mechanization of cotton production and the impact of the Agricultural Adjustment Act on the tenant farmer and sharecropper. Ultimately, the displaced cotton farmer found himself searching for work in urban areas, thereby undercutting the Farm Demonstration Movement's initial efforts to make rural life more attractive, profitable, and desirable. In short, reformers never really solved the paradox, and it simply faded away with the relentless encroachment of technological innovation that made modernization all but inevitable.

CHAPTER FOUR

The Poor White Problem as the "New Race Question"

Every white man in the Southern States rightly attaches supreme importance to White Supremacy. We cannot therefore contemplate without
concern this process of degeneration going on among the white children,
while, at the same time the child of the negro, barred out of the factories,
has the opportunity to acquire an education and is not subjected during
the tender years of childhood to the exhausting and enervating toil that
the white child endures. As a consequence, ten years hence, such negro
children will presumably be better equipped for life, both physically and
mentally, than their less fortunate white contemporaries.

— ALFRED E. SEDDON

White illiteracy is a body of death.

— ROBERT C. OGDEN

In April 1902 the *Arena* published a national article cautioning that the
South now faced a greater problem than the "negro question." S. A.
Hamilton, from Roaring Spring, Pennsylvania, described how this "new
'race question'" had "approached so insidiously, and from so unexpected a
quarter, that few persons have realized in it a danger to existing political and
social institutions in the South." The "new 'race question'" Hamilton identified was not the problem of Native Americans, Chinese exiles, or Southeastern
European immigrants but the problem of poor whites. Most Americans might
have been surprised to discover that men such as Hamilton viewed lower-class
whites as a specific racial type. But, as he explained, if one came across a "typical one" who had wandered from the pine woods, the encounter would leave
"the observer with the conviction that extreme cases of reversion are possible

even to such highly-bred races as the English, Scotch, Irish, and French . . . when any of their members are neglected by civilization for several hundred years."[1] The question of whether poor whites were racially degenerate or simply the victims of environmental circumstances (or even both) underscored the paradox of the New South in yet another way. This class of poor whites jeopardized the reintegration of the South into the nation-state and threatened to compromise an American national identity rooted in whiteness. As Albert Bushnell Hart charged, the South had a "Caucasian problem."[2]

In the early twentieth century, reformers and philanthropic organizations identified the region's large group of poor southern whites as an especially conspicuous and alarming problem for several reasons. First, many poor whites were small cotton farmers caught in a cycle of spiraling debt engendered by the crop lien. It was unclear whether they could extricate themselves from debt and become productive members of the industrial body politic. Second, poor whites suffered from disproportionately higher rates of illiteracy. Reformers argued that a lack of education prevented poor whites from exercising their claims as informed democratic citizens. Third, the medical community singled out several diseases that appeared to be largely confined to the southern regions of the United States. Poor whites suffered from such distinctive illnesses as hookworm and pellagra in far greater numbers than any other social or racial group. The enervating effects of these diseases led to a loss in economic production and raised questions about poor whites' ability to lift themselves out of poverty. Finally, disease coupled with extreme poverty and illiteracy among lower-class whites nurtured social scientific anxieties about racial degeneration at the very moment the white South tried to delineate the boundaries of the color line through the codification of Jim Crow. Growing evidence of the possibility of a degenerate white race moving backward toward a state of barbarism rather than forward toward a state of civilization muted the distinctions between black and white and challenged the fiction embodied in whites' efforts to keep the races separated socially.

Not only did southern whites endeavor to circumscribe the lives of African Americans and define the meaning of blackness, they also struggled to shore up the whiteness of poor whites. At times, northern reformers stayed purposefully on the sidelines when the needs of southern blacks drew national attention, and they invested considerable time and finances into the declining condition of poor whites. The vast literature on segregation and the New South connects the consolidation and policing of the color line with the passage of segregation statutes and antimiscegenation laws, the disfranchisement of the black race, the construction of special clauses designed to ensure that poor whites kept the vote, and the federal government's failure to live up to the promise of the Fourteenth and Fifteenth Amendments. Yet the construction of Jim Crow also included a sweeping effort to regulate, monitor, and reshape the social lives of poor whites whose questionable racial attributes tested the legitimacy of the color line. In the early years of Jim Crow the language of class occasionally merged with theories of racial essentialism, and the problems of poor whites muddied the boundaries between black and white. While mountain whites received special attention from reformers, they were not typically included in the category of poor whites since their presumed contact with African Americans and slavery was minimal.[3]

The existence of a class of poor whites in the South also hindered sectional reconciliation. Their alleged lack of civilized behavior, illiteracy, and indolent farming habits did not reflect the values of the nation-state. Thus the perception of these attributes raised questions as to whether poor whites in the South could become productive republican citizens in the Jeffersonian tradition let alone develop into democratic, industrial citizens in the emerging progressive nation. At moments, the South appeared to face two race problems. Whiteness often came to be identified with a specific kind of white person, and the moniker "poor white trash" served to reinforce southern distinctiveness and led to the racialization of the region. At times reformers tried to make distinctions between poor whites in the Appalachian mountains, who were thought to be the purest representatives of the Anglo-Saxon race, and poor whites who resided in the lowlands of the southern states, who were seen as suffering from more questionable attributes. In addition, reformers worried that poor whites not only were sinking to the level of poor blacks but also shared certain characteristics with people of color in the newly acquired colonies, such as illiteracy, tropical disease, and a similar manner of backward living. Reformers and social scientists used the rhetoric of uplift in describing all three groups, and their emphasis on industrial training, education, and public health reflected a global pattern of reform dominant during the Progressive Era. In one sense, the problem of poor whites at home had the power to undermine white prestige overseas and imperial power in colonial locales. "Poor whiteism" (as it was referred to in South Africa by Americans and Afrikaners) called for domestic civilizing missions that could shore up civilizing missions abroad.

Yet, paradoxically, poor whites taken as a whole were decidedly American in nature, not colonized people, and worth redeeming for the sake of nation building. On a broader level the national emphasis on southern rural backwardness, particularly among the poor white population, served a purpose in denoting national character and identity. In pointing out the existence of regional dysfunction, by marking the boundaries of what was normal, the nation-state upheld the values of civic competence and economic productivity. While northern travelers had commented on the problem of poor whites as far as back as the antebellum period, in the late nineteenth and early twentieth centuries the fascination with the poor white problem reflected a moment in which social scientific methods of reform undergirded the project of nationalism and liberal state-building. Poor whites became as much a problem for white northerners as they did for white southern liberals. Social science provided a new solution to the process of readjustment as reformers worked to juggle the seeming incompatibility of faith in the ability to improve the status of poor whites with growing apprehension that this reform project was immune to state intervention because of some inherent biological inferiority in the group.

The Evolution of the "Caucasian Problem"

In the midst of New South promises of progress, a new generation of middle-class educated whites took it upon themselves to hasten the process of southern advancement and looked askance at poor whites who appeared to be holding it back. Broadus Mitchell, an economic historian who began his career at Johns Hopkins in the 1920s, explained in his work on southern cotton mills, "The term 'poor white' is not easily defined, although every Southerner knows pretty accurately what it means."[4] In contrast to the New South ideologues who celebrated and praised the American Anglo-Saxon element in the South (especially that found in the mountain whites), this generation of liberal whites raised concerns about the mass of uneducated, diseased poor whites that seemed to have been left behind during the wave of industrial progress sweeping the region. "I tell you, the sorry white man in the South is the real curse of the land," Walter Hines Page wrote in a letter to his wife. "He is at once the worst and the most persistent product of slavery."[5] William Garrott Brown, a southern reformer and writer, remarked that not only was the "sleeping lazy black man" a characteristic feature of the New South but the "idle, listless, child-like poor white" was a defining trait too. Brown concluded that as depressing as the black man was to the outside traveler, "the illiterate southern white man is more depressing still."[6] Andrew Sledd, a professor at Emory College, linked the root of the poor white problem to the antebellum period. While poor whites constituted a numerical majority before the war, he explained, they existed "in an almost hopeless state of poverty, subordination and contempt," and their condition "was inconceivable to those who [had] not seen it in all of its wretchedness and filth and beastliness." Sledd described how poor whites in the New South had changed very little and were still responsible for "some features of Southern life that bring odium (not undeserved) on all the section." He blamed them for southern lawlessness, southern illiteracy, and agricultural backwardness as well as providing the "rich soil in which all sorts of political weeds take root and flourish."[7]

While southerners may have recognized the standard figure of the poor white, some northern travelers and reformers were especially shocked at the level of backwardness among rural poor whites in the South and questioned whether or not these whites could easily meet the standards of modern civilized life. Like Andrew Sledd, many explained the poor white problem as a consequence of the institution of slavery, which they claimed devalued the nature of certain kinds of work and led to unwanted race-mixing. Albert Bushnell Hart was particularly fascinated with the condition of poor whites. In the account of his winter 1907–1908 trip through the South, Hart described a family of poor whites as "undersized, ill-fed, anaemic [sic], unprogressive" and moving with their goods because they could no longer pay the rent on their tenant farm. He noted that they were traveling with quite a bit of property, including animals, furniture, and personal belongings, evidence that perhaps they were seeking to improve their lives and acquire the "main props of civilization." Most northern visitors, according to the Harvard professor, were often struck by the crudeness and backwardness of the poor whites. "There is a turbulence and uncontrolled passion," he explained, "sometimes a ferocity, among the rural people which is to be matched in the North only in the slums. . . . A large proportion of poor whites in the South and many of the better class go armed and justify it because they expect to have need of a weapon. Tobacco juice flows freely in hotel corridors, in railroad stations, and even in the vestibules of ladies' cars; profanity is rife, and fierce talk and unbridled denunciations, principally of black people. There is doubtless just the same thing in the Northern places, if you look for it, but in the South it follows you."[8]

While Hart drew comparisons between urban northern immigrants and southern poor whites, he identified two features that set the South apart from the rest of the nation despite the superficial similarities that existed between the two groups. First, a sharp social division existed between the races that accounted for lingering racial tensions in the region between poor whites and poor blacks. Second, there were "peculiar" social and economic divisions among the white people. According to the Harvard professor, most southerners called the lower-class whites "'Tar Heels' in North Carolina; 'Sand Hillers' in South Carolina; 'Crackers' in Georgia; 'Clay Eaters' in Alabama; 'Red Necks' in Arkansas; 'Hill Billies' in Mississippi; and 'Mean Whites,' 'White Trash,' and 'No 'Count' everywhere else." In general, the "less prosperous and progressive portion" of the white population was commonly called "Poor Whites," and the chief problem among this class was backwardness. Hart made certain to distinguish this group from the white mountaineers who were not "typical Southerners" or like any other group found in the North. He also explained how outsiders not familiar with the region's social landscape had the tendency to conflate the poor white with the small southern white farmer, when in reality these two social classes were very different.[9]

Although many spoke about the class differences between poor whites and other groups of whites, which hinted at the possibility of improvement, there were some who viewed the poor white as a specific degenerate racial type, such as S. A. Hamilton writing in the *Arena* in 1902 or Wickliffe Rose who commented on the Forkemites in 1911 (see chapter 3). In his piece on the "new 'race question,'" Hamilton described how poor whites had degenerated into a racially backward class with virtually no social markers of civilization, which posed significant problems. Hamilton, who coined the term "new race question," explained how the poor white, or "Cracker," was a degenerate racial type who had little contact historically with "civilization." Consequently, poor southern whites had "degenerated from the beginning into a besotted, ignorant, and vicious class," and they were "multiplying with the usual fecundity of the poverty-stricken." When speaking about the relationship between poor southern whites and southern blacks, Hamilton identified poor whites as a similarly dispossessed racial group. Indeed, he explained how in the antebellum period, the poor black or slave viewed the poor white with the kind of revulsion that one "pariah race" feels for another. In his discussion of the alienation that had developed between southern aristocrats and poor whites, Hamilton made racial distinctions between the two groups rather than explaining their discord in class terms. More often than not he conflated the categories of race and class. While he described the Crackers as a "poor white class," he used words such as "reversion," "degenerated," and "civilization" in his discussion, which invoked the racialized discourse of evolution so often used to explain the condition of foreign races at the turn of the century. Hamilton also reported that one of "the most potent factors in the elevation of the Crackers" in the post–Civil War years had been their inclination to intermarry with the aristocrats. The resulting group, known as "half-strainers," embodied the best "racial" traits of each side; they were blessed with "the mental traits and abilities of the aristocrats" and a "generous supply of physical strength" from the poor whites.[10] Hamilton did not suggest that these half-strainers had emulated the traits of the upper class. He focused on the hybrid character of the offspring that had resulted from the intermarriage between the two groups of whites, reinforcing the notion that poor whites in the South were a separate racial group whose genetic worth could be improved by intermarriage with another group occupying a higher place in the racial hierarchy. Hamilton did conclude on a sanguine note when he suggested that the superior, newly educated half-strainers would be the ones to join hands with the northern capitalists and uplift the South.

Hamilton's identification of this "new race question" marked the beginning of a growing social scientific interest in the level of backwardness in rural poor whites in the South and their inability to meet Anglo-Saxon standards of civilization. Anxiety about possible white degeneration in the South hindered sectional reconciliation, an ideology predicated on the celebration of whiteness across regional divides. The point is not to deny that whiteness could operate as a powerful hegemonic construct. Nor do I mean that poor whites did not benefit from their racial status in certain contexts. What the discourse about the poor white problem suggests is that whiteness was an unstable racial category that had to be continually reinforced and redefined. Recent historians studying the evolution of white identity in the nineteenth and twentieth centuries have pointed to the hybridity of whiteness. For example, in his work on poor white, black, and Mexican sharecroppers and tenant farmers in central and east Texas, Neil Foley states that whiteness was not simply the "pinnacle of ethno-racial status" but "a complex social and economic matrix wherein racial power and privilege were shared, not always equally by those constructing Anglo-Saxon identities." Foley describes how the rise of industrialized agribusiness farms and the influx of Mexican laborers and sharecroppers "ruptured whiteness as a normative racial identity" by contributing to the landlessness of white tenant farmers. Forced to deal with angry white sharecroppers and laborers demanding their rights, many landowners began to justify their preference for Mexican labor by ascribing to poor whites those permanent characteristics they had once used to mark blacks and Mexicans — such as laziness, deceitfulness, and shiftlessness — as well as criticizing poor whites for failing to achieve or keep ownership of land. Foley adds that the growing eugenics movement in the early twentieth century only added fuel to the fire by claiming that whiteness had come to mean a particular kind of white person.[11]

As the eugenics movement discovered, one of the principal ways used to reinforce and redefine the boundaries of whiteness involved the authority of science. Yet paradoxically, new modes of scientific classification ruptured the binary between black and white by providing a nomenclature attuned to both the fluid and fixed nature of racial taxonomies. Reformers and social scientists often viewed poor whites as another variation of the southern "race question." The rise of "white trash studies" within the social scientific community (which were not always regionally specific) provided a broader context within which to situate the southern white problem.[12] Part of the process of political and cultural reunion entailed reconstituting and reforming an inferior stock of whites in the South. To some extent, the language of class became racialized and complicated understandings about the feasibility of this reform project. If poor southern whites were a degenerate racial type, then what did that say about the South's ability to lay claim to a national identity rooted in a belief in the supremacy of the white race? In turn, the region as construct and category became racialized, as the classification of poor whites and white trash increasingly came to be associated with the South.

The social scientific interest in poor whites persisted into the 1920s and 1930s, focusing particularly on those in the cotton fields. While the belief in racial degeneration largely fell by the wayside because of shifts in anthropological thought based on work by the environmentalist Franz Boas, it still occasionally made its way to the surface. The image of the backward, shiftless white cotton-grower continued to serve as a common trope in social scientific studies, politics, and fiction, highlighting the paradox of American progress and southern backwardness.[13] Several studies in the 1920s and 1930s, including Frank Tannenbaum's *The Darker Phases of the South* (1924), Rupert Vance's *Human Factors in Cotton Culture: A Study in the Social Geography of the American South* (1929), and Charles S. Johnson, Edwin R. Embree, and W. W. Alexander's *The Collapse of Cotton Tenancy* (1935), presented a cultural cartography of the Cotton Belt. For social scientists studying the cultural landscape of the Cotton Belt, one of the more shocking aspects of this regional "human ecology" was the high percentage of white farmers who had been reduced to a state of dependency, idleness, and ignorance. Although many associated cotton with black laborers, others exposed the "hidden" class of white tenant farmers and sharecroppers suffering from the vengeance of what Tannenbaum described as the "white plague" of cotton afflicting the "beautiful sunny South."[14] One writer in a northern magazine explained how photographs and illustrations "invariably show[ed] you broadly smiling darkies in the cotton field," but if you looked more closely, he asserted, poor white cotton pickers could be seen in high numbers too.[15] Because the traits social scientists frequently identified in anemic white cotton-growers — such as laziness and idiocy — were typically attributed to the nonwhite races at home and abroad, the question of racial degeneration never entirely disappeared. Rupert Vance even speculated that hereditary, not just cultural, factors might play some role in the "inherent deficiencies in character, energy, and intelligence" of the average white cotton farmer.[16] If heredity played a role in the social makeup of the white southern cotton grower, then it said very little about the fitness of the white race as a whole.

Even as late as 1937 George Schuyler, a black intellectual and writer who was friendly with H. L. Mencken, explained to his mutual admirer that he long believed the "Southern cracker" was a "peculiar type." Invoking some of the similar concerns that social reformers had stressed almost forty years earlier, he drew comparisons between poor whites and colonized people. He opined:

> There was hope at one time that the cracker might become one of the vanishing races like the Maoris and Tahitians. Indeed, it was a probability, what with

pellagra, hookworm, rickets, malaria and other maladies to which he is heir. But latterly the Uplift has turned from saving the Armenians, Dravidians and Solomon Islanders and invaded the eroded habitat of the cracker, teaching him to read *True Stories*, the funnies and the current Ku Klux Weekly, fetching him salvarsan, quinine and tomato juice, instructing him in the use of soap and water, and douche bags and condoms. . . . But I still doubt that his basic nature can be changed by these heroic efforts in his behalf and at our expense. . . . He may sew up and wash his overalls. He may go to work steadily. He may move from his sagging shack to a new WPA cabin. He may cease his incestuous ways even do away with his rutting camp meetings and his prodigious sessions with the jug, but let him sniff the frying carcass of a blackamoor and at once he will revert to his true self and scramble for a toe or a knuckle.[17]

Schuyler's assessment of poor whites was biting and sardonic, as was the satirical piece he published in Mencken's *American Mercury* titled "Our White Folks," which mocked the assumptions of white supremacists.[18] Undoubtedly he felt he could be brazen in his language since Mencken had recently written to him, "the Southern cracker . . . seems to be hardly human, and if it were proposed seriously to proceed against him with machine guns I'd certainly not object."[19] But Schuyler's inclination to describe social reform as uplift and to racialize poor whites, in part, drew from an older colonial rhetoric. Situating poor whites within the context of degeneration theory and Social Darwinism, he questioned the power of the liberal state to rehabilitate this group.

Regardless of whether the paradox of racial degeneracy and environmentalism could ever be resolved with any degree of satisfaction, many observers found the primitive and distinctive characteristics of poor whites in the Cotton Belt appalling. Frank Tannenbaum saw cotton tenancy as largely a "white man's problem" and pointed out that it had "pauperized the rural South," made "people narrow, single-grooved, helpless," and bred a deadening form of "spiritual numbness." Tannenbaum described how cotton tenant families lived without books, newspapers, music, art, access to doctors and dentists, regular schooling, and suitable leisure such as picnics, dances, or meetings. This lack of access to civilized goods and the accoutrements of modern life contributed to the monotony of the southern cotton grower's life, which Tannenbaum regarded as an "empty existence."[20] Charles S. Johnson, Edwin R. Embree, and W. W. Alexander presented a similar dismal social topography in

The Collapse of Cotton Tenancy, issued at the height of the Great Depression when farmers across the country were suffering, although they still partly believed in the idiosyncratic nature of the South. Their investigation, which represented a collaboration between Fisk University and the University of North Carolina at Chapel Hill, reported, "The cultural landscape of the cotton belt has been described as a 'miserable panorama of unpainted shacks, rain-gullied fields, straggling fences, rattle-trap Fords, dirt, poverty, disease, drudgery, and monotony that stretches for a thousand miles across the cotton belt.'" They agreed with this assessment and mentioned that the life of a cotton grower was scarcely above the "level of bare animal existence."[21] In a nod to more environmental explanations, Johnson, Embree, and Alexander concluded that two-thirds of the farmers and their families were white; thus the "meager and pinched way of living" was not a "racial trait" but merely an outgrowth of the system of cotton tenancy. The group cited a letter written to the *Dallas News* by attorney T. N. Jones, which aptly captured the misery of the cotton grower and the humiliation these tenants brought upon the South. Jones proclaimed, "In the South, there is more abject poverty and illiteracy than in any other country on earth in which a high state of civilization is supposed to exist. The squalid condition of the cotton raisers of the South is a disgrace to all southern people. They stay in shacks, thousands of which are unfit to house animals, much less human beings. Their children are born under such conditions of medical treatment, food and clothing as would make an Eskimo rejoice that he did not live in a cotton growing country."[22] Two years later, Mencken simply deemed the living conditions of these poor whites a "ghastly spectacle."[23]

In addition, most social and anthropological studies of white cotton growers noted how they harbored no misgivings about putting their children and wives to work in the fields (see fig. 6). The emasculated animal-like cotton farmer, unable to extricate himself from debt and forced to make his family work, stood in contrast to the archetypal liberal citizen who was progressive, manly, and resourceful. As early as 1912, Lyman Abbott, the editor of the *Outlook*, which was a national magazine with a reformist bent, published an article on King Cotton in the *Independent* that included a shocking front-page photograph of a very young white toddler standing amid the rows of cotton plants holding a large picking sack. The startling caption read, "If a baby ventures into the cotton field, it is 'get busy.'" Abbott insinuated that white "adult male labor of the South" lacked proper masculine traits because their

FIGURE 6. "Millie, four years old and Nellie, five years old. Cotton pickers on a farm near Houston, Millie picks eight pounds a day and Nellie thirty pounds. This is nearly every day. Home conditions bare and bad. Location: Houston [vicinity], Texas." 1913. Photograph by Lewis Wickes Hine. Library of Congress, Prints & Photographs Division, National Child Labor Committee Collection [reproduction number LC-DIG-nclc-05536].

inefficient ways of growing cotton entailed the use of female and child labor. He predicted that one of the few things that might free the cotton grower and his family from this emasculating situation was the mechanization of cotton picking. Only then could the wife attend to the home, the children go to school, and the farmer harvest the cotton with the help of a single son.[24] Abbott's assessments implied that the high incidence of women working in the cotton fields contributed to the lack of civilized living because these women had no time to take care of their proper domestic duties within the confines of the home. Years later, Bradford Knapp, president of Oklahoma A&M College and son of Seaman A. Knapp, stated this more clearly when he remarked, "I know the world wants cheap cotton to clothe its nakedness, but may God forgive the man who wants it at the price of the labor of women and children in the field."[25]

White Slavery in the Southern Mills

To underscore the difference between the uncivilized South and the nation's industrial democracy, Frank Tannenbaum drew upon the intellectual heritage of the idea that the institution of slavery was inimical to democratic progress. Using the metaphor of bondage when speaking about poor whites, Tannenbaum concluded that cotton had ensured that "the people of the South, old and young, are its slaves" and that one-crop agriculture had "subject[ed] them to what one man has called 'the new slavery.'"[26] As if to highlight the horrors of this new form of slavery, Alabama journalist and social critic Clarence Cason invoked the specter of Harriet Beecher Stowe and declared in a piece titled "Southern Slavery Revised" that cotton tenancy for poor whites and blacks was worse than "Simon Legree and his bloodhounds."[27] Another permutation of white slavery involved the experience of poor whites who labored in the cotton textile mills. While the term "white slavery" ultimately became associated with prostitution and the alleged kidnapping of white women for the purposes of sexual exploitation, in the early years of the twentieth century it shared allegorical space with the labor exploitation of southern whites, particularly children.[28] A 1902 cartoon in the *New York American and Journal* bearing the caption "White Slavery: Northern Capital and Southern Child Labor" captures the heinous nature of the situation by evoking the image of a slave auction. The illustration shows two gaunt, ragged white children standing on a platform bearing the sign "For Sale to the HIGHEST BIDDER" who are surrounded by plump wealthy men in top hats marked as northern capitalists. One capitalist squeezes the boy's leg, another grasps the girl's arm, and the third with dollars hanging out of his pocket and pen and paper in hand assesses the cost of the young boy and girl. The cartoon is designed to elicit a sense of horror as these helpless white children are prodded for likely use in northern-invested cotton mills in the South (see fig. 7).[29]

Although published twenty-two years after the white slavery cartoon, Frank Tannenbaum's collection of essays compiled in *The Darker Phases of the South* not only drew attention to cotton-growing white slaves but reinforced the impression that white slavery predominated in the cotton mills. As the Columbia professor lamented, the South had "buried its Anglo-Saxons." Workers in the production of textiles (the spinning and weaving rooms) were exclusively white, and while this was mostly accomplished by tradition, South

FIGURE 7. "White Slavery: Northern Capital and Southern Child Labor." *New York American and Journal*. Reprinted in *Literary Digest* 25 (October 18, 1902).

Carolina actually passed The Segregation Act (1915) that prohibited the mixture of races in cotton textile mills. During his extended tour of the region, Tannenbaum visited several cotton mill villages and described the "forgotten" men and women working in these mills as childlike in appearance and deportment. "They *are* like children," he wrote in surprise, "rather strange, lost-looking, and bereaved. Their faces seem stripped, denuded, and empty." This group of "washed out, destroyed" people had been "reduced to a state of childish impotence where they have to be taken care of and where they produce nothing." Tannenbaum's account painted a portrait of a puerile, weak class of poor whites who had failed to generate men of great worth such as politicians,

lawyers, leaders, poets, and businessmen. The only way the South could rescue these buried Anglo-Saxons would be to relieve them of a "state of spiritual dependence upon the mill-owner." Tannenbaum was not clear about how
this should be accomplished, but he remained convinced that such an action
would bring the necessary "manhood, integrity, and self-reliance" to the region.[30] Ironically, although Tannenbaum viewed the rescue of the white South
in masculine terms, the mills' owners embraced white women and children
with open arms since they provided a substantial source of unskilled cheap
labor. From 1880 to 1910 manufacturers noted that at least 25 percent of cotton textile workers were below the age of sixteen, and historians estimate this
number is even greater due to underreporting.[31]

Tannenbaum's description of adult white cotton-mill workers as "childlike"
is perhaps not surprising given the great numbers of laboring mill children
as well as the national campaign against child labor that showed particular interest in the textile labor force in the South. Samuel Gompers and the
American Federation of Labor launched the first anti–child labor campaign
in the South and sent Irene Ashby, a British woman who had organized working girls, to Alabama in December 1900 where she visited twenty-five cotton
mills. In 1887 the Alabama legislature had passed a law limiting children and
women to eight hours a day of work and restricting children under fourteen
from working, but it was repealed in 1894 in response to pressure from the
northern Dwight Manufacturing Company. The *Minneapolis Tribune*, which
summarized Ashby's travels six years after the law's rescission, reported that
she said she was "familiar with the slums of two continents" and had "never
witnessed a more pitiful sight than these mill children of the South" who were
"pale, bowed, shrunken, and looked as if their minds were hypnotized and
their souls paralyzed." She largely blamed the northern capitalists who had invested in southern mills but was willing to implicate southern mill owners
too. Ashby stressed that even the British colonies involved with manufacturing had banned child labor unlike the U.S. South, which had readopted "old
barbarous methods." The ease with which Ashby drew comparisons between
poor white southern children, native British laborers, and British colonial subjects suggests the way in which southern labor problems were global in concept.[32] In this instance the racialized southern poor whites, British working
class, and nonwhites in British colonies constituted part of a broader web of
capitalist exploitation. Yet, as Ashby implied, the British were more civilized

than Anglo-Saxon northern capitalists who were willing to put the southern children of their own race to work.

While in Alabama, Irene Ashby connected with Edgar Gardner Murphy, author of the *Problems of the Present South* and a prominent leader in reforming child labor in the cotton mills. Murphy served as head of the Alabama Child Labor Committee (ACLC) founded in 1901 and helped shape national policy as one of the architects of the National Child Labor Committee (NCLC) in 1904. The all-male ACLC, with the support of Alabama women's clubs, was designed to be a propaganda machine that targeted the owners of northern-invested mills and southern manufacturers who did not support compulsory education or child labor laws. By 1903, the ACLC had issued twenty-eight thousand pamphlets with anti–child labor arguments as well as photographs of young mill workers working twelve to fourteen hours a day, material created to inform the region and the nation of the horrors of working white southern children.[33] Labor activists and reformers initially targeted Alabama because it had the highest percentage of northern-owned mills than any of the Piedmont states, but soon the anti–child labor lobby expanded across the South and left a patchwork of laws with various age and hour limits in place. Southern liberal Edgar Gardner Murphy was a public critic of southern backwardness but also believed in the possibilities of southern progress. He saw promise in the industrial advancement made by the New South cotton mills and was willing to concede that "the factory is to take its place beside the church, the schoolhouse, the home, as one of the effectual and characteristic forces of civilization" in the South. Nonetheless Murphy was keenly aware of the deadening effects of child labor exploitation and maintained that the system symbolized "arrested development in the individual, for ignorance and industrial helplessness" as well as "in the social class to which the child belongs."[34]

The condition of white children in the mills pointed to the paradox embedded in the broader movement to reform the South especially as it pertained to the question of race. Anti–child labor reformers such as Edgar Gardner Murphy believed in redemption and viewed poor white children as "an uncorrupted stock" with inherent potential.[35] Others supported Murphy's commitment to the reclamation of poor whites but spoke more explicitly about the dangers of racial de-evolution. Reverend Alfred E. Seddon, who investigated conditions in Mississippi, described how white children in "the atmosphere of the mill" were "growing up anaemic [sic], deficient in size and weight, illiterate and apt to degenerate morally."[36] In a paper titled "The Child Labor Problem — A Study in Degeneracy" given before the American Association for the Advancement of Science, Alexander J. McElway, a native of North Carolina and the assistant secretary of the NCLC, asserted there was "no greater catastrophe than race degeneracy," which had already befallen "the little child slaves of our southern cotton mills."[37] Yet only two months later McElway recounted a journey he took on a train of fifty people bound for the South Carolina cotton mills and deemed them the "purest American stock." Indeed, the assistant secretary's discourse embodied the tension in child labor reform, which walked the rhetorical line between issuing admonitions about the degeneration of the white race but not pushing the alarmist language so far as to suggest that poor whites were beyond rescuing. McElway viewed children as the "saviour [sic] of the race," and he framed the problem of child labor in the South as a "national question" precisely because in New England the child labor question involved the children of "foreigners" but in the southern states it was "the breed of American" that faced the threat of degeneration. Salvaging whiteness in the southern cotton mills was crucial to maintaining the prestige of American national identity, since McElway also viewed the training of these children as a prerequisite for military service to their country.[38]

Anti–child labor reform advocates also drew contrasts between poor whites and African Americans to emphasize the exigency of protecting the white South from racial and moral degeneration. In the first two decades of the twentieth century the NCLC employed fieldworkers to conduct investigations of southern cotton mills, and their reports were rife with descriptions of dirty, uneducated, and apathetic white children. In many instances, the NCLC representatives pointed out how black families sent their well-dressed children to school while white families sent their children to waste away in the mills. The Reverend Alfred E. Seddon noted how this situation was "paving the way for the elevation of the colored man and the degradation of the white man in the South." Many reformers called for their state legislatures to pass compulsory education laws to limit high illiteracy rates and ensure that white children attended school. In his report on Mississippi, Seddon described the crisis in stark racial terms. He wrote how white men feared "degeneration" among white mill children and that "White Supremacy" was in desperate need of fortification since black children were making gains in school and soon would outperform white children.[39] Ironically, in this context the insistence that blacks not intermingle with whites in the Jim Crow South worked to the mill children's disadvantage and actually weakened white supremacy's claims to power.

Industrial Training as a Solution to the "Forgotten Man"

The precarious position of the "forgotten child" enmeshed in a system of white slavery underscored the dangers to Anglo-Saxon democracy posed by child labor as well as the necessity for widespread educational reform.[40] Compulsory attendance laws offered only one solution to the perceived problem that the gains of black children, and even the children of colonized peoples abroad, had come at the expense of poor white children. Questions about what kind of education might best facilitate national reunion and the development of an industrial democracy dominated the discussion of educational reformers. Men such as Robert C. Ogden, Edwin A. Alderman, Walter Hines Page, and Lyman Hall advocated a form of industrial training for poor white men in addition to the establishment of compulsory education for southern children. Echoing the remarks made by Edwin L. Godkin thirteen years earlier in his *Nation* article "The White Side of the Question," Jacobus D. Droke wrote that "how to deal with this class so as to convert them into intelligent, industrious American citizens is one of the great problems which to-day confronts the New South."[41] The crusade to provide industrial training to poor white men embodied a narrow view of democracy, an Anglo-Saxon democratic vision committed to industry, self-discipline, and advancement. Those reformers who focused on the ability of poor whites to redeem themselves through industrial education typically believed in the force of the environment on progress and did not explicitly touch on the theme of white racial degeneration. As early as 1897, Walter Hines Page spoke of a particular class he called the "forgotten and neglected men" and argued that in the making of a civilization it was these men that had to be taken into account more than any other class. Indeed, the very term "forgotten" implied that these men could be redeemed.[42]

In a speech delivered before the State Normal and Industrial College for Women at Greensboro, North Carolina, Walter Hines Page challenged his audience to consider the most important undeveloped resource in the state, the men themselves. He informed the crowd that common people furnished the structural foundation of civilization in part because "the security and the soundness of the whole body [was] measured at last by the condition of its weakest part." According to Page, the great evil was not posed by illiteracy itself but rather by the social and psychological condition it engendered. He explained how "the forgotten man was content to be forgotten" and "became not only a dead weight, but a definite opponent of social progress." In short, it was the poor white man, through no fault of his own, who was responsible for the lack of movement forward in the New South. Page did not go so far as to suggest that the "forgotten man" was of degenerate stock or intrinsically of "a lower order of intelligence than any other people of Anglo-Saxon stock." As he put it, the "white trash" in the South was "not poorer nor 'trashier' than the rural population of New Jersey or Pennsylvania or New York or New England were several generations ago" because these men were merely in a state of "arrested development." Page explained that by instructing poor white men to become useful citizens through industrial training the South might eliminate "poverty in living, poverty in thinking, [and] poverty in spiritual life" and become more national in orientation.[43]

Ironically Page issued his call to redeem the "forgotten men" of the South at a school of industrial training for southern women. For the most part, reformers interested in the poor white problem in the early twentieth century paid less attention to the specific role of women. Two years after Page's speech at the North Carolina State Normal and Industrial College, the *Outlook* published an article titled "The Forgotten White Woman of the South." D. F. St. Clair took issue with the lack of interest in white southern women (with the exception of the school in North Carolina) and pronounced, "The South's forgotten white woman has, of course, been more profoundly forgotten than ever her brother was." St. Clair explained how the problem of forgotten white women lay at the heart of illiteracy in the South since teaching was a female profession. She stressed that with proper training white women could educate a new populace intent on leading the South down the path of civilization. St. Clair praised the work of Dr. Charles D. McIver at the Normal College and explained how McIver had presented the South with "a woman who may not be quite so beautiful and charming as her aristocratic antebellum sister was, but a great deal better equipped to meet and master the civilization that cold-blooded practical Northern men have in the past generation developed in this Republic."[44] In St. Clair's account, however, progress in the New South was still framed as masculine in nature since southern white women in search of civilized life now deemphasized the femininity of their antebellum ancestors and embraced the hard masculinity of northern men.

The emphasis on developing the squandered resources of manhood in the New South as an approach to southern problems was a consistent theme. The call for the development of vigorous Anglo-Saxon men echoed throughout the South as the key to facilitating southern industrialization and the economic integration of the region into the nation. Dr. Lyman Hall, the president of the Georgia Institute of Technology, said that the most productive thing in the world was not one dollar, or two dollars, or a million dollars, but the "American boy." He reasoned that wealth invested in the stock market could not be predicted to return a profit and therefore should not be relied upon. Rather, Americans should view the southern boy himself as the valuable investment. As Hall described it, this boy was "alive and bristling with energy and horsepower" and ready to build empires, conquer "savage beasts and men," and steer the ships and trains. These young southern men were full of "ambition to perform great deeds of industry and progress" in the New South but needed training facilities to instruct them in how to utilize their talents. Like Page, Hall advocated a form of industrial training for white men. He maintained that the growth of industry in the South demanded "staunch, sturdy, powerful, workingmen."[45] In addition, these men's belief that virile, sturdy, aggressive white men were an essential component of a successful commercial civilization in the New South mirrored broader cultural shifts occurring in American society at the time. Reformers believed a skillful progressive masculine labor force could serve as the prime catalyst to industrialization in the New South.

Even so, Page and other reformers were conscious that their program of industrial training was almost identical to the program of moral uplift and industrial training advocated at black institutions such as Hampton Institute and Tuskegee Institute as well as those used in colonial settings such as the Philippines. Those committed to the education of poor whites typically harbored an interest in solving the broader "race problem" as well, and the comparisons to be made were evident. For example, Robert C. Ogden, the northern philanthropist who became a national advocate of reforming southern educational problems, served on the Board of Trustees of Hampton Institute. The institute was founded by General Samuel Chapman Armstrong, who was inspired to open the industrial training school based on his experience with mission schools in Hawaii. Hampton Institute enrolled a small number of students from Puerto Rico with the intention of training them in American habits of discipline and frugality, and in 1900 the governor of the island colony petitioned Ogden personally suggesting that he could offer "representative children, bright and alert" who would benefit from attending.[46] But reformers who acknowledged the similarities between poor whites and people of color walked a slippery slope as the language of class was always in danger of becoming racialized. As Edgar Gardner Murphy stressed, "the racial heritage of the white man must be clearly accepted and recognized" when it involved industrial training.[47]

Poor Whites in a Global Context

The need for an industrious white manhood in the South ready to contribute to industrial progress and forge new empires in distant lands, as Lyman Hall suggested, demonstrated a recognition that the poor white problem had global ramifications. In part what lent American imperialism its power abroad was the assertion of the superiority of the Anglo-Saxon male, thus the existence of a degenerate poor southern white population pointed to the fiction of such a claim. In colonial settings around the world such as the Dutch Indies, India, Barbados, and Kenya the problem of poor whites was an integral part of social policy. Imperialists' attempts to police the poor white population in the colonies and on domestic soil reflected a broader effort to regulate the racial and class boundaries of the colonizers themselves. European colonizers adopted a variety of strategies in regulating white subversives. Some established relief funds and engaged in reform efforts to refashion the poor white population into an industrious citizenry through such efforts as schooling and psychiatric treatment. In other situations, such as the Dutch colonies, those in charge made the decision to repatriate poor whites.[48] The commitment to rehabilitate poor whites did not prohibit them from laying claim to some of the benefits of whiteness. "The populations that fell within these contradictory colonial locations," Ann Stoler argues, "were subject to a frequently shifting set of criteria that allowed them privilege at certain moments and excluded them at others."[49] Their very presence eroded the boundaries between the colonizers and colonized and created divisions that undermined racial strategies of colonial domination. It is hardly a coincidence that in the context of empire, reformers and social scientists began to scrutinize the poor white population in the United States, particularly in the southern states.

Of course the U.S. South was not a colonized foreign country, but its noticeable population of poor whites (and poor blacks) informed transnational discussions and reflected a global circuit of expert knowledge and reform. The connections between the Carnegie Corporation, Columbia University, and South Africa offer the best example.[50] In his 1919 will, Andrew Carnegie requested that money be set aside for the Dominions and Colonies Fund, which was designed to provide support for social scientific projects in the overseas colonies of the British Empire. Frederick Paul Keppel, formerly dean of Columbia College (the undergraduate campus), assumed the presidency of the Carnegie Corporation in 1923 with a broad international mandate in mind, using as a template African American educational studies initiated in the U.S. South by Thomas Jesse Jones, the director of the Phelps-Stokes Fund. Jones, who had received a doctorate in sociology at Columbia University and spent eight years working in the research department at Hampton Institute, authored a two-volume report in 1917 titled *Negro Education: A Study of the Private and Higher Schools for Colored People in the United States*, based on collaboration between the Phelps-Stokes philanthropic organization and the U.S. Bureau of Education. Shortly thereafter, he wrote a parallel report on his observation of the state of education in Africa, emphasizing the need for agricultural and industrial training as he had for African Americans in the U.S. South.[51] The Carnegie Corporation was particularly interested in South Africa since it believed white southerners could offer guidance to South Africans on the "race problem."

A dense web of transnational links among the corporation, the university, and South Africa developed in the 1920s and 1930s. The Teachers College at Columbia enrolled a significant number of white South Africans, and the Fund financed an exchange of visits between the United States and South Africa, creating a transnational network that moved in both directions. One such recipient of a Carnegie Visitors' Grant was August D. Luckhoff, who supervised the philanthropic work of the Dutch Reformed Church in South Africa and traveled to the United States seeking counsel on "its work for the uplifting of the Poor Whites."[52] Inspired by Jones's global framework and prompted by Mabel Carney, an instructor at the Teachers College and an expert on rural education and race relations, Keppel had traveled to Australia, New Zealand, and South Africa in 1927 in search of possible reform projects.[53] While in South Africa, Keppel met with Ernst G. Malherbe, director of the National Bureau for Educational and Social Research and a Columbia University graduate. Although Keppel arrived thinking in terms of the black race, Malherbe successfully persuaded Keppel that the "most urgent problem" in South Africa at the time was that of poor whites. In an article Malherbe began writing at Columbia in 1921 and later published in the *Cape Times*, the South African educator cautioned, "Today we have over 100,000 so-called poor whites living in our very midst" and they are "a menace to the self-preservation and prestige of our white people." This threat to the integrity of the white race, he determined, was "the cumulative result of some maladjustment of our society in the past."[54] In the southern states reformers struggled with the problem of readjustment, whereas in South Africa reformers faced the problem of maladjustment.

As a result of Frederick Keppel's conversation with Ernst G. Malherbe and others, the Carnegie Corporation decided to fund a multiyear project undertaken by the Commission of Investigation into the Poor White Question, which resulted in the publication in 1932 of a five-volume report titled *The Poor White Problem in South Africa*. "This term," the commission decided, "is used to denote principally the economic and social retrogression of a considerable part of a white rural (or originally rural) population of our country." The working group included such South Africans as Ernst G. Malherbe; Dr. Raymond W. Wilcocks, a professor of psychology at Stellenbosch University, who traveled to the U.S. South on a Carnegie Visitors' Grant and later drafted an unpublished essay comparing poor whites in South Africa with poor whites in the southern states; and Dr. Charles T. Loram, who studied at Columbia University with Mabel Carney, subscribed to the belief that black industrial education at Hampton Institute and Tuskegee Institute proffered the best example for "native" education in South Africa, and ultimately relocated to Yale University in 1931 as a professor of education with the intent of studying global race relations.[55] The commission identified many problems including poor whites' inability to adjust to "modern economic conditions"; illiteracy due to an inferior educational system; unsanitary conditions leading to disease and fecal pollution of food and water; backward, unproductive methods of farming; women's ignorance of child rearing; and poor whites' retrogressive psychological attributes. In their findings they advocated following the U.S.

Department of Agriculture's farm extension work first initiated by Seaman A. Knapp in the U.S. South. At times the report was scathing in its denunciation of the immorality of this class of whites and identified such character traits as "irresponsibility," "untruthfulness," "lack of self-respect," "ignorance," and "unsettledness of mode of life." Like the American reformers working to uplift southern poor whites, South African social scientists sometimes grappled with the same question of causation: Was it the environment (isolated conditions), "social heredity," or both which accounted for the decline of poor whites?[56] Since the Carnegie Corporation financed the work of the Eugenics Record Office in Cold Spring Harbor, New York, and some of the Carnegie men were close with Madison Grant, an admonisher of race mixing and the author of *The Passing of the Great Race* (1916), it stood ready to offer the expert advice of eugenics reformers to South Africans concerned about the possibility of degeneration among poor whites. As Ellen Condliffe Lagemann writes in her history of the Carnegie Corporation, the trustees were all "guided in their grant decisions by an acknowledged wish to protect Anglo-Saxon prerogatives, customs, and genes."[57]

Indeed, Frederick Keppel, Charles T. Loram, and Raymond W. Wilcocks decided that the Poor White Commission should have input from American social scientists given Americans' broad and extensive training in sociological questions. Loram was partial to Thomas Jesse Jones since he viewed Jones as "the leading authority in the world on the education of backward peoples" and admired his theory of "the four legs of the race adjustment table" involving "Governments, missionaries, settlers, and the Natives."[58] However, the two experts the Carnegie Commission decided to send to South Africa to proffer advice on the poor white issue were Charles W. Coulter, a professor of sociology from Ohio Wesleyan University, and Kenyon L. Butterfield, a member of Theodore Roosevelt's Commission on Country Life and a nationally recognized rural sociologist who had studied agricultural conditions in Europe. During the course of their investigation, South African planners and fieldworkers consulted an American "Poor White Bibliography" mailed to them by Keppel, which had been put together by Howard W. Odum for the Social Science Research Council.[59] Coulter spent many months advising on the problem of poor whites and Butterfield spent four months in South Africa assessing agricultural conditions and two weeks traveling with the Poor White Commission.[60] South African psychologists and social scientists conferred with the American experts on such issues as public health, home life, agricultural poverty, and labor relations. When Butterfield returned to New York, the Carnegie Corporation published his report on "Rural Conditions and Sociological Problems in South Africa" in which he included a section on "Agriculture and Country Life in the Two 'U.S.A.'s.'" The comparisons to be drawn between the Union of South Africa and the United States were limited, Butterfield explained, because of "so many differences that one comparison immediately contradicts the other"; however, he did see parallels between potentially redeemable "virile European stock" in both places as well as a similar system of agricultural research, education, and demonstration.[61]

Members of the commission in South Africa were very open to the idea that the poor white problems in both the U.S. South and South Africa had a great deal in common. Like others before him, R. W. Wilcocks traveled to the United States with the assistance of a Carnegie Visitors' Grant to study the "psychological nature" of the poor white problem, and when he returned he drafted an unpublished comparative study titled "Rural Poverty among Whites in South Africa and in the South of the United States" that entered the transnational circuit of knowledge on poor whites.[62] He denoted a poor white as "a person who is wholly or chiefly dependent on farming for a livelihood or is of comparatively recent rural origin." This included principally South African share-tenants and unskilled laborers; southern tenants, sharecroppers, and mill workers; and inhabitants of the Appalachian mountains. Wilcocks acknowledged that in both South Africa and the United States there existed "a certain disinclination" to use the term "poor white" because of its "derogatory sense" and the desire to make distinctions between southern poor whites and Appalachian poor whites, but he concluded that it was necessary to "envisage the problem as a whole" and there seemed to be no other "suitable inclusive term." Often Wilcocks and others simply referred to the problem as "poor whiteism."[63] Although these social scientists had been trained to pay attention to schemes of classification and nuance, they willingly embraced the more elastic notion of "poor whiteism," which inherently minimized differences between groups of whites since the term was useful in capturing a prevalent understanding of what it meant to be backward, uncivilized, and living in rural poverty. James Bertram, the secretary of the Carnegie Corporation, read Wilcocks's paper and wrote to Frederick Keppel that he found the legitimacy of the analogy between South Africa and the United States lacking since the study did not distinguish between different groups of whites in the U.S. South.[64] However, the perceived commonality of the threat poor whites posed to agricultural prosperity in both countries was an effective illustration to make for those working in the mission field and struggling to identify the origins of the problem.

One characteristic that accounts for the inclination to draw comparisons between the U.S. South and South Africa, in spite of some reformers' acknowledgment of the elusiveness of the phrase "poor-whiteism," was the envisioned similarity between each country's history of race relations. Social scientists and reformers viewed the history of blacks and whites intermingling in one locale as a global problem involving the relationship between the "civilized" and "backward" races. As early as 1915, Maurice S. Evans, a British transplant to the East African colony of Natal and author of the book *Black and White in South East Africa* (1911), traveled to the southern states to study race relations "from a South African point of view." The larger purpose of Evans's ensuing book *Black and White in the Southern States* (1915) was to provide a counterexample of what would happen if South Africa did not impose full-scale segregation in all areas of life.[65] It is no accident that fascination with the poor white problem in both the U.S. South and South Africa coincided with the rise of Jim Crow and apartheid. Discussions about degeneration and indolence among poor whites reflected an anxiety with the inviolableness of what Evans's friend Edgar Gardner Murphy called "race integrity."[66] As Saul DuBow notes in his study on South Africa, "The language of degeneration reflected — simultaneously and contradictorily — an overweening sense of whites' biological superiority, and a perception of their social vulnerability."[67] If poor whites could be reformed and kept separate from blacks then it would minimize the erosion of Anglo-Saxon superiority and colonial power.

Although South Africa suffered from an intransigent poor white problem, the problem of poor whites in the U.S. South proved to be especially problematic. Repatriation as a solution used in some colonies was not an alternative for obvious reasons: the number of poor whites was too great, the region was not a true colony, and there was no metropole to which poor whites could be sent. In truth, the only alternative was reform. However, the tendency to describe the agricultural, public health, and educational reform of poor whites as uplift continually pulled the issue back into the orbit of the colonial world and pointed to the protean boundaries of racial categories marking black and white. Reformers' and scientific experts' commitment to reforming the southern "forgotten man" through a form of industrial training resonated with the program of moral uplift and industrial training advocated at black institutions such as Hampton Institute and Tuskegee Institute and schools in the overseas colonies.[68] During his trip to Asia, southern reformer Clarence H. Poe witnessed the introduction of industrial education to young children in the Philippines and boldly declared that "right here is a valuable lesson for those of us who are interested in getting practical training for white boys and girls in America as we are for brown boys and girls in the Philippines." Poe maintained that one of the reasons the United States had fallen behind the Philippines was because it had focused on industrial education for adults only. He also was startled to discover that in Japan "brown Mongolian farmers," whom Americans viewed as "backward 'heathen,'" had better educational facilities and more parental commitment to their children's uplift than what was given to "our white farm boys and girls . . . who have in their veins the blood of a race which has carried the flag of human progress for a thousand years."[69] The emphasis on cultivating an industrial work ethic in poor white children in the South underscored the anxiety about the power and imperviousness of the Anglo-Saxon race.

While Poe was part of a transnational web of agricultural reformers and genuinely seeking lessons in the "Orient," others were more disparaging about the unequal distribution of resources that seemed to benefit the overseas colonies more than the U.S. South. Speaking to a crowd of reformers, Governor Charles Henderson of Alabama thundered, "Will you do for your own people in Alabama what you have done so freely and cheerfully for those in foreign countries?"[70] William H. Skaggs explained how children attended public school 200 days out of the year in the Philippines, 165 days out of the year in Puerto Rico, and only 113.3 days in Alabama. What he found particularly disturbing was Congress's relative lack of interest in southern educational problems as compared to the educational problems of the colonies. He described how William Jennings Bryan had undertaken a combined tour of the southern states and the West Indies and had only reported to the House Committee on Insular Affairs on the grave need for schools, better roads, and hookworm eradication programs in Puerto Rico but not for the U.S. South. Skaggs chastised Bryan for neglecting the region which had voted for Bryan in substantial numbers during the presidential election of 1908.[71] Charles W. Dabney, educational reformer and president of the University of Tennessee, encouraged southern states to consider accepting national aid for education in the South by appealing to their patriotic sensibilities. He stressed how white southerners had willingly served their country in defense of the "Cuban people" and died in a "war for aliens" and thus were entitled to national support for their own children. Like Skaggs he also noted the incongruity between establishing schools for Puerto Ricans and Filipinos but neglecting white southern children at home.[72] Skaggs and Dabney's decision to compare poor whites with Filipinos and Puerto Ricans, as opposed to northern immigrants or African Americans, highlighted the most dreadful repercussion of the "southern problem," the uncanny commonalities between a large group of southern whites and nonwhites overseas.

Education and "Re-nationalizing" the South

William H. Skaggs and Charles W. Dabney's plea that social reformers pay more attention to the education of poor whites reflected a broader shift in focus on those who would benefit from educational reform. The southern educational reform movement initiated during Reconstruction had focused exclusively on reducing illiteracy rates among the newly freed slaves, and in the years immediately following Reconstruction white philanthropists continued to direct most of their efforts at African Americans. What is noteworthy is that at the turn of the century the educational reform movement shifted in orientation and directed almost all of its attention to the inadequacies of poor whites. Liberal southern reformers and northern philanthropists who advocated the ideal of the manly, progressive white citizen in the South embraced not just the value of a specialized area, such as industrial training, but also highlighted the importance of education as a whole in cultivating American citizenship and productivity. They viewed the task of educating the southern populace, particularly poor whites, as both a regional and national project. Reformers frequently cited statistics using northern rates of literacy as a reference point from which to judge the South and argued that democratic education was the key to national reconciliation. As the *Presbyterian Standard* noted in 1901, "The education of the ignorant is no sectional question since the nation may sometimes suffer through the suffrage of the unintelligent."[73] The paper hinted that while white southerners had long harbored regional anxieties about black suffrage in the South, the possibility of illiterate poor whites voting was a graver problem still, since in the end their participation in the political process would injure the nation. Andrew Sledd put it more bluntly when he said, "The South is the most ignorant section in the Union."[74]

Efforts to revive the quality of southern education and reduce the level of "civic degeneracy" began as early as Reconstruction when northern churches and philanthropists entered the region to educate the freed slaves.[75] Edgar W. Knight, professor of education at Trinity College (later Duke University), explained how the South during this period was "looked upon as a vast missionary field."[76] When the federal government pulled its last federal troops out of the South in 1877, public education suffered tremendously because of the Redeemer governments' policy of retrenchment. State appropriations for public schools were appallingly low, and the average length of the school term in the South decreased by 20 percent.[77] A minority of local southern reformers and northern supporters continued to advocate better educational opportunities in the region, but they lacked state support and had to search for alternative funding, often from the North. George Peabody, a Georgia-born investment banker from New York, donated $3.5 million for the promotion of education in those portions of the South that had suffered the most in the wake of the Civil War. Jabez Lamar Monroe Curry, a southern crusader for education from Alabama, was appointed to administer the Peabody Fund for the Peabody Foundation in 1881 and later worked with the Slater Fund, another northern educational endowment initiated by Jon Fox Slater, a Connecticut industrialist.[78] Curry, like most educational reformers, supported the congressionally defeated Blair Education Bill of 1883, which had promised to extend federal appropriations for education based on the proportion of illiteracy in the various states. Of course if it had passed, the South would have received the lion's share of the money as it had the highest rate of illiteracy. Other early proponents of southern education included General Samuel Chapman Armstrong. The years following the Civil War left behind the blueprint for educational reform in the South, but until the turn of the century whatever philanthropic support existed tended to target African Americans.

Buoyed by the increase in social scientific experts during the early years of the Progressive Era and propelled by the codification of Jim Crow, educational reformers began to shift their attention toward the problem of poor whites. Thirty-five years after the Civil War, the South still lagged far behind the North in terms of the amount of money spent per pupil, the length of the school year, and the highest grade achieved. In 1908 Samuel C. Mitchell complained that "the disadvantaged people — for whom the philanthropists and reformers of the North should have lifted up their voices — were not the slaves, but the disinherited and neglected masses of the white population."[79] Indeed, the shocking situation of white illiteracy made for especially stunning headlines. William H. Skaggs wrote a letter to the editor of the *Birmingham Age-Herald* regarding the deplorable educational facilities and opportunities in his home state of Alabama. The startling headline of his editorial read, "INDICTMENT OF SOUTH'S EDUCATION GROWS APPALLING. Wm. H. Skaggs, Former Talladega Man, Presents Some Gruesome Facts. SEES DARK AHEAD FOR OUR WHITE CHILDREN. Says Educational Conditions Among Southern White People Are the Most Deplorable in the Civilized World." Skaggs had collected documentation after making a personal investigation of the educational situation in the southern states and reported that he could "furnish evidence of ignorance, poverty and physical and civic degeneracy" among the white class. He warned that what he had discovered would make every person in the state "stand aghast." In fact, Skaggs noted that not only were blacks rapidly accumulating more property and becoming more literate than poor whites but also that Puerto Rico was "making greater progress than the South."[80]

In response to these educational deficiencies, a group of southern reformers with ties to northern philanthropists initiated a broad campaign to promote an educational awakening in the South and draw attention to the region's backward plight. They tapped into northern concern about the South and made the fight against illiteracy and southern backwardness a national issue. The interest in correcting southern educational deficiencies began with the first meeting of the Conference for Education in the South in Capon Springs, Virginia, in 1898. The participants elected New Yorker Robert C. Ogden as president of the conference. Ogden served in this capacity until his death in 1913 and was celebrated as the chief evangelist in the movement. The task of uplift was even broader in nature and involved ensuring that the poor white population was fit to exercise its citizenship rights as educated democratic citizens. Initially, the annual sessions at the first meeting attracted little attention except from religious educators interested in improving black education and providing relief for the poor white inhabitants of the Appalachian mountains. Within three years the movement had expanded to a nationally backed campaign to solve the educational problem predominantly in poor white communities across the South.[81] Ogden stated clearly the movement's intentions to a friend: "I represent a group of broad indeed patriotic men and women who are extremely desirous to aid, up to the limit of their ability, the existing illiteracy in our backward States, and this applies with a great deal more force to the white than the Negro race."[82] Just prior to the 1903 Conference for Education in the South held in Richmond, Virginia, Ogden privately told James H. Kirkland, the chancellor of Vanderbilt University, that he did not plan to issue invitations to black educators because he could not confirm that white participants would support this action and he preferred to avert any possibility of dissension within the group.[83]

Three years after the first meeting, the conference participants voted to create the Southern Education Board (SEB), an association designed to oversee the Conference for Education in the South, as well as a Bureau of Information and Investigation. The original board of the SEB founded in 1901 included eleven members, six from the South and five from the North. Robert C. Ogden served as the president of the SEB. The southern board members included Walter Hines Page; Charles W. Dabney; Edwin A. Alderman; Charles D. McIver, president of the North Carolina State Normal and Industrial College for Women; and Hollis B. Frissell, principal of Booker T. Washington's alma mater, the Hampton Institute. Edgar Gardner Murphy assumed the position of executive secretary in 1902, and other liberal white southerners who joined the board over the next few years included Samuel C. Mitchell; James Hardy Dillard, president of the Jeanes Fund and the John F. Slater Fund; and James H. Kirkland.[84] The board members designed the SEB to be a propaganda machine, not a distributor of funds. Ogden described the New York City–based operation as a "voluntary, self-perpetuating body" with "no capital fund" whose goal was to disseminate "propaganda for popular education upon the Jeffersonian doctrine of a 'crusade for education.'"[85] Its mission included distributing broadsides, publishing its findings in southern and national newspapers, and cultivating support from businessmen, church leaders, and educators. The issues the group hoped to draw attention to included taxing citizens to support education, compulsory education, lengthening of school terms, education of teachers, and improvement and cleanup of schools. In the early years of the SEB, George Peabody furnished the organization with financial support but the members of the board looked forward to a much larger donation. The philosophy of the SEB impressed John D. Rockefeller Jr. so much that he encouraged his father to establish the General Education Board (GEB), an institution committed to providing financial assistance for school improvement in the United States. Between 1902 and 1909, Rockefeller bestowed fifty-three million dollars on the GEB. The bulk of the funds went to the South in support of black and white public school education and the farm demonstration projects just beginning at several agricultural and normal schools.[86]

In 1901, the year these reformers in the "Ogden movement" created the SEB, Ogden chartered a train from the Pennsylvania Railroad and loaded it with almost eighty philanthropists, reformers, clergymen, and educators who planned to attend the annual conference and travel through the South for two weeks inspecting the region's educational conditions.[87] The entourage included such prominent individuals as John D. Rockefeller Jr., George Peabody, Walter Hines Page, and Lyman Abbott. They visited Hampton Institute, North Carolina College for Women, Atlanta University, and Tuskegee University. Ogden would continue leading these train excursions until 1906, issuing hundreds of invitations to northerners and southerners alike (see fig. 8). On these voyages, Ogden and his companions wound their way through the South, visiting various educational facilities and meeting important southern educational leaders. Future groups continued to stop at some African American schools, but the greatest number of the visits involved white schools. Indeed, Edgar Gardner Murphy once warned Ogden that if the New York philanthropist ever decided to substitute a black school for a white school on a train trip it would lead to "deep resentment and humiliation" and inflame political partisanship.[88] Yet hostility and suspiciousness were already evident throughout the South as the travelers continued to arrive. Seizing upon a familiar staple of southern criticism of the North, the *Manufacturer's Record* accused the "Ogden movement" of preaching racial equality and entertaining black Americans in white homes.[89]

Passengers making the trip called it the "Ogden Special" and the "Special School for Uplift," reflecting imperial overtones.[90] Some newspapers dubbed the train "the millionaires' special."[91] Edward Ingall, managing editor of the *Manufacturer's Record* in Baltimore and a prominent New South ideologue, described with great derision the New York philanthropist's train as being equipped "with state rooms, bathrooms, barber-shop, etc." and full of "Mr. Ogden's collection of millionaires, educators, philanthropists, and sundry

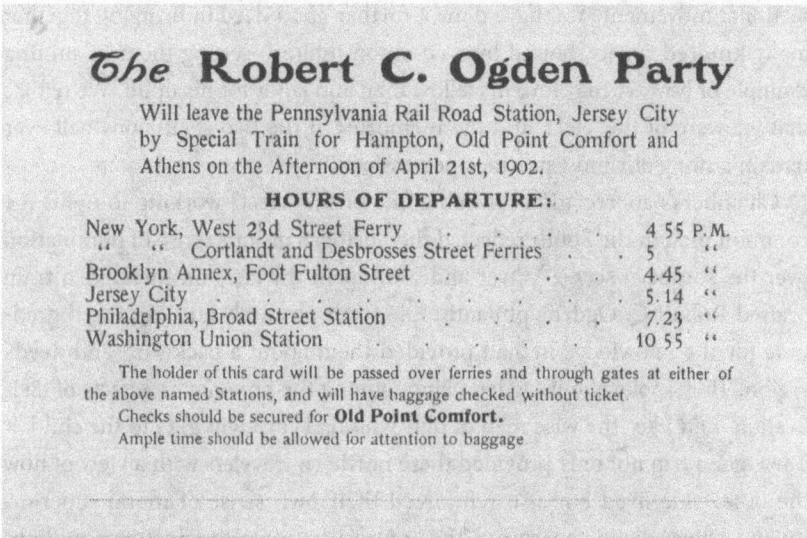

The Robert C. Ogden Party

Will leave the Pennsylvania Rail Road Station, Jersey City by Special Train for Hampton, Old Point Comfort and Athens on the Afternoon of April 21st, 1902.

HOURS OF DEPARTURE:

New York, West 23d Street Ferry	4.55 P.M.
" " Cortlandt and Desbrosses Street Ferries	5 "
Brooklyn Annex, Foot Fulton Street	4.45 "
Jersey City	5.14 "
Philadelphia, Broad Street Station	7.23 "
Washington Union Station	10.55 "

The holder of this card will be passed over ferries and through gates at either of the above named Stations, and will have baggage checked without ticket.
Checks should be secured for **Old Point Comfort.**
Ample time should be allowed for attention to baggage

FIGURE 8. Train ticket for the "The Robert C. Ogden Party." Library of Congress, Manuscript Division, The Papers of Robert C. Ogden.

curios."[92] No better instance of southern neo-orientalism can be found. The South became a spectacle, a foreign land to be surveyed, catalogued, and scrutinized by northern eyes. One man from Cambridge, Massachusetts, recounted a story in which a Parisian asked him if he was planning on traveling to Europe that summer. "'No,' I answered, 'I am going on a much more interesting journey.' 'But what can be more interesting than Europe?' he asked. I said, 'Mr. Ogden's trip through the Southern States has a fascination that no European trip can equal.'"[93] At the conclusion of one such train voyage, the various passengers presented Ogden with a notebook, containing personal messages to their benefactor and recorded observations of the trip. Frederick T. Gates wrote, "Dear Mr. Ogden: It was the trip of my life. I saw many instructive sights; I heard many wise words; I learned some valuable lessons, I learned some deep impressions." Gates likened Ogden to the Apostle Paul and commended him on the "extraordinary achievement" of this "great educational excursion." Frank R. Chambers, from Bronxville, New York, inscribed to Ogden, "The 'Propaganda' has been, as you have told us, the work of many men, but surely to you belongs the credit for having interested most effectively a host of the North's best people, thereby creating a national sympathy for a sectional movement. You have done a further good deed in bringing together many kindred spirits, bound by a common interest, setting them in shining example of how we may love his fellow man and labor for his uplift. We rejoice that we were of the 'elect' and the memories of the two excursions will ever remain among our most precious possessions."[94]

Chambers's appreciation for being one of the "elect" working to uplift the common man in the South reflected the northern group's sense of domination over the southern scene.[95] Over and over again travelers on the Ogden train praised Robert C. Ogden's philanthropic spirit profusely and expressed gratitude for the knowledge he had provided them about a backward and needy region. They spoke about Ogden being "among the honored architects of civilization" and like "the wise men of old" who had "brought gifts to the child."[96] The Ogden trip not only provided these northern travelers with a view of how the other side lived but also reinforced their own sense of moral superiority and paternalistic generosity. The contrast between the northern millionaires and the backward, uneducated poor whites in the South could not have been starker. These expeditions provided fertile ground for the development of northern missionary practice in the region, a concept that supporters of the educational movement sometimes referred to explicitly and critics often condemned.

In addition, a transnational circuit of educational reformers and ideas also created the opportunity for men seeking to uplift nonwhite people abroad to use the South as a training ground or blueprint. In 1904 Ogden received a letter from a graduate student at Harvard University who was getting ready to head to the Philippines to work under Governor-General Cameron Forbes; he inquired whether he could join one of Ogden's journeys as preparation for his service in the colonial government.[97] Puerto Rico also provided an analogous social laboratory, both for educational reform and hookworm eradication. The secretary of the NCLC informed Edgar Gardner Murphy that he would transmit notes on Murphy's experience with the SEB to the new commissioner of education in Puerto Rico with the hope "that the good work of the Southern Education Board may be extended that far South."[98] The concept of a broader global South incorporating the U.S. South with the colonies in the Caribbean included the commitment to uplift unenlightened people. As Samuel C. Mitchell wrote after Ogden's death, "It is noteworthy that, just at the time when

Mr. Ogden became identified with the popular movement for education in the South, the American people were led, as the result of the war with Spain, to undertake the training of backward peoples in the Philippines, Porto Rico [sic] and Hawaii. Here was projected upon a world stage the same task and the same principle of education in the making of a race which the South was at that time exemplifying." He added, "The meaning of this social effort will be lost unless it is realized that the principle and process used here are applicable in every country that aspires to progress under democratic freedom."[99]

Those white southerners, hostile to what they perceived as northern interference and interest in uplifting poor whites, labeled this educational movement the "Ogden circus" or "Ogdenism."[100] These attempts to remake the U.S. South socially and culturally often precipitated a wave of vitriol on the part of native white southerners, including some New South ideologues. One southern newspaper advised its readers to resist "the special trains loaded with distinguished parties of Southerners and Northerners" who were "making a conquest of the South and Southern sentiment."[101] Richard H. Edmonds conceded that the forgotten white man might benefit from some education and training in self-reliance, but Edmonds felt that "begging a few dollars from Ogdenism" would ultimately have a countereffect. Turning philanthropic rhetoric on its head, Edmonds argued that southerners who petitioned for charitable help while "a bountiful Providence [was] pouring more than $7,000,000 into their laps" were in danger of losing their former manly self-reliance. "Would you sap the virility, the sturdy character, the manliness of a boy?" Edmonds asked. A white man who took charity looked prosperous on the outside, but inside, Edmonds declared, there was "decay, rottenness, [and] death." In addition, the editor of the *Manufacturer's Record* maintained that the state of dependency generated by an overreliance on charity not only produced degeneration in the individual person but also reflected a greater degeneration in the nation. "Outwardly there may be signs of real life, of manhood, of progress upward," he proclaimed, "but at the heart there may be a fatal disease gnawing at the very vitals of all true national character and life."[102] Edmonds insisted the South remained poised at a critical juncture in its evolutionary path. The region had made great commercial progress but these "false teachers," northern philanthropists, were prepared to "pauperize the manhood of the South" with their alms. Perhaps Edmonds could not reconcile his faith in the progress of the New South with such nationally publicized southern problems as illiteracy and cultural backwardness. He rejected the efforts of reformers to train the forgotten white men of the South for industrial progress, because in his mind the commercial development that would result from such training had already been accomplished.

While the beneficent motives of these reformers should be acknowledged as well as their remarkable success in reducing illiteracy rates, the racial implication of their project lurked beneath the propaganda and was frequently noted in private conversations as well as public orations. The reformers may have had more in common with Edmonds than he realized. Both white and northern reformers believed that widespread educational reform would redress the failings of questionable members of the Anglo-Saxon race and reinforce their whiteness. Robert C. Ogden laid the problem out this way: "The great present need of the South is the uplift of its backward populations. . . . Through the country the urgent need is for a white civilization that the black man can respect. Only this can eliminate the dangers of the future."[103] Ogden and his supporters viewed education as the key to racial harmony in a segregated system since if poor whites could be taught to meet the standards of civilized life then blacks would ultimately defer to them. At times, the proponents of southern education were apprehensive about the ability of poor whites to better themselves and noted that African Americans, unlike lower-class whites, never had to be persuaded to send their children to school.[104] Some members of the SEB petitioned for the public advocacy of compulsory attendance laws for whites; they insisted that, without prodding, these whites would continue to drag the region down and contribute to enduring racial tensions.[105] In a piece endorsing compulsory education in the southern states, Erwin Craighead from Mobile, Alabama, explained how, in a democracy, "the primary object of education has been to make good, intelligent, loyal sovereigns." Without education white southern people would be unable to develop into an "intelligent, prosperous, and orderly citizenship."[106]

While these reformers did not utilize the language of the race-baiting southern demagogues, they still remained committed to an idea of democracy that included the social separation of the races and black disfranchisement. The philanthropic interest in black education, at such places as Hampton Institute and Tuskegee Institute, did not fade completely but remained devoid of any hint of political activism or the call for civil rights. On many occasions,

Robert C. Ogden supported the "honest enforcement" of southern laws designed to exploit the loopholes of the Fourteenth and Fifteenth Amendments and encouraged discussion of black suffrage only from an academic point of view.[107] Educating white illiterates was simply part of a broader process to solidify the color line with as little racial antagonism as possible.

Despite the occasional southern protest against northern aid and intervention, the SEB and the GEB represented a successful collaboration between the North and South to eliminate the educational problems of the rural South and remake the region in the image of the North. The formation of the GEB marked the beginning of a new era in which powerful northern philanthropies made the South a laboratory for social change. Prominent northern capitalists and businessmen played a significant role in the educational rehabilitation of the South and worked in conjunction with liberal southern reformers. In 1904 Ogden warned, "There are more white illiterates in our Southern States than black ones. . . . If we do not lift this mass of ignorance, both black and white, they will pull down the South and be a dead weight to the best interests of the country."[108] These liberal reformers viewed the educational movement as the key to national power and the cultivation of democracy. Lyman Abbott, one of the many northern passengers on Ogden's train, described the New South as a "new-born democracy" and explained how the process of training a new democracy "to understand either its rights or its duties" always took time.[109] Century magazine informed its editorial readers that the effort to reduce illiteracy in the South was "an enterprise of the highest patriotism, of the most genuine nationalism" and a "movement of humanitarianism which will have fruits not only on our own continent but in distant parts of the world."[110] Here the progress of the South was coupled with the future success of imperial projects. The proper education of each American citizen not only played a key role in developing nationalist sentiment but also contributed to the legitimacy and supremacy of American authority abroad.

Ogden and his southern supporters harbored concerns not just about the effect the uneducated would have on the nation-state's power as a whole but also on the ability of the sections to reunite in the long wake of the Civil War. Reformers consistently stressed educational reform as the key to national reconciliation between sections and identified the reeducation of poor whites as vital to this process. They believed in redeeming poor whites who had been the victims of aristocratic traditions, old values, and southern antebellum ideals as well as those left behind in the drive for social and economic progress engendered by industrialization in the New South. Samuel C. Mitchell blamed slavery as the real cause of illiteracy among the poor whites whom the southern aristocracy had neglected and socially "disinherited." Mitchell explained how slavery had "separated the South from the rest of the country by sectional idiosyncrasies" and "paralyzed the effect of those spiritual affinities which constitute alone the real bonds of a modern nation under democracy." He described "the school as the exponent of democracy in the South" and the key to the emancipation of the common white man and, ultimately, the emancipation of the nation."[111] Charles W. Dabney, head of the SEB propaganda machine, simply described the southern educational campaign as the process of "re-nationalizing the South."[112]

In short, education would play a crucial role in facilitating the transition of the South from a provincial backward region to a modern progressive region in tune with the ideals of a national industrial democracy for whites only. Educational reformers viewed poor southern whites as the South's greatest untapped resource, the key to facilitating southern industrialization and national reunion. The crusade to bring education to the southern populace embodied a certain view of democracy, a national democratic vision that highlighted the importance of industry, self-discipline, and progress.

While the discourse on the "southern problem" focused on many issues, poor whites repeatedly elicited attention in multiple arenas including public health, agriculture, labor, and education. What was to become of the poor white population in the South, and how could these poor whites be made into useful American citizens? The existence of poor whites highlighted the paradox of the New South — the tension between the ideologues who championed industrial progress, racial harmony, and white supremacy and those detractors who believed "poor whiteism" threatened the advancement of civilization both regionally and nationally. At times, reformers juggled contradictory ideas regarding the root of the problem and their ability to solve it. Was it the social environment or some intrinsic racial trait that accounted for such problems as lazy farming, lack of initiative, low intelligence, and arrested development? Some reformers such as Walter Hines Page advocated industrial training for these "forgotten men" and viewed poor whites as the most promising undeveloped resource in the region. Page saw potential in this group and maintained that investing in their future would yield the rewards of industrial prosperity and democracy. Yet in advocating industrial training for poor whites, educational reformers had to walk a fine line, being careful not to advance the suggestion that poor whites and poor blacks were racially equal, even while they employed a similar rhetoric of uplift when discussing both groups.

The formation of the SEB in 1901 and the subsequent support of John D. Rockefeller Jr. for the GEB marked an important commitment to not just industrial training for men but the education of the southern population as a whole. The apparent lack of literacy in the poor white population raised questions about their ability to exercise the rights of citizenship in a modern democracy that valued a self-informed and self-sufficient body politic. Reformers called for compulsory education and described the school as the center of democracy and the most effective means for unifying northerners and southerners. Indeed, reformers repeatedly described this wave of educational reform as crucial to national reconciliation and the key to the reintegration of a backward yet improving region into the modern industrial nation-state. The task of cultivating citizenship and productivity through the education of poor white children was viewed as both a regional and a national problem. Many southern problems such as child labor, or what many reformers simply referred to as "white slavery," underscored the imperative need to educate white children in preparation for assuming their roles as white citizens in the American nation-state.

Finally, during a moment when new questions about empire dominated the national landscape, educational reformers abruptly turned their eyes toward the millions of poor whites in the South. Reformers such as Robert C. Ogden and William H. Skaggs observed that poor southern whites shared many of the characteristics of the peoples of color in overseas colonies. Poor whites suffered from similar diseases, retrograde agricultural practices, and illiteracy, among other deficiencies. These reformers also advocated using the U.S. South as an educational training ground for those working in colonial settings abroad. The similarity in rhetoric and the strategies of reform used in these transnational locations points to a broader conception of a global South that included both the southern states and countries South of the United States. Later in the 1920s this transnational movement of ideas and people between the southern states and the overseas colonies animated discussions about another poor white problem in an imperial setting. South African social scientists sought the help of American social scientists and this group drew on their expertise with both African Americans and native Africans. Scattered populations of potentially degenerate poor whites threatened to undermine not only the authority of empire abroad but also the southern color line during the rise of Jim Crow and the ultimate emergence of apartheid in South Africa.

CHAPTER FIVE

The "Race Problem" and the Fiction of the Color Line

Among the chief problems which have vexed the country for the last century and threaten to give yet more trouble in the future, is what is usually termed "The Negro Question." To the South, it has been for nearly forty years the chief public question, overshadowing all others, and withdrawing her from due participation in the direction and benefit of the National Government. It has kept alive sectional feeling; has inflamed partizanship [sic]; distorted party policies; barred complete reconciliation; cost hundreds of millions of money, and hundreds if not thousands of lives, and stands ever ready, like Banquo's Ghost, to burst forth even at the feast.

— THOMAS NELSON PAGE

We have a way in America of wanting to be "rid" of problems. It is not so much a desire to reach the best and largest solution as it is to clean the board and start a new game. For instance, most Americans are simply tired and impatient over our most sinister social problem, the Negro. They do not want to solve it, they do not want to understand it, they want to simply be done with it and hear the last of it.

— W. E. B. DU BOIS

In the summer of 1890 over one hundred white philanthropists, reformers, politicians, newspaper editors, and clergymen from across the country met to discuss the "Negro question" at Lake Mohonk in Ulster County, New York. It was not the first such gathering at Lake Mohonk. Many of the same men and women, including former President Rutherford B. Hayes, Samuel Chapman Armstrong, and Lyman Abbott had attended previous Mohonk Conferences on Native Americans in the United States. At the seventh Mohonk Conference on Indian Affairs, President Hayes urged the audience to hold a symposium on the status of African Americans, and later he wrote to the founder of the Mohonk meetings that he viewed it as a conference "for uplifting the Negroes of the South."[1] The following year the group nominated Hayes to serve as their chairman and both Hayes and the group spent several days at the Mohonk Mountain House trying to identify the key components of the "Negro question." Papers at the conference sessions addressed such issues as industrial training, home life, labor, lynching, and higher education. In the opening address Chairman Hayes encouraged the attendees to eschew partisanship and sectionalism and seek solutions on "the educational, the benevolent, and the religious side of the question." "If the Negroes remain as co-occupants and co-citizens of the States, and we do not lift them up," he concluded, "they will drag us down to industrial bankruptcy, social degradation, and political corruption."[2] In 1891 the Mohonk participants gathered for yet a second conference on the "Negro question." Ostensibly both meetings sought to address the problems African Americans faced in the post-Reconstruction South, but more was at stake. A resolution of the "Negro question" also stood to benefit southern and northern whites, who believed that with luck the solution would avoid the thorny political issues that had driven a wedge between the North and South over the course of the nineteenth century. Conference organizers specifically decided not to invite any African Americans to Mohonk lest their presence agitate white southern participants and provoke political dissension. Reverend A. D. Mayo, from the Bureau of Education in Washington, D.C., confirmed the alleged wisdom of this decision in his declaration that the conference would yield optimistic "Christian insight" during a time in which "partisan politics seems to pause in uncertainty on the steep edge of a dark abyss, when noble and humane people all over the country seem to be falling into despondency," over the question of race in the South.[3]

The Mohonk gatherings of prominent white southern and northern reformers on the "Negro question" initiated a new era of engagement with the "race problem" in the South, which evaded the question of federal support and political intrusion and focused on the philanthropic and social scientific side of the question. What these conferences illustrate is that the problems of Emancipation and Reconstruction had not been resolved entirely. Perhaps it was fitting that President Hayes, the beneficiary of the Compromise of

1876, headed the first national conference since the political agreement had ceded the presidency to Hayes and the Republican Party and all but ensured the complete loss of African Americans' political and civil liberties in the Democratic South. In the late nineteenth and early twentieth centuries, the perplexing question of race stoked a protracted and vigorous debate about the place of black Americans in the South. Indeed, the persistent problem of race in the South continually tested and challenged the fictions embodied in the reconciled New South. As David W. Blight writes, "Race was so deeply at the root of the war's causes and consequences, and so powerful a source of division in American social psychology, that it served as the antithesis of a culture of reunion. The memory of slavery, emancipation, and the Fourteenth and Fifteenth Amendments never fit well into a developing narrative in which the Old and New South were romanticized and welcomed back to a new nationalism."[4] Endless discussion about the nature of the color line — what it was, where it existed, whether it could be stabilized, and what happened if the boundaries were crossed — contributed to an inexhaustible discussion on the nature of race in the South.

Interest in identifying and solving the "Negro question," alternately known as the "Negro problem," the "race question," and the "race problem," cannot be attributed to any one individual, group, or institution.[5] For example, the term was utilized by white segregationists to complain about the general behavior of southern blacks, by northern philanthropists to refer to southern areas in need of reform, and by middle-class black Americans to signify the relentless injustice of life in the Jim Crow South. Much like the idiom the "southern problem," the concept of the "race problem" was elastic in meaning. The problem referenced a range of issues, including politics, labor, disease, education, industrial training, segregation, violence, social relations, home life, and "miscegenation." While a few sporadic references to a "Negro problem" or a "Negro question" appear in some antebellum and Civil War writings, the term is largely a postbellum construct used by participants in this dialogue to describe the past, present, and future state of race relations between blacks and whites.[6]

Because the discourse of the "race problem" had the power to collapse the boundaries between black and white by drawing attention to inconsistencies in the ideology of the color line, it proved to be extremely malleable. Sometimes the participants in this discourse engaged in dialogue with one another. At other times the discussions followed separate but parallel courses.

The ubiquitousness of the topic opened up spaces for black intellectuals to voice their concerns about the issue of race in both the South and the nation. Prominent black leaders and experienced and novice social scientists such as W. E. B. Du Bois, Kelly Miller, Booker T. Washington, Archibald Grimke, and William S. Scarborough published numerous books as well as articles about the problem of race in the South. Southern white liberals such as Edgar Gardner Murphy, Walter Hines Page, and George Washington Cable tackled the issue head-on, occasionally antagonizing their fellow white southerners by advocating paternalistic racial solutions rather than a hardline racist approach. White segregationists such as Thomas Nelson Page and Alfred Holt Stone offered their own interpretation of a problem they argued was best left to white southerners to resolve on southern soil. Northern liberals, such as Albert Bushnell Hart and Ray Stannard Baker, a muckraking journalist who wrote a series of articles based on interviews he did with blacks and whites, traveled through the South and published books and scores of articles based on their outside observations of the region. Transoceanic visitors from other countries recorded their southern journeys in search of answers to their own racial problems in the colonies or back at home. A kaleidoscope of dialogue on the "race problem" so dominated the national press, the lecture circuit, and the publishing world that it prompted Kelly Miller, the founder of sociology at Howard University and a prolific writer, to remark: "The national opinion concerning the negro is formed and re-formed with such startling rapidity that only the process of instantaneous photography can preserve its shifting phases."[7]

However several sweeping assumptions anchored this discourse on universal ground. First, the "race problem," as in the context of the United States, almost universally referred to something southern in nature. It was a problem that squarely set the South apart from the rest of the nation. While the participants in this discourse acknowledged that other regions of the United States had their own racial problems to contend with, they viewed the "race problem" in the South as particularly acute and distinctive. Second, almost all of the commentators viewed the problem as a remnant of Reconstruction, an unresolved tension that had not been worked out by federal interference or even by southern whites granted the freedom to deal with the situation as they saw fit. Thus the existence of the "race problem" rendered any form of reconciliation — such as reunion between North and South or a regional understanding between blacks and whites — extremely difficult. Third, the "race problem" was viewed as a particularly volatile social issue that stood ready to erupt at any moment. Fear of an impending race war or some unspoken, unidentifiable conflict contributed to the disorientation and hesitation of those commentators broaching the subject in multiple forums. Over time the constructs of race and region developed in mutually reinforcing patterns of dependence as Americans increasingly began to associate the South with a distinctive racial milieu marked by strife, disequilibrium, and potential calamity. Finally, even while commentators on southern race relations viewed the situation as unique to the South, they consistently agreed that the South's racial troubles were part of a world problem, one recently magnified by the exigencies of western imperialism. A transnational community of scholars and reformers held joint symposia, exchanged intellectual ideas, and encouraged each other to situate the "race problem" in a global context.[8] The collaborators in this conversation both imported and exported their racial ideologies. A large number of British and South African imperialists traveled to the South in search of answers to their own race questions, and likewise, domestic American reformers often looked to American and British colonialists in foreign contexts for strategies in solving southern racial problems.

Because of the sheer magnitude of printed material on the "race problem" and the multiplicity of subtopics, this chapter will focus largely on how social scientists and self-proclaimed experts on the issue theorized about general social relations between the races, the place of mixed-race peoples in the South, and the capacity for progress and evolution in a global context. The imprint of social science as a tool of knowledge production is evident in almost all of this writing on the "race problem." The shift toward education, social reform, and philanthropy as viable solutions represented a movement away from the Reconstruction focus on free labor ideology, civil rights, and black suffrage thought to prolong sectional tensions. Yet even as these professional and amateur scholars tried to eschew questions of traditional politics, they still acknowledged that the "race problem" in the South made the region unique and was an enduring sectional issue rooted in the legacy of the Civil War. Furthermore, the distinctiveness of the South from the North emerged in sharper form when measured against the race problems overseas. Race theorists adopted a broader perspective and observed that the state of race relations in the southern states appeared to share much in common with other countries such as South Africa, Jamaica, Cuba, and Brazil.

Social Science and Race

The late nineteenth and early twentieth centuries ushered in a new generation of social scientists intent on using social scientific methodologies to solve modern-day problems engendered by the widespread social transformations of the Gilded Age and Progressive Era. Industrialization, the consolidation of wealth, escalating class conflict, growing immigration, and American imperialism coincided with the professionalization of such fields as economics, history, sociology, and political science. The social scientific interest in rationality, objectivity, and progress reflected social scientists' expectations of a better world.[9] The establishment of social science as a prominent intellectual discipline and tradition in the American academy provided a venue for professionals to address the issue of race relations at home and abroad. Some observers who theorized about race relations in the South but were not professional social scientists or affiliated with academic communities nevertheless were influenced by social scientific precepts. The question of race as it related to the modern liberal society was one of the central topics of interest in the growing body of literature on the "race problem," a dilemma that was viewed as global in nature and an inevitable outgrowth of western imperialism.

Participants in the "race problem" dialogue often struggled to reconcile the question of race in the South with the precepts of liberalism. For white social scientists and self-professed experts on the subject, the liberal belief in progress toward a higher state of civilization diverged from the seemingly irreconcilable nature of racial problems in the South. In 1913 James Bardin, a psychologist from the University of Virginia, explained how many students of the southern race problem "[had] as their ideal the creation through evolutionary processes of a state in which the whites and the Negroes live side by side, each group partaking of the same civilization on a basis of ethical equality, and each playing its part in government and society according to its ability." He remarked that theoretically this "bi-racial state" should have a single civilization encompassing a "complex, though organically homogenous, society," but those studying southern racial problems failed to recognize that it was an "ethical ideal" and "not a working formula." In short, Bardin maintained there was an inherent tension between theory and practice in the belief that all men are created equal.[10] As many scholars have noted, the theoretical concept of liberalism advocates ideas of universality and inclusion even as it engages in systematic patterns of exclusion.[11] Thus it is not unexpected that early on the field of social science could embrace the ideology of liberal individualism as a leading concept yet still support racialist thinking embodied in evolutionary biology and racial anthropology. Social scientific experts and liberal social reformers observing the southern "race problem" could declare their support for a universal society while simultaneously constructing racial hierarchies and practicing racially exclusionary policies.

Moreover, the field of social science itself existed in a constant state of evolution. Many social scientists espoused incompatible theories, sometimes hanging onto old frameworks while seeking to incorporate new models. For example, ideas about racial essentialism existed uneasily with new theories about the impact of culture and the environment on racial development. At the turn of the century, the ideas of Social Darwinism and the belief in inherent racial defects guided social scientific thought and many social reform projects. In the late nineteenth century, Franz Boas, a prominent German anthropologist, first introduced arguments against the idea of innate racial inferiority and challenged the established paradigm of scientific racism. Boas's ideas both subverted and overlapped with earlier sociological understandings about fixed racial identities and the biological differences between races. Ultimately, the environmentalist tradition triumphed over racial determinism as the disciplines of social science matured over the course of the twentieth century. However, the protean nature of the disciplines in the first few decades of the twentieth century fostered an intellectual environment that welcomed competing theories, contradictions, and unresolved questions.[12] The South furnished an ideal racial laboratory in which to test many of these developing claims. Both black and white social scientists participated in these discussions and even grappled with the same incongruities, although not always in direct dialogue with one another. The era in which publications on the "race problem" proliferated was, as John David Smith describes, a moment "when the lines were blurred between amateur and professional social scholars — before the 'professionalization' of academe became complete and when lay-scholars competed head-to-head with professors for notoriety."[13]

The Progressive reform impulse, with its focus on rationality and scientific answers, spawned a wealth of information on the "race problem" that eclipsed the amount of material written on the subject in previous times. The number of conferences, lectures, periodical articles, travelers' accounts, sermons, editorials, and sociological studies on the "race problem" during this period is staggering. In the late nineteenth and early twentieth centuries hundreds of books and articles appeared that documented and discussed every possible aspect of the evolving "race problem" in North America. Philanthropic organizations and reform societies advocated a professional and scientific approach to the study of race relations and touted the merits of sociological practices and theories. Many encouraged investigation of the "race problem" at leading universities in the South. Vice president of the University of Florida, Professor James M. Farr, thought that each university should "organize a class in sociology to study the race problem, largely by the laboratory method, using the town and county in which the university is located as the field for investigation."[14] At the University of Virginia and the University of Georgia, students under the auspices of the Young Men's Christian Association engaged in a systematic study of the "race problem" outside of their regular coursework.[15] Over the course of several decades, these men held a number of national conferences dedicated to resolving the repercussions of the "race problem": the First Mohonk Conference on the Negro Question (1890), the Second Mohonk Conference on the Negro Question (1891), the First Annual Conference Held Under the Auspices of the Southern Society for the Promotion of the Study of Race Conditions and Problems in the South (1900), and the Annual Conferences Held by the American Negro Academy (1897–1924). Other social reform associations held regular conferences including the Commission of Southern Universities on Southern Race Questions (1912–1917) and the Southern Sociological Congress (1912–1915). Academic organizations such as the American Economic Association, the American Historical Association, the American Sociological Society, the American Academy of Political and Social Science, and the Association for the Study of Negro Life and History regularly addressed various facets of the "race problem" at their meetings. In addition, informal and impromptu conferences and gatherings sprang up across the country and the issues discussed at these unofficial venues often made their way into the national press.

A strong social scientific tradition also developed in the black intellectual and professional community. Leading black thinkers such as Kelly Miller and W. E. B. Du Bois advocated the sociological approach in studying race questions as early as the late nineteenth century. Miller published many books and articles on "race friction," "miscegenation," and the problem of racial adjustment

in democratic nations.[16] Du Bois published scores of articles in national journals and magazines on the sociological approach to the race question and
undertook a series of lengthy sociological studies, including *The Philadelphia
Negro: A Social Study* (1897) and the Atlanta University studies, which led the
way in black social science.[17] Fisk University and Howard University developed
strong social science departments and trained students in a variety of social
problems, addressing such topics as the rural South and urban youth. During
the 1930s Charles S. Johnson, who studied with renowned sociologist Robert
Park at the University of Chicago, headed the department of social science at
Fisk and initiated and participated in many studies on the rural South.[18] This
small contingent of black sociologists contributed extensively to the discourse
of the "race problem." Alexander Crummell, a seventy-four-year-old prominent clergyman and black activist, established the American Negro Academy
(ANA) in 1897. Crummell created this black learned and cultural society to address the question of race in American life as well as in a transnational context.
He and a small group of black intellectuals, including W. E. B. Du Bois, Kelly
Miller, and William S. Scarborough, constituted this forty-member organization which remained in existence for thirty-one years. Later members of the
organization included Alain L. Locke, Carter G. Woodson, and James Weldon
Johnson. The ANA dedicated itself to the promotion of black scholarly works,
the publication of papers to counter racist propaganda, and assistance to black
youth in the attainment of higher culture. Members of the ANA published a
number of books and articles, both individually and through the auspices of
the association, contributing to the broader discourse on the "race problem."[19]

Although both white and black intellectuals spoke frequently about cooperation between the races on the subject of race relations, these intellectual societies and social reform organizations remained largely segregated.
While a number of northern and southern liberal whites were committed to
improving certain conditions for black Americans they did not typically invite black reformers and intellectuals to participate in their conferences, with
the possible exception of Booker T. Washington, who was entreated to attend
when white intellectuals sought the so-called expertise of a race leader. At the
First Mohonk Conference on the Negro Question, Albion Tourgée criticized
his colleagues for their failure to seek the opinions of leading black intellectuals and reformers, and he chastised the white participants for their self-
congratulatory attitudes and paternalistic sensibilities. "He [the black person]

is the poor patient, we are told, who is shut out of the council of the wise physicians for his own sake," Tourgée pronounced. "He is not even allowed to detail his own symptoms. Why should he? The physician has a theory: why should he trouble himself about facts? We do not promise justice, but are over-flowing with mercy."[20] William S. Scarborough offered a similar criticism and targeted the Mohonk Conference's exclusion of black Americans, which convinced him there was "a great deal of insincerity on the part of many so-called advocates of the race." "What makes the affair appear more absurd," he added, "is that the negro's views of the 'negro question' were given by a white man."[21] At the Montgomery Conference (as it was referred to) held by the Southern Society for the Promotion of the Study of Race Conditions and Problems in the South, black men and women were permitted to observe the discussion from the gallery only and were not given the chance to offer their own opinions and reflections on their lives. The only form of black participation observed was applause, stomping feet, and loud shouts when a white speaker mentioned something they approved of.[22] Eight years later at the Conference for Education in the South held in Memphis, Tennessee, black Americans were also relegated to the gallery and not invited to participate in the conversation.[23] Some professional associations, such as the American Historical Association, would occasionally invite guest speakers from a small select group of educated blacks to address their members on race-related topics, such as W. E. B. Du Bois. One of the few social reform organizations to invite black delegates to attend was the Southern Sociological Congress, although whites largely dominated the organization and maintained control over the intellectual agenda. Only a few professional associations included a handful of black members, such as the American Academy of Political and Social Science. Overall, black intellectuals were largely excluded from the wider intellectual debates on the question of race relations taking place in the white intellectual community.

The Peril of "Race Friction"

The exclusion of African Americans from so many white social scientific discussions on race lent credence to a growing belief that blacks and whites could not work together amicably without a resurgence of political and social tensions. During the late nineteenth and early twentieth centuries many Americans came to fear that general interaction between blacks and whites in the South had become a source of irrepressible social conflict. Some even proposed that southern race relations had reached an acute stage of irritation or a period of recrudescence. Scholars of the culture of reunion have argued that the process of sectional reconciliation between North and South not only reflected a belief in harmony between the races but also erased purposefully the presence of African Americans from the historical record.[24] Yet there exists a large body of social scientific literature from this period written by professionals and amateurs that emphasized the very lack of harmony between southern whites and blacks and the hazards this posed. Even Henry Grady, the New South ideologue usually associated with the culture of reunion and the New South creed, publicly acknowledged that the race question remained sectional in nature and jeopardized the national commitment to sectional reconciliation. In a lengthy speech delivered before the annual banquet of the Boston Merchants Association in 1889, Grady informed the audience that "the continuous estrangement of the North from the South could be tied to the inability of "two utterly dissimilar races on the same soil" to live in harmony.[25] Two years earlier at the Texas State Fair in Dallas, Grady had proclaimed "the problem of the South is to carry on within her body politic two separate races, equal in civic and political rights, and nearly equal in numbers." The region "must carry those races in peace, for discord means ruin," he added, and "must carry them separately, for assimilation means debasement."[26] Albert Bushnell Hart observed wisely, "'The South' in Grady's mouth really means the white South" because white men and women had no intention of permitting African Americans to participate in any discussions on the state of race relations in the South.[27]

Intellectual, popular, and social scientific interest in the adjustment between the so-called advanced and backward races generated a universal vocabulary that theorized about the dynamics of racial interactions in the South. Commentators on the matter invoked such terms as "race friction," "race antagonism," "race feeling," "race aversion," "race conflict," "race revulsion," and "racial antipathy" to explain the growing hostility between southern whites and blacks. Those embroiled in the debate over "What makes the color line?" as George Washington Cable asked in the *Chicago American* in 1889, tried to identify the source and nature of the lines of demarcation.[28] Was "a certain antagonism between the white and black races" a natural, inborn, instinctual emotion or an arbitrary "artificial" sentiment? Who drew the color line? Were the boundaries political, social, economic, or psychological? What effect did race mixing have on the distinctions between black and white? Was the color line a practical configuration that served the needs of southern blacks and whites or did it engender perpetual dissidence and bewilderment? And finally, as the Executive Committee at the Montgomery Conference queried, "Is race antipathy a curse, or a blessing to both races?"[29] Endless theorizing about the nature of the color line tested the fiction of racial harmony, raised questions about the systemic weaknesses in the social separation of the races, and reflected anxieties about the threats African Americans posed to the lines drawn by Jim Crow. "The blacks and Whites [sic] in the South are two members of a pair of shears, so clumsily put together that they gnash against each other continually," Albert Bushnell Hart concluded. "Though one side be silver and the other only bronze, neither can perform its function without the other, but there is a terrible strain upon the rivet which holds them together."[30]

The nature and history of "race friction" became a staple topic at the professional meetings of various academic disciplines and involved input from both trained and self-proclaimed social scientists. In 1907 the American Sociological Society invited Alfred Holt Stone, a plantation owner from the Mississippi Delta, to give a paper in Madison, Wisconsin, titled "Is Race Friction between Blacks and Whites in the United States Growing and Inevitable?" Stone had garnered a reputation as an internationally known race expert given his predilection to gather a vast array of primary and secondary material on the "race problem," his participation in the Montgomery conference in 1900, his practical experiments managing three hundred black tenant farmers on his Dunleith plantation, his presentations at such professional associations as the Mississippi Historical Society and the American Economic Association, and his research on race relations for the Carnegie Institution that included a visit to the West Indies.[31] The American Sociological Society allowed eight respondents to reply to Stone's precirculated paper, including John Spencer Bassett; W. E. B. Du Bois; and Walter F. Willcox, a statistician and political science professor at Cornell University who had collected demographic data in such places as Puerto Rico and South Africa. In his presentation in Madison, Stone defined friction between the races as a "'lack of harmony' or a 'mutual irritation'" and explained how this disharmony between the races could be attributed to something called "racial antipathy," an "abstract mental quality" that involved an "instinctive feeling of dislike, distaste or repugnance, for which sometimes no good reason can be given." He also blamed African Americans for the sustained racial conflict because of black men and women's insistence on being treated equally. Stone asserted that all "race problems and race prejudices" were rooted in inherent racial differences such as physical appearance, psychological makeup, and mental ability. On the surface Stone's statement read clearly as a blunt defense of white southern racism, but northern academics at the meeting found much they agreed with.[32] The Mississippi planter's sociological model of "race friction" was so elastic as to include "the thousand and one things keenly and clearly appreciable, yet sometimes elusive and indefinable," thus providing a wide-ranging framework for those involved in the national debate.[33] All of the participants, with the exception of John Spencer Bassett and W. E. B. Du Bois, believed that "race friction" was the inevitable product of emancipation and only the maintenance of segregation with northern acquiescence would enable the South to resolve the problem.

W. E. B. Du Bois was not able to secure funding to attend the meeting, nor did the conference participants read his paper aloud, but his remarks were later published in the *American Journal of Sociology* with the other statements of the mostly northern and midwestern attendees. Du Bois laid out his candid response with a series of questions in the first paragraph: "First, Is the old status of acknowledged superiority and inferiority between the white and black races in America longer possible? Secondly, Are the race differences in this case irreconcilable? And thirdly, Is racial separation practicable?" The answer to all three questions was a resounding no. Du Bois pointed out how the antebellum treatment of blacks as inferior was purely linked to coercion and that it was dangerous for those "who expect to keep up with modern civilization, to base their hope of peace and prosperity on the ignorance" of humankind. This is what "we expect and cultivate in dogs," he said, "but not in men." Du Bois explained how African Americans were laboring hard, becoming educated, and acquiring substantial property; with patience for change, there need not be "race friction." The root of the "race problem" in the pre–Civil War era was that whites viewed black intellectuals and abolitionists such as William Cooper Nell with a "tolerant contempt or amusement or irritation" and now, in the postemancipation world, the "attitude toward his [Nell's] descendants is that of consternation and perplexity and more or less veiled dislike." Du Bois advocated the social scientific study of race as a useful tool for solving the "race problem," but he was critical of what national white social scientists had achieved so far. He accused them of engaging in shallow scientific work on race, which had produced "a most ludicrous and harmful conglomeration of myth, falsehood, and desire." Finally, he concluded that the "unbiased" environmental model of Franz Boas was the proper model to follow and affirmed that the separation of the races in the southern states and in places such as the Philippines would never provide the right solution due to the importance of the expanding global economy.[34]

While commentators continued to disagree over the cause of the South's racial troubles, almost all those writing on the adjustment of the races agreed that the southern situation had deteriorated significantly in the years following Reconstruction. Much of the literature on the "race problem" echoed a sense of foreboding and apocalyptic fear. Some commentators described the problem as a latent irritation, festering beneath the surface and ready to erupt like a volcano at any second. In 1890 Andrew D. White, former president of Cornell University, explained how he arrived at the First Mohonk Conference on the Negro Question with "a heavy heart" because after traveling through the South he "constantly heard talk seeming to point toward a terrible future" in which white and black men struggled for control over the region. White explained how nineteenth-century Americans had fooled themselves into believing that human progress was an evolutionary process marked by "an unfolding of good into better." While he acknowledged the existence of a hypothetical peaceful process of evolution, he insisted that evolution was more often dominated by "catastrophe" and "cataclysm."[35] For many, the South stood at the crossroads of progress and racial conflict, unsure of which direction to move in as it approached the dawn of the twentieth century. Race riots in Wilmington, North Carolina, in 1898; in New Orleans, Louisiana, in 1900; and in Atlanta, Georgia, in 1906 only confirmed the country's feeling that "race friction" in the South had reached a boiling point. William P. Trent, a Virginian who taught at the University of the South and Columbia University, confided to his southern liberal friend Edwin Mims that "there is a danger at any time that race riots may grow into a race war" and "the spectre [sic] that rises before my mind is a race war begun and finished before education has really taken hold of the Southern masses."[36] Nationally, black boxer Jack Johnson's defeat of two heavyweight champions in 1908 and 1910 sparked race riots across the country. These events embodied literally the strife that many perceived to exist between blacks and whites in the first decade of the twentieth century.

The insistence that older relations of intimacy and familiarity in the ante-bellum South had given way to the racial friction of the postbellum era dominated much of the discussion on the "race problem." Paradoxically, the sense that race relations in the Jim Crow era had deviated from a previously amicable path (which conveniently ignored the social and political struggle during Reconstruction) resonated with the romantic plantation imagery and the myth of the happy slave at the turn of the century. Most historians have pointed to the national popularity of the plantation school of literature as evidence of the reunion between North and South, a reconciliation rooted in white supremacy and a willingness to put aside the issue of race.[37] Paul Gaston describes this process as one in which this group of writers indulged in "a national love feast for the Old South."[38] Yet these two sets of images could not exist without one another. Nostalgic feelings for faithful slaves and the idyllic race relations of the antebellum South were often juxtaposed with descriptions of rising racial hostility and antagonism in the Jim Crow era, which was attributed to persistent sectional tensions between North and South. In his book *The Negro: The Southerner's Problem* (1904), Thomas Nelson Page, one of the architects of the romantic plantation myth, lamented, "The old relation of intimacy and affection that survived to a considerable extent even the strain and stress of the reconstruction period, and the repressive measures that followed it, has passed away." Instead, he reported, "indifference and contempt" from the whites and "indifference or envy" from the blacks had taken its place.[39] The wistful longing for an imaginary past proved to be so powerful precisely because of the fear and apprehension about the future. Nostalgia for the loyal slaves of the antebellum South did not necessarily deflect attention away from the racial problems of the New South, nor did a focus on the pleasantries of the past exist within a rhetorical vacuum. An idyllic portrait of the Old South existed in opposition to the presumed racial animosity of the present and the future and underscored the paradox of the New South with its competing claims of harmony and trouble.

In the eyes of many southern whites, the problem could be linked to a new generation of African Americans who were allegedly more insolent and rebellious than their forbears. These whites drew attention to the dichotomy between what commentators labeled the "new Negro" and the "old Negro." Anxiety about the "new Negro" often accompanied sentimental reminiscences of the "old Negro" from plantation days.[40] Ray Stannard Baker explained in a piece titled "Following the Color Line" that white southerners simply longed for and mourned the disappearance of "the faithful, simple, ignorant, obedient, cheerful, old plantation Negro." In short, he announced, "They want the New South, but the old Negro." The problem was that the "new Negro" didn't jest and laugh as much because being free was "grim business."[41] Even white southern liberals mourned the loss of this allegedly picturesque older generation of African Americans because the mythology of the Old South held such a tenacious grip on the minds of all white southerners. John Spencer Bassett partly blamed the influence of northern culture for the "loss of picturesqueness," the "rich old darkey dialect," and "the plantation songs . . . passing into coon songs." He noted that "even so strong a race trait as the curliness of the negro's hair" had been threatened by the onslaught of northern advertisements for hair straightening products and cried, "Is there nothing of the genuine old negro which you good people will leave us?"[42]

Similarly, black leaders and intellectuals such as W. E. B. Du Bois and Kelly Miller reminisced about a time when the social relations between the races were more pleasant and agreeable, although they did not necessarily lay blame for ongoing racial tensions at the feet of African Americans nor did they recycle pernicious caricatures (fig. 9). Like many of their white counterparts, they agreed that blacks and whites had drifted further apart in the social realm in the postbellum period, resisting a new set of racial relations that had replaced a collection of familiar racial associations. Miller explained how the interaction between the races had become more businesslike and formal now that slavery was no longer in place to maintain equilibrium in the social system.[43] Du Bois bemoaned the fact that the rigid drawing and enforcement of the color line had caused this older affection to disappear and that "nothing has come to replace that finer sympathy and love between some masters and house servants." Ironically, Du Bois noted, despite "much physical contact and daily intermingling" in the New South there was "almost no community of intellectual life or points of transferrence [sic] where the thoughts and feelings of one race can come with direct contact and sympathy with the thoughts and feelings of the other." Du Bois and Miller were hardly proslavery advocates and they did not advocate further segregation as a solution to the problem; they simply presumed that the "adjustment of the races" had been rendered more problematic now that the intimacies of slavery had vanished. The two black sociologists advocated cultivating better relations between whites and blacks,

FIGURE 9. Kelly Miller, 1863–1939. Moorland-Spingarn Research Center, Howard University.

which they believed could dissolve the racial conflict of the present. Even two years before Du Bois published *The Souls of Black Folk* (1903), a seminal work that took the white race to task for its unrelenting oppression of blacks, he urged the country to adopt a "scheme of friendliness and philanthropy" that might lead to a "generous fellowship" between the races.[44]

In general, almost all liberal white and black intellectuals blamed "race friction" not on a new generation of assertive African Americans but rather on an intransigent population of white southerners. These theorists insisted that any antagonism between the races was not of necessity a reciprocal feeling because "race friction" only flowed in one direction. In his article titled "Stirring Up the Fires of Race Antipathy," John Spencer Bassett avowed that racial hostility was not a mutual sentiment but involved solely the white man's contempt for the black man. He explained how African Americans were open to equality and harbored no reservations about worshiping, eating meals, and attending the theater in interracial settings.[45] Other observers more openly critical of the South scoffed at white southerners' irrational fear of black domination and averred that an underlying incessant apprehension constituted the root of the problem. "It is only where a people are moved by the fear of 'Negro supremacy,'" George Washington Cable maintained, "that the simple *belief* in a divinely ordered race antagonism is used to justify the withholding of impersonal public rights which belong to every man because he is a man, and with which race and its real or imagined antagonisms have nothing whatever to do."[46] These outspoken critics suggested that "race friction" was the result of the white race demanding its superiority and simultaneously expecting the black race to accept its inferiority. In pointing out white demand for black subordination, as well as southern whites' concrete efforts to ensure their own supremacy through such things as disfranchisement and segregation, liberal intellectuals like Bassett and Cable implied that "race antipathy" was not innate or natural. Historical conditions shaped the sense of growing "race friction" between the races and thus racial tensions could not be blamed on some biologically programmed racial antagonism immune to progressive solutions.

By offering an environmental interpretation of the racial hostilities in the New South, this group of critical reformers and intellectuals contested the dominant nineteenth-century model of scientific racism. George Fredrickson has called this perspective a "moderate liberalism" or "accommodationist racism." These new white liberals celebrated the ideals of southern paternalism but looked forward to an era of social cooperation and human progress.[47] Unlike those struggling to solve the question of race during Reconstruction, white liberals did not offer political or military solutions but instead turned to social scientific practices and philanthropy to reshape the southern environment and facilitate the adjustment of the races. Mia Bay explains how "liberal environmentalism" was a far less revolutionary ideology in the black intellectual community since black thinkers were long accustomed to considering the influence of culture and environment on racial differences. Yet, unlike in the white intellectual community, no broadly received paradigm developed in black racial thought because intellectuals such as W. E. B. Du Bois and Kelly Miller continually grappled with the idea of racialism in the context of black nationalist movements that accepted the idea of an essential racial identity. Paradoxically, black intellectuals moved back and forth between advocating racial essentialism and relying on the framework of environmentalism in explaining racial problems in the South.[48] The concepts of sociocultural evolutionism and social Darwinism that were fashionable among some white intellectuals and used to support ideas of racial hierarchy and superiority also appealed to some black intellectuals who reworked it into a social theory about black uplift.

Thus debates over whether "race friction" was innate or artificial reflected intellectual efforts to come to terms with the conflict between scientific racism and the environmental perspective first advanced by anthropologists such as Franz Boas. Some social scientists and reformers pointed out the inconsistencies in the arguments made by those who advocated segregation as a solution to "race antagonism" or who took the pessimistic view that the races could never live side-by-side in peace. Many questioned the logic of inherent "race antipathy," particularly in the intimate spaces and domains of daily life. In short, tension between the races boiled down to a white fear of social equality and a desire to preserve the color line in furtherance of protecting the purity of the white race. In a classic exposition on the ironies of segregation, George Washington Cable called attention to the fact that if the black race allegedly and naturally repulsed the white race then why did white southerners entrust their children to black nursemaids?[49] The problem, he concluded, had less to do with a mutual "race aversion" and more to do with the specter of "social equality." In his book *Race Adjustment* (1908), Kelly Miller explained how the "gentlemen" driving to the railroad station and sitting "cheek to jowl" with a black coachman could not bear to be made a "joint occupant" with a black passenger on the train. But this had absolutely nothing to do with an innate physical repulsion. The concept of "race friction" was merely a mask for deeper prejudices rooted in the desire to maintain white supremacy and a fear of the black man's desire to be equal with the white man.[50] White southerners permitted contact in certain intimate spaces as long as the relations of power were not disrupted and the color line remained intact.

The "Mulatto Problem" Undermines the Color Line

The belief that one could reduce the "race problem" to a simple explanation such as the existence of an innate racial antipathy was emblematic of a deep faith in the practice of social science, but it often raised more questions than answers. For white conservatives the concept of "race friction" reflected the desire to justify white dominance and draw a permanent color line in the New

South. White liberal commentators viewed the existence of racial conflict as a call to champion reform but their calls for change were always situated within the context of segregation. Even the most liberal participants in the dialogue on the "race problem" could never fully abandon a belief in inherent racial differences rooted in a taxonomic worldview. This logic lent a natural authority to Jim Crow and disfranchisement since reciprocal race repulsion implied not only that the two races would choose to live apart but also that segregation provided the only sensible solution for a society handicapped by "race friction." Yet the logic threatened to unravel in the face of one particular southern problem: interracial sex. If the black and white races naturally eschewed contact due to some inherent mutual feeling of repugnance, then how did one explain the pervasiveness of interracial sex or the existence of a mixed-race population that clearly furnished evidence of sex across the color line?

Turning the logic of inherent racial antipathy on its head, Kelly Miller declared that whether real or imagined, the color line could only be maintained by artificial stimulation such as legislative action because it would always "break down in the face of [the] cosmic urge to multiply and replenish the earth."[51] In short, the human body's biological sex urge had the power to obliterate a color line artificially inscribed in southern law and custom. Miller observed sardonically that if there truly was such a thing as natural race antipathy, the black man already would have been "rent asunder" from within due to the animosity of the cohabitating black and white parts inside of himself.[52] Overall, many social scientists agreed with Miller that two races living side-by-side in the same geographical and spatial areas would invariably turn to "amalgamation" or "race blending" and that in reality no artificial boundaries could keep them apart.

The subtext of "miscegenation," while not always explicit, consistently underlay the "race problem" theme. University of Virginia Professor H. E. Jordan stated it bluntly when he warned, "The United States has something more than a 'negro problem'; it has a 'mulatto problem.'"[53] The popular and academic focus on the contact of the races invariably drew attention to the racialized physical body and its biological and sexual function. The effort to classify, catalog, and map the black body in the social scientific world refocused interest on sexual conduct as part of the larger social behavior of the biological organism while simultaneously locating this body in a particular social environment or geography.[54] Many feared that the placid, daily, intimate, and physical (meaning nonsexual) contact between the races during slavery had given way to a new kind of subversive intimacy unencumbered by the legal and social proscriptions of Jim Crow. This modern sexual intimacy was not the same as the intimacy claimed to have existed during slavery. The nostalgic longing for the warm, intimate affection between master and slave went hand in hand with anxiety about the races moving further apart in the postbellum period. Yet, in a curious irony, wistful commentators found themselves arguing that now too much intimacy, or the wrong kind of intimacy, existed in the New South. Others, particularly those in the social scientific world, did not necessarily argue for the subversive nature of this contact but tried to draw attention to the inevitability of race mixing and to theorize more abstractly about its repercussions. And yet another group preferred not to, or could not, acknowledge what Andrew Sledd called "an idea so coarse and repugnant to every finer feeling" that it could have only originated "in the brain of the wild theorist, ignorant of conditions, and hurried by his Negrophile propensities."[55] White southerners horror-stricken by the prospect of sex across the color line responded quite vehemently to other writers who insisted that "miscegenation" was ubiquitous. The very fact that some self-professed experts on the "race problem" felt the need to deny the existence of interracial sex demonstrates how much the subject had permeated popular and social scientific literature on the question of race.[56]

The preoccupation with the "mulatto problem" in the post-Reconstruction South manifested itself in many contexts. In the late nineteenth and early twentieth centuries a proliferation of statutes outlawing marriage and sexual relations between the races sprang up across the southern landscape. Laws passed to regulate sexual boundaries increasingly provided guidelines on how to determine an individual's race since white southerners had to classify the black person who could not marry a white person. Many states legally defined a person as black if they had at least one-eighth "black blood." Others resorted to the "one-drop" rule (or what sociologists called the rule of "hypodescent"), which determined that any person with black heritage was an African American. Although over time the one-drop rule often took precedence, for many decades the effort to impose fractional definitions was a fluid and unpredictable process.[57] The specter of "amalgamation" haunting the region also precipitated a wave of apprehension about the mythic "black beast" rapist and the threat he posed to southern white womanhood. These stories became a staple of the southern demagogue's political lore and alarmed the majority of southern white men and women in the Jim Crow South.[58] However, the fear of voluntary race mixing caused just as much consternation as the mythology of the oversexed black rapist. The problem of interracial sex engendered a whole other set of fears about "invisible blackness" as one might be legally black but visually appear white. Many writing on the subject speculated about the extent of this passing and struggled to define the nature of blackness and whiteness.[59] Did being white simply mean having a phenotypical white skin color, or was it an attitude and set of cultural behaviors? Who or what determined someone's race?

The shift between the fluidity and fixity of racial identities underscored the mobility of mixedness as a category. Social scientists and reformers who attempted to study and document the problem of "miscegenation" ironically wound up acknowledging the idiocy of the one-drop rule (that one was either black or white and not something else) since they began with the premise that evidence of racial mixture could be found throughout the South. On one level, theorizing about the problem of "miscegenation" was an inadvertent rebuttal to the one-drop rule. In 1908 Ray Stannard Baker captured the complexity of the situation in the opening statement of his article "The Tragedy of the Mulatto" when he wrote, "I had not been long engaged in the study of the race problem when I found myself face to face with a curious and seemingly absurd question: 'What is a Negro?'" Baker illustrated the incredible diversity of physical characteristics among the southern men and women recognized as black and noted that even white southerners could not always visually identify a "black" person.[60] Reverend C. J. Ryder from the American Missionary Association also illuminated the preposterousness of trying to draw rigid boundaries when he rhetorically asked the supporters of colonization at the Second Mohonk Conference on the Negro Question, "If you send them to Africa, where would you draw the line? Shall the white black girl go and the black white girl stay?"[61]

In 1931 George Schuyler published a novel titled *Black No More*, which explored the ludicrousness of categorizing race in a racially conscious world marked by interracial sex. The main protagonist Junius Crookman invents a secret formula that has the power to turn any black American white. In large numbers, African Americans begin to visit established "Black No More" clinics and as a result the nation's "race problem" virtually disappears. Over the course of the narrative, however, Schuyler demonstrates how the "race problem" has merely been replaced with a "mulatto problem" because the resulting color change does not pass to one's offspring. Unsuspecting white women who marry or consort with "white men" (who were formerly black men) suddenly find themselves giving birth to mixed-race children. In search of the answer to this perplexing phenomenon, white Democrats in the story turn to meticulous genealogical research only to uncover evidence of black relatives in their own family lineage, thereby exposing another "mulatto problem" that is even greater than the one they initially feared. Ultimately, when Dr. Crookman reports that the new "Caucasians" are several shades lighter than the old "Caucasians," white Americans begin to look for ways to darken their skin, such as tanning, in an effort to prove they are authentically white and not intrinsically black. Schuyler's clever satire illustrates how the southern effort to retain the color line in the face of so much confusion over who was truly white and who was truly black could reach the absolute height of absurdity.[62]

While social scientists and satirical writers grappled with the problem of "miscegenation," average citizens unaffiliated with the academic or scientific communities felt compelled to speak publicly on the topic too. In the early twentieth century, the sexual peccadilloes of elite and middle-class white men came under special scrutiny in local communities. Albert Bushnell Hart cautioned that an investigation of interracial sex in the South was "especially delicate and hazardous" and there was "no easy or pleasant way of alluding to it," but that did not prevent some white southerners from broaching the subject.[63] The power of sex to potentially dissolve racial distinctions and physical boundaries caused tremendous consternation among many local citizens. In 1907 J. H. Currie, the district attorney in Meridian, Mississippi, addressing the jury in a case on interracial sex, maintained, "The accursed shadow of miscegenation hangs over the South to-day like a pall of hell. . . . We have tolerated this crime long enough, and if this country is to be run by policy and not by law then it is time to rise up and denounce the sin of the earth."[64] One white woman in the Mississippi Delta wrote to the editor of a Louisiana paper to report that in her town interracial sex was quite common and that any white man who had "isolated himself from feminine society" was suspected of keeping a black mistress. Calling her sisters to arms, she declared that "if some daring woman, not afraid of being dubbed a Carrie Nation, were to canvass the delta counties of Mississippi, taking the census, she would find so many cases of miscegenation and their resultant mongrel families, that she would bow her head in shame for the flower of Southern chivalry gone to seed."[65] In Vicksburg, Mississippi, whites organized an "Anti-Miscegenation League" to thwart the growing sexual relationships between white men and black women, collect evidence of men suspected of engaging in interracial sex, and publicly announce their names, addresses, and alleged social habits.[66] Likewise, in Francisville, Louisiana, local white men and women held meetings to organize against what they deemed "the yellow peril" and established a vigilance committee to draw public attention to the coupling of white men and black women.[67] The editor of the Louisiana *Times Democrat* went so far as to advocate using mobs to break up couples engaging in interracial sex, since in his view white men who condemned interracial sex but still practiced it were more dangerous to the white race than outspoken black leaders.[68]

While some southern whites were willing to blame white men for the crime of interracial sex, the black intellectual community did not find this a surprising allegation since it had always been willing to address the sexual transgressions of white men. Ida B. Wells is best known for her public condemnation of the myth that black men harbored an insatiable urge to rape white women and her assertion that it was white men who raped black women in far greater numbers.[69] Like Wells, T. Thomas Fortune, a leading black journalist and the editor of the *New York Age*, debunked the myth that black men were responsible for "the extensive hybridization of the race" and pointed the finger at white men whose wealth and social position enabled them to seduce and corrupt chaste black women. He denounced these white men for not showing "the same manly honor and Christian self-denial" found in black men and condemned white men's tendency to "whine like babies over their supposed misfortune" when they really only deserved contempt.[70] George Allen Mebane, a black man writing in the *Arena*, criticized the double standard that permitted "white men of high social standing" to live with and financially support "negro families" but cast aspersions on the character and reputation of black women. As he explained, it was the black women and their "fatherless half-white children" that had "to bear all the odium."[71]

In blaming white men for the "mulatto problem," critics and commentators could not help but draw attention to the hypocrisy of white southern culture and its obsession with the purity of the white race. Indeed, as Albert Bushnell Hart pointed out, interracial sex was "the most glaring contradiction of the supposed infallible principles of race separation and social inequality."[72]

Evidence of interracial sex completely invalidated the social scientific theory of a natural, intrinsic "race antipathy" and suggested that antagonism between the races might be purely the product of structural and environmental circumstances. Those who blamed the "mulatto problem" on the sexually unrestrained behavior of white men had to either acknowledge the hypocritical implications of white men's deeds or turn a blind eye to their actions. If white men truly harbored an innate aversion or antipathy to black physical bodies and contact then how could they justify their interracial sexual encounters? Kelly Miller lambasted southern racists who refused to acknowledge "the bleaching breath of Saxon civilization" and the inconsistencies between "the attitude and action" of the "loud-mouthed advocates of race purity." He scathingly advised white southerners, including Thomas Dixon Jr., to put aside their philanthropic efforts to uplift the black race and engage in their own "missionary work" among the men of the white race.[73]

In the late nineteenth and early twentieth centuries, southern apprehension about the dangers to white racial purity concealed even deeper fears about the phenomenon of passing. What if mixed-race people could no longer be identified as black and subsequently crossed over the color line? No one was quite sure how many mixed-race people had passed for white in the South. "Legislatures have repeatedly attempted to define where black leaves off and white begins," Ray Stannard Baker explained, yet even those southern people who prided themselves on being able "to distinguish a drop of dark blood in the white face" were frequently deceived.[74] Frances Hoggan, a British doctor who campaigned against lynching in the South, warned that blacks who passed as white could mislead "even judges and experienced persons."[75] In 1911, in a short piece titled "When Is a Caucasian Not a Caucasian," the northern magazine the *Independent* informed its readers that the "conundrum" was no laughing matter and happened to be a very serious issue in the state of Louisiana.[76] One year later James Weldon Johnson anonymously published *Autobiography of an Ex-Colored Man* (1912), which made it quite clear how easy it was for a light-skinned black man to pass as white while traveling through the South. In 1925 *Century Magazine* published an anonymous autobiographical account of an educated black man from Harlem who passed as white during his travels in the South and explained how southern whites would be shocked to learn of the number of black men who had traversed the color line. Even more ominous, these men had secretly gathered much "information about what white people are doing and thinking."[77] Many observers, documenting the rising trend of passing in the South, offered stories of African American communities duplicitously working to protect their friends and family members from being detected by southern white communities.[78] Thus the "mulatto problem" proved more dangerous and resistant to change than the "race problem" since it often made identification of the very problem itself exceedingly difficult.

The identification of a "mulatto problem" not only reflected a concern about the erasure of those visual cues associated with the color line but also revealed consternation about certain behavioral changes on the part of the so-called "new Negro." Whiteness did not merely entail the bleaching of one's skin. Both skin color and behavior dictated what made a person white and what made a person black in the South. Many white social scientists and popular writers theorized about the development of the mixed-race person's peculiar characteristics engendered by the infusion of "white blood." They argued that mixed-race people were more intelligent and gifted than "pure" blacks.[79] The more reactionary thinkers warned that the "mulatto's" intelligence only led to discontent and restlessness thereby pushing the mixed-race person into the role of an agitator working to induce rebellion in the black masses against white supremacy. Alfred H. Stone warned that the "mulatto" wielded tremendous influence over the average African American "through the medium of race papers, and magazines, the pulpit, industrial and political gatherings and associations," and he maintained that the "the negro's mind is being constantly poisoned with the radical teachings and destructive doctrines of the mulatto."[80] These reactionary critics often pointed to W. E. B. Du Bois as the prototypical example of this specific danger.[81] Much of the literature on the "mulatto" insisted that mixed-race peoples harbored an insatiable urge to behave and be recognized as white although social scientists interested in the subject did not always agree on the reason for this particular yearning. One group argued for a biological racial determinism and attributed the mixed-race people's unrelenting desire to pass as a member of the "advanced race" to the genetic mixture of "white blood." The other group maintained that it was no surprise mixed-race people demanded the social and civil rights extended to the white race because being recognized as white afforded certain tangible advantages. As Ray Stannard Baker noted astutely, "The ideal is whiteness: for whiteness stands for opportunity, power, and progress."[82]

Inevitably the belief that mixed-race southerners would always demand that they be recognized as white raised the question of political and social equality. In fact, the term "social equality" frequently functioned as a euphemism for interracial sex and marriage and it was invoked by white southerners often to the point of excess. Professor William Smith of Tulane University spoke for many southerners when he argued that if whites entertained blacks as social guests and let them eat at white tables, black men and women soon would be seeking to marry white men and women. "Remove the barrier between two streams flowing side by side," he alleged, and "immediately they begin to mingle their molecules."[83] All aspects of the "race problem" — whether political, social, religious, educational, or class or labor related — were subject to the demon of social and sexuality equality. This racial domino theory stressed how the chain reaction of "social equality" could be set in motion by just one simple Anglo-Saxon action of tolerance in any domain.

Finally, although popular and academic writers on "miscegenation" framed the "mulatto problem" in regionally specific terms, they made clear the troublesome national implications of the problem. Commentators from all sides of the political spectrum offered their opinions of the effect of interracial sex on the nation and insisted that it was not just a southern problem but a situation of grave national concern. Scientific and public debates about the purported increase in mixed-race peoples and their propensity to subvert white supremacy through agitation and resistance threatened the nation-state's racial taxonomies and the illusion of the imperviousness of a white national identity. In 1926 Ernest Sevier Cox, a leading white supremacist who advocated colonization as a solution to the "race problem," published a tract titled *The South's Part in Mongrelizing the Nation,* which expressed this lingering horror about the region's primary role in undermining the white nation-state. Clearly fears about "amalgamation" informed Cox's nationalist agenda and led him to argue that rampant interracial sex in the region threatened the overall well-being of the national body politic.[84] But his analogy between the "mulatto" body and the political body of the mongrelized South resonated with a public that had come to view the South as a diseased space given the public health work undertaken by the Rockefeller organizations and federal experts' commitment to "clean farming." Both the southern physical body and the political body threatened to pollute the white race and the white nation. Apprehension about "mongrelization" in one part of the country engendered concern about the sanctity of white identity in the entire country. Even George Washington Cable, who was criticized by white southerners for his exceedingly liberal views on race, made it absolutely clear that he found private social equality "monstrous." Like Cox he also used the sexualized rhetoric of national identity and maintained that national unity or reconciliation between the North and South did not require "mongrelization" because "nationalization by fusion of bloods" was a mark of "barbarous times."[85] In an effort to avoid advocating a hybrid national unity, Cable made distinctions between the impersonal civil rights of the public arena, which declared all individuals deserving of the full protection of the law, and the private social associations rooted in personal, individual decisions. He believed that in most cases, if given the opportunity, blacks and whites would not choose to pursue social equality.[86]

The ability of sex to potentially dissolve the color line ensured that the subject of "miscegenation" would always haunt national discussions of the "race problem." Because sex constituted one form of contact between the races, the social scientific study of "race contact" and "race adjustment" in the late nineteenth and early twentieth centuries invariably drew attention to the repercussions of interracial sex. Modern social scientific interest in the "race problem," with its tendency to categorize and classify the black body, meant that the question of sexuality could not be divorced from race. The physical separation of the races and the "one-drop" rule, which deemed anyone with the slightest trace of African heritage black, did not entirely alleviate southern fears about the purity of the white race as social scientists and others continued to struggle to understand the nuances of "race contact" and the possible consequences. Interracial sex tended to be such an explosive topic exactly because it undermined the assumption of white supremacy that underlay the system of Jim Crow. The notion of a natural "race antipathy" or "race friction" seemed illogical in the face of sex across the color line.

Global "Race Adjustment"

The belief in an inexorable conflict between the races and persistent evidence of interracial sexual contact not only underscored the unsteady foundation of whiteness in the U.S. South but also mirrored the problems vexing the architects of empire around the globe. The traditional narrative of sectional reconciliation offered by historians of the United States suggests that racism functioned as a unifying force that cut across sectional lines and obliterated philanthropic or political interest in African Americans. In their account, imperialism, best embodied in the Spanish-American War and the subsequent colonization of the Philippines, solidified the reunion between North and South and put the race question at home to rest. Yet the American acquisition of the colonial possessions overseas generated fresh debates about how and if people of color could be incorporated into the American body politic. The pursuit of civilizing missions in these new foreign lands led to the creation of social and racial taxonomies articulating who should be included and who should be excluded from the colonial state, thereby throwing attitudes and ideologies into flux. This in turn refocused attention on the relationship between black Americans and the domestic American body politic and encouraged social scientists and self-proclaimed experts writing on the "race problem" to identify the southern problem as simply one component of a global problem in the context of western imperialism.

As the American and European engagement with imperialism provided a context in which to discuss racial tensions in the U.S. South, both black and white intellectuals in the United States began to draw attention to the similarities between regional and global race questions. Indeed, W. E. B. Du Bois recognized the importance of this transnational framework in many of his speeches and writings. In a 1900 address at the Pan-African Congress in London, and later in 1903 in his book *The Souls of Black Folk*, Du Bois asserted, "The problem of the twentieth century is the problem of the color line." For more than a century, this legendary remark has been cited and referenced innumerable times, but those who quote Du Bois's celebrated statement often truncate it, failing to acknowledge the larger global implications. The full quotation reads, "The problem of the twentieth century is the problem of the color line — the relation of the darker to the lighter races in Asia and Africa, in America and the islands of the sea."[87] Three years later Du Bois published an article in *Collier's Weekly* titled "The Color Line Belts the World" where he made a similar declaration and wrote, "The Negro problem in America is but a local phase of a world problem."[88] Du Bois's observations that the question of race was transnational should come as no surprise. At the turn of the century, it was not unusual for black historians to address the international dimensions of African American history and place the history of American race relations in a global context.[89]

204 • CHAPTER FIVE

This was a moment in which the white intellectual community sought to situate American history in a transnational setting too. Several years after Du Bois's piece in *Collier's Weekly*, Ulysses G. Weatherly, a professor from Indiana University, borrowed the same discourse in his essay "A World-Wide Color Line" and outlined the various kinds of "race contacts" developing in an era in which "world interests ha[d] begun to override national and continental interests." He stated that Americans had a tendency to believe the "color problem" was peculiar to the United States when in reality "the race struggle covers the whole world, wherever whites and blacks are brought together under common political and social forms."[90] In the early years of the professionalization of history, a project that coincided with the creation of the modern nation-state and the objective pursuit of scientific knowledge, the influence of transnational perspectives and shared global discourses was significant. As Ian Tyrrell has shown, a new breed of historians began to focus on the "interplay between ideas of nation and ideas of empire." This momentary interest in transnational and comparative approaches evolved out of the need to articulate the boundaries of the American nation-state and to construct a new "genealogy" that involved identifying and theorizing about the destiny and evolution of nations and their citizens. Professional historians sought to explain the history of America in relationship to what came before in Europe.[91]

In fact, Du Bois and other intellectuals' assertions that the "race problem" was a worldwide problem can be traced as far back as the Civil War. As early as the mid-nineteenth century, white leaders and intellectuals around the globe began to theorize about interracial contact, especially as it pertained to the development of democracy. British liberals such as James Bryce, Goldwyn Smith, and Charles Pearson from Oxford and Cambridge visited the United States during and after the Civil War to study American political issues including the "Negro question." They conferred with Americans such as Charles Elliot Norton, a social critic; Wendell Phillips, a Boston abolitionist with ties to William Lloyd Garrison; and Herbert Baxter Adams, a professor of history at Johns Hopkins with a doctorate from a German university and secretary of the American Historical Association. The development of what Marilyn Lake and Henry Reynolds call a transnational "racial regime" involving England and the United States animated questions about empire, the nature of citizenship, and national sovereignty. These transnational intellectuals viewed Reconstruction in the United States as a catastrophic failure and asked themselves, "How could the two races coexist in a democratic republic?"[92] At the heart of that question was the paradox that theorists such as Bryce faced; how did one reconcile faith in the creed that "all men are created equal" with the belief in the inferiority of nonwhite races? Bryce believed the "Negro problem" was the gravest problem American democracy faced and wrote it was "most likely to stand a source of anxiety, perhaps of danger, for generations to come."[93] In the late nineteenth and early twentieth centuries these transnational observers considered multiracial democracy an intractable and potentially unsolvable dilemma. Bryce is best known for his magnum opus *The American Commonwealth* (1888), a study of the American polity that he revised many times to address evolving historical conditions. In this work, he identified a fundamental "social problem raised by the coexistence on the same soil, under the same free government, of two races so widely different that they do not intermingle."[94] In another work, *The Relations of the Advanced and Backward Races of Mankind* (1902), Bryce described this contact between "the advanced and backward races" as "a crisis in the history of the world, which will profoundly affect the destiny of mankind."[95] Bryce developed close friendships with Theodore Roosevelt and Edwin L. Godkin, the editor of the *Nation* who wrote two early articles on the "southern problem" in 1880. Others theorizing about race in such places as the southern states, the Caribbean, South America, Latin America, and South Africa cited Bryce consistently as a specialist on global racial issues.

James Bryce and other self-proclaimed race experts interested in transnational questions of race viewed the contact between the white and nonwhite races not only as a new problem evident in the existence of four million emancipated slaves in the southern states but also as one engendered by the inevitable spread of empire. They portrayed the expansion of white civilization as an inexorable force relentlessly creeping into the far corners of the globe, bringing with it the possibility of what Bryce and others labeled as "race antagonism." Studies such as Bryce's *The Relations of the Advanced and Backward Races of Mankind* and Basil Mathews's *The Clash of Colour: A Study in the Problem of Race* (1925) sought to explain the political, social, and economic dilemmas engendered by the association of two races in the same locale or nation. Benjamin Franklin Riley, author of *The White Man's Burden* (1910) and a Baptist minister from Alabama, argued that while conditions in South Africa, the Philippines, and the United States varied materially, "one cardinal principle alike" guided the British and American efforts to deal with racial issues, particularly those arising out of imperialism. The question was how to find the "means of which the recalcitrant elements" could "be brought into friendly and easy relations with the powers that be." Riley saw no inconsistencies in labeling the southern black population the United States' domestic version of the "white man's burden."[96] Yet he did not foresee any viable solution but disfranchisement and the complete separation of the races. Many decades later in his crowning achievement *Black Reconstruction in America* (1935) W. E. B. Du Bois denounced white men such as Riley as imperialists who had used African Americans as cheap labor and as creators of a southern "oligarchy similar to the colonial imperialism of today."[97]

In the first two decades of the twentieth century social scientists and reformers interested in resolving the "race problem" organized conferences and contemplated other means of sharing knowledge in a transnational setting. In 1901 the American Academy of Political and Social Science held a symposium at their annual meeting in Philadelphia where ten experts on the subject, ranging from W. E. B. Du Bois to Colonel Hilary A. Herbert, ex-secretary of the Navy and a native of Alabama, read papers on race relations in the Philippines, Hawaii, Cuba, Puerto Rico, and the U.S. South.[98] Although at this conference they did not always explicitly make comparisons between the southern states and the overseas colonies in their individual papers, it is significant that the academy paired the lectures on southern race relations with the lectures on the colonial possessions. The conference participants could just have easily juxtaposed a discussion on the U.S. South or in the overseas colonies with a discussion on the problem posed by the influx of immigrant populations in the North, given that nativists initially viewed southeastern European immigrants as separate and inferior races too.[99] During his presentation, Herbert praised the academy for its interest in resolving a variety of race problems since American imperialism had recently stimulated the need to consider them in a broader context. The United States found itself "dealing now not only with its Negroes in the South, but with the Cuban and Porto Rican [sic] and Philippine populations." He celebrated the power of scientific inquiry to resolve the "Negro question," a question that had intensified and expanded more widely than the sectional one embodied in the troubles of the Civil War and Emancipation.[100] Likewise, Herbert's fellow Alabama native Edgar Gardner Murphy agreed with the analogy made between the experience of southern blacks and the status of people of color overseas. Murphy had grand

visions of inaugurating a publication that would inspire intellectuals and reformers interested in the broad "problem of racial adjustment." In a confidential memorandum sent to Walter Hines Page, he pleaded with his liberal friend
to assist him with the production of a monthly "readable magazine" titled *Race
Problem — A Journal of Information and Discussion*. The purpose of the journal
would be to disseminate information on the "phases of a great world problem with which Christian civilization has been called to deal, particularly the
problem of southern blacks, Native Americans, Filipinos, Puerto Ricans, and
Cubans." "I feel that the opening of pages of such a journal to the discussion
of the race problems of 'greater America,'" Murphy explained, "will give us
distinct aid in the discussion of the especial race problem of 'little America.'"[101]

The concept of a "little America" or hemispheric global South expanded
more universally a decade later when delegates representing fifty countries met
in London to attend the first Universal Races Congress. Ulysses G. Weatherly
revealed that several concerns made this conference a necessity including "a
striking development of race consciousness accompanied by a quickening of
sensitiveness" that imperiled "inter-racial unity" and the existence of "practical
questions growing out of extended conquests and colonization of European
peoples in the lands inhabited by backward peoples of dark skin in all the
outlying parts of the earth."[102] However, the objective of the conference was
to apply the modern scientific model to an investigation of the relationship
between the "so-called white and so-called coloured [sic] races with a view
to encouraging between them a fuller understanding, the most friendly feelings, and a heartier co-operation."[103] The delegates adopted an environmental rather than a biological approach to the question of race, attempting to
move beyond the sociological notion of inherent "race friction" and "race
antipathy." The conference planning and promotion involved members of the
London Ethical Culture Society, including its founder Felix Adler, a lecturer
named Gustav Spiller, and John E. Milholland, a New York City philanthropist
and businessman with ties to W. E. B. Du Bois. The British hosts avoided the
topic of imperialism and advocated racial equality in the spirit of the Social
Gospel.[104]

One year after the first Universal Races Congress gathered, Booker T.
Washington hosted the Tuskegee International Conference on the Negro,
partly in response to his lack of participation in the Universal Races Congress.
The gathering drew in 120 delegates representing eighteen countries, including

members of missionary societies based in the North who worked with Africans and African Americans. The *Tuskegee Student* reported in its press release that "the purpose of this conference will be to bring together not only students of colonial and racial questions, but more particularly those who, either as missionaries, teachers or government officials, are actually engaged in any way in practical and constructive work, which seeks to build up Africa by educating and improving the character and condition of the native peoples."[105] Washington's intention, in fact, was even more broadly conceived; his objective was to provide a forum "for a general interchange of ideas" about education and uplift not just for peoples in Africa but also for those of African descent in the countries and colonies of Europe, the Caribbean, South America, and South Africa. He implored his participants to ask how the models of Hampton Institute and Tuskegee Institute might directly apply to colonial settings overseas.[106] The conference attendees spent three days focusing on one topic each day — "Conditions," "Missions," and "Methods."[107]

Washington not only attracted observers to the southern states but also sent personnel outward to Africa, forging a broader global South linking ideas about race, labor, and the political economy. After Washington gave his famous exposition address, German imperialists turned their eyes to the southern states in search of ideas about growing cotton in colonial locales. In the first decade of the twentieth century Washington initiated the Tuskegee cotton expedition to Togo, which involved African Americans teaching New South practices of discipline and industrial training to Germans on an experimental cotton farm.[108] By the time of the Tuskegee International Conference the majority of reformers and social scientists had already embraced the belief that the model of race relations in the U.S. South had much to offer the colonial world. Even African American clubwomen in this period, such as Halie Quinn Brown and Mary Church Terrell, adopted a transnational focus, traveling to the 1899 and 1904 meetings of the International Conference on Women where they spoke about the experiences of southern blacks in the face of Jim Crow. Margaret Murray Washington, the wife of Booker T. Washington, founded and assumed leadership of the International Council of Women of the Darker Races in 1924, likely influenced by her husband's long-standing interest in situating the South's race problems in a transnational setting.[109]

Washington was not the only educator who advocated using the U.S. South as a transnational testing ground for racial reform. He also had learned this way of thinking at his alma mater, Hampton Institute. Samuel Chapman Armstrong, the founder, had been reared in Hawaii and established Hampton as a school for industrial training based on the similarities he saw between African Americans and Hawaiians.[110] Andrew Zimmerman explains how "Armstrong refashioned a progressive American pedagogical tradition of manual education by incorporating a colonial pedagogy designed for white rule over perceived racial inferiors.[111] Hollis B. Frissell, who took over control of Hampton Institute after the death of Armstrong, dedicated his life to stimulating interest in southern educational problems. He was a member of the SEB and the GEB and participated in the Conference for Education in the South, always drawing other reformers' attention to the global implications of educational reform. Ray Stannard Baker reported how Frissell believed "that our own South should be utilized as a great experimental laboratory in race relationships," particularly its experience with industrial training. Hampton continued to host overseas visitors on a regular basis who were looking for answers to their own colonial race troubles.[112] Likewise, Kelly Miller concurred, stating that the U.S. South provided the "world's most interesting laboratory for working out the intricate issues of race adjustment."[113]

The racial situation in the U.S. South attracted a large number of British and South African travelers who not only came to the United States to study the sociological implications of the region's specific solution to the "race problem," but also published lengthy monographs about Jim Crow. Segregationists and imperialists such as Maurice S. Evans, William Archer, William P. Livingstone, William Laird Clowes, and Sir Harry Hamilton Johnston all traveled through the U.S. South from several weeks to several months.[114] These men were welcomed and assisted by prominent reformers and journalists interested in southern problems, including Walter Hines Page, Edgar Gardner Murphy, and Ray Stannard Baker. James Bryce corresponded with Edgar Gardner Murphy regarding his interest in the southern situation after reading Murphy's work, which described the attempt of modern nation-states and the southern states to contend with the relations between whites and nonwhites as "the distinctive task of a democratic imperialism or of an imperial democracy."[115] Harry Hamilton Johnston and Maurice S. Evans attended Booker T. Washington's International Conference on the Negro. Many of these Britons and South Africans made combined tours of the southern states, the West Indies, and Latin America. Johnston had spent several years observing the situation in colonial Africa and while researching his book on the "Negro question" in the New World he traveled to the southern states, Haiti, Jamaica, Barbados, Central America, Trinidad, Guiana, and Brazil.[116] Livingstone had previously studied the "race problem" and British colonial policies in Jamaica but traveled to the U.S. South in search of clearer answers.[117] William Archer included a visit to Cuba, Jamaica, Panama, Cartagena, and Trinidad as part of his whirlwind tour of the southern United States and reported that even while visiting the West Indies he was still in "Afro-America" observing certain aspects of the broader "colour-problem."[118] Some of these British and South African visitors hoped to return with newfound knowledge of how to govern as imperial powers in the modern world. Archer justified his interest in the U.S. South by suggesting that sociological studies of the region could aid the British in solving their own colonial problems. "My interest, then, in the colour-question in the South was not a mere abstract interest in an alien problem," he decided, "nor was it due solely to the special sympathy for America and all things American. . . . It was a personal interest which ought, I think, to be shared by every Englishman who is so far an Imperialist as to feel that he cannot simply wash his hands of the problems of Empire."[119]

While these foreign travelers to the U.S. South observed similarities between the region's racial troubles and the difficulties involved in administering a colonial government in a tropical context, they still identified the region as a distinctive locale. Like their American counterparts who feared that southern race relations bordered on the verge of a catastrophic race war, these British and South African men averred that the "race problem" was, as William Archer concluded, in "its acutest and most fully developed form" in the U.S. South.[120] They decided that "race antipathy" and "race friction" were more severe in the southern states because of the particular demographic configuration and the intensifying assertiveness of black Americans. William P. Livingstone expounded on how the U.S. South differed from the West Indies because "race-hatred" was most evident when contact between the two races was extremely close. In the British Empire, "the main body of the black inhabitants" was "located far distant from the main body of the whites" and the two did not "come into direct contact and competition with one another." In the U.S. South, in spite of the system of segregation, the races existed in a perpetual state of economic and social friction. Livingstone postulated that black Americans behaved as if they had achieved "racial and social equality," unlike the "black inhabitants of the Empire" who acknowledged their subordinate position, accepted the paternalistic model of governance, and welcomed the philanthropic intentions of the British imperial state. Thus what made the southern situation particularly complex and troublesome was the theoretical assertion that all were equal before the law. The U.S. South's misfortune, these visitors asserted, lay in the ill-fated attempt to facilitate the adjustment of the backward races to a democratic structure that southern whites presupposed could realistically accommodate African Americans.[121]

Finally, international visitors carefully observed that the "Negro question" in the southern states was an intractable problem because it was not only a conflict between black and white in one locale but also a question of regional strife between the North and South within the circumstance of empire. William P. Livingstone captured this situation most clearly when he conceptualized the North as "white America" and the South as "black America." The whites in "white America" and the whites in "black America" did not always pursue the same policies, he noted, since the former assemblage of whites behaved like British imperialists applying colonial strategies to a situation they were physically removed from. The crux of the matter was the latter group of whites living in "black America" who refused to follow colonial prescriptions. "The problem is, therefore, not simply a question of white against black," Livingstone claimed, "but of white against white and black, or to express it more conveniently, of the North, where negroes are relatively few, against the South, where they swarm." The "race problem" in the United States was characterized by regional and imperial conflict. First, this was a sectional dilemma in which northern and southern solutions to the "race problem" were consistently at odds. Second, Livingstone framed the southern situation as a problem of internal colonialism in which competing factions of white imperialists bickered over the acceptable means of racial reform and the evolutionary capacity of black Americans. What made the South distinctive was the fact that its white citizens sometimes resisted northern attempts to colonize the region and resolve the simmering "race problem."[122]

Indeed, the conceptual and linguistic reliance on colonial strategies such as uplift and industrial education guided much of the discussion among educators, philanthropists, and social scientists on the American version of the "race problem." The rhetoric of colonialism was present consistently in discussions on the U.S. South, particularly in the emphasis on words and ideas such as "discipline," "restraint," "progress," "civilization," "imitation," "child-like," "self-government," "education," "evolution," "inferior races," "missionaries," and "citizenship." Moreover, the popularity of sociocultural evolutionary thinking at the height of imperialism engendered descriptions of childlike races in need of proper discipline and guidance in both the U.S. South and the overseas colonies. Reformers and educators working in the region depicted black Americans as simple and childlike. At the First Mohonk Conference on the Negro Question, Reverend A. D. Mayo, from the Bureau of Education in Washington, D.C., reminded the audience that the "Negro" was a "perpetual child" who lacked the capacity to be a "citizen of a republican government." He went on to explain how "the child race must be cared for by a paternal organization of society, and that element of paternalism is just what every good American citizen declares he will not have in his government." Mayo concluded that without the help of "private benevolence and missionary zeal" the national government would be incapable of incorporating millions of southern blacks into the American body politic.[123] A year later, at the Second Mohonk Conference on the Negro Question, President W. H. Hickman of Clark University spoke of the duties that the "stronger race" had toward the "weaker race" because, he said, "The Negro is weak" and "is a grown up child."[124] Yet as Albion Tourgée aptly noted at the first Mohonk Conference, these white philanthropists and reformers had no desire to consult black Americans as equals regarding their needs.[125] Instead, they treated them as childlike colonial subjects in need of parental tutelage. Not surprisingly, Du Bois's paper the *Crisis* took exception to the idea that the black race was "in the infant or bottle stage of civilization" and insisted that Americans had overlooked the fact that black Americans had been in the United States nearly as long as whites. Instead, he indicated that at the very least the black race "was in a stage of civilization approximating youth."[126]

In their efforts to bring the black race up to the standards of civilization, Edgar Gardner Murphy and others advocated a program similar to President Taft's notion of "benevolent assimilation" in the Philippines. On the one hand, the practice of governance embraced philanthropic sensibilities. It constituted a form of "democratic tutelage," and educators aimed to instruct Filipinos to learn how to govern themselves. Colonial supervision in such areas as industrial education, labor relations, and public health would serve as a method of benevolent reform. On the other hand, this act of white paternalism necessitated a program of discipline. The success of colonial rule depended upon the marriage of an ideology of benevolence with the rigorous practice of discipline and restraint.[127] In Edgar Gardner Murphy's book on race relations, *The Basis of Ascendancy* (1910), he stressed that "restraint, direction, discipline, order are the essence of utilization," particularly in relation to the progress of "the ignorant masses of our colored population." The use of military force alone to ensure the development of a "republican form of government" among the "negro masses" was bound to lead to catastrophe. Murphy advocated a philanthropic curriculum that focused on industrial education and training in suffrage in conjunction with a disciplinary strategy. Only then, he added, would "the pupils in the school of society . . . be effectually prevented from destroying the school."[128]

Educators and philanthropists such as Murphy who advocated the colonial model of paternalistic reform in the southern states employed the discourse of empire making on the broadest scale to buttress the state's authority in disciplining and aiding the black race. Archibald R. Colquhoun explained how segregation in the U.S. South had created "this anomaly—a nation within a nation." He did not believe that transplanting the black race to either Africa or the Philippines (a suggestion made by some) would solve the problem since African Americans had become an "integral part" of the United States.[129] Nor did he believe that letting the situation alone to work itself out would succeed either. The solution, many concluded, was to treat the southern blacks as a colonized population in the setting of empire rather than as national citizens in the United States. Ironically, the segregated system of Jim Crow linked regional and national visions of whiteness, even while it simultaneously disrupted the idea of unanimity in American nationalism by treating a large population in the South as a separate nation within the American nation.

The discourse of the "race problem" drew attention to the fact that neither Reconstruction nor Redemption had managed to resolve the question of race. The spate of conferences, speeches, editorials, journal articles, sermons, sociological studies, and travelers' accounts on the subject testify to the inconsistencies, fictions, and tensions built into the edifice of white supremacy. The problem of the color line—whether it was expedient, stable, or feasible—eroded confidence in the mythology of a national reconciliation between sections predicated on the belief that race was no longer a sectional issue. Alternatively, social scientists and reformers agonized over the possible repercussions of "race friction," which they attributed to the actual physical presence of African Americans in the distinctive South. Sentimental and nostalgic longings for the idyllic relations between master and slave in the antebellum South were juxtaposed with fears about the presumed animosity between the races in the postbellum world. Preoccupation with "race antagonism" reflected a collective lamentation over the imagined loss of days gone by when blacks and whites supposedly lived side-by-side in a state of mutual affection and understanding. Leading African American writers and intellectuals also worried about mounting racial tensions but highlighted how the true causes of the so-called problem could be attributed to segregation and disfranchisement. Black men and women's demand for political and civil rights at the turn of the century drew attention to the contradiction between African Americans' lived experiences and the theoretical promises of democracy and citizenship. At times white liberal reformers were forced to acknowledge this paradox — that black southerners were an intrinsic part of the American system and that the social separation of the races might not provide the most adequate or practical solution. In addition, the "mulatto problem" provided plenty of evidence that the system of Jim Crow contained within it an inherent contradiction. The renewed attention to the status and condition of the black race in America and the place of mixed-race people in this period had evolved into a question of philanthropy and uplift rooted in social scientific principles rather than a question of sheer politics. The dilemma facing the United States was how to reconcile socially two supposedly dissimilar races (or "nations") on the same soil.

Yet "race friction" was much larger than a regional or national problem. Social scientific efforts to understand the nature of the relationship between black and white through the theoretical concepts of "adjustment," "friction," "antipathy," and the "mulatto problem" were never limited solely to a discussion of the U.S. South; the discourse had been global in orientation since the Civil War and peaked during the expansion of American empire. This transnational circulation of intellectuals, governing strategies, reform practices, and scientific theories linked regional, national, and global spaces together, strengthening the conviction that the domestic "race problem" was not only a hemispheric global southern problem but a broader world problem as well. Foreign visitors traveled to the U.S. South, confident that what they found there would enable them to restructure the racial systems in South Africa and the British colonies. They harbored seemingly contradictory views, a belief that the problem of the color line in the southern states was transnational in nature, yet also simultaneously distinctive. Individuals such as Booker T. Washington, Walter Hines Page, and Edgar Gardner Murphy welcomed these imperialists and took into account what lessons the global visitors could offer with regard to the U.S. South. The colonies overseas and the southern states became laboratories of racial reform and uplift, demonstrating that civilizing missions were both domestic and global in orientation. Yet, the broad connections made between such places as the Philippines, Hawaii, Puerto Rico, South Africa, and the southern states guaranteed that questions surrounding the meaning of citizenship could never be dismissed entirely in the U.S. South. The people of color encountered abroad were not American citizens either in practice or theory but their existence rejuvenated debates about the political and social consequence of democracy since African Americans theoretically held full citizenship rights. Ironically, these were issues that white Americans thought they had left behind with the end of Reconstruction.

The tragedy, of course, is that the discourse of the "race problem" in the late nineteenth and twentieth centuries continues to shape discussions on race in America today. There is a history behind why Americans have rendered certain peoples problematic. Social issues such as idleness, crime, illegitimacy, and the degeneration of the family in the black community still draw attention currently and are ideological remnants of the social scientific and popular debates that took place more than a hundred years ago.[130] Anxieties about brewing "race friction" and "race antagonism" resonate with claims made today by some politicians and policymakers that ungrateful minority groups have failed to acknowledge the benefits that have been ceded to them over the past generation. The tendency to view African Americans as objects rather than as subjects is a product of both the past and the present and only serves to validate whiteness and delegitimize people of color as historical actors in their own right. Kelly Miller's observation made a century ago still rings true: "In seeking a solution to the 'race problem' the white man is mainly anxious for the effect upon his lordly self. The African is not regarded in his own rights and for his own sake, but merely with reference to the effect which his presence and activity produce upon the dominant Aryan. . . . The black object is always projected against a white background, producing a grotesque and gloomy silhouette."[131]

The Enduring Paradox
of the South

So often in the South the stage seems all set for remarkable progress in public opinion and then something happens that swings us back into the old orbit of political and social immobility and decadence. . . . The liberals of the South are quite as well aware of these paradoxes as anyone else, but we insist that peoples of other sections should lay emphasis on the signs of progress rather than on those of reaction.

— EDWIN MIMS

The hordes of Yankeedom plainly regard themselves, not only as thoroughly competent critics, but in some measure as missionaries told off to preach the gospel violently in a heathen land. This is remarkable. When the messianic delusion infects an entire population, causing it to spend fifty years, and incalculable tons of paper and ink, not to mention spoken words, in discussion of a section that but rarely pays attention to its critics, the thing is surely traceable to some definite cause.

— GERALD W. JOHNSON

I n 1926, Edwin Mims, chair of the literature department at Vanderbilt University, wrote in *The Advancing South* that "the conflict between the forces of progress and reaction has been going on ever since Appomattox." Writing on the heels of the Scopes trial in Dayton, Tennessee, which pitted the fundamentalist southern guard against the modernist forces who embraced the theory of evolution, Mims described how a wave of people and organizations were "carrying on a veritable war of liberation in the Southern States." He considered himself, along with individuals such as Walter Hines Page and Edgar Gardner Murphy, a model for a new generation of southern liberals fighting a reinvigorated and reactionary strain of conservatism. On the surface, Mims's book appeared to underscore the persistent paradox of the South — the simultaneous pairing of provincialism with advancement — but he suggested optimistically that the "more outspoken, more belligerent, more apparently victorious" forces of traditionalism were in truth dying out. Indeed, Mims viewed the Scopes trial as a cultural aberration on an ever-changing southern landscape. In his book the Vanderbilt professor pledged not to discuss "abstract" southern problems and instead proffered a more cheerful interpretation of southern progress in industry, agriculture, literary thought, and even race relations.[1] After reading Mims's work, author Ellen Glasgow advocated placing it in all southern schools as evidence of "balance and sanity" and a civilized southern intellect. "Yet even as I read," she confessed, "I wonder if the whole country, not the South alone is becoming intoxicated upon the same ancient deadly brew of fanaticism, intolerance, and hypocrisy?" Perhaps in subtle defense of the South or with a hint of skepticism about Mims's sanguinity, she asked, "Is this the witches' cauldron beginning to boil over again in the Land of the Free?"[2] In short, was the nation becoming more like the Problem South or had the problems been national all along?

Mims's assessment of the South paralleled two other strains of thought in the 1920s and 1930s embodied in the work of H. L. Mencken and Howard W. Odum. Following World War I, interest in the "southern problem" did not wane although it evolved in several directions. Mencken and his compatriots relished the savagery and absurdity of southern backwardness and made poking fun of the South a national pastime. Some of his fellow social critics included Gerald W. Johnson of North Carolina, Grover C. Hall of the *Montgomery Advertiser*, Nell Battle Lewis of the *Raleigh-News and Observer*, and Julian Harris (the son of Joel Chandler Harris) and Julia Collier Harris of the *Columbus Enquirer-Sun*. The explosive growth of the Ku Klux Klan, the resurgence of religious evangelicalism, the Scopes trial, persistent racial violence, and even more flagrant examples of peonage provided fertile subject matter for musings on the South and in part contributed to a burgeoning southern literary renaissance in this period.[3] Mencken established his own journal, the *American Mercury*, soliciting contributions on national and regional topics and often serving as a mentor to aspiring writers. The viciousness with which Mencken attacked the South eclipsed anything that had come before it. Charles Angoff, managing editor to the *Mercury*, recalled that Mencken once called the region the "bunghole of the United States, a cesspool of Baptists, a miasma of Methodism, snake-charmers, phony real-estate operators, and syphilitic evangelists."[4] Mencken was fond of speaking about the "Ku Klux klergy," southern "yokels," and "Kulture in the South," and he viewed Arkansas as a place "still so barbarous that a mere lynching, without special tortures, is regarded down there as a lemonady sport for women and children."[5]

Howard W. Odum continued the tradition of envisaging the South as a colossal social laboratory, invigorating the field of sociology with the establishment of the *Journal of Social Forces* in 1922 and the Institute for Research in Social Science in 1924 at the University of North Carolina. In general, the 1920s saw a shift in sociological attention to southern problems, as social scientists solidified the field and entered the university system in greater numbers, thinking less in terms of general social reform and more in terms of large-scale welfare projects involving systematic planning.[6] Odum maintained there was "no reasonable doubt" that "the South needs criticism, and severe criticism," but he blamed "the unscientific, provincial, professional, amateurish agitators from without and the unscientific, provincial regional patriots within" for hindering regional progress with their censure.[7] Odum understood regionalism to be academic, cooperative, enterprising, and technological; its purpose was to serve the nation-state. He saw sectionalism as unpatriotic, stagnant, conflict driven, and resistant; it thought of the nation only in relationship to itself.[8] Odum published several books over the course of his career including *Southern Pioneers in Social Interpretation* (1925), which was a collection of essays paying tribute to Walter Hines Page and other southern progressives; a semiautobiographical account, *An American Epoch* (1930); and of course the massive tome *Southern Regions of the United States* (1936). Published just a few years after Frederick Jackson Turner's *The Significance of Sections in American History* (1932), *Southern Regions* reflected Odum's posture as a sociologist in contrast to Turner's training as a historian.[9] As early as 1907 Turner had advocated using the concept of sectionalism to understand the history of the United States as one involving sections behaving as if they were separate nations. Turner described American history as the story of economic colonization and the conquest of separate provinces, with the Northeast acting as its own nation-state in an "imperial" fashion (see chapter 1). Odum's treatise on the South advocated regional planning as a solution to southern failings although he made it clear that he no longer believed in the ability to measure the existence of "the South." Instead he thought it wiser to recognize "many Souths."[10] In embracing regionalism, Odum stressed the importance of nationalism and declared that any remaining southern deficiencies were a "national problem" not a "sectional issue."

However, Odum still could not move beyond the contradiction of the New South, acknowledging that there was "a paradoxical South, now rapidly developing, now receding, an eager and puzzled South trying to take stock of itself and its role in the changing nation." Odum used the very familiar terms "readjustment" and "reconstruction" to illustrate the project of regionalism in the South. He described the region "as one of those vast American regional empires vibrant with the emotions and unplanned activities of a great people, working heroically to overcome multiple handicaps, conscious of their power, yet also sometimes conscious of their limitations and the need for help." Not astonishingly, Odum stressed the importance of the utilization of rich southern resources in his description of this regional empire, which resonated with both the New South creed and the discourse of colonialism, even as he acknowledged there were lingering distinctive problems. In short, the South was both empire and colony. In several letters to H. L. Mencken he identified the stubbornly distinctive southern issues of "ecclesiastical dogmatism," "demagogy," and poor whites, although he was never quite sure if he believed there was a verifiable group who could be called "'poor white trash.'"[11]

H. L. Mencken, Howard W. Odum, and Edwin Mims were three prominent figures who represented the persistence of regionalism in the interwar years, and in fact each of them lived long enough to see a rearticulation of the Problem South during the early years of the civil rights movement in the 1950s.[12] Odum and Mims had been strong proponents of modernization in the South, as many southern and northern liberals before them, although their assessment of southern progress differed in degree. Odum was more realistic than Mims, open to discussing concrete southern problems and using the region as a Petri dish for investigation while the Vanderbilt professor was forever optimistic about how far the South had already progressed. At times both men still grappled with the baffling paradoxical nature of the South, a conundrum that had beset observers of the region for many years. Mencken was not interested in promoting the transformation of the South, however, and well-nigh thought the situation hopeless. He had harsh words for Mims's book *The Advancing South*, and wrote in his review that the Scopes trial never would have occurred if "Mims and his fellow pussy-footers" had been willing to publicly and vigorously criticize provincial southern thinking.[13] But the liberal progressive current pushing for modernization in the South, or what at the turn of the century had previously been denoted civilization, continued onward throughout the twentieth century. Two years after World War II ended, Odum communicated to Mencken, "All I am asking the public to do is to understand the South in the same way in which it tries to understand other cultures in other parts of the world."[14] The words of the sociologist from Chapel Hill demonstrated clearly that the notion of the South as a foreign country could never entirely be shaken off.

NOTES

INTRODUCTION. *Regional, National, and Global Designs*

1. Citations for headings are Andrew Sledd, "The Negro: Another View," *Atlantic Monthly* 90 (July 1902): 65; and Cash, *Mind of the South*, viii. H. L. Mencken, "The Sahara of the Bozart," in *Prejudices, Second Series*, 136–39, 141. For select studies of Mencken's life and works see Hobson, *Mencken*; Fitzpatrick, *H. L. Mencken*; and Teachout, *Skeptic*.

2. Paul Green to H. L. Mencken, December 20, 1924, Correspondence of H. L. Mencken, box 48, New York Public Library Microfilm, Special Collections, Enoch Pratt Free Library.

3. For historians who argue that Mencken made fervent criticism of the South a new national pastime and that "The Sahara of the Bozart" marks the genesis, see Tindall, "Benighted South"; and Hobson, *Serpent in Eden*.

4. For a history of Odum and the work done at the Institute for Research in Social Science see Hobson, *Tell about the South*, 180–243; Tindall, "Significance of Howard W. Odum"; Sosna, *In Search of the Silent South*, 42–59; and O'Brien, *Idea of the American South*, 31–93.

5. Tindall explains how the mythology of the backward South did not really gain steam until the onset of rapid urbanization combined with increasing poverty in the rural South, religious fundamentalism, and nativism, best embodied in the rebirth of the Ku Klux Klan. See Tindall, "Benighted South." Paul Gaston, in *New South Creed*, 228–29, also makes the case that the 1920s signaled a new moment in which the South's deficiencies became the target of social scientific liberals.

6. Ayers and Onuf, *All over the Map*, 9.

7. While the literature is vast, one of the best surveys on the history of southern regionalism is Cobb, *Away Down South*. Thomas Jefferson listed these characteristics in a letter to the Marquis de Chastellux in 1785. See Smith and Cohn, *Look Away!*, 9. Also see Grant, *North over South*; John David Cox, *Traveling South*; Bertelson, *Lazy South*; Taylor, *Cavalier and Yankee*; Hobson, "Savage South"; and Foner, *Free Soil*, 40–72.

For an exploration of how the South was configured as the "antipode" of the nation in American literature see Greeson, *Our South*.

8. The conventional understanding of the relationship between North and South in the late nineteenth and early twentieth centuries minimizes, if not erases, the persistence of regionalism and stresses the primacy of a unified American nationalism buoyed by imperialism, military ventures overseas, and the development of a national patriotism. Historians argue this period was marked by a national interest in cultural reunion that downplayed sectional grievances, celebrated racial and industrial harmony, reflected a shared belief in the supremacy of the white race, and involved a collective engagement in mythmaking about the meaning of the Civil War and Reconstruction. In short, this body of scholarship suggests that the "culture of reunion" made it easier to overlook the South's problems. See Blight, *Race and Reunion*; Silber, *Romance of Reunion*; Blum, *Reforging the White Republic*; Hale, *Making Whiteness*; Grantham, *Southern Progressivism*; Gaston, *New South Creed*; Buck, *Road to Reunion*; and Foster, *Ghosts of the Confederacy*. Silber explicitly states that the focus on domestic harmony allowed the nation to overlook the South's problems, especially the poverty of poor whites (*Romance of Reunion*, 11). Also see Watts, *One Homogeneous People* for a discussion about how the formation of a white southern identity resonated with national ideals and enabled the South to avoid becoming "the disruptive section of American history" (90). This book contends that this group of scholars have overemphasized the extent to which cultural symbols, literature, and sentimental and historical memories facilitated the process of reunion. Subsequently, they have overlooked material actions taken by people and institutions to resolve southern problems. The interplay between memory and ideology certainly is powerful, yet cultural iconography does not always correspond to the behavior of real people. In turn, actions initiated on the ground level can generate new mythologies that may run counter to other mythologies.

9. Gerstle, "Protean Character of American Liberalism," 1046.

10. Sklar, *Corporate Reconstruction*, 1.

11. Rodgers, "In Search of Progressivism," has shaped my thinking on Progressivism as various strains of discourse or "languages of discontent."

12. For a history of liberalism in the Progressive Era South see Clayton, *Savage Ideal*; Bailey, *Liberalism in the New South*; and Doherty, "Voices of Protest." For a discussion of southern liberals' views on the race question see Sosna, *Silent South*.

13. For a history of this development see Stocking, *Victorian Anthropology*; and Bowler, *Invention of Progress*.

14. One of the most powerful ways to mark boundaries and draw distinctions between who belongs and who does not belong is to invoke the authority of science.

Science played a key role in generating new authoritative knowledges about the South that reinforced the binary opposition between the nation and the region. According to Pierre Bordieu, the symbols or stigmata used to identify a region are not objective criteria but reflect struggles over classification (often under the guise of empirical science) and over "the monopoly of power" to get people to observe, believe in, and recognize a particular social world. Science is one field that plays a prominent role in the battle to create particular representations of regions. In short, these are struggles over the power to "*make and unmake groups.*" Bordieu argues that regionalist discourse is performative in nature and the mere act of revealing or showing can be both complicitous or critical. Regionalist discourse as performance leads people to view the region in opposition to some dominant definition that is considered the locus of normality and legitimate authority. See Bordieu, "Identity and Representation," 220–28.

15. The term "rational interventions" is used by Gerstle, "Protean Character of American Liberalism," 1046. The bulk of the historiography on the Progressive Era in the South has either followed a synthetic top-down approach, thereby minimizing distinctions between regions and emphasizing the continuities between southern and national Progressive reformers, or it has focused on local communities, actions, and concerns in the South. The two most helpful overviews of southern Progressivism are Grantham, *Southern Progressivism*; and Link, *Paradox of Southern Progressivism*. Link not only considers the motivations of the reformers but is far more attentive to the social context of reform. He comes closest to making regional distinctions when he argues that the reformers' social policies of centralization and interventionism in state and local governments precipitated local community resistance in the South marked by fierce traditions of individualism. Also see Kirby, *Darkness at the Dawning*, for a history of race and southern Progressivism.

16. I argue the Progressive movement in the South followed a different trajectory than it did in the North. Historians writing on southern Progressivism have struggled to define the features and characteristics of the movement much like those historians writing about Progressivism in general. For a brief overview of the trajectory of the historiography of Progressivism, at least through the early 1980s, see Rodgers, "In Search of Progressivism." For a discussion of the conflict surrounding the historiography of southern Progressivism see William A. Link, "The Social Context of Southern Progressivism, 1880–1930," in Cooper and Neu, *Wilson Era*; Richard Watson, "From Populism Through the New Deal," in Boles and Nolen, *Interpreting Southern History*. Also see Grantham, "Contours of Southern Progressivism."

17. Rodgers, *Atlantic Crossings*, 6–7.

18. The field of southern history has long been preoccupied with the North–South

224 · NOTES TO INTRODUCTION

or region–nation dichotomy. At times the word "nation" is used to denote the North. One classic example of this binary history is C. Vann Woodward's book *American Counterpoint*. Woodward's attention to the North–South counterpoint in the postbellum period is rooted in his belief that the West largely became an extension of the East with the closing of the frontier at the turn of the century. The persistent debate among contemporary southern historians over the distinctiveness of the South has kept the scholarship mired in the traditional North–South binary framework. The historiographical debate often is a product of these historians' failure to interrogate the distinctiveness question as a historical phenomenon and reconsider global connections. The historical actors themselves not only set apart the South from the rest of the nation but also made comparisons with other foreign locales to highlight the region as a deviant geographical space. White, "Nationalization of Nature," has enabled me to think about how framing history on multiple spatial scales alters the historical picture.

19. For general histories of Progressivism in a global context see Rodgers, *Atlantic Crossings*; Kloppenberg, *Uncertain Victory*; and Tyrrell, *Reforming the World*. For the influence of postcolonialism on the interdisciplinary field of southern studies see Smith and Cohn, *Look Away!*; Schmidt, *Sitting in Darkness*; Taylor, *Disturbing Calculations*; Greeson, *Our South*; Duck, *Nation's Region*; Handley, *Postslavery Literatures*; Aboul-Ela, *Other South*; and Smith, McKee, and Romine, "Special Issue, Part I and II." For other work on the relationship between the South and empire see Guterl, *American Mediterranean*; and Zimmerman, *Alabama in Africa*. For a history of how the colonial model was used at Tuskegee Institute see Sehat, "Civilizing Mission." Stoler's essay "Tense and Tender Ties" has shaped my understanding of the relationship between postcolonialism and U.S. history.

20. My thinking on this is inspired by Ann Stoler and Frederick Cooper who suggest the history of colonialism should include research into "the extent to which models of rule passed back and forth across different kinds of imperial territory." See Ann Laura Stoler and Frederick Cooper, "Between Metropole and Colony: Rethinking a Research Agenda," in Stoler and Cooper, *Tensions of Empire*, 23. Paul Kramer has shown how American governmental officials and experts began to acknowledge that their own practices of imperialism and colonialism were part and parcel of a global pattern of imperialism. Kramer explains that "the architects of colonial rule often turned to rival powers as allies, foils, mirrors, models, and exceptions." See Kramer, "Empires, Exceptions, and Anglo-Saxons," 1315–16.

21. An example of comparative history would be Cell, *Highest Stage of White Supremacy*; Fredrickson, *Black Liberation*; and Fredrickson, *White Supremacy*, both of which juxtapose the U.S. South with South Africa.

22. Michael Salman argues that national debates surrounding the Civil War and Reconstruction provided the context for future disagreement over patterns of American colonial intervention in the Philippines (a country grappling with the legacy of its own system of slavery); see Salman, *Embarrassment of Slavery*, 27, 50. For a literary discussion of how U.S. imperial imagery reflected and was shaped by colonial domination of the South during Reconstruction see Greeson, *Our South*, 227–89. In his work on the literary output of former slave societies, George Handley states "the South essentially was the first colony of U.S. imperial expansion." See Handley, *Postslavery Literatures*, 20.

23. For a history of southern underdevelopment and the southern colonial economy see Woodward, *Origins*; and Bensel, *Political Economy*, 19–100. Also see Gavin Wright, *Old South, New South* for a discussion of the South's isolated labor market; and Persky, *Burden of Dependency* for a history of how southerners perceived the South to be a colonial economy beginning in the seventeenth century.

24. Scholars interested in colonialism have examined how colonial states were constructed and sustained in addition to exploring the myriad ways in which the colonized resisted the hegemony of the colonial state. Those who study how colonial regimes maintain their rule have focused on the relationship between the production of knowledge and power, the categories used to classify and survey the colonized, and the way in which colonies served as "laboratories" for modernity, social engineering, and civilizing experiments. This includes topographical surveys, social engineering, the collection of massive amounts of data and statistics as well as the use of professional experts to analyze and interpret the material collected. For some examples see Stoler, *Carnal Knowledge*; Arnold, *Colonizing the Body*; Stoler and Cooper, *Tensions of Empire*; and Dirks, *Colonialism and Culture*.

25. For a theoretical study of how travel writing functioned as a colonial strategy of hegemony see Pratt, *Imperial Eyes*.

26. In recent years American historians have examined how international relations shaped a dominant imperial culture at home, and they suggest we need to rethink empire as central to American history. American historiography traditionally has defined American exceptionalism as inherently anti-imperialist. Too often the annexation of colonial possessions at the turn of the century is viewed as a historical anomaly in the ongoing process of state expansion that the United States has actively pursued since its founding. Rather, the United States has a long history of both external and internal colonialism. See Amy Kaplan, "'Left Alone With America': The Absence of Empire in the Study of American Culture," in Kaplan and Pease, *Cultures of United States Imperialism*; Donald Pease, "U.S. Imperialism: Global Dominance without Colonies," in Schwartz and Ray, *Companion to Postcolonial Studies*; Salman,

Embarrassment of Slavery; Stoler, *Haunted by Empire*; Hoganson, *Fighting for American Manhood*; Kaplan, *Anarchy of Empire*; Wexler, *Tender Violence*; Kramer, *Blood of Government*; Renda, *Taking Haiti*; and "Editor's Introduction." For a panel discussion on situating colonial studies in the context of U.S. history see "Forum: Empires and Intimacies."

27. C. Vann Woodward, "The Irony of Southern History," in Woodward, *Burden of Southern History*, 190.

28. John Smith and Deborah Cohn, "Introduction: Uncanny Hybridities," in Smith and Cohn, *Look Away!*, 2. Smith and Cohn also cite Fred Hobson's argument that "poverty, frustration, failure, and a *felt* knowledge of history also apply, even more strongly if for quite different reasons, to black southerners"; see Hobson, *South to the Future*, 2.

29. For commentary on the use of the concept of American exceptionalism see Fredrickson, "From Exceptionalism to Variability"; Daniel T. Rodgers, "Exceptionalism," in Molho and Wood, *Imagined Histories*; Tyrrell, "American Exceptionalism"; and Adas, "Settler Colony to Global Hegemony."

30. Hobson, *South to the Future*, 1–2.

31. For an introduction to the term "new regional studies" see Ayers and Onuf, *All over the Map*. For examples of this scholarship in the past twenty years see Duck, *Nation's Region*; Powell, *Critical Regionalism*; Kermes, *Creating an American Identity*; Conforti, *Imagining New England*; Morrissey, *Mental Territories*; "AHR Forum"; Dorman and Wilson, *New Regionalism*; Jordan, *Regionalism Reconsidered*; and Kowalewski, "Writing in Place." The historiographical focus on nationalism, nation-state construction, and national identity likely contributed to this renewed interest in regionalism. Celia Applegate has suggested that Benedict Anderson's concept of an "imagined community" in the process of nation making could just as easily be used to think about how regions themselves are imagined and configured. Applegate, "A Europe of Regions," 1176. For the classic texts that have influenced theoretical discussions on nationalism and nation-state construction in the past two decades see Anderson, *Imagined Communities*; Hobsbawm, *Nations and Nationalism*; and Gellner, *Nations and Nationalism*.

32. The literature on the South as an idea is extensive and too lengthy to list in its entirety. For some examples see O'Brien, *Idea of the American South*; Gray, *Writing the South*; Grantham, *Regional Imagination*; Gerster and Cords, *Myth and Southern History*; Grantham, *South and the Sectional Image*; Stephen A. Smith, *Myth, Media*; Singall, *War Within*; Gaston, *New South Creed*; Davenport, *Myth of Southern History*; and Vandiver, *Idea of the South*. Also see Kirby, *Media-Made Dixie*; and Karen L. Cox, *Dreaming of Dixie*.

33. O'Brien, "On Observing the Quicksand," 1203; and Laura F. Edwards, "Southern History as U.S. History."

34. Howard W. Odum, "Regionalism vs. Sectionalism in the South's Place in the National Economy," *Social Forces* 12 (March 1934): 338.

35. Murphy, *Problems of the Present South*, 22–24. For another example asserting that northerners claimed "the nation meant the North and did not include the South," see "Editor's Announcement," *South Atlantic Quarterly* 4 (April 1905): 108.

36. See Albert Bushnell Hart, *Southern South*, 1.

37. Rafael, "Regionalism, Area Studies," 1208–9. For an example of how southerners in the Appalachian mountains were celebrated for their tradition and Anglo-Saxon purity in spite of their rural poverty and alleged backwardness see Whisnant, *All That Is Native;* and Shapiro, *Appalachia on Our Mind.*

38. Grantham, *Regional Imagination,* explores the influence of regionalism and the commitment to social scientific study of the South in the first two decades of the twentieth century.

39. For these terms see Benedict Anderson, *Imagined Communities;* and Hobsbawm, *Invention of Tradition.* For an example of the way in which exclusionary prescriptions fashioned national identity see Uday S. Mehta, "Liberal Strategies of Exclusion," in Cooper and Stoler, *Tensions of Empire,* 59–86.

40. See McCurry, *Masters of Small Worlds,* 39. In the same year I finished my PhD dissertation, which this book is based on, a graduate student in geography was simultaneously making an argument about the South and "internal orientalism." See Jansson, "Internal Orientalism in America" and "American National Identity." James Cobb cites David Jansson's concept of "internal orientalism" to describe the process of using the South as the conceptual antithesis of the United States. See Cobb, *Away Down South,* 3. Jane Schneider's edited collection of essays entitled *Italy's "Southern Question": Orientalism in One Country* suggests that postcolonial intellectual theory has relevance within the context of one nation contending with its own backward southern region. For a history of the Italian struggle with the "southern question" also see Dickie, *Darkest Italy;* Lumley and Morris, *New History;* and Moe, *View from Vesuvius.* For work that explicitly makes the comparison between the Italian South and the American South see Dal Lago and Halpern, *American South and Italian Mezzogiorno;* Doyle, *Nations Divided;* and Susanna Delfino, "The Idea of Southern Economic Backwardness: A Comparative View of the United States and Italy," in Delfino and Gillespie, *Global Perspectives.*

41. Said, *Orientalism,* 20, 22.

42. McLeod, *Beginning Postcolonialism,* 45–46.

43. See Greeson, *Our South.*

CHAPTER 1. *The "Southern Problem" and Readjustment*

1. Headings are Murphy, *Problems of the Present South*, 20; and Brown, *Lower South*, 270–71. Roosevelt is cited in Tremain, *Sectionalism Unmasked*, 13.

2. Larry J. Griffin, "Why Was the South a Problem to America?" in Griffin and Doyle, *South as an American Problem*, 14.

3. "Our Student Ambassador to the Court of St. James: Character Sketch," *New York Sun*, 1913, typescript, Letters Sent to Walter Hines Page from Various Correspondents, American Period, box 21, MS Am 1090, Houghton Library, Harvard University.

4. Edmonds, *South's Redemption*, 3–4.

5. Ibid., 5.

6. Edmonds, *Facts about the South*, 37.

7. For late nineteenth and early twentieth-century examples of an optimistic faith in the South's current and future progress see Edmonds, *South's Redemption*; Grady, *New South*; Harrison, *How to Get Rich*; Robertson, *Road to Wealth*; Cowlam, *Undeveloped South*; Bruce, *Rise of the New South*; McClure, *South*; Schurz, *New South*; Droke, *From the Old South*; Kelley, *Old South and the New*; Atkinson, *Resources of the Southern States*; Edmonds, *Facts about the South*; Morris, *Old South and the New*; and Hillyard, *New South*. The number of journal articles espousing the New South creed are too numerous to list.

8. Edmonds, *South's Redemption*, 3–5.

9. Kelley, *Old South and the New*, 162.

10. Walter Hines Page, "The Arisen South," *World's Work* 14 (June 1907): 8925.

11. Frederick Jackson Turner, "The Frontier in American History," in *Frontier in American History*, 1. This is a reprint of Turner's paper read at the American Historical Association meeting in Chicago in 1893.

12. Samuel C. Mitchell, "Nationalization of Southern Sentiment," *South Atlantic Quarterly* 7 (April 1908): 110.

13. "Editor's Announcement," *South Atlantic Quarterly* 4 (April 1905): 107–8.

14. Hamilton Wright Mabie, "The New North," *South Atlantic Quarterly* 4 (April 1905): 111–14. Mabie's quotation is cited in Edwin Mims, "Autobiographical Fragment — Education in the South, etc.," Edwin Mims Papers, box 19, folder 7, Special Collections and University Archives, Vanderbilt University.

15. Robert Bingham, "Sectional Misunderstandings," *North American Review* 179 (September 1904): 370.

16. Robert Bingham to Edwin Mims, May 27, 1907, Edwin Mims Papers, box 1.

17. See Saxton, *Rise and Fall*; Bederman, *Manliness and Civilization*; Hale, *Making Whiteness*; and Lears, *Rebirth*.

18. Gaston, *New South Creed*, 95.

19. Joshua W. Caldwell, "The South Is American," *Arena* 8 (October 1893): 607–17.

20. Thompson, *New South*, 193.

21. Wallace Putnam Reed, "The Old South on Deck," *Independent* 50 (November 24, 1898): 1497.

22. Gaston, *New South Creed*, 125.

23. See Tourgée, *A Fool's Errand*; and Elliott, *Color-Blind Justice*.

24. Jones, "Sectional Fiction."

25. Tourgée, *A Fool's Errand*, 337, 340.

26. Edwin L. Godkin, "The Southern Question in the Canvass," *Nation* 31 (July 29, 1880): 72.

27. Edwin L. Godkin, "The White Side of the Southern Question," *Nation* 31 (August 19, 1880): 126–27.

28. Hugh Bailey, *Liberalism in the New South*, 24.

29. George Washington Cable, "The Freedmen's Case in Equity," *Century Magazine* 29 (January 1885): 413. Cable's article elicited a flood of letters protesting his statements, as many readers mistakenly assumed that Cable also had advocated social equality (a code phrase for "miscegenation"). Three months later, *Century Magazine* published a response by preeminent New South proponent Henry Grady, who justified segregation, insisted that separate but equal was truly equal, and attacked Cable for misrepresenting both white and black southerners who did not desire civil rights or any form of "social intermingling." Henry Grady, "In Plain Black and White. A Reply to Mr. Cable," *Century Magazine* 29 (April 1885): 909–17.

30. See Cable, *Silent South*.

31. Walter Hines Page, "Study of an Old Southern Borough," *Atlantic Monthly* 47 (May 1881): 648, 652–53, 655, 657–58.

32. Bailey, *Liberalism in the New South*, 108.

33. For works on Walter Hines Page see Cooper, *Walter Hines Page*; and Hendrick, *Training of an American*.

34. Page, *Southerner*, xiii.

35. Straker, *New South Investigated*, iv–v, 16.

36. Reed, "Old South on Deck," 1496–97.

37. Du Bois, *Souls of Black Folk*, 9.

38. McCulloch, *Call of the New South*, 7.

39. Chatfield, "Southern Sociological Congress: Organization of Uplift"; and Chatfield, "Southern Sociological Congress: Rationale of Uplift."

40. Harold A. Caparn, "The Question of Civic Improvement," *Sewanee Review* 15 (October 1907): 497.

41. For some examples see John Lee Coulter, "The Rural Life Problem of the South," *South Atlantic Quarterly* 12 (January 1913): 60; John Carlisle Kilgo, "Some Phases of Southern Education," *South Atlantic Quarterly* 2 (April 1903): 138; Editorial, "The Immigration Problem" *Outlook* 97 (February 18, 1911): 354; Carl Schurz, "Present Aspects of the Indian Problem," *North American Review* 132 (July 1881): 1; Prof. E. W. Gilliam, "The African Problem," *North American Review* 139 (November 1884): 417; Monroe N. Work, "The South's Labor Problem," *South Atlantic Quarterly* 19 (January 1920): 1; Willis, *Our Philippine Problem*; Lebbeus Redman Wilfley, "America and the Far Eastern Question," *Outlook* (May 29, 1909): 282; William V. Pettit, "Porto Rico," *Atlantic Monthly* 83 (May 1899): 634; Editorial, "The Pellagra Problem Solved," *World's Work Magazine* 34 (August 1917): 365; John Carlisle Kilgo, "Some Phases of Southern Education," *South Atlantic Quarterly* 2 (April 1903): 138; Frederick J. Turner, "The Problem of the West," *Atlantic Monthly* 78 (September 1896): 288; and Lyman Abbott, "The Rights of Man: A Study in Twentieth Century Problems," *Outlook* 68 (May 11, 1901): 117.

42. Walter Hines Page to Daniel Coit Gilman, May 9, 1894, Letters Sent to Walter Hines Page, box 10, MS Am 1090(421).

43. For a history of this phenomenon see Mott, "Magazine Revolution."

44. For his praise of Booker T. Washington see John Spencer Bassett, "Stirring Up the Fires of Race Antipathy," *South Atlantic Quarterly* 2 (October 1903): 299.

45. Edwin Mims and William G. Glasson, "Editors' Announcement," *South Atlantic Quarterly* 4 (April 1905): 106.

46. Hobson, *Tell about the South*, 167.

47. The serial is Nicholas Worth, "The Autobiography of a Southerner since the Civil War, Part I–IV," *Atlantic Monthly* 98 (July–October 1906): 1–12; 157–76; 311–25; 474–88. The novel was originally published as *The Southerner: A Novel; Being the Autobiography of Nicholas Worth*. See Page, *Southerner*.

48. Page, *Southerner*, 108–10, 134–35.

49. Nicholas Worth, "The Autobiography of a Southerner since the Civil War [Part IV]," *Atlantic Monthly* 98 (October 1906): 474–75.

50. William Watson Davis to Walter Hines Page, October 22, 1908, Letters Sent to Walter Hines Page, box 7, MS Am 1090(304).

51. "Mr. Page on 'The Evil of Our Land,'" unnamed newspaper, n.d., February 1898, Walter Hines Page Papers, box 1, MS Am 1090.3, Houghton Library, Harvard University.

52. "The Passing Throng," *Montgomery Advertiser*, Scrapbook, March 1900, Edgar Gardner Murphy Papers, box 2, folder 11, vol. 1, Southern Historical Collection, Wilson Library, University of North Carolina at Chapel Hill.

53. Walter Hines Page to Daniel Coit Gilman, May 9, 1894, Letters Sent to Walter

Hines Page, box 10, MS Am 1090(421). For another reference to the Nineteenth Century Club see Horace Edward Deming to Walter Hines Page, November 1, 1892, Letters Sent to Walter Hines Page, box 7, MS Am 1090(311).

54. Topics of the Times, "News From the South," *Century Magazine* 5 (March 1903): 797–98.

55. *Yearbook of the New York Southern Society*, 5.

56. "Mr. St. John Explains," *New York Times*, January 10, 1890; and "Heated Southern Blood," *New York Times*, January 11, 1890.

57. See Sutherland, "Southern Fraternal Organizations in the North."

58. Albert Bushnell Hart to Oswald Garrison Villard, March 2, 1905, Albert Bushnell Hart Papers, box 1, "Southern Questions and Slavery," University Archives, Harvard University. One of Hart's southern academic friends, Samuel C. Mitchell, expected him to write an Olmsted-like multivolume account of conditions when traveling through the back country of the South. See Albert Bushnell Hart to Samuel Chiles Mitchell, October 10, 1907, Albert Bushnell Hart Papers, box 1, "Southern Questions and Slavery."

59. Albert Bushnell Hart to Edgar Gardner Murphy, October 1, 1907, Albert Bushnell Hart Papers, box 1, "Southern Questions and Slavery."

60. Albert Bushnell Hart, "Conditions of the Southern Problem," *Independent* 58 (March 23, 1905): 644.

61. Albert Bushnell Hart, "Remedies for the Southern Problem," *Independent* 58 (May 4, 1905): 993.

62. Albert Bushnell Hart, "The South's 'Backwardness,'" *Times-Dispatch*, March 22, 1905; and Albert Bushnell Hart, "The South's Progress," *Times-Dispatch*, April 6, 1905.

63. Albert Bushnell Hart to Edgar Gardner Murphy, June 1 1905, Edgar Gardner Murphy Papers, box 1, folder 3.

64. Edgar Gardner Murphy to Albert Bushnell Hart, October 8, n.d., Albert Bushnell Hart Papers, box 2, "Southern Trips."

65. Mrs. H. L. Harris, "A Southern Woman's Impressions of New York City," *Independent* 60 (February 22, 1906): 430.

66. "By a Southern Visitor: Northern Men and Women," *Independent* 55 (March 12, 1903): 600–601. Mrs. Harris is the likely author of this article. For other examples of Mrs. Harris's discussion of northern criticism of the South see Mrs. H. L. Harris, "North and South: The Difference," *Independent* 58 (June 15, 1905): 1348–50; and Mrs. H. L. Harris, "The South's Way," *Independent* 65 (December 3, 1908): 1274–77. For a liberal southerner's discussion of southern resistance to criticism as well as commentary on the usefulness of external and internal criticism of the South see Edwin Mims, "The Function of Criticism in the South," *South Atlantic Quarterly* 2 (October 1903): 341–45.

67. "Governor Vardaman," *Vicksburg Mississippi Post*, December, 10, 1904, U.S.

Department of Agriculture, Record Group 7, Southern Field Crop Insect Investigations, Newspaper Clippings, box 10, National Archives, Washington, D.C. (hereafter cited as USDA, RG, and SFCII).

68. Thompson, "The New South, Economic and Social," in Gardner, *Southern History and Politics*, 315.

69. See Bowler, *Invention of Progress*.

70. Stocking, *Victorian Anthropology*, 186–237.

71. For a literary analysis of how the discourse of civilization was employed to make sense of the New South see Jeremy Dwight Wells, "Civilization and the South." Wells states that texts about the postbellum South were obsessed with the idea of civilization, but he maintains that the discourse of civilization in the South functioned differently in the immediate years following the Civil War than it did at the turn of the century. Wells maintains that early on the region was criticized for its lack of civilization. However, by the late nineteenth century, and in conjunction with the spread of empire overseas, writers almost always celebrated the greatness of southern civilization. Wells's work does not account for the existence of the paradox of the New South that this book addresses. Indeed, liberal southerners, northern philanthropists, and government experts often wrote and spoke about the *absence* of southern civilization in the early twentieth century. See Wells, *Romances of the White Man's Burden* for an expansion on his dissertation.

72. Dr. John E. White, "The Significance of the Southern Sociological Congress," in McCulloch, *South Mobilizing for Social Service*, 16.

73. "Free Speech in the South," *Independent* 55 (January 15, 1903): 131.

74. Rev. John E. White, "The True and False in Southern Life," *South Atlantic Quarterly* 5 (April 1906): 101.

75. See Bederman, *Manliness and Civilization*, 45–76.

76. Walter Hines Page, "The Last Hold of the Southern Bully," *Forum* 1 (November 1893): 303–14. Page also criticized "the brute," or black rapist, for inciting the savage behavior of whites, but he was inclined to argue that both the white and black races in the South were responsible for holding back the progress of civilization.

77. See Davis, *Slavery and Human Progress*, xvii.

78. Atticus G. Haygood, *New South*, 14.

79. Charles B. Spahr, "America's Working People, Part II: The New Factory Towns of the South," *Outlook* 61 (March 4, 1899): 514; William W. Ball, "The Industrial Revolution in South Carolina," *Sewanee Review* 19 (April 1911): 9; and Samuel C. Mitchell, "Robert Curtis Ogden: A Leader in the Educational Renaissance of the South," Robert Curtis Ogden Papers, box 27, folder 1, Library of Congress, Washington, D.C., Manuscript Division. For examples of references to slavery as an incubus, see Richard H. Edmonds,

Facts about the South, 1; and William P. Trent, "Dominant Forces in Southern Life," *Atlantic Monthly* 79 (January 1897): 47.

80. Walter Hines Page, *Rebuilding of Old Commonwealths*, 121, 138.

81. Nicholas Worth, "The Autobiography of a Southerner since the Civil War [Part III]," *Atlantic Monthly* 98 (September 1906): 324.

82. Murphy, *Problems of the Present South*, vii, ix.

83. Elmer Ellsworth Brown, "One View of National Unity," *Arena* 22 (August 1899): 186.

84. Murphy, *Problems of the Present South*, x.

85. Tremain, *Sectionalism Unmasked*, 2.

86. Clarence H. Poe, "The South: Backward and Sectional or Progressive and National?" *Outlook* 114 (October 11, 1916): 328.

87. Murphy, *Problems of the Present South*, 22–24. For another example asserting that northerners claimed "the nation meant the North and did not include the South" see "Editor's Announcement," *South Atlantic Quarterly* 4 (April 1905): 108. Albert Bushnell Hart also noted that the three regions of the North, Midwest, and West were often lumped together as "the North" to the exclusion of the South. See Albert Bushnell Hart, *Southern South*, 1.

88. Frederick J. Turner, "Is Sectionalism in America Dying Away?" *American Journal of Sociology* 13 (March 1908): 661, 673. For another example of Turner's commentary on his disagreement with Elihu Root see Frederick J. Turner, "Sections and Nation," in Turner, *Significance of Sections*, 325–26. For biographies of Turner's life see Billington, *Frederick Jackson Turner*; and Bogue, *Frederick Jackson Turner*.

89. See Tyrrell, "Making Nations/Making States." Tyrrell suggests that even in the 1920s and 1930s "the desire to situate the United States within a wider history survived." It was not until after World War II that the "dominance of nation-centered historiography" was fulfilled.

90. Turner, "Sectionalism in America," 662–63.

91. Turner, "Geographic Sectionalism in American History," 85.

92. Michael Heffernan, "Inaugurating the American Century: 'New World' Perspectives on the 'Old' in the Early Twentieth Century," in Slater and Taylor, *American Century*, 119.

93. Cash, *Mind of the South*, viii.

94. Stoler, "Tense and Tender Ties," 862.

95. Editorial, *New Republic* 4 (August 21, 1915): 56.

96. See Mackie, *From Cape Cod to Dixie*.

97. Archer, *Through Afro-America*, xv–xvi.

98. Albert Bushnell Hart, *Southern South*, 4.

99. Albert Bushnell Hart, *Obvious Orient*, 9; and Albert Bushnell Hart, *Southern South*, 2–3.

100. See Salman, *Embarrassment of Slavery*.

101. Walter Hines Page, "The End of the War, and After," *Atlantic Monthly* 82 (September 1898), 430–31. Pushing the southern blueprint for colonization back even further, Burton J. Hendrick, the editor of Walter Hines Page's correspondence, wrote that the North Carolina reformer believed the solution to the colonial problem in the Philippines could be solved by extending Thomas Jefferson's principles of uplifting the common man in remote areas. Hendrick himself made comparisons between Virginia and the Philippines. He encouraged colonizers to train the Filipinos in the "essentials of self-government" as Jefferson did in eighteenth-century Virginia, including teaching them to read and write, training them in agriculture, trades, and mechanic arts, and encouraging them to practice proper sanitary habits and build roads and highways. See Hendrick, *Training of an American*, 268.

CHAPTER 2. *The Menace of the Diseased South*

1. Headings are Poe, *My First Eighty Years*, 199–200; and Grady, *Race Problem*, 543. James McCulloch, "Introduction," in McCulloch, *Battling for Social Betterment*, 3.

2. Charles E. Rosenberg, "Disease in History," 1–15.

3. O'Brien, *Idea of the American South*, xiii.

4. Scholars writing on the history of medicine in the South tend to address disease as a material reality. They have focused largely on the existence and identification of diseases distinctive to the region; the role played by state boards of health in eradicating yellow fever, malaria, and hookworm; the significance of the development and growth of public health education in the region; and the influence of Progressive Era Protestant values on public health reform. See Savitt and Young, *Disease and Distinctiveness*; Ettling, *Germ of Laziness*; Link, "Privies, Progressivism, and Public Schools"; Fee, *Disease and Discovery*; Carrigan, *Saffron Scourge*; Humphreys, *Yellow Fever*; Humphreys, *Malaria*; Etheridge, *Butterfly Caste*; and Rose, *Plague of Corn*. The scholarship on hookworm in the South has done a thorough job of emphasizing both the impact of this parasite in the lives of poor whites and of exploring how the identification of this distinctly southern infectious disease shaped Progressive Era reform in the region. See Ettling, *Germ of Laziness*; Tullos, "Great Hookworm Crusade"; Link, "The Harvest Is Ripe"; Alan I. Marcus, "The South's Native Foreigners: Hookworm as a Factor in Southern Distinctiveness," in Savitt and Young, *Disease and Distinctiveness*; Boccaccio, "Ground Itch"; Twyman, "Clay Eater"; Cassedy, "'Germ of Laziness.'" Historians of medicine in the South have paid less attention to the conceptual

framework physicians and scientists employed in surveying and interpreting the character of the region and how this framework reflected national and international policy and thought. One recent exception is Moran, *Colonizing Leprosy*. Wray's chapter on the hookworm crusade in *Not Quite White* (96–132) makes some arguments similar to those in this chapter; however, see Ring, "Inventing the Tropical South," for an earlier articulation than Wray of the South as a diseased space and the role of class and race in understanding the Rockefeller philanthropies' efforts to eradicate hookworm in the South.

5. My idea on this metaphor of the doctor and patient representing the South and North is borrowed from Nelson Moe's work on a similar situation in Italy. See Nelson Moe, "The Emergence of the Southern Question in Villari, Franchetti, and Sonnino," in Schneider, *Italy's "Southern Question,"* 68–69.

6. For an argument suggesting the opposite — that northerners and southerners' cooperative efforts to eradicate the yellow fever epidemic in 1878 erased sectional tensions and therefore contributed to national reconciliation — see Blum, "Crucible of Disease."

7. See Fee, *Disease and Discovery*; Tomes, *Gospel of Germs*; Hoy, *Chasing Dirt*; Ettling, *Germ of Laziness*; Humphreys, *Yellow Fever*; John Farley, "Parasites and the Germ Theory of Disease," in Rosenberg and Golden, *Framing Disease*; and Michael Worboys, "The Emergence and Early Development of Parasitology," in Warren and Bowers, *Parasitology*. For an example of a conceptual shift in ideas about disease and geography in a Latin American context see Peard, *Race, Place, and Medicine*.

8. For a history of tropical medicine see Michael Worboys, "The Emergence of Tropical Medicine: A Study in the Establishment of a Scientific Specialty," in Lemain, MacLeod, Mulkay, Weingart, *Emergence of Scientific Disciplines*; Warwick Anderson, *Colonial Pathologies*; Haynes, *Imperial Medicine*; Arnold, *Warm Climates*; Packard, *Making of a Tropical Disease*; and Hewa, *Colonialism, Tropical Disease*.

9. Richard E. Brown, *Rockefeller Medicine Men*, 4–5, 8–9.

10. For studies of the Rockefeller Foundation's international public health work see Farley, *To Cast Out Disease*; Birn, *Marriage of Convenience*; Palmer, *Launching Global Health*; Cueto, *Missionaries of Science*; Brannstrom, "Polluted Soil, Polluted Souls"; Richard E. Brown, "Public Health in Imperialism"; Gadelha, "Conforming Strategies"; and Hewa, *Colonialism, Tropical Disease*.

11. For the story of how public health was redefined and professionalized in this period see Fee, *Disease and Discovery*. Medical historian Margaret Humphreys (*Yellow Fever*) argues that efforts to control yellow fever in the South in the nineteenth century contributed to the prevalence of southern and national public health agencies. I would suggest that periodic outbreaks of yellow fever might have sparked the creation of some rudimentary and poorly funded boards of public health scattered across the South that

were occasionally supported by federal assistance, but it was not until Rockefeller philanthropy entered the picture to eradicate hookworm that the systematic expansion of professional state boards of health took place across the region.

12. Allen W. Freeman, "Rural Sanitation," *Southern Medical Journal* 4 (December 1911): 869. For another example of a statement of the problem see J. Howell Way, "Rural Sanitation in the South. Two Vital Forces: The Whole-Time County Health Officer and Specialized Units of Health Work by State Boards of Health," *Southern Medical Journal* 3 (March 1916): 217–21.

13. See Leloudis, *Schooling the New South;* and Link, "Privies, Progressivism and Public Schools."

14. R. N. Whitfield, "Sanitating a Rural Home," *Southern Medical Journal* 3 (March 1916): 221–22.

15. For a history of American public health see Duffy, *Sanitarians.*

16. Tomes, *Gospel of Germs,* 2–5.

17. For a theoretical explication of how disease created social categories see Charles E. Rosenberg, "Introduction," in Rosenberg and Golden, *Framing Disease,* xvii–xix.

18. "A Bill," n.d., Rockefeller Sanitary Commission for the Eradication of Hookworm, box 5, folder 98, Rockefeller Archive Center (hereafter cited as RSC).

19. "Preliminary Draft of Text for a Story Intended for the Use of School Teachers in the Public Schools of the South to Enable Them to Tell an Interesting Story on Hookworm Disease to Children Who May Then, with the Use of Poster Stamps That Are Being Provided, Prepare a Story of Their Own," International Health Board, Record Group 5, series 2, box 22, folder 22, Rockefeller Archive Center (hereafter cited as IHB and RG).

20. "Press Article, North Carolina State Board of Health, August 5, 1914, PHILADELPHUS, North Carolina's Most Progressive Rural Community," RSC, box 9, folder 47; "Citizens Called on by Health Officer to Aid Big Clean-up Campaign," IHB, RG 5, series 2, box 4, folder 31; and "To the Public," RSC, box 12, folder 182.

21. "Citizens Called."

22. Charles Cross and George G. Hampton, "Hookworm and Health Campaign Reports from Field Directors: Preliminary Report on an Intensive Health Campaign in Lee County, Mississippi, From July, 1919 to December 31, 1919," IHB, RG 5, series 3, box 45; Charles Cason, "Recent Visits to Some Experiments and Demonstrations of the International Health Board of the Rockefeller Foundation in Malarial Control," IHB, RG 5, series 2, box 3, folder 23; and Rockefeller Foundation Pamphlet Collection, box 6, folder 86, Rockefeller Archive Center (hereafter cited as RFPC).

23. "Reports Southern States 1916," IHB, RG 5, series 3, box 5.

24. "A Picture of an 'Ulcer' that New Orleans Is Going to Have Cured by Summer

Time," *Times-Picayune*, March 29, 1920; and "Clio Dump Conditions Astound Orleanians," *Times-Picayune*, March 30, 1920, located in USDA, RG 7, SFCII, General Correspondence, box 2.

25. "Picture of an 'Ulcer.'"

26. For a history of the public health movement's focus on privy building in the South see Link, "Privies, Progressivism, and Public Schools."

27. W. H. Rowan to W. S. Leathers, February 1, 1912, RSC, box 9, folder 134.

28. Charles Wardell Stiles, "The Sanitary Privy," RSC, box 3, folder 77.

29. L. L. Lumsden, "The Privy as a Public Health Problem," *American Journal of Public Health* 10 (January 1920): 45–46.

30. Charles Wardell Stiles to U.S. Surgeon General, July 17, 1913, RSC, box 3, folder 75; Charles Wardell Stiles to Wickliffe Rose, January 12, 1914, RSC, box 3, folder 76; and Charles Wardell Stiles to Wickliffe Rose, September 8, 1914, RSC, box 3, folder 76.

31. Charles Wardell Stiles, circular letter, April 5, 1914, RSC, box 3, folder 76; and Charles Wardell Stiles, "Confidential Letter to the Most Prominent Citizens. Fight Flies, Filth, and Fever!!!," September 1914, RSC, box 3, folder 76.

32. See Marion Hamilton Carter, "The Vampire of the South," *McClure's Magazine* 33 (October 1909): 618.

33. Rockefeller Sanitary Commission for the Eradication of Hookworm Disease, *Fourth Annual Report*, fig. 3.

34. See Carter, "Vampire of the South," 617.

35. Charles Wardell Stiles, "Some Recent Investigations into the Prevalence of Hookworm Disease among Children, June/July 1910," RSC, box 3, folder 77.

36. For examples of the use of metaphors of war in describing disease see Livingston Farrand, "Tuberculosis Takes More Lives Than War. Dr. Livingston Farrand Makes Statement. Wants America Made Healthy for Democracy," July 7, 1918, IHB, RG 5, series 2, box 3, folder 20; Handbill, RFPC, box 6, folder 85; "Flies for War Use," undated newspaper article, IHB, RG 5, series 2, box 4, folder 31; and Cyrus Edson, "Defenses against Epidemic Diseases, *Forum* 9 (June 1890): 481.

37. Bledstein, *Culture of Professionalism*.

38. Rosenberg, "Disease and Social Order in America," 269. For a late nineteenth-century example of this point of view see Paul Gibier, "The Physician and the Social Question," *North American Review* 160 (April 1895): 461–69; and Henry J. Nichols, "The Influence of Tropical Medicine on General Medicine," *American Journal of Tropical Diseases and Preventive Medicine* 3 (December 1915): 314–20.

39. George E. Vincent, "Public Welfare and Public Health," IHB, RG 5, series 2, box 3, folder 20.

40. The analogy of a place or locale as a laboratory for public health work on disease

eradication was a common one. The Bureau of Science in the Philippines referred to the country as a huge laboratory and the American colonial project as a great experiment in racial hygiene. See Warwick Anderson, *Colonial Pathologies*, 3, 5–6.

41. George Thomas Palmer M.D., "The Diagnosis of the Sick City," *American Journal of Public Health* 3 (July 1913): 648.

42. "Our National Health Is Physically the Greatest National Asset. Hookworm Disease and Sanitation," *Eufaula Times and News*, April 18, 1912, RSC, box 4, folder 81.

43. John M. Swan, "Tropical Diseases and Health in the United States," *Southern Medical Journal* 4 (July 1911): 497.

44. Lewellys F. Barker, "The Wider Influence of the Physician," *Southern Medical Journal* 12 (December 1919): 719. For other examples using the analogy of the social organism see W. S. Rankin, "Diseases of the Social Organism," in McCulloch, *Call of the New South*, 141–47; Edward Alsworth Ross, "The Diseases of Social Structures," *American Journal of Sociology* 24 (September 1918): 139–58; and Cyrus Edson, "The Microbe as a Social Leveler," *North American Review* 161 (October 1895): 421–26. For a history of how the Southern Sociological Congress used the conception of the "organic society" to understand southern conditions see Chatfield, "Rationale of Uplift."

45. Barker, "Wider Influence of the Physician," 720.

46. Ibid., 723.

47. Cited in Hobson, *Tell about the South*, 108.

48. Foucault, *Birth of the Clinic*, 34–35.

49. See Borges, "'Puffy, Ugly, Slothful and Inert'"; and Bourdaghs, "Disease of Nationalism."

50. Moe, "Emergence of the Southern Question," 68–70.

51. Wright, *Old South, New South*, 3–10, 57, 60–65.

52. L. O. Howard, "Insects as Carriers and Spreaders of Disease," in *Yearbook of the United States Department of Agriculture 1901*, 177; H. H. Howard, "Annual Report of Hinds County, Antimalarial Campaign for the Period June 13, 1918 to December 31, 1919," IHB, RG 5, series 2, box 14, folder 79; and Watson S. Rankin, "Recommendation in Regard to Appropriations for Rural Health Work in North Carolina 1919," IHB, RG 5, series 2, box 17, folder 95.

53. Watson S. Rankin, "Recommendation in Regard to Appropriations," IHB, RG 5, series 2, box 17, folder 95.

54. "Public Health and Public Welfare," IHB, RG 5, series 2, box 64.

55. C. N. Leach and K. F. Maxey, "Analysis of Typhoid Morbidity in a Southern State," IHB, RG 5, series 2, box 3, folder 19.

56. For a history on the interest in rural problems at the turn of the century see

Bowers, *Country Life Movement in America;* and Lowry, *Rural Sociology.* Also see chapter 3 of this book.

57. F. W. Dershimer, "All Time Health Officer," unknown newspaper clipping, n.d., IHB, RG 5, series 2, box 4, folder 31. For another story about how Barney learns to feed his children as well as he feeds his mules see F. W. Dershimer, "Starving Children," unknown newspaper clipping, n.d., IHB, RG 5, series 2, box 4, folder 31.

58. "Undernourishment Is Misunderstood", newspaper clipping in "County Health Work, Kentucky Reports 1923," IHB, RG 5, series 3, box 31. For another example of an analogy between children and pigs and cattle see M. A. Fort, "Sangs [sic] and Sermons," Georgia State Board of Health, IHB, RG 5, series 3, box 30.

59. "The Problem of Soil Pollution," *Southern Medical Journal* 12 (January 1919): 52.

60. F. W. Dershimer, "Why They Went," unknown newspaper clipping, n.d., IHB, RG 5, series 2, box 4, folder 31.

61. "State Crop Pest Commission Year," *New Orleans Daily Picayune*, September 1, 1909, USDA, RG 7, SFCII, Newspaper Clippings, box 18. For a history of efforts to eradicate the cattle tick in the South see Strom, *Making Catfish Bait.*

62. Barker, "Wider Influence of the Physician," 723–26.

63. F. W. Dershimer, "Health County Means Bigger Price for Lands," unknown newspaper clipping, n.d., IHB, RG 5, series 2, box 4, folder 31.

64. M. W. Dinsmore to Wickliffe Rose, January 5, 1912, RSC, box 4, folder 79.

65. "Outline of Activities in the Investigation and Control of Malaria Tennessee Department of Public Health July 1, 1924–June 30, 1925," IHB, RG 5, series 2, box 18, folder 197.

66. "South Carolina Co-operative Malaria Control Work Period — August 1919 to December 31, 1922, Narrative and Statistical, 1922," IHB, RG 5, series 3, box 79.

67. J. A. LePrince, "Malaria Control — the Business Man's Problem," *Southern Medical Journal* 8 (August 1919): 471.

68. W. E. Noblin M.D., "How Does Malaria Affect Your Business?" Bulletin No. 4, Yazoo County Health Department, May 1923, IHB, RG 5, series 3, box 47. For another example of this argument made by the Yazoo County Health Department see W. E. Noblin M.D., "Malaria Mathematics," Bulletin No. 3, Yazoo County Health Department, April 1923, IHB, RG 5, series 3, box 47.

69. W. G. Stromquist, "Malaria Control from the Engineering Point of View," *American Journal of Public Health* 10 (June 1920): 497, 500–501.

70. Editorial, "The Cost of Bad Health," *Southern Medical Journal* 7 (June 1914): 507–8.

71. Sidney Porter to Dr. Jas C. Burdette, December 9, 1910, RSC, box 6, folder 121.

72. Handbill, RSC, box 7, folder 125.

73. R. N. Whitfield to W. S. Leathers, September, 19, 1914, RSC, box 8, folder 137; W. S. Leathers to Wickliffe Rose, January 19, 1912, RSC, box 8, folder 133; and "Changes in a Small Town Brought about by the Health Department," IHB, RG 5, series 2, box 1, folder 2.

74. "These Pictures Show What Relief from Hookworm Disease Meant to One Family," *Huntsville Weekly Mercury*, December 4, 1912, RSC, box 4, folder 81.

75. Charles Cason, "Recent Visits to Some Experiments and Demonstrations of the International Health Board of the Rockefeller Foundation in Malaria Control," IHB, RG 5, series 2, box 3, folder 23.

76. Louis I. Dublin, "The Economics of World Health," *Harpers Monthly Magazine* 153 (November 1926): 734.

77. Samuel C. Mitchell, "The Challenge of the South for a Better Nation," in McCulloch, *South Mobilizing for Social Service*, 51.

78. Stromquist, "Malaria Control," 497.

79. Ferrell, "Hookworm Disease," 188–89.

80. J. N. McCormack to Wickliffe Rose, January 15, 1913, RSC, box 6, folder 115.

81. Charles Wardell Stiles to Wickliffe Rose, September 2, 1912, RSC, box 3, folder 74.

82. Handbill, IHB, RG 5, series 2, box 3, folder 21.

83. D. B. Stevenson to Dr. Thompson, August 10, 1914, RSC, box 8, folder 137.

84. See Bederman, *Manliness*, 170–216.

85. J. F. Siler to Surgeon General of the U. S. Army, December 7, 1908, IHB, RG 5, series 2, box 3, folder 20.

86. "Report of the Hookworm Infection Survey in the U.S. Army, Southern Department," IHB, RG 5, series 2, box 3, folder 18; H. H. Howard, "Memorandum: The Examination and Treatment of Hookworm Disease of Southern Bred Recruits to the United States Army," IHB, RG 5, series 2, box 3, folder 19; and Watson S. Rankin, "Recommendation in Regard to Appropriations," IHB, RG 5, series 2, box 17, folder 95.

87. "Enlist, Your Country Needs You!," IHB, RG 5, box 6, folder 82.

88. Professor Irving Fisher to Walter Hines Page, December 24, 1908, Letters of Walter Hines Page, box 9, MS Am 1090(368), Houghton Library, Harvard University.

89. For an excellent history of the rise of tropical medicine as a special discipline see Worboys, "Emergence of Tropical Medicine."

90. See David Arnold, "Introduction," in Arnold, *Warm Climates and Western Medicine*, 5–10. For an example on how "medico-topographical surveys" conducted by British colonizers helped invent tropicality in nineteenth-century India see Arnold, *Colonizing the Body*.

91. Foucault, *Birth of the Clinic*, 24.

92. See Curtin, *Death by Migration*.

93. David N. Livingstone, "Human Acclimatization," 360.

94. See Warwick Anderson, *Colonial Pathologies*. For a history of the relationship between medicine and the military in India see Arnold, *Colonizing the Body*.

95. Ernst C. Meyer, "Creating Social Values in the Tropics," *American Journal of Sociology* 21 (March 1916): 665.

96. Earl Baldwin McKinley, *Geography of Disease*, xxiii.

97. Arnold, "'Illusory Riches,'" 7. For other examples addressing this duality see Arnold, "Inventing Tropicality"; Frenkel, "Jungle Stories"; and Stephan, "Tropical Nature."

98. Crowther, *Romance and Rise*, v.

99. See David N. Livingstone, "Race, Space and Moral Climatology."

100. For an example of how a tropical region was conceptualized as the Other see Frenkel, "Geographical Representations of the 'Other.'"

101. Carl F. Westerberg, "Revolt in the Tropics," *North American Review* 231 (January 1931): 257–63. Indeed, Westerberg included the U.S. South in his sightline as he explained, "The great common characteristic of all tropical countries is poverty, of the type which exists among our Southern mountaineers [southern poor whites]" (257).

102. See Kupperman, "Fear of Hot Climes"; and David N. Livingstone, "Human Acclimatization."

103. Mackie, *From Cape Cod to Dixie*, 153, 169. For an analysis of the significance of the image of the swamp in nineteenth-century America see David C. Miller, *Dark Eden*.

104. See Silber, *Romance of Reunion*, 66–92.

105. See Dunn, "Florida"; and Tarr, "Eden Revisited."

106. McIntyre, "Promoting the Gothic South," 33.

107. Swan, "Tropical Diseases and Health in the United States," 499–500. Swan also said the immigrant was as much a problem as the "home-coming" citizen.

108. Editorial, "The American Society of Tropical Medicine," *Southern Medical Journal* 4 (February 1911): 175–76. For a history of how anxiety about yellow fever entering the southern states through Cuba contributed to declaring war on Spain in 1898 see Espinosa, "Threat from Havana."

109. Editorial, *American Journal of Tropical Diseases and Preventive Medicine* 1 (July 1913): 1. For an early reference also see Editorial, "The Existence of Tropical Diseases in the South," *Southern Medical Journal* 1 (October 1908): 269.

110. R. A. Henry, "The White Man and the Tropics," IHB, RG 5, series 2, box 64.

111. On the relationship between exhibitions and empire see Rydell, *All the World's a Fair;* and Kramer, "Making Concessions." For a history of medical and public health exhibits at international expositions see Julie K. Brown, *Health and Medicine on Display*.

112. International Health Commission, Rockefeller Foundation, "Countries by Groups, in Which Hookworm Infection Has Been Demonstrated," RFPC, box 4, 58.

113. Walter H. Page, "The Hookworm in Civilization," *World's Work* 24 (September 1912): 504.

114. Huntington, *Civilization and Climate*, 24, 35.

115. Warwick Anderson, *Colonial Pathologies*, 104–29.

116. "Intensive Community Work for the Relief and Control of Hookworm Disease in the Southern States," IHB, RG 5, series 2, box 3, folder 20.

117. Palmer, *Launching Global Health*, 22–54.

118. See David N. Livingstone, "Human Acclimatization"; and Kennedy, "Perils of the Midday Sun."

119. Warwick Anderson, "Immunities of Empire," 94–100, 104–105.

120. Truxtun Beale, "The White Race and the Tropics," *Forum* 27 (July 1899): 534–36.

121. For more specific attention to the role race played in colonial medicine see Warwick Anderson, "Immunities of Empire," 94–118.

122. Dr. Charles T. Nesbitt, "The Health Menace of Alien Races," *World's Work* 27 (November 1913): 74.

123. Hunter, *To 'Joy My Freedom*, 202–3.

124. L. C. Allen, "The Negro Health Problem," *American Journal of Public Health* 5 (March 1915): 194–96. Also see A. G. Fort, "The Negro Health Problem in Rural Communities," *American Journal of Public Health* 5 (March 1915): 191–93; Editorial, "The Negro Menace to Public Health," *Southern Medical Journal* 9 (May 1916): 468–70; Marvin L. Graves, "Tropical Diseases and Public Health: The Negro a Menace to the Health of the White Race," *Southern Medical Journal* 9 (May 1916): 407–13; and C. E. Terry, "The Negro, A Public Health Problem," *Southern Medical Journal* 7 (June 1914): 458–67. For a different perspective from W. E. B. Du Bois see Du Bois, *Health and Physique*. For a discussion of white employers' fears that black servants carried tuberculosis into white homes see Hunter, *To 'Joy My Freedom*, 187–218. Also see Roberts, *Infectious Fear* for a broader history of tuberculosis and African Americans during Jim Crow.

125. Surgeon L. D. Fricks, "Malaria Control in the United States — Retrospect and Prospect, N.M.C. Meeting, November 12–13, 1923," IHB, RG 5, series 2, box 1, folder 4.

126. "To Fight Hookworm: Dr. Crook Sounds First Note of State Campaign: Tennessee First to Move," *Jackson Whig*, January 23, 1910, RSC, box 1, folder 20; Retired U.S. Navy Surgeon W. F. Arnold, "Hookworm Disease in the South," 1906, RSC, box 1, folder 11; American Press Association, "Hookworm: The Greatest Menace to the American Family," RSC, box 1, folder 6; Dr. H. H. Howard, "Winston County Mississippi. THE NEGRO VS. HOOK WORM DISEASE," RSC, box 8, folder 134; John Wilkerson to C. W.

Stiles, August 8, 1910, RSC, box 4, folder 78; Editorial, "The Hookworm Disease in the South," *Southern Medical Journal* 2 (October 1909): 1049; and Nesbitt, "Health Menace of Alien Races," 74.

127. Carter, "Vampire of the South," 631.

128. Huntington, *Civilization and Climate*, 42–43.

129. Carter, "Vampire of the South," 617.

130. Wickliffe Rose to Frederick T. Gates, June 28, 1911, IHB, RG 5, series 2, box 19, folder 113.

131. J. N. McCormack to Wickliffe Rose, September 22, 1913, RSC, box 6, folder 117. For other references to poor white "aborigines" in the South see "Narrative Report for Work in Harlan County, Kentucky, Quarter Ending 9/30/20," in "County Health Work and Hookworm Disease. Kentucky Reports, 1918–1920," IHB, RG 5, series 3, box 31; and Mitchell and Mitchell, *Industrial Revolution in the South*, 274.

132. See Chamberlin and Gilman, *Degeneration*; Pick, *Faces of Degeneration*; Kershner, "Degeneration"; and Borges, "'Puffy, Ugly, Slothful and Inert.'"

133. DuBow, *Scientific Racism*, 180.

134. Nancy Stepan, "Biological Degeneration: Races and Proper Places," in Chamberlin and Gilman, *Degeneration*, 97–120. Also see Gilman, "Degeneracy and Race in the Nineteenth Century." In the Brazilian context race mixing was believed to have an elevating or "whitening" effect on the national race. See Borges, "'Puffy, Ugly, Slothful and Inert,'" 237; and Skidmore, *Black into White*."

135. For a history of the development of Lamarckian ideas over the course of the nineteenth century see Bowler, *Eclipse of Darwinism*.

136. For a history of the development of a white national identity see Saxton, *Rise and Fall*; and Hale, *Making Whiteness*.

137. Editorial, "Hookworm Disease: A World Disease of Long Duration," *American Journal of Tropical Diseases and Preventive Medicine* 1 (April 1914): 671.

138. Warshaw, *Malaria*, ix.

139. On malaria as the South's biggest problem see Stromquist, "Malaria Control," 497. On malaria as a national health problem see "Malaria as a Public Health Problem," *American Journal of Public Health* 6 (December 1916): 1297.

140. "Abbeville. Invasion of Mosquitoes Is Worst Ever Known," *Louisiana Times-Democrat*, July 10, 1910, USDA, RG 7, SFCII, Newspaper Clippings, box 18.

141. "Southern Bishop Warns People to Shun Northerner: Says Teach New Tricks to Southern "Barbarians," unidentified newspaper article, General Education Board Records, series 1.2, box 262, folder 2711, Rockefeller Archive Center (hereafter cited as GEB).

142. Wickliffe Rose to Olin West, June 27, 1910, RSC, box 11, folder 171.

143. In 2007 economist Hoyt Bleakley used differential analysis, among other strategies, to assess the effectiveness of the Rockefeller Sanitary Commission's efforts in the South and came to the conclusion it was very successful. Bleakley determined that 40% of southern children were infected with hookworm prior to treatment. These school-aged children had a 20% "lower probability" of attending school and if infected throughout their childhood they could expect to make 40% less in adult wages. See Bleakley, "Disease and Development," 75–77.

CHAPTER 3. *The White Plague of Cotton*

1. Headings are Johnson, *Collapse of Cotton Tenancy*, 1; and Murchison, *King Cotton*, 2. G. L. Fossick, "Ailing King Cotton," *Independent* 117 (November 20, 1926): 580.

2. Historians writing on the history of agriculture or industry in the New South usually find that they cannot avoid the question of southern economic distinctiveness. Discussions tend to revolve around the degree to which the South industrialized in the postbellum period, the persistence of the planter class in positions of economic and social authority, and whether or not an agrarian or commercial ethos dominated the region. For examples see Woodward, *Origins*; Wiener, *Social Origins*; Ransom and Sutch, *One Kind of Freedom*; Wright, *Old South, New South*; Woodman, *New South, New Law*; Hahn, *Roots of Southern Populism*; and Carlton, *Mill and Town*. For a discussion of these questions with regard to the nature of the antebellum southern economy see Wright, *Political Economy*; Genovese, *Political Economy of Slavery*; and Woodman, *Slavery and the Southern Economy*. For a history of the influence of cotton mills on the southern economy, including the social impact of the migration of poor whites from the countryside to more industrial areas and class conflict between mill workers and mill owners, see Hall, *Like a Family*; Flamming, *Creating the Modern South*; Simon, *Fabric of Defeat*; Carlton, *Mill and Town*; and Tullos, *Habits of Industry*.

3. Henry S. Reed, "Financing the Cotton Crop," *Annals of the American Academy of Political and Social Science* 35 (January 1910): 19–20.

4. See Woodward, *Origins*, 291–320; and Wright, *Old South, New South*.

5. Vance, *Human Factors in Cotton Culture*, vii.

6. Burkett and Poe, *Cotton*, 53.

7. Ibid., 55.

8. Wilcox, "Great White Way," 78.

9. Murchison, *King Cotton*, 48.

10. Hale, *Making Whiteness*, 146, 155–60.

11. T. S. Miller, *American Cotton System*, 1.

12. Harvie Jordan, "Cotton in Southern Agricultural Economy," *Annals of the Academy of Political and Social Science* 35 (January 1910): 4.

13. "Why the Deadly Boll Weevil, Bringing Revolution with Him, Is Called the 'Prosperity Bug,'" *New York Times*, January 9, 1910, USDA, RG 7, SFCII, Newspaper Clippings, box 18.

14. *Prospectus of the Cotton States*.

15. *Official Guide*, 23–24.

16. "Report of the Representative of the Department of Interior," USDA, RG 33, Records of the Extension Service, Records Concerning the Tennessee Centennial Exposition, Nashville, 1897, box 1, folder "Department of Interior, n.d.," National Archives, Washington, D.C.

17. Perdue, *Race and the Atlanta Cotton States Exposition*, 99.

18. Clarence H. Poe, "The Rich Kingdom of Cotton, *World's Work* 9 (November 1904): 5488.

19. Scherer, *Cotton*, 3–4.

20. Beckert, "Emancipation and Empire, 1405–6.

21. J. L. Watkins, "The Future Demand for American Cotton," in *Yearbook of the Department of Agriculture, 1901*, 203.

22. Watkins, *King Cotton*, 10.

23. Pepperell Manufacturing Company, *Cotton: From Plant to Product* (Boston: Pepperell Manufacturing Company, n.d.), 9, in Warshaw Collection, box 1, Cotton, folder 18, Smithsonian Institution, Washington, D.C.

24. Bederman, *Manliness and Civilization*.

25. Turpin, *Cotton*, 3, 5.

26. Scherer, *Cotton*, 358, 383.

27. Bryce, *Relationship*, 8.

28. For a discussion of the imperial fascination with eastern markets as a solution to American "overproduction" and the Open Door Policy see LaFeber, *New Empire*; William Appleman Williams, *Tragedy of American Diplomacy*; and Jacobson, *Barbarian Virtues*, 15–38.

29. "Cotton Still King Despite Drawbacks," *Daily Picayune*, September 1, 1909, USDA, RG 7, SFCII, Newspaper Clippings, box 18.

30. For a specific example of the argument that the southern states needed to secure eastern markets for their monopoly on cotton see John Lowndes M'Lauring, "The Commercial Democracy of the South," *North American Review* 173 (November 1901): 658.

31. See Scherer, *Cotton*, 4; Burkett and Poe, *Cotton*, 13; and Turpin, *Cotton*, 36.

32. Mercier and Savely, *Knapp Method*, 97. For other references to cotton as a tropical

plant see T. S. Miller, *American Cotton System*, 2; Collings, *Production of Cotton*, 2–4; and Brooks, *Story of Cotton*, 22.

33. Edward Atkinson, "The Future Situs of the Cotton Manufacture of the United States," *Popular Science Monthly* 36 (January 1890): 289–319.

34. See Poe, *Where Half the World*, viii, 15–16, 18, 25–26, 185, 261–62, 265–68, 270–73. During his life, Poe also visited Denmark, England, and Ireland looking for ways to improve southern agricultural practices. In his memoirs Poe attributes the phrase "comparative view of the world" to his friend Dr. Timothy Richards who argued it was the key to China's great success. Poe, *My First Eighty Years*, 186–87.

35. Cited in "Science and Invention: Possibilities of Tropical Agriculture," *Literary Digest* 21 (August 18, 1900): 193.

36. Wilcox, *Tropical Agriculture*. Wilcox held many posts at the USDA over the years. He based some of this work on his experience as head of the Hawaii Agricultural Experiment Station and the visits he made to Florida, California, and Cuba.

37. O. F. Cook, "Agriculture in the Tropical Islands of the United States," in *Yearbook of the Department of Agriculture 1901*, 348–68.

38. "Partial Programme of Southern Commercial Congress at the Williard, Washington D.C., Dec. 6th and 7th, 1909," Letters of Walter Hines Page, box 7, MS Am 1090 (1265), Houghton Library, Harvard University.

39. Brooks, *Story of Cotton*, 210.

40. Crawford, *Heritage of Cotton*, v.

41. For a history of the celebration of the "agrarian myth" see Hofstader, *Age of Reform*, 23–59.

42. Otken, *Ills of the South*, 10–11.

43. D. D. Wallace, "Southern Agriculture: Its Condition and Needs," *Popular Science Monthly* 64 (January 1904): 260, 248–49.

44. U.S. Congress, *Report*, iii–iv, v–viii, xxi, 294, 298, 366, 397.

45. For a history of the decline of cotton factorage see Woodman, *King Cotton*, 268–94.

46. For a detailed explanation of the workings of the cotton exchange and the futures market see Boyle, *Cotton;* and "Arthur R. Marsh, "Cotton Exchanges and Their Economic Functions," *Annals of the American Academy of Political and Social Science* 38 (September 1911): 571–98.

47. U.S. Congress, *Report*, viii.

48. Ibid., xi.

49. Crawford, *Heritage of Cotton*, 217.

50. U.S. Congress, *Report*, 4.

51. Ibid., 56, 64.

52. For statistics and analysis on the increase in cotton production and demand during this period see Wright, *Old South, New South*, 55–56, 121–23.

53. For a history of the impact of the boll weevil on "cotton culture" in the South see Helms, "Just Lookin' for a Home"; and Daniel, *Breaking the Land*, 3–22.

54. E. S. Peters to Walter D. Hunter, August 1, 1905, USDA, RG 7, SFCII, General Correspondence, box 2.

55. Helms, "Just Lookin' for a Home," 32, 45–46, 49.

56. Colonel Hiram Hawkins, "The Boll Weevil," *Baton Rouge Louisiana Times*, February 29, 1909, USDA, RG 7, SFCII, Newspaper Clippings, box 16.

57. "The Boll Weevil," *Kansas City Journal*, June 11, 1904, USDA, RG 7, SFCII, Newspaper Clippings, box 5; "The Boll Weevil," *New Orleans Democrat*, February 3, 1906, USDA, RG 7, SFCII, Newspaper Clippings, box 10; "Says Weevil Yarn Is Fake," *New York Tribune*, February 13, 1911, USDA, RG 7, SFCII, Newspaper Clippings, box 17.

58. "Great Alarm Felt on Account of Weevil," *Columbia South Carolina State*, November 14, 1904, USDA, RG 7, SFCII, Newspaper Clippings, box 6.

59. "National Boll Weevil Menace Convention, Endorsements from Men of Affairs," USDA, RG 7, SFCII, General Correspondence, box 1.

60. For an excellent history of the use of these metaphors in the fields of agricultural and medical entomology see Russell, "War on Insects." Russell's subsequent book focuses on a more narrow time period beginning with World War I. See Russell, *War and Nature*.

61. Richard Bruce, "Notes on Some Insect and Other Migrations Observed in Equatorial America," Warshaw Collection, box 1, Insecticides, folder "Reldeid, RB."

62. "Hammond's Slug Shot," Warshaw Collection, box 1, Insecticides, folder "Hammond."

63. "Fight on Weevil," *Huntsville Mercury*, December 18, 1904, USDA, RG 7, SFCII, Newspaper Clippings, box 10. For other examples of the use of military metaphors in the war on the boll weevil and other pests see E. L. D. Seymour, "The War on Agricultural Pests," *World's Work* 28 (May 1914): 93–98; and Terrific Warfare of Real Lilliputians," *Kansas City Post*, April 18, 1909, USDA, RG 7, SFCII, Newspaper Clippings, box 16.

64. "Will the Boll Weevil Control the Mississippi?" *Louisiana Dispatch*, October 21, 1906, USDA, RG 7, SFCII, Newspaper Clippings, box 11. For an example framing the arrival of the boll weevil as a foreign invader that the "Caucasian" race must engage in warfare against see "Louisiana Cotton Planters," *Shreveport Times*, November 4, 1904, USDA, RG 7, SFCII, Newspaper Clippings, box 6. While entomologists, farm demonstration agents, and newspaper writers frequently alluded to the fact that the boll weevil had entered the United States from Mexico, surprisingly few accounts racialized their

descriptions of the situation. This is striking given the fact that Mexican immigration peaked during 1890–1920 and generated extreme levels of xenophobia and fervent nativist debates in the United States. For a history of nativist reaction to Mexican immigration in this period see Gutiérrez, *Walls and Mirrors*, 39–68. I did find isolated references to the "'greaser' weevil," the "Mexican invader," and the "Mexican marauder." See "Boll Weevil Ravages in Cotton," *New York Mail and Express* May 21, 1904, USDA, RG 7, SFCII, Newspaper Clippings, box 6; "The Boll Weevil and the Negro," *Chicago Post*, February 17, 1911, USDA, RG 7, SFCII, Newspaper Clippings, box 18; and "Shreveport Boll Weevil Convention," *Shreveport Times*, November 29, 1904, USDA, RG 7, SFCII, Newspaper Clippings, box 10. Also one newspaper in Houston, Texas, described the boll weevil as a "distinctly Mexican product and a very undesirable immigrant to the United States." See "To Kill the Boll Weevil," *Houston Post*, April 16, 1901, USDA, RG 7, SFCII, Newspaper Clippings, box 1. Walter D. Hunter of the Bureau of Entomology solely blamed Mexico for the weevil's persistence because he argued that Mexicans were "more liable to resort to prayer than science to eliminate their pests." See "Boll Weevil History," *New Orleans Democrat*, October 20, 1906, USDA, RG 7, SFCII, Newspaper Clippings, box 11. Scientists from the USDA did travel to Mexico and established communication with the Mexican government regarding the boll weevil. See T. E. Holloway to Walter D. Hunter, August 13, 1912, USDA, RG 7, SFCII, Newspaper Clippings, box 14.

65. For examples see "Shortage in Rice Crop a Worm Caused Damage," *Austin Tribune*, October 6, 1904, USDA, RG 7, SFCII, Newspapers Clippings, box 2; untitled, *Jacksonville Times-Union*, December 1, 1910, USDA, RG 7, SFCII, Newspapers Clippings, box 17; "Plan to Exterminate Boll Weevil in Texas," *Houston Chronicle*, March 11, 1910, USDA, RG 7, SFCII, Newspaper Clippings, box 18; "The Boll Weevil Parasite," *Mobile Register*, December 20, 1909, USDA, RG 7, SFCII, Newspaper Clippings, box 18; "Boll Weevil Threatens America's Entire Cotton Industry," *New York Herald*, June 21, 1903, USDA, RG 7, SFCII, Newspaper Clippings, box 1; "The Boll Weevil, *Knoxville Sentinel*, July 13, 1909, USDA, RG 7, SFCII, Newspaper Clippings, box 17; "The Mexican Boll Weevil," *New Orleans Trade Index*, n.d., August 1903, USDA, RG 7, SFCII, Newspaper Clippings, box 1; "Important Papers at Weevil Meeting," *San Antonio Light*, December 13, 1904, USDA, RG 7, SFCII, Newspaper Clippings, box 6; "Editorial," *Northern Bedford Massachusetts Mercury*, May 20, 1904, USDA, RG 7, SFCII, Newspaper Clippings, box 6; "The Shreveport Boll Weevil Convention," *Shreveport Times*, November 29, 1904, USDA, RG 7, SFCII, Newspaper Clippings, box 10; and "The Cotton Lands of Texas, unnamed newspaper, n.d., USDA, RG 7, SFCII, Newspaper Clippings, box 6.

66. *Biddeford Maine Journal*, February 15, 1911, USDA, RG 7, SFCII, Newspaper Clippings, box 18.

67. See Fred Reinlein, "Review of the Work Incident to Solving the Boll Weevil Problem," Pamphlet, USDA, RG 7, SFCII, General Correspondence, box 11.

68. "To Inoculate the Boll Weevil," *Austin Statesman*, October 7, 1904, USDA, RG 7, SFCII, Newspaper Clippings, box 5; "Trying Bacteria Cultures for Leguminous Plants," *New Orleans Picayune*, October 3, 1904, USDA, RG 7, SFCII, Newspaper Clippings, box 5; "Inoculate Cotton," *Dallas News*, September 10, 1904, USDA, RG 7, SFCII, Newspaper Clippings; "Three Thousand Weevil Will be Turned Loose," *Waco Texas Herald*, July 14, 1904, USDA, RG 7, SFCII, Newspaper Clippings, box 5; and "Azotogen Bacteria-inoculation-matter for Leguminous Plants," Warshaw Collection, box 4, Fertilizers, folder "General Works."

69. "Killing of Johnson Grass," *Galveston News*, July 2, 1904, USDA, RG 7, SFCII, Newspaper Clippings, box 5.

70. "Boll Weevil Battle," *New Orleans Picayune*, May 27, 1904, USDA, RG 7, SFCII, Newspaper Clippings, box 5; "Weevil Spread," *Austin Texas Post*, August 13, 1904, USDA, RG 7, SFCII, Newspaper Clippings, box 5. For examples of the Bureau of Plant Industry's interest in setting up quarantines to protect California see "Cotton Boll Weevil," *Los Angeles Times*, September 13, 1908, RG 7, SFCII, Newspaper Clippings, box 14; and Walter D. Hunter to L. O. Hunter, May 29, 1912, USDA, RG 7, SFCII, General Correspondence, box 11.

71. Mercier and Savely, *Knapp Method*, 97.

72. "Louisiana's Campaign against the Boll Weevil," *New York Journal of Commerce*, May 19, 1904, USDA, RG 7, SFCII, Newspaper Clippings, box 6; and "Weevil Spread," *Houston Post*, August 13, 1904, USDA, RG 7, SFCII, Newspaper Clippings, box 5.

73. "Health and Crop Problems," *Petersburg Appeal*, May 25, 1904, USDA, RG 7, SFCII, Newspaper Clippings, box 6.

74. "Precautions to Prevent Advent of Boll Weevil in the State of Mississippi," *Vicksburg Post*, August 20, 1904, USDA, RG 7, SFCII, Newspaper Clippings, box 5. Leland Howard was once asked whether the boll weevil could be transported in clothing and he agreed it certainly was a possibility. See "Cannot Be Exterminated," *Boston Transcript*, April 13, 1904, USDA, RG 7, SFCII, Newspaper Clippings, box 5.

75. "Weevils Causing an Exodus," *Charleston News*, December 28, 1908, USDA, RG 7, SFCII, Newspaper Clippings, box 18.

76. "Fleeing before the Boll Weevil," *New Orleans Democrat*, n.d., USDA, RG 7, SFCII, Newspaper Clippings, box 16.

77. "The Boll Weevil and the Negro," *Chicago Post*, February 17, 1911, USDA, RG 7, SFCII, Newspaper Clippings, box 18.

78. "Negro and the Boll Weevil," *Galveston News*, October 10, 1904, USDA, RG 7, SFCII, Newspaper Clippings, box 5.

79. See "New Era in Cotton States," *Charleston Courier*, January 18, 1909, USDA, RG 7, SFCII, Newspaper Clippings, box 15.

80. "Weevils Cause an Exodus," *New York City Sun*, December 27, 1908, USDA, RG 7, SFCII, Newspaper Clippings, box 16; and "New Era in Cotton States," *Charleston Courier*, January 18, 1909, USDA, RG 7, SFCII, Newspaper Clippings, box 15.

81. "Boll Weevil 'Panic' in Louisiana and Mississippi," *Dallas Morning News*, December 25, 1908, USDA, RG 7, SFCII, Newspaper Clippings, box 16.

82. "Boll Weevil on the Y. & M. V.," *Natchez Democrat*, January 3, 1911, USDA, RG 7, SFCII, Newspaper Clippings, box 18.

83. For a history of the development of rural sociology see Nelson, *Rural Sociology*. For a study of cotton farmers' participation in the agrarian reform movement, see Herbin, "Healing the Land."

84. Hugh MacRae, "Vitalizing the Nation and Conserving Human Units through the Development of Agricultural Communities," *Annals of the Academy of Political and Social Science* 63 (January 1916): 278, 280, 284–85. For another example of how the farm or countryside was viewed as a "practical laboratory" see Edwin Mims, "The South Realizing Itself, Second Article, Redeemers of the Soil," *World's Work* 23 (November 1911): 48–49.

85. Butterfield, *Chapters*, 15.

86. For a history of the country life movement see Bowers, *Country Life Movement*.

87. U.S. Senate, *Report*, 4, 6, 8–9.

88. Martin, *Demonstration Work*, 24; and Wallace Buttrick, "Seaman A. Knapp's Work as an Agricultural Statesman," *American Monthly Review of Reviews* 43 (June 1911): 685.

89. Martin, *Demonstration Work*, 8.

90. Knapp, *Recent Foreign Explorations*.

91. Martin, *Demonstration Work*, 8.

92. Ibid., 8.

93. Ibid., 27–28.

94. O. B. Martin, "A Great Agricultural Statesman," GEB, series 1.2, box 209, folder 2012.

95. Seaman A. Knapp, "Farmer's Co-operative Demonstration Work and its Results," in Southern Education Board, *Proceedings of the Ninth Conference*, 114.

96. Lecture Delivered Before State Teacher's Association of South Carolina at Chick Springs, Seaman Asahel Knapp Papers, box 2, folder 10, Southwest Collection/Special Collections, Texas Tech University.

97. For references to cotton as the "lazy man's crop" see "How to Destroy the Boll Weevil," *Atoha Oklahoma Citizen*, November 28, 1907, USDA, RG 7, SFCII, Newspaper

Clippings, box 14; and U.S. Congress, *Report,* 286. Also see untitled, *Shreveport Journal,* November 5, 1904, USDA, RG 7, SFCII, Newspaper Clippings, box 6.

98. W. D. Bentley to Seaman A. Knapp, July 14, 1906, USDA, RG 33, Records of the Extension Service, Letters Received by Seaman A. Knapp from County Demonstration Agents, box 2; W. M. Bamberge to Seaman A. Knapp, May 27, 1906, USDA, RG 33, Records of the Extension Service, Letters Received by Seaman A. Knapp from County Demonstration Agents, box 1; and O. F. Cook, "Cotton Improvement on a Community Basis," in *Yearbook of the Department of Agriculture 1911,* 408.

99. "Heading Off the Weevil," *Atlanta Journal,* January 3, 1907, USDA, RG 7, SFCII, Newspaper Clippings, box 13.

100. Martin, *Demonstration Work,* 252.

101. "Memorial Exercises in Honor of Dr. S. A. Knapp," *Washington Herald,* March 23, 1922, Seaman Asahel Knapp Papers, box 2, folder 16.

102. Seaman A. Knapp, "The Farmers' Cooperative Demonstration Work," in *Yearbook of the Department of Agriculture 1909,* 160.

103. Seaman A. Knapp, "Back to the Farm," Manuscript, Seaman Asahel Knapp Papers, box 2, folder 8.

104. See Susanna Delfino, "The Idea of Southern Economic Backwardness: A Comparative View of the United States and Italy," in Delfino and Gillespie, *Global Perspectives,* 107–8.

105. Seaman A. Knapp, "Causes of Southern Rural Conditions and the Small Farm as an Important Remedy," in *Yearbook of the Department of Agriculture 1908,* 313.

106. "Doctrine of Diversification," *Jackson Mississippi Evening News,* December 16, 1908, USDA, RG 7, SFCII, Newspaper Clippings, box 15.

107. Reinlein, "Review of the Work Incident."

108. John Lee Coulter, "The Cooperative Farmer," *World's Work* 23 (November 1911): 63.

109. Seaman A. Knapp to Editor of the *World's Work,* Seaman Asahel Knapp Papers, box 2, folder 14.

110. Knapp, "Causes of Southern Rural Conditions," 316.

111. Knapp, "Back to the Farm."

112. For a concurrent argument made while I was in the early stages of my project see John M. Heffron, "Nation-Building for a Venerable South: Moral and Practical Uplift in the New Agricultural Education, 1900–1920," in Urban, *Essays.*

113. Everett W. Smith, "Raising a Crop of Men," *Outlook* 89 (July 18, 1908): 608, 603.

114. Martin, *Demonstration Work,* 24, 36. Also see Seaman A. Knapp, "An Agricultural Revolution," *World's Work* 12 (July 1906): 7734; and Knapp, "Causes of Southern Rural Conditions," 319.

115. Knapp, "An Agricultural Revolution," 7736.

116. Coulter, "Cooperative Farmer," 61. For a discussion on Seaman A. Knapp's philosophy of "demonstration work as business help" see Bradford K. Knapp, "Some Results of the Farmers' Cooperative Demonstration Work," in *Yearbook of the Department of Agriculture 1911*, 295–96.

117. U.S. National Emergency Council, *Report on Economic Conditions*, 1, 8.

CHAPTER 4. *The Poor White Problem as the "New Race Question"*

1. Headings are Robert C. Ogden to W. H. Baldwin Jr., February 26, 1904, Robert Curtis Ogden Papers, "Special Correspondence," box 13, Manuscripts Division, Library of Congress, Washington, D.C.; and Alfred E. Seddon to A. J. McKelway, November 29, 1907, National Child Labor Committee Records, box 3, folder, "Mississippi Cotton Mills, 1908," Manuscripts Division, Library of Congress.

See S. A. Hamilton, "The New Race Question in the South," *Arena* 27 (April 1902): 352–53.

2. Albert Bushnell Hart, *Southern South*, 68–69.

3. Southern whites in the Appalachian mountains were often praised for their Anglo-Saxon purity and genuine American traits. For example, Nina Silber argues that at the turn of the century, northerners "had begun to minimize the strangeness of the mountain region" as part of the process of sectional reconciliation and the commemoration of a white national identity. See Nina Silber, "'What Does America Need So Much as Americans?': Race and Northern Reconciliation with Southern Appalachia, 1870–1900," in Inscoe, *Appalachians and Race*, 245. However, other scholars have argued that the destitution and presumed backwardness of Appalachia whites continued to draw attention well into the twentieth century. See Billings, Norman, and Ledford, *Confronting Appalachian Stereotypes*.

4. Mitchell, *Rise of Cotton Mills*, 162.

5. Hendrick, *Training of an American*, 393.

6. William Garrott Brown, *Lower South*, 251, 267.

7. Andrew Sledd, "Illiteracy in the South," *Independent* 53 (October 17, 1901): 2473–74. Andrew Sledd is perhaps best known for his article "The Negro Another View," *Atlantic Monthly* 90 (July 1902): 65–73, which provoked a very public and vitriolic backlash from white southerners who resented his critique of lynching and his assertion that the "inferiority" of the black race did not warrant such "dehumanizing" treatment of African Americans. Sledd was ultimately forced to resign by the trustees of Emory and became the president of the University of Florida in 1904. For an excellent summary of this controversy see Warnock, "Andrew Sledd."

8. Albert Bushnell Hart, *Southern South*, 42, 64–65.

9. Ibid., 68.

10. Hamilton, "New Race Question," 352–53, 357–58.

11. Foley, *White Scourge*, 7–8, 38–39, 73–74, 86. For histories of the eugenics movement in the South see Larson, *Sex, Race, and Science*; and Dorr, *Segregation's Science*. For a history of the development of the American idea of "white trash" from the colonial period through the 1920s see Wray, *Not Quite White*.

12. See Rafter, *White Trash*.

13. See Duck, *Nation's Region*.

14. Frank Tannenbaum, "The Single Crop: Its Social Consequence in the South," *Century Magazine* 106 (October 1923): 816. Playing with the same metaphor, Neil Foley argues in his work on Texas that the development of a tenant class of "white trash" proved to be as much of a "white scourge" to the South as the cotton crop itself. See Foley, *White Scourge*, 5–8, 64–91.

15. L. J. Abbott, "King Cotton," *Independent* 72 (March 7, 1912): 510.

16. Vance, *Human Factors*, 309–10.

17. George S. Schuyler to H. L. Mencken, January 12, 1937, Correspondence of H. L. Mencken, box 100, New York Public Library microfilm, Enoch Pratt Free Library.

18. George S. Schuyler, "Our White Folks," *American Mercury* 12 (December 1927): 385–92.

19. H. L. Mencken to George Schuyler, January 5, 1937, Correspondence of H. L. Mencken, box 100.

20. Tannenbaum, "Single Crop," 817, 821–22, 824–25.

21. Johnson, Embree, and Alexander, *Collapse*, 14.

22. Vance, *Human Factors*, 217.

23. H. L. Mencken to George Schuyler, January 23, 1937, Correspondence of H. L. Mencken, box 100.

24. Abbott, "King Cotton," 509–10, 514. For a discussion of manhood, gender, and "agrarian whiteness" see Foley, *White Scourge*, 141–62.

25. Vance, *Human Factors*, 211.

26. Tannenbaum, "Single Crop," 816.

27. Clarence E. Cason, "Southern Slavery Revised," *Independent* 121 (July 14, 1928): 33–34.

28. For an analysis of the white slavery phenomenon as it pertains to prostitution, see Keire, "Vice Trust."

29. Reprinted in *Literary Digest* 28 (October 18, 1902).

30. Tannenbaum, *Darker Phases of the South*, 42, 56, 182–83.

31. Jacquelyn Dowd Hall, *Like a Family*, 56.

32. See Clune, "'From Light Copper'" for a discussion of New South industrialist and cotton mill owner Daniel Augustus Thompkins and his particular racialized global view of labor.

33. Devine, "Southern Prosperity," 453–54.

34. Murphy, *Problems*, 102, 123.

35. Ibid., 232.

36. Alfred E. Seddon, "The Education of Mill Children in the South," *Annals of the Academy of Political and Social Science* 32 (July 1908): supp., 74.

37. Alexander J. McElway, "The Child Labor Problem — A Study in Degeneracy," *Annals of the American Academy of Political and Social Science* 27 (March 1906): 55.

38. Alexander J. McElway, "Child Labor in the Southern Cotton Mills," *Annals of the American Academy of Political and Social Science* 27 (March 1906): 259, 261–62, 269.

39. Mississippi Report by Alfred E. Seddon, NCLC Records, box 3, Folder "MS. Cotton Mills, 1908," National Child Labor Committee Records.

40. The phrase "forgotten child" is used by Murphy, *Problems*, 94.

41. Droke, *From the Old South*, 8.

42. Walter Hines Page, "The Forgotten Man," in Page, *Rebuilding of Old Commonwealths*.

43. Page, "The Forgotten Man," 1–9, 22, 26, 34–35; and Walter Hines Page, "The Rebuilding of Old Commonwealths," in Page, *Rebuilding of Old Commonwealths*, 122, 139, 141, 144. Also see Walter Hines Page to Clark Howell, February 9, 1910, Letters of Walter Hines Page, box 12, MS Am 1090(533), Houghton Library, Harvard University. For other references to developing "human resources" as opposed to natural resources such as forests and industries see Editorial, "The Southern Education Board — A New Patriotic Force," *World's Work Magazine* 3 (December 1901): 1479–80; and Editorial, "The Southern Educational Conference," *World's Work Magazine* 4 (June 1902): 21–44.

44. D. F. St. Clair, "The Forgotten White Woman of the South," *Outlook* 63 (October 21, 1899): 457, 459.

45. Dr. Lyman Hall, "Needs of the New South," *Annals of the American Academy of Political and Social Science* 22 (September 1903): 22–23. For an example of another call for the South to "develop its manhood resources" see Mims, *Advancing South*, 26.

46. Governor Charles H. Allen to Robert C Ogden, December 8, 1900, Robert Curtis Ogden Papers, "Special Correspondence," box 6, folder "1900."

47. Edgar Gardner Murphy, "The Task of the South: An Address before the Faculty and Students of Washington and Lee University, Lexington, Virginia, December 10th, A.D., 1902," Hoole Alabama Collection, 24–25, W. S. Hoole Special Collections Library, University of Alabama, Tuscaloosa.

48. For examples see Stoler, *Carnal Knowledge*; Keller, "Madness and Colonialism"; Buettner, "Problematic Spaces"; and Lambert, "Liminal Figures."

49. Stoler, *Carnal Knowledge*, 36, 39–40.

50. For a discussion of these connections see Bell, "American Philanthropy"; and Magubane, "American Construction."

51. Thomas Jesse Jones, *Education in Africa*.

52. August D. Luckhoff to Hon. Secretary, Carnegie Corporation Visitors' Grants Committee, December 20, 1929, Carnegie Corporation of New York Records, Grant Files, series IIIA, box 208, folder 2, Rare Book and Manuscript Library, Columbia University.

53. For a history of Mabel Carney's career, her allegiance to the Country Life Movement, and her involvement in the United States, Africa, and Britain see Glotzer, "Career of Mabel Carney."

54. Ernst Gideon Malherbe, "The Carnegie Poor White Investigation: Its Origin and Sequels," Carnegie Corporation of New York Records, Grant Files, series IIIA, box 295, folder 7, 87. For a history of Malherbe's work with the South African National Bureau for Educational and Social Research and his dedication to social science as a tool of change see Fleisch, "Social Scientists as Policy Makers."

55. For a history of Charles T. Loram's experience chairing the South African Visitor's Grants Committee for the Carnegie Corporation, his participation in "the white liberal movement in race relations," and his direction of a series of conferences on race and acculturation at Yale University see Heyman, "C. T. Loram." Loram's belief that the "impingement of one civilization upon another" was an inevitable global problem reflected his interest in studying race relations between Hawaii, the Philippines, Japan, India, Africa, and the Dutch East Indies. See Charles T. Loram to Frederick Keppel, May 17, 1932, Carnegie Corporation of New York Records, Grant Files, series IIIA, box 206, folder 1; and Charles T. Loram, "Overseas Students at Yale University," Carnegie Corporation of New York Records, Grant Files, series IIIA, box 206, folder 1.

56. Carnegie Commission of Investigation of the Poor White Question in South Africa, *Poor White Problem*, 1:v, viii–ix, xiv, xvii. For a broad study of this commission see Willoughby-Herard, "Waste of a White Skin." For a brief discussion of the Commission and the transnational connections see Stoler, "Tense and Tender Ties," 857–61.

57. Lagemann, *Politics of Knowledge*, 30, 80–81.

58. Charles T. Loram to Hon. E. G. Jansen, December 14, 1929, Carnegie Corporation of New York Records, Grant Files, series IIIA, box 295, folder 8.

59. Frederick Keppel to Charles T. Loram, September 18, 1928, Carnegie Corporation of New York Records, Grant Files, series IIIA, box 295, folder 8.

60. Charles T. Loram and Frederick Keppel had a very pointed discussion in their correspondence about whether Kenyon L. Butterfield had been the right choice for South Africa because of a "nervous" condition and his greater interest in studying Christian missionary practice rather than lecturing on the poor white situation in a university setting. Charles W. Coulter was called in when it became clear that Butterfield was better suited for visiting churches rather than touring with the poor white survey group. Frederick Keppel to Charles T. Loram, January 30, 1920; Charles T. Loram to Frederick Keppel, February 28, 1929; and Charles T. Loram to Frederick Keppel, March 21, 1929, Carnegie Corporation of New York Records, Grant Files, series IIIA, box 295, folder 8.

61. Carnegie Corporation of New York, "Report of Dr. Kenyon L. Butterfield on Rural Conditions and Sociological Problems in South Africa" (New York, 1929), Kenyon L. Butterfield Papers, box 54, folder "Rural Life," 14–15, Manuscript Division, Library of Congress.

62. R. W. Wilcocks, to Dr. Keppel, November 3, 1932, Carnegie Corporation of New York Records, Grant Files, series IIIA, box 295, folder 6.

63. R. W. Wilcocks, "Rural Poverty among Whites in South Africa and in the South of the United States," Kenyon L. Butterfield Papers, box 7, folder "African Agriculture." Also see Correspondent in Pretoria, "The Poor-White Problem," 297.

64. Memorandum to F. P. K., Carnegie Corporation of New York Records, Grant Files, series IIIA, box 295, folder 6.

65. See Evans, *Black and White*, xiv.

66. Evans, *Black and White*, 185, 193.

67. DuBow, *Scientific Racism*, 167.

68. See Schmidt, *Sitting in Darkness*. In this postcolonial analysis of New South fiction and education, Schmidt advocates what he calls "a new analytical frame — Jim Crow colonialism — for understanding the paradoxical mix of citizen-building and subjection at the heart of Progressivist discourse at home and abroad" (14).

69. Poe, *Where Half the World*, 17, 169.

70. Hastings H. Hart, *Social Problems*, 10.

71. "Some Newspaper Articles Regarding the Educational Situation and Other Civic Matters in the Southern States: Alabama in Particular," Hoole Alabama Collection, 16–17.

72. Untitled typescript, Charles W. Dabney Papers, subseries 5.2, box 26, folder 1, Southern Historical Collection, Wilson Library, University of North Carolina at Chapel Hill.

73. *Presbyterian Standard*, November, 20, 1901, Southern Education Board Records, subseries 1.1, box 1, folder 3, Southern Historical Collection, Wilson Library, University of North Carolina at Chapel Hill (hereafter cited as SEB).

74. Sledd, "Illiteracy in the South," *Independent* 53 (October 17, 1901): 2471.

75. For a general history of black education during Reconstruction see Charles Morris, *Reading*; Butchart, *Northern Schools*; and Nieman, *African Americans*.

76. Edgar W. Knight, "Some Fallacies Concerning the History of Public Education in the South," *South Atlantic Quarterly* 13 (October 1914): 373.

77. Woodward, *Origins*, 61–62.

78. For a history of the Peabody Fund see Earle H. West, "The Peabody Education Fund and Negro Education, 1867–1880," in Nieman, *African Americans*. For a history of the Slater Fund see Roy E. Finkenbine, "'Our Little Circle': Benevolent Reformers, the Slater Fund, and the Argument for Black Industrial Education, 1882–1908," in Nieman, *African Americans*.

79. Samuel C. Mitchell, "Phases in the Educational Movement of the Day," *Sewanee Review* 16 (January 1908): 19.

80. "Some Newspaper Articles," 5, 10.

81. Charles W. Dabney, "Report from the Bureau of Investigation and Information of the Southern Education Board," in Southern Education Board, *Proceedings of the Conference for Education in the South, the Sixth Session*, 44.

82. Robert C. Ogden to George W. Boyd, February 27, 1904, Robert Curtis Ogden Papers, "Special Correspondence," box 13. For a history of Ogden and the education movement's increasing commitment to whites see Harlan, "Southern Education Board."

83. Robert C. Ogden to Dr. J. H. Kirkland, February 19, 1903, Robert Curtis Ogden Papers, "Special Correspondence," box 13.

84. For a history of the alliance between southern university presidents and northern philanthropists for southern educational reform see Dennis, *Lessons in Progress*.

85. "Released for Publication May 3rd, Ninth Conference for Education in the South, Lexington, Ky., President's Annual Address," Robert Curtis Ogden Papers, "Speeches," box 21, folder 1906.

86. Woodward, *Origins*, 403.

87. For brief histories of the Ogden train trip and its influence on the development of educational reform in the South see Leloudis, *Schooling the New South*, 145–51; Woodward, *Origins*, 396–404; and Hendrick, *Training of an American*, 403–12.

88. Edgar Gardner Murphy to Robert C. Ogden, April 8, 1904, Robert Curtis Ogden Papers, "Special Correspondence," box 7, folder "April 6–10, 1904."

89. "Southern Education: Whither?" Pamphlet published by *Manufacturer's Record*, Baltimore, 1908, GEB, series 1.2, box 262, folder 2711. Robert C. Ogden also was repeatedly criticized by Thomas F. Dixon Jr., the North Carolina Baptist minister, state legislator, and playwright who was nationally known for his virulent racism and writing the

novel that became the film *Birth of a Nation*. Dixon harbored a fanatical abhorrence of Ogden and once accused the northern philanthropist of hugging Booker T. Washington in public. See Hugh C. Bailey, *Liberalism in the New South*, 90. For an excellent collection of essays on Thomas F. Dixon Jr. see Gillespie and Randal L. Hall, *Thomas Dixon, Jr.*

90. Notebook, SEB, subseries 6.1, box 9, folder 272.

91. Chernow, *Titan*, 481.

92. Ingle, *Ogden Movement*, 14.

93. John Graham Brooks, "The Larger Meaning of the Conference," in Southern Education Board. *Proceedings of the Fifth Conference*, 82. The Massachusetts man is identified as John Graham Brooks in Samuel C. Mitchell, "Robert Curtis Ogden: A Leader in the Educational Renaissance of the South," Robert Curtis Ogden Papers, "Speeches, Writings, and Related Materials," box 27.

94. Notebook.

95. As Edward Said states, "Orientalism depends for its strategy on this flexible *positional* superiority, which puts the Westerner in a whole series of possible relationships with the Orient without ever losing him the relative hand" (Said, *Orientalism*, 7).

96. Notebook.

97. W. A. Locke to Robert C. Ogden, April 1, 1904, Robert Curtis Ogden Papers, "Special Correspondence," box 7, folder "April 1–5, 1904."

98. Samuel M. Lindsay to Edgar Gardner Murphy, December 9, 1904, Edgar Gardner Murphy Papers, box 1, folder 2, Southern Historical Collection, Wilson Library, University of North Carolina at Chapel Hill.

99. Mitchell, "Robert Curtis Ogden," vii, 173.

100. Hendrick, *Training of an American*, 404–5.

101. Cited in Editorial, "The University of Virginia," *Independent* 57 (December 29, 1904): 1521.

102. Edmonds, *South's Prosperity*, 7, 2–3.

103. Robert C. Ogden to Col. Archibald Hopkins, May 6, 1903, Robert Curtis Ogden Papers, "Special Correspondence," box 13.

104. "Compulsory Attendance Laws," Robert Curtis Ogden Papers, box 18, folder "Education in the South."

105. "Summer Meeting of the Southern Education Board," Robert Curtis Ogden Papers, August 5–8, 1907, box 17, folder "Education in the South, 1907."

106. Erwin Craighead, "Compulsory Education and the Southern States," *Sewanee Review* 16 (July 1908): 298.

107. For an example see Robert C. Ogden to Prof. S. G. Atkins, Robert Curtis Ogden Papers, December 21, 1903, "Special Correspondence," box 13.

108. Robert C. Ogden to Colonel A. C. Kaufman, February 13, 1904, Robert Curtis Ogden Papers, "Special Correspondence," box 13.

109. Editorial, "The New South," *Outlook* 92 (July 17, 1909): 627.

110. "News From the South," *Century Magazine*, 5 (March 1903): 798.

111. Samuel C. Mitchell, "The School as the Exponent of Democracy in the South," *Sewanee Review* 16 (January 1908): 18–20.

112. "The South Again Nationalized," Charles W. Dabney Papers, subseries 5.2, box 25, folder 318.

CHAPTER 5. *The "Race Problem" and the Fiction of the Color Line*

1. Headings are Thomas Nelson Page, "The Negro: The Southerner's Problem," *McClure's Magazine* 22 (March 1904): 548; and W. E. B. Du Bois, "The Color Line Belts the World," *Collier's Weekly* 38 (October 20, 1906): 30. Fishel, "'Negro Question,'" 281.

2. *First Mohonk Conference*, 9. For a history of the Mohonk conferences see Fishel, "'Negro Question.'"

3. *First Mohonk Conference*, 39.

4. Blight, *Race and Reunion*, 4.

5. I will keep quotation marks around these terms when using them in the context of discussing historical understandings of the meaning of race and the way in which it was categorized and marked.

6. For rare examples of earlier works utilizing these terms in the titles see Carlyle, "Occasional Discourse" in 1849; New-York Merchant, *Negro Labor Question* in 1858; and Read, *Negro Problem Solved* in 1864. For an example of a late nineteenth-century assertion that the "Negro question" was a product of the New South and not the Old South see the review of Thomas Nelson Page's *The Old South: Essays Social and Political* in "The Old South," *Sewanee Review* 1 (November 1892): 92. For a brief discussion of the literature on the "Negro question," "Negro problem," "race question," and "race problem" see Hollandsworth, *Portrait of a Scientific Racist*, 6–8. Hollandsworth notes that the use of these phrases drops off significantly after World War I.

7. Kelly Miller, "The Negro and Education," *Forum* 30 (February 1901): 693.

8. In a piece on the practice of comparison in North American history and postcolonial studies, Ann Stoler notes, "Category making produced cross-colonial equivalencies that allowed for international conferences and convinced their participants — doctors, lawyers, policy makers, and reformers — that they were in the same conversation, if not always talking about the same thing." See Stoler, "Tense and Tender Ties," 863.

9. See Ross, *Origins of American Social Science*, xiii. For another history of the professionalization of social science see Haskell, *Emergence of Professional Social Science*.

Ross explains how the discipline of social science was "imbedded in the classical ideology of liberal individualism." Questions about the capitalist market, industrialization and urbanization, and the liberal vision of citizenship informed the subject matter of social scientists in the United States. Although Ross makes the case for the dominance of American exceptionalism in the discipline, other scholars have demonstrated that the same kinds of questions animated social scientists and intellectuals in European countries undergoing similar social and economic transformations. See Kloppenberg, *Uncertain Victory*; Rodgers, *Atlantic Crossings*; and Butler, *Critical Americans*.

10. James Bardin, "The Psychological Factor in Southern Race Problems," *Popular Science Monthly* 83 (October 1913): 369–70.

11. See Uday, "Liberal Strategies of Exclusion."

12. For a history of the idea of race and its impact on social science and popular thought see Gossett, *Race*.

13. John David Smith, "High Authority," 198.

14. University Commission on Southern Questions, *Minutes*, 5, 9, 11.

15. Charles Hillman Brough, "Work of the Commission of Southern Universities on the Race Question," *Annals of the American Academy of Political and Social Science* 49 (September 1913): 48–49.

16. There is surprisingly very little scholarship on Kelly Miller's life. See W. D. Wright, "Thought and Leadership"; Roberts, "Kelly Miller and Thomas J. Dixon"; and Hutchinson, "Whitman and the Black Poet." Also see Young, "Early Traditions."

17. For a history of W. E. B. Du Bois's sociological approach see Reiland, *Against Epistemic Apartheid*; Turley, "Black Social Science "; and Green and Driver, *W. E. B. Du Bois*. For a history of Du Bois's sociological study on Philadelphia see Gaines, *Uplifting the Race*, 152–78.

18. For a history of the black sociological tradition, particularly at Howard University, see Holloway, *Confronting the Veil*.

19. Moss, *American Negro Academy*, 24.

20. *First Mohonk Conference*, 110.

21. W. S. Scarborough, "The Race Problem," *Arena* 2 (October 1890): 562.

22. Isabel C. Barrows, "The Montgomery Conference," *Outlook* 65 (May 19, 1900): 160. For a discussion about southern whites' exclusion of blacks from this conference see John David Smith, "'No negro is upon the program.'"

23. Archer, *Through Afro-America*, 41–42.

24. See, in particular, Blight, *Race and Reunion*; and Hale, *Making Whiteness*.

25. Grady, *Race Problem*, 537.

26. Henry W. Grady, "The South and Her Problems," in Shurter, *Complete Oration*,

26. An essay in the *Southern Workman* by Moorfield Storey cites Grady's statement but

adds the phrase "equal in civic and political rights." See Moorfield Storey, "National Aspects of the Negro Problem," *Southern Workman* 49 (August 1920): 349. The original quotation does not contain the phrase "equal in civic and political rights."

27. Albert Bushnell Hart, *Southern South*, 151.

28. George Washington Cable, "What Makes the Color Line?" in Cable, *Negro Question*, 187–90.

29. Southern Society for the Promotion of the Study of Race Conditions and Problems in the South, *Race Problems of the South*, 11.

30. Ibid., 68.

31. For a history of Stone's life and work see Hollandsworth, *Portrait of a Scientific Racist*; John David Smith, "Alfred Holt Stone"; and John David Smith, "High Authority or Failed Prophet?"

32. For a history of northern Progressive reformers and their racist ideology regarding the "Negro Question" see Southern, *Malignant Heritage*.

33. Alfred Holt Stone, "Is Race Friction between Blacks and Whites in the United States Growing and Inevitable?" *American Journal of Sociology* 13 (March 1908): 677–78. For an explication of Stone's participation in this meeting see Hollandsworth, *Portrait of a Scientific Racist*, 197–208.

34. W. E. B. Du Bois in "Discussion of the Paper by Alfred H. Stone, 'Is Race Friction between Blacks and Whites in the United States Growing and Inevitable?'" *American Journal of Sociology* 13 (March 1908): 834–36.

35. *First Mohonk Conference*, 117–19.

36. William P. Trent to Edwin Mims, July 21, 1903, cited in "Mims Autobiography: Chpt XVI, A Harvest of Letters," Edwin Mims Papers, box 18, folder 10, Special Collections and University Archives, Vanderbilt University.

37. For a history of plantation romance literature see Blight, *Race and Reunion*; and Silber, *Romance of Reunion*. For studies on turn-of-the-century deep nostalgia for cheerful slaves such as the figure of Mammy see McElya, *Clinging to Mammy*; and Manring, *Slave in a Box*.

38. Gaston, *New South Creed*, 170.

39. Thomas Nelson Page, *Negro*, 53, 166. For other comments in the same period on the erosion of the intimate master and slave relationship see Riley, *White Man's Burden*, 15; and W. D. Weatherford, "Race Relationship in the South," *Annals of the American Academy of Political and Social Science* 49 (September 1913): 165–66.

40. For an early twentieth-century articulation of the "old-time Negro" versus the "new Negro" see Thompson, *New South*, 142–45. For a historical discussion of white southerners' obsession with the "New Negro" see Litwack, *Trouble in Mind*, 197–216.

41. Ray Stannard Baker, "Following the Color Line in the South," in Baker, *Following the Color Line*, 44.

42. John Spencer Bassett, "Fragment of Speech re. Slater School of Winston Salem at Boston?" John Spencer Bassett Papers, box 47, folder 6, Library of Congress, Manuscripts Division, Washington, D.C.

43. Kelly Miller, "A Brief for the Higher Education of the Negro," in Kelly Miller, *Race Adjustment*, 264.

44. W. E. B. Du Bois, "The Relation of the Negroes to the Whites in the South," *Annals of the American Academy of Political and Social Science* 18 (July 1901): 138, 136–37.

45. John Spencer Bassett, "Stirring Up the Fires of Race Antipathy," *South Atlantic Quarterly* 2 (October 1903): 298.

46. George Washington Cable, "A Simpler Southern Question," *Forum* 6 (December 1888): 397.

47. Fredrickson, *Black Image*, 283–319.

48. Bay, *White Image*, 187–202.

49. George Washington Cable, "The Negro Question," in Cable, *Negro Question*, 132.

50. Kelly Miller, "Social Equality," in Kelly Miller, *Race Adjustment*, 113.

51. Kelly Miller, *House of Bondage*, 42–43. Several years later Miller stated this idea more explicitly when he argued that "the sex urge is a deeper and more profound instinct than race preference, or race pride." See Kelly Miller, "Is the American Negro to Remain Black or Become Bleached?" *South Atlantic Quarterly* 25 (July 1926): 243.

52. Kelly Miller, "Is the American Negro," 248.

53. H. E. Jordan, "The Biological Status and Social Worth of the Mulatto," *Popular Science Monthly* 82 (June 1913): 573.

54. See Roberts, *Infectious Fear*. For a later example of the preoccupation with black bodies in science see Reverby, *Examining Tuskegee*.

55. Andrew Sledd, "The Negro: Another View," *Atlantic Monthly* 90 (July 1902): 66.

56. For examples of authors who claimed that "miscegenation" was an imaginary problem or that census data proved a decrease in the number of mixed-race people over time see Ernest Hamlin Abbott, "The South and The Negro: Social Equality versus Social Service," *Outlook* 77 (July 9, 1904): 590; Ulysses G. Weatherly, "Race and Marriage," *American Journal of Sociology* 15 (January 1910): 444; Bruce, *Plantation Negro as a Freeman*, 53–55; Phillip Alexander Bruce, "Evolution of the Negro Problem," *Sewanee Review* 19 (October 1911): 389; and Letter from Bishop Atticus B. Haygood cited at the *First Mohonk Conference*, 85. Joseph LeConte argued that the level of mixing between the races was exaggerated and predominantly an urban phenomenon only. See LeConte, *Race Problem*, 373. Even one of the most liberal southerners, George

Washington Cable, agreed there was not much evidence for "miscegenation" in the South. See George Washington Cable, "Silent South," in Cable, *Negro Question*, 112–13.

57. See Pascoe, *What Comes Naturally*; Wallenstein, *Tell the Court*; Williamson, *New People*; Hollinger, "Amalgamation and Hypodescent"; Berry, "Judging Morality"; Zackondik, "Fixing the Color Line"; and Elliott, "Telling the Difference."

58. For works addressing the myth of the "black beast rapist" see Hall, "'Mind That Burns'"; Feimster, *Southern Horrors*; Williamson, *Crucible of Race*; and Gilmore, *Gender and Jim Crow*.

59. For some examples of historical and literary scholarship on the phenomenon of passing see Ginsberg, *Fictions of Identity*; Fabi, *Passing*; Wald, *Crossing the Line*; Pfeiffer, *Race Passing and American Individualism*; and Susan Prothro Wright, *Passing*.

60. Ray Stannard Baker, "The Tragedy of the Mulatto," *American Magazine* 65 (April 1908): 582.

61. *Second Mohonk Conference*, 73.

62. Schuyler, *Black No More*. For an analysis of the importance of *Black No More* to the discourse on race in the context of the Harlem Renaissance see Ferguson, *Sage of Sugar Hill*, 212–44. For a general biography of Schuyler that stresses his later conservatism see Arthur R. Williams, *George S. Schuyler*.

63. Albert Bushnell Hart, *Southern South*, 151–52.

64. Evans, *Black and White*, 595.

65. Ibid., 187–88. For the entire cited letter to the editor see Baker, "Tragedy of the Mulatto," 595.

66. Holm, *Holm's Race Assimilation*, 263–64; Albert Bushnell Hart, *Southern South*, 157; Baker, "Tragedy of the Mulatto," 594–95.

67. Baker, "Tragedy of the Mulatto, 595.

68. Evans, *Black and White*, 188.

69. Wells, *Southern Horrors*.

70. T. Thomas Fortune, "Notes on Living Problems of the Hour," *Arena* 3 (December 1890): 116. For other examples of authors and speakers who blamed white men for the problem of "miscegenation" in the South see Evans, *Black and White*, 185; Archibald H. Grimke A.M., "The Heart of the Race Problem," *Arena* 35 (March 1906): 274–75; and *First Mohonk Conference*, 113.

71. George Allen Mebane, "Have We an American Race Question?" *Arena* 24 (November 1900): 459–60.

72. Albert Bushnell Hart, *Southern South*, 155.

73. Kelly Miller, "As to the Leopard's Spots: An Open Letter to Thomas Dixon, Jr.," in Kelly Miller, *Race Adjustment*, 51. For other examples of Miller's assertion that it was hypocritical for white men to advocate race purity when they were not practicing it

themselves see Kelly Miller, *Everlasting Stain*, 127; and Kelly Miller, *Out of the House of Bondage*, 48.

74. Baker, "Tragedy of the Mulatto," 582.

75. Frances Hoggan, "The American Negro and Race Blending," *Sociological Review* 2 (October 1909): 354.

76. Editorial, "When Is a Caucasian Not a Caucasian?" *Independent* 70 (March 2, 1911): 478–79.

77. Anonymous, "White, but Black: A Document on the Race Problem," *Century Magazine* 109 (February 1925): 492–99.

78. Baker, "Tragedy of the Mulatto," 593; and Hoggan, "American Negro and Race Blending," 355.

79. See address by John Roach Straton in Southern Society for the Promotion of the Study of Race Conditions and Problems in the South, *Race Problems*, 149; William Benjamin Smith, *Color Line*, 44; E. B. Reuter, "The Superiority of the Mulatto," *American Journal of Sociology* 23 (July 1917): 83–106; George T. Winston, "The Relation of the Whites to the Negroes," *Annals of the Academy of Political and Social Science* 18 (July 1901): 108; Bruce, *Negro as a Freeman*, 143; and Shannon, *Racial Integrity*, 82. For an environmental and social argument challenging some of the authors listed above who argued that "mulatto" intelligence was an innate characteristic see Robert E. Park, "Mentality of Racial Hybrids," *American Journal of Sociology* 26 (January 1931): 534–51.

80. Alfred H. Stone, "The Mulatto Factor in the Race Problem," *Atlantic Monthly* 91 (May 1903): 661.

81. For examples see Ray Stannard Baker, "An Ostracized Race in Ferment," in Baker, *Following the Color Line*, 224–25; Shannon, *Racial Integrity*, 19; Evans, *Black and White*, 92; and Thompson, *New South*, 145–46.

82. Baker, "Tragedy of the Mulatto," 598.

83. William Benjamin Smith, *Color Line*, 8.

84. Earnest Sevier Cox, *South's Part*.

85. Cable, "Silent South," 130. For a study on the relationship between sexuality, "miscegenation," and both white and black nationalism see Barbara Bair, "Remapping the Black/White Body: Sexuality, Nationalism, and Biracial Antimiscegenation Activism in 1920s Virginia," in Hodes, *Sex, Love, Race*, 399–419. Also see William A. Edwards, "Racial Purity."

86. See Cable, "Silent South," 88–98. In this article, Cable felt compelled to defend charges by Henry Grady that Cable was advocating national social equality among the races in his well-known article "The Freedmen's Case in Equity." For Grady's criticism see Grady, "In Plain Black and White."

87. Du Bois, *Souls of Black Folk*, 9. At the Pan African Congress Du Bois issued

his statement about the "problem of the color line" in a slightly different version. See W. E. B. Du Bois, "To the Nations of the World," in Lewis, *W. E. B. Du Bois: A Reader*, 639.

88. Du Bois, "The Color Line Belts the World," 30.

89. See Kelley, "But a Local Phase."

90. U. G. Weatherly, "A World-Wide Color Line," *Popular Science Monthly* 79 (November 1911): 474, 479. Weatherly initially taught European history at Indiana University and then later moved into the field of sociology. He traveled to the Caribbean to study race relations with sociologist Robert E. Park.

91. Tyrrell, "Making Nations/Making States," 1021, 1023. Ian Tyrrell argues that at the turn of the century historians, for a short moment, considered the connections between empire and nation. This intellectual inclination, while not dominant in the years that followed, occasionally made an appearance until it disappeared around World War II. Yet in the 1950s, Herbert Aptheker and C. Vann Woodward alluded in passing to the links between domestic racism and American imperialism and claimed that it was no coincidence that the rise of segregation and disfranchisement in the South coincided with the expansion of the American empire. Aptheker wrote, "When American monopoly capitalism turned its attention seriously to overseas investments and to the appropriation of Hawaii, Puerto Rico, Cuba and the Philippines, it simultaneously turned its attention seriously to investments in the South and to the establishment of terrorist domination of the Southern masses and especially of the Negro people." Woodward declared that when "America shouldered the White Man's Burden, she took up at the same time many Southern attitudes on the subject of race." In Woodward's account the "wave of southern racism" could not be isolated from the expansion of a jingoistic imperial state. See Herbert Aptheker, "American Imperialism and White Chauvinism," in Aptheker, *Toward Negro Freedom*, 90; and Woodward, *Strange Career of Jim Crow*, 74. Also see Woodward, *Origins of the New South*, 324–26.

92. Lake and Reynolds, *Drawing the Global Colour Line*, 6–9, 53–55, 61. Also see Kramer, "Empires, Exceptions, and Anglo-Saxons," for another history of this British-American exchange at the turn of the twentieth century.

93. James Bryce, "Thoughts on the Negro Problem," *North American Review* 153 (December 1891): 641.

94. Bryce, *American Commonwealth*, 532.

95. Bryce, *Relation of the Advanced*, 7.

96. Riley, *White Man's Burden*, 14–15.

97. Du Bois, *Black Reconstruction*, 195.

98. American Academy of Political and Social Science, *America's Race Problems*.

99. For a history of how European immigrants became white at the turn of the

century see Jacobson, *Whiteness of a Different Color*. At the American Academy of Political and Social Science meeting, Edward A. Ross, professor of sociology at the University of Nebraska, acknowledged the racial component of the northern experience with European immigrants by including a brief discussion of European immigrants in his opening address titled "The Causes of Race Superiority," in American Academy of Political and Social Science, *America's Race Problems*, 88–89.

100. Col. Hilary A. Herbert, "The Race Problem at the South," in American Academy of Political and Social Science, *America's Race Problems*, 98–99.

101. "From Edgar Gardner Murphy," Walter Hines Page Papers, "American Letters," box 15, MS Am1090.3, Houghton Library, Harvard University.

102. Ulysses G. Weatherly, "The First Universal Races Congress," *American Journal of Sociology* 17 (November 1911): 315.

103. Evans, *Black and White*, 10–11.

104. Luker, *Social Gospel*, 312–13.

105. "A News Item in the *Tuskegee Student*," in Harlan, *Booker T. Washington Papers*, 512.

106. Booker T. Washington, "An Announcement of a Conference at Tuskegee Institute," ca. March 1911, in Harlan, *Booker T. Washington Papers*, 72.

107. "Tuskegee International Conference on the Negro," *Journal of Race Development* 3 (July 1912): 118.

108. See Zimmerman, *Alabama in Africa*.

109. See Rief, "Thinking Locally, Acting Globally."

110. *Race Problems of the South*, 95. For a discussion of Armstrong's educational program as an extended project of colonialism and the comparisons he made between Hawaiians and black southerners see Jeremy Dwight Wells, "Civilization and the South," 129–43. Also see Sehat, "Civilizing Mission."

111. Zimmerman, *Alabama in Africa*, 42–43.

112. Ray Stannard Baker, "A Statesman of the Negro Problem," *World's Work* 35 (January 1918): 308–9. For another example of a southern reformer who advocated using the U.S. South as a training ground for American and European colonial projects see Murphy, *Basis of Ascendancy*, 222.

113. Kelly Miller, *Appeal to Conscience*, 13–15.

114. Evans, *Black and White*; Archer, *Through Afro-America*; W. P. Livingstone, *Race Conflict*; Clowes, *Black America*; and Johnston, *Negro in the New World*.

115. James Bryce to Edgar Gardner Murphy, November 20, 1909, Edgar Gardner Murphy Papers, box 1, folder 6, Southern Historical Collection, Wilson Library, University of North Carolina at Chapel Hill; James Bryce to Edgar Gardner Murphy,

June 27, 1910, Edgar Gardner Murphy Papers, box 1, folder 7; Murphy, *Basis of Ascendancy*, 222.

116. Sir Harry Hamilton Johnston to Edgar Gardner Murphy, September 24, 1909, Edgar Gardner Murphy Papers, box 1, folder 6. Johnston's other books include *Britain across the Seas, History of the Colonization of Africa by Alien Races*, and *Opening Up of Africa*.

117. See W. P. Livingstone, *Black Jamaica*.

118. Archer, *Through Afro-America*, xv–xvi.

119. Ibid., x.

120. Ibid.

121. Archer, *Through Afro-America*, 187; and W. P. Livingstone, *Race Conflict*, 18–21.

122. W. P. Livingstone, *Race Conflict*, 22.

123. *First Mohonk Conference*, 40.

124. *Second Mohonk Conference*, 62.

125. *First Mohonk Conference*, 110.

126. Editorial, *Crisis* 6 (July 1913): 129.

127. See Rafael, *White Love*, 21–23. For a contemporary example making the explicit comparison between the need for a similar form of discipline in the Philippines, Puerto Rico, and the South see Archibald R. Colquhoun, "The Future of the Negro," *North American Review* 176 (May 1903): 666.

128. Murphy, *Basis of Ascendancy*, 17, 19. For another example of a writer advocating "training and discipline" as a means of encouraging the black race to reach "the highest civilization" see Walter G. Hamm, "The Three Phases of Colored Suffrage," *North American Review* 168 (March 1899): 296.

129. Colquhoun, "Future of the Negro," 658–59. For other examples of the assertion that black southerners were a nation within a nation see D. Allen Willey, "The Negro and the Soil," *Arena* 23 (May 1900): 553; and A. D. Mayo, "The Progress of the Negro," *Forum* 10 (November 1890): 337.

130. For an example of these very issues being discussed at the Montgomery Conference on Race Problems over a hundred years ago see Isabel C. Barrow, "The Montgomery Conference," *Independent* 52 (May 24, 1900): 1257–58.

131. Kelly Miller, "The Negro and Education," *Forum* 30 (February 1901): 704.

EPILOGUE. *The Enduring Paradox of the South*

1. Citations for headings are "Little Known of the Real South," *New York Times*, May 6, 1926; and Gerald W. Johnson, "The South Takes Offensive," *American Mercury* 2 (May 1924): 70. Mims, *Advancing South*, vii–x, 1. For an exploration of Edwin Mims's

analysis of the New South see O'Brien, "Edwin Mims: An Aspect of the Mind of the New South Considered, I," and O'Brien, "Edwin Mims: An Aspect of the Mind of the New South Considered, II."

2. Ellen Glasgow to Edwin Mims, May 12, 2926, Edwin Mims Papers, box 1, Special Collections and University Archives, Vanderbilt University.

3. See Cobb, *Away Down South*, 99–129; Fitzpatrick, *Gerald W. Johnson*; Hobson, *South-Watching*; Leidholt, *Battling Nell*; Lisby, *Someone Had to Be Hated*; and Hollis, *An Alabama Newspaper Tradition*.

4. Angoff, *H. L. Mencken*, 126. For a look at Angoff's career see Angoff and Yoseloff, *Man from the Mercury*.

5. "H. L. Mencken, "Civil War in the Confederacy," *Baltimore Evening Sun*, July 30, 1928; H. L. Mencken, "Below the Potomac," *Baltimore Evening Sun*, June 18, 1923; and "Untitled," 1921, H. L. Mencken Collection, Clipping Book IV, Special Collections, Enoch Pratt Free Library.

6. See Grantham, *Regional Imagination*, 6–7.

7. Howard W. Odum, "Need of Self-Criticism" and "A More Articulate South," *Journal of Social Forces* 2 (November 1924): 730.

8. See Howard W. Odum, "Regionalism vs. Sectionalism in the South's Place in the National Economy," *Journal of Social Forces* 12 (March 1934): 338–54.

9. Hobson, *Tell about the South*, 196.

10. Odum, "Regionalism vs. Sectionalism," 345.

11. Ibid., 340, 345; and Howard W. Odum to H. L. Mencken, Sept. 25, 1923, and September 13, 1923, Correspondence of H. L. Mencken, box 88, New York Public Library Microfilm, Special Collections, Enoch Pratt Free Library.

12. Howard W. Odum died in 1954, H. L. Mencken in 1956, and Edwin Mims in 1959.

13. H. L. Mencken, "The South Looks Ahead," *American Mercury* 8 (August 1926): 508.

14. Howard W. Odum to H. L. Mencken, March 29, 1947, Correspondence of H. L. Mencken, box 88.

BIBLIOGRAPHY

ARCHIVAL MATERIAL AND MANUSCRIPTS

Columbia University, Rare Book and Manuscript Library, New York, New York
    Carnegie Corporation of New York Records
Enoch Pratt Free Library, Special Collections, Baltimore, Maryland
    H. L. Mencken Collection
    Correspondence of H. L. Mencken, New York Public Library Microfilm
Harvard University, Houghton Library, Cambridge, Massachusetts
    Letters sent to Walter Hines Page from Various Correspondents, American
        Period
    Walter Hines Page Papers
Harvard University, University Archives, Cambridge, Massachusetts
    Albert Bushnell Hart Papers
Library of Congress, Manuscripts Division, Washington, D.C.
    John Spencer Bassett Papers
    Kenyon L. Butterfield Papers
    National Child Labor Committee Records
    Ray Stannard Baker Papers
    Robert Curtis Ogden Papers
National Archives, Washington, D.C.
    United States Department of Agriculture
        Records of the Bureau of Entomology and Plant Quarantine, Record Group 7
            Records of the Division of Cotton Insect Investigations
            Records of the Division of Southern Field Crop Insect Investigations
        Records of the Extension Service, Record Group 33
            Correspondence
            Records Concerning Farmers' Cooperative Demonstration Work in the South
            Records Relating to Departmental Participation in Fairs and Expositions
        Bureau of Plant Industry Records, Record Group 54

Rockefeller Archive Center, Tarrytown, New York
    General Education Board Records
    International Health Board Records
    Rockefeller Foundation Pamphlet Collection
    Rockefeller Foundation Photograph Collection
    Rockefeller Sanitary Commission for the Eradication of Hookworm Records
Smithsonian Institution, National Museum of American History, Washington, D.C.
    Warshaw Collection of Business Americana
Southern Historical Collection, Wilson Library, University of North Carolina at
    Chapel Hill
    Charles W. Dabney Papers
    Edgar Gardner Murphy Papers
    Howard W. Odum Papers
    Southern Education Board Records
Southwest Collection/Special Collections, Texas Tech University, Lubbock, Texas
    Seaman Asahel Knapp Papers
Special Collections and University Archives, Vanderbilt University, Nashville,
    Tennessee
    Edwin Mims Papers
W. S. Hoole Special Collections Library, University of Alabama, Tuscaloosa
    Hoole Alabama Collections

PRINTED U.S. GOVERNMENT DOCUMENTS

Knapp, Seaman A. *Recent Foreign Explorations, as Bearing on the Agricultural
    Development of the Southern States, Bureau of Plant Industry, Bulletin No. 35.*
    Washington, D.C.: Government Printing Office, 1903.
United States Congress. *Report of the Committee of Agriculture and Forestry on
    Conditions of Cotton Growers in the United States, the Present Prices of Cotton, and
    the Remedy; and on Cotton Consumption and Production.* 53rd Cong., 3rd Sess.,
    Report 986. Vols. 1 and 2. Washington, D.C.: Government Printing Office, 1895.
United States Department of Agriculture. *Agricultural Yearbooks.* Washington, D.C.:
    Government Printing Office, 1896–1910.
United States National Emergency Council. *Report on Economic Conditions in the
    South. Prepared for the President by the National Emergency Council.* Washington,
    D.C.: Government Printing Office, 1938.
United States Senate. *Report of the Country Life Commission: Special Message from
    the President of the United States Transmitting the Report of the Country Life
    Commission.* 60th Congress, 2nd Sess., Document No. 705. Washington, D.C.:
    Government Printing Office, 1909.

SERIALS

American Journal of Public Health
American Journal of Sociology
American Journal of Tropical Diseases and Preventive Medicine
American Magazine
American Mercury
American Monthly Review of Reviews
Annals of the American Academy of Political and Social Science
Arena
Atlantic Monthly
Century Magazine
Collier's Weekly
Commonweal
Cosmopolitan
Country Gentleman
Country Life in America
Crisis
Forensic Quarterly
Forum
Harper's Monthly Magazine
Independent
Journal of Social Forces
Literary Digest
McClure's Magazine
Nation
New Republic
New York World
North American Review
Outlook
Pan-American Magazine
Pearson's Magazine
Popular Science Monthly
Quarterly Journal of Economics
Scribner's Magazine
Sewanee Review
Sociological Review
South Atlantic Quarterly
Southern Medical Journal
Southern Workman

Survey
Virginia Quarterly Review
World's Work Magazine

PRIMARY SOURCES

Alderman, Edwin A. *The Growing South: An Address Delivered before the Civic Forum in Carnegie Hall, New York City, March 22, 1908*. New York: Civic Forum, 1908.

American Academy of Political and Social Science. *America's Race Problems: Addresses at the Annual Meeting of the American Academy of Political and Social Science, Philadelphia, April Twelfth and Thirteenth, MCMI*. 1900. Reprint, New York: Negro Universities Press, 1969.

Archer, William. *Through Afro-America: An English Reading of the Race Problem*. London: Chapman & Hall, 1910.

Atkinson, Edward. *The Development of the Resources of the Southern States: An Address to the Atlanta Chamber of Commerce*. Boston: n.p., 1898.

Baker, Ray Stannard. *Following the Color Line: American Negro Citizenship in the Progressive Era*. Edited by Dewy Grantham. 1908. Reprint, New York: Harper Torchbook, 1964.

Banks, Enoch Marvin. *Economics of Land Tenure in Georgia*. New York: AMS Press, 1905.

Battle, A. D. *The Negro Problem: From the Standpoint of an Extreme Southerner*. New Orleans: J. G. Hawser Printer, 1899.

Black, David. "Slaughter of the Innocents," *Iron Molder's Journal* 37 (December 1901): 754–55.

Blair, Lewis H. *A Southern Prophecy: The Prosperity of the South Dependent upon the Elevation of the Negro*. Edited with an introduction by C. Vann Woodward. 1889. Reprint, Boston: Little, Brown, 1964.

Boyle, James E. *Cotton and the New Orleans Cotton Exchange*. Garden City, N.Y.: Country Life Press, 1934.

Brooks, Eugene Clyde. *The Story of Cotton and the Development of the Cotton States*. Chicago: Rand McNally, 1911

Brown, William Garrott. *The Lower South in American History*. New York: Macmillan, 1902.

——. *The New Politics and Other Papers*. Boston: Houghton Mifflin, 1914.

Bruce, Philip Alexander. *The Plantation Negro as a Freeman: Observations on His Character, Condition, and Prospects in Virginia*. New York: G. P. Putnam's Sons, 1889.

———. *The Rise of the New South.* Philadelphia: G. Barrie & Sons, 1905.

Bryce, James. *The Relationship of the Advanced and Backward Races.* Oxford: Clarendon Press, 1902.

Burkett, Charles William, and Clarence Hamilton Poe. *Cotton: In Cultivation, Marketing, Manufacture, and the Problems of the Cotton World.* New York: Doubleday, Page, 1908.

Butterfield, Kenyon L. *Chapters in Rural Progress.* Chicago: University of Chicago, 1907.

Cable, George Washington. *The Negro Question: Selection of Writings on Civil Rights in the South.* Edited by Arlin Turner. 1890. Reprint, New York: W. W. Norton, 1958.

———. *The Silent South, Together With the Freedmen's Case in Equity and the Convict Lease System.* New York: C. Scribner's Sons, 1889.

Carlyle, Thomas. "Occasional Discourse on the Negro Question." *Fraser's Magazine* 40 (December 1849): 670–79.

Carnegie Commission of Investigation of the Poor White Question in South Africa. *The Poor White Problem in South Africa.* Vols. 1–5. Stellengosch, South Africa: Proecclesia-drukkery, 1932.

Cash, Wilbur J. *The Mind of the South.* Garden City, N.Y.: Doubleday, 1941.

Chamberlain, Daniel Henry. *Present Phases of Our So-Called Negro Problem: Open Letter to the Right Honorable James Bryce.* n.p., 1904.

Chew, Morris. *History of the Kingdom of Cotton and Cotton Statistics of the World.* New Orleans: W. B. Stansbury, 1884.

Clowes, W. Laird. *Black America: A Study of the Ex-Slave and His Late Master.* 1891. Reprint, Westport, Conn.: Negro Universities Press, 1970.

Collings, Gilbeart H. *The Production of Cotton.* New York: John Wiley & Sons, 1926.

Cook, Joseph, ed. *Our Day: A Record and Review of Current Reform.* Vol. 5. Boston: Our Day, 1890.

Correspondent in Pretoria. "The Poor-White Problem in South Africa." *British Medical Journal* 2 (August 12, 1933): 296–97.

Cowlam, George B. *The Undeveloped South. Its Resources and the Importance of Their Development as a Factor in Determining the Future Prosperity and Growth of Wealth in the United States.* Louisville, Ky.: Courier-Journal, 1887.

Cox, Earnest Sevier. *The South's Part in Mongrelizing the Nation.* Richmond, Va.: White American Society, 1926.

Crawford, M. D. C. *The Heritage of Cotton: The Fibre of Two Worlds and Many Ages.* New York: Grossett & Dunlap, 1924.

Crowther, Samuel. *The Romance and Rise of the American Tropics.* New York: Double Day Doran, 1929.

Cross, Samuel Creed. *The Negro and the Sunny South*. Martinsburg, W. Va.: S. C. Cross, 1899.

Devine, Edward T. "Southern Prosperity Is Not Shackled to Child Labor. An Interview. Edgar Gardner Murphy. Chairman Alabama Child Labor Committee." *Charities* 10 (May 2, 1903): 453–56.

Droke, Jacobus. *From the Old South to the New*. Harriman, Tenn.: Progress, 1895.

Du Bois, W. E. B. *Black Reconstruction in America: An Essay Toward a History of the Part Which Black Folk Played in the Attempt to Reconstruct Democracy in America, 1860–1880*. Introduction by David Levering Lewis. 1935. Reprint, New York: Oxford University Press, 2007.

———. *The Souls of Black Folk*. 1903. Reprint, New York: Dover Publications, 1994.

Edmonds, Richard H. *Facts about the South*. Baltimore: Manufacturer's Record, 1902.

———. *The South's Prosperity, Its Danger: Strength of Character Needed as Never Before*. Baltimore: Manufacturer's Record, 1907.

———. *The South's Redemption: From Poverty to Prosperity*. Baltimore: Manufacturer's Record, 1890.

Evans, Maurice S. *Black and White in South East Africa: A Study in Sociology*. New York: Longmans, Green, 1911.

———. *Black and White in the Southern States: A Study of the Race Problem in the United States from a South African Point of View*. London: Longmans, Green, 1915.

———. *Black and White in the Southern States: A Study of the Race Problem in the United States from a South African Point of View*. Introduction by George M. Fredrickson. Columbia: University of South Carolina, 2001.

Falkiner, W. Robbins. *The South and Its People*. Richmond, Va.: P. Keenan, 1890.

Ferrell, John A. "Hookworm Disease, Its Ravages, Prevention and Cure." *Atlanta Journal-Record of Medicine* 61 (July 1914): 178–96.

First Mohonk Conference on the Negro Question Held at Lake Mohonk, Ulster County, New York, June 4, 5, 6, 1890. Reported and edited by Isabel C. Barrows. Boston: George H. Ellis, printer, 1890.

Five Letters to the University Commission on Southern Race Questions. Charlottesville, Va.: Michie, 1927.

Fleming, Walter Lynwood. *The South in the Building of the Nation: A History of the Southern States Designed to Record the South's Part in the Making of the American Nation; To Portray the Character and Genius, to Chronicle the Achievements and Progress and to Illustrate the Life and Traditions of the Southern People*. Vols. 1–13. Richmond, Va.: Southern Historical Publication Society, 1909–1913.

Fries, Henry. *In Memory of Robert Curtis Ogden: True Friend, Patriotic Citizen, Unofficial Statesman, Christian Gentleman*. Privately published, 1916.

Gaines, Francis Pendleton. *The Southern Plantation: A Study in the Development and Accuracy of a Tradition*. New York: Columbia University Press, 1925.

Galpin, Charles Josiah. *Rural Social Problems*. New York: Century, 1924.

Gardner, J. W., ed. *Studies in Southern History and Politics: Inscribed to William Archibald Dunning*. New York: Columbia University Press, 1914.

George, Henry. *Progress and Poverty: An Inquiry into the Cause of Industrial Depressions, and of Increase of Want with Increase of Wealth; the Remedy*. New York: Henry George, 1879.

Glotzer, Richard. "The Career of Mabel Carney: The Study of Race and Rural Development in the United States and South Africa." *International Journal of African Historical Studies* 29 (1996): 309–36.

Grady, Henry Woofin. *The New South*. New York: Robert Bonner's Sons, 1890.

———. *The Race Problem: A Lecture*. Philadelphia: J. D. Morris, 1900.

Grant, Madison. *The Passing of the Great Race*. New York: C. Scribner, 1916.

Harrison, William H. *How to Get Rich in the South. Telling What to Do, How to Do It and the Profits Realized*. Chicago: W. H. Harrison Jr., 1888.

Hart, Albert Bushnell. *The Obvious Orient*. New York: D. Appleton, 1911.

———. *The Southern South*. New York: D. Appleton, 1910.

———. "The South's 'Backwardness.'" *Times-Dispatch*, March 22, 1905.

———. "The South's Progress." *Times-Dispatch*, April 6, 1905.

Hart, Hastings H. *Social Problems of Alabama: A Study of the Social Institutions and Agencies of the State of Alabama as Related to Its War Activities Made at the Request of Governor Charles Henderson*. New York: Russell Sage Foundation, 1918.

Haygood, Atticus G. *The New South: Gratitude, Amendment, Hope: A Thanksgiving Sermon For November 25, 1880*. Oxford, Ga.: n.p., 1880.

"Heated Southern Blood." *New York Times*, January 11, 1890.

Hebert, Hilary A. *Why the Solid South? Or Reconstruction and Its Results*. Baltimore: R. H. Woodward, 1890.

Hendrick, Burton J. *The Life and Letters of Walter H. Page*. Vol. 1. Garden City, N.Y.: Doubleday, Page, 1923.

———. *The Training of an American: The Earlier Life and Letters of Walter Hines Page, 1855–1913*. Boston: Houghton Mifflin, 1928.

Hillyard, M. B. *The New South: A Description of the Southern States, Noting Each State Separately and Giving Their Distinctive Features and Their Most Salient Characteristics*. Baltimore: Manufacturer's Record, 1887.

Holm, John James. *Holm's Race Assimilation or the Fading Leopard's Spots: A Complete Scientific Exposition of the Most Tremendous Question That Has Ever Confronted Two Races in the World's History*. Naperville, Ill.: J. L. Nichols, 1910.

Huntington, Ellsworth. *Civilization and Climate*. 3rd ed. New Haven, Conn.: Yale University Press, 1924.

Ingle, Edward. *The Ogden Movement: An Educational Monopoly in the Making*. Baltimore: Manufacturer's Record, 1908.

"Is Laziness Due to a Germ?" *Public Opinion* 33 (December 11, 1902): 756.

Johnsen, Julia E. *Selected Articles on the Negro Problem*. New York: H. W. Wilson, 1921.

Johnson, Charles S., Edwin R. Embree, and W. W. Alexander. *The Collapse of Cotton Tenancy: Summary of Field Studies and Statistical Surveys 1933–1935*. 1935. Reprint, Freeport, N.Y.: Books for Libraries Press, 1972.

Johnston, Sir Henry Hamilton. *Britain across the Seas: Africa, a History, and a Description of the British Empire in Africa*. London: National Society's Depository, 1910.

———. *A History of the Colonization of Africa by Alien Races*. Cambridge, U.K.: University Press, 1913.

———. *The Negro in the New World*. London: Methuen, 1910.

———. *The Opening Up of Africa*. New York: H. Holt, 1911.

Jones, C. H. "Sectional Fiction." *Appleton's Journal: A Magazine of General Literature* 9 (December 1880): 563–70.

Jones, Thomas Jesse. *Education in Africa: A Study of West, South, and Equatorial Africa by the Education in Africa Commission*. New York: Phelps-Stokes Fund, 1922.

———. *Negro Education: A Study of the Private and Higher Schools for Colored People in the United States*. Washington, D.C.: Government Printing Office, 1917.

Kelley, William D. *The Old South and the New: A Series of Letters*. New York: G. P. Putnam, 1888.

Krock, Arthur, ed. *The Editorials of Henry Watterson*. New York: George H. Doran, 1923.

LeConte, Joseph. *The Race Problem in the South*. 1892. Reprint, Miami, Fla.: Mnemosyne, 1969.

"Little Known of the Real South." *New York Times*, May 6, 1926.

Livingstone, W. P. *Black Jamaica: A Study in Evolution*. London: S. Low Marston, 1900.

———. *The Race Conflict: A Study of Conditions in America*. London: S. Low, Marston, 1911.

Mackie, John Milton. *From Cape Cod to Dixie and the Tropics*. New York: G. P. Putnam, 1864.

Martin, Oscar Baker. *The Demonstration Work: Dr. Seaman A. Knapp's Contribution to Civilization*. Boston: Stratford, 1921.

Mathews, Basil. *The Clash of Colour: A Study in the Problem of Race*. Edinburgh: Edinburgh House Press, 1925.

McClure, Alexander. *The South: Its Industrial, Financial and Political Condition.* Philadelphia: J. B. Lippincott, 1885.

McCulloch, James, ed. *Battling for Social Betterment: Southern Sociological Congress, Memphis, Tennessee, May 6–10, 1914.* Nashville, Tenn.: Southern Sociological Congress, 1914.

——. *The Call of the New South: Addresses Delivered at the Southern Sociological Congress, Nashville, Tennessee, May 7–10, 1912.* Nashville, Tenn.: Southern Sociological Congress, 1912.

——. *The South Mobilizing for Social Service: Addresses Delivered at the Southern Sociological Congress Atlanta, Georgia, April 25–29, 1913.* Nashville, Tenn.: Southern Sociological Congress, 1913.

McKinley, Carlyle. *An Appeal to Pharaoh: The Negro Problem, and Its Radical Solution.* 3rd ed. Columbia, S.C.: State, 1907.

McKinley, Earl Baldwin. *A Geography of Disease: A Preliminary Survey of the Incidence and Distribution of Tropical and Certain Other Diseases.* Washington, D.C.: George Washington University Press, 1935.

Mecklin, John. *Democracy and Race Friction: A Study in Social Ethics.* New York: Macmillan, 1914.

Mencken, H. L. *Prejudices, Second Series.* New York: Alfred A. Knopf, 1920.

Mercier, W. B., and H. E. Savely. *The Knapp Method of Growing Cotton.* New York: Doubleday, Page, 1913.

Merriam, George S. *The Negro and the Nation: A History of American Slavery and Enfranchisement.* 1906. Reprint, Westport, Conn.: Negro Universities Press, 1969.

Miller, Kelly. *An Appeal to Conscience: America's Code of Caste a Disgrace to Democracy.* Introduction by Albert Bushnell Hart. New York: Macmillan, 1918.

——. *The Everlasting Stain.* Washington, D.C.: Associated Publishers, 1924.

——. *Out of the House of Bondage: A Discussion of the Race Problem.* New York: T. Y. Crowell, 1914.

——. *Race Adjustment: Radicals and Conservatives and Other Essays on the Negro in America.* 1908. Reprint, New York: Schocken, 1968.

Miller, T. S., Sr. *The American Cotton System Historically Treated: Showing Operations of the Cotton Exchanges. Also Cotton Classification with Numerous Practical Domestic and Foreign Commercial Calculations.* Austin, Tex.: Austin Printing, 1909.

Mims, Edwin. *The Advancing South: Stories of Progress and Reaction.* Garden City, N.Y.: Doubleday, Page, 1926.

Mitchell, Broadus. *The Rise of Cotton Mills in the South.* 1921. Reprint, Gloucester, Mass.: P. Smith, 1966.

Mitchell, Broadus, and George Sinclair Mitchell. *The Industrial Revolution in the South*. Baltimore: Johns Hopkins University Press, 1930.

Morris, Charles. *The Old South and the New: A Complete Illustrated History of the Southern States, Their Resources, Their People, Their Cities, and the Inspiring Story of Their Wonderful Growth in Industry and Riches*. Philadelphia: n.p., 1907.

"Mr. St. John Explains." *New York Times*, January 10, 1890.

Murchison, Claudius T. *King Cotton Is Sick*. Chapel Hill: University of North Carolina Press, 1930.

Murphy, Edgar Gardner. *The Basis of Ascendancy: A Discussion of Certain Principles of Public Policy Involved in the Development of the Southern States*. New York: Longmans, Green, 1909.

———. *The Problems of the Present South*. New York: Macmillan, 1904.

New-York Merchant. *The Negro Labor Question*. New York: J. A. Gray, 1858.

Odum, Howard W., for the Southern Regional Committee of the Social Science Research Council. *Southern Regions of the United States*. Chapel Hill: University of North Carolina Press, 1936.

Olmsted, Frederick Law. *A Journey in the Back Country, 1853–1854*. 1860. Reprint, New York: Schocken, 1870.

———. *A Journey in the Seaboard Slave States with Remarks on Their Economy*. New York: n.p., 1856.

Official Guide to the Cotton States and International Exposition Held at Atlanta, Ga., U.S.A. September 28–December 31, 1895. Atlanta: Franklin Printing, 1895.

Otken, Charles H. *The Ills of the South; or Related Causes Hostile to the General Prosperity of the Southern People*. New York: G. P. Putnam's Sons, 1894.

Page, Thomas Nelson. *The Negro: The Southerner's Problem*. New York: Charles Scribner's Sons, 1904.

Page, Walter Hines. *The Rebuilding of Old Commonwealths: Essays Toward the Training of the Forgotten Man in the Southern States*. New York: Doubleday, Page, 1902.

———. *The Southerner*. Edited and with an introduction by Scott Romine. 1909. Reprint, Columbia: University of South Carolina Press, 2008.

Pickett, William P. *The Negro Problem: Abraham Lincoln's Solution*. 1909. Reprint, Westport, Conn.: Negro Universities Press, 1969.

Poe, Clarence Hamilton. *My First Eighty Years*. Chapel Hill: University of North Carolina Press, 1963.

———. *A Southerner in Europe. Being Chiefly Some Old World Lessons for New World Needs as Set Forth in Fourteen Letters of Foreign Travel*. Raleigh, N.C.: Mutual, 1908.

———. *Where Half the World Is Waking Up: The Old and New in Japan, China, the Philippines, and India.* Garden City, N.Y.: Doubleday, Page, 1911.

Prospectus of the Cotton States and International Exposition Held at Atlanta, Ga., U.S.A. September 28–December 31, 1895. Atlanta: Franklin Printing, 1895.

Race Problems of the South. Proceedings of the First Annual Conference. Published for the Southern Society for the Promotion of the Study of Race Conditions and Problems in the South. Richmond, Va.: B. F. Johnson, 1900.

Read, Hollis. *The Negro Problem Solved: or Africa as She Was, as She Is, and as She Shall Be; Her Curse and Her Cure.* 1864. Reprint, New York: Negro Universities Press, 1969.

Reed, John C. *The Old South and the New.* A. S. Barnes, 1876.

Reuter, Edward Byron. *The American Race Problem: A Study of the Negro.* New York: Thomas Y. Crowell, 1927.

———. *The Mulatto in the United States: Including a Study of the Role of Mixed-Blood Races throughout the World.* 1918. Reprint, Westport, Conn.: Negro Universities Press, 1969.

———. *Race Mixture: Studies in Intermarriage and Miscegenation.* New York: McGraw-Hill, 1931.

Riley, Benjamin Franklin. *The White Man's Burden: A Discussion of the Interracial Question with Special Reference to the Responsibility of the White Race to the Negro Problem.* 1910. Reprint, Westport, Conn.: Negro Universities Press, 1969.

Robertson, Eugene C. *The Road to Wealth Leads through the South: Solid Facts from Settlers along the Lines.* Cincinnati: n.p., 1894.

Rockefeller Sanitary Commission for the Eradication of Hookworm Disease. *Second Annual Report.* Washington, D.C.: Offices of the Commission, 1911.

———. *Fourth Annual Report for the Year 1913.* Washington, D.C.: Office of the Commission, 1914.

Royce, Josiah. *Race Questions, Provincialism, and Other American Problems.* New York: Macmillan, 1908.

Scherer, James A. B. *Cotton as a World Power: A Study in the Economic Interpretation of History.* New York: Frederick A. Stokes, 1916.

Schurz, Carl. *The New South.* New York: American News, 1885.

Schuyler, George. *Black No More.* 1931. New York: Modern Library, 1999.

Second Mohonk Conference on the Negro Question Held at Lake Mohonk, Ulster County, New York, June 3, 4, 5, 1890. Reported and edited by Isabel C. Barrows. Boston: George H. Ellis, printer, 1891.

Shannon, A. H. *Racial Integrity and Other Features of the Negro Problem.* 1907. Reprint, New York: Books For Libraries Press, 1972.

Shurter, Edwin DuBois, ed. *The Complete Oration and Speeches of Henry W. Grady.* New York: Hinds, Noble & Eldredge, 1910.

Sinclair, William. *The Aftermath of Slavery: A Study of the Condition and Environment of the Negro.* Boston: Small, Maynard, 1905.

Skaggs, William H. *The Southern Oligarchy: An Appeal on Behalf of the Silent Masses of Our Country against the Despotic Rule of the Few.* New York: Bonnell, Silver, 1907.

Smith, William Benjamin. *The Color Line: A Brief in Behalf of the Unborn.* New York: McClure, Phillips, 1905.

Southern Education Board. *Proceedings of the Conference for Education in the South, the Sixth Session, Richmond Virginia.* New York: Committee on Publication, 1903.

——— . *Proceedings of the Eighth Conference for Education in the South, Columbia, S.C., April 26-28, 1905.* New York: Committee on Publication, 1905.

——— . *Proceedings of the Fifth Conference for Education in the South Held at Athens Georgia, April 24, 25, and 16, 1902.* New York: Southern Education Board, 1902.

——— . *Proceedings of the Ninth Conference for Education in the South, Lexington, KY, May 2-4, 1906.* Chattanooga, Tenn.: Times Printing, 1906.

Southern Society for the Promotion of the Study of Race Conditions and Problems in the South. *Race Problems of the South. Report of the Proceedings of the First Annual Conference Held Under the Auspices of the Southern Society for the Promotion of the Study of Race Conditions and Problems in the South, at Montgomery, Alabama, May 8, 9, 10, A.D. 1900.* Richmond, Va.: B. F. Johnson, 1900.

Stone, Alfred H. *Studies in the American Race Problem. With an Introduction and Three Papers by Walter F. Willcox.* New York: Doubleday, Page, 1908.

Straker, David Augustus. *The New South Investigated.* 1888. Reprint, New York: Arno Press, 1973.

Tannenbaum, Frank. *The Darker Phases of the South.* New York: G. P. Putnam's Sons, 1924.

Thompkins, Daniel Augustus. *A Builder of the New South: Being a Story of the Life Work of Daniel Augustus Thompkins.* Garden City, N.Y.: Doubleday, Page, 1920.

Thompson, Holland. *The New South: A Chronicle of Social and Industrial Education.* New Haven, Conn.: Yale University Press, 1919.

Todd, John A. *The World's Cotton Crops.* London: A & C Black, 1915.

Tourgée, Albion. *A Fool's Errand by One of the Fools.* New York: Fords, Howard, & Hulbert, 1879.

Tremain, Henry Edwin. *Sectionalism Unmasked.* 1907. Reprint, New York: Negro
Universities Press, 1969.

Turner, Frederick Jackson. *The Frontier in American History.* New York: Henry, Holt,
1920.

———. "Geographic Sectionalism in American History." *Annals of the American
Association of Geographers* 16 (June 1926): 85–93.

———. *The Significance of Sections in American History.* New York: Henry Holt, 1932.

Turpin, Edna Henry Lee. *Cotton.* New York: American Book, 1924.

———, ed. *The New South and Other Addresses by Henry Woodfin Grady With
Biography, Critical Opinions, and Explanatory Notes.* New York: Charles E. Merrill,
1904.

"Tuskegee International Conference on the Negro." *Journal of Race Development* 3
(July 1912): 117–20.

Universal Races Congress. *Papers on Inter-racial Problems Communicated to the
First Universal Races Congress, Held at the University of London, July 26–29, 1911.*
London: P. S. King & Son, 1911.

University Commission on Southern Questions. *Minutes of the University Commission
on Southern Race Questions.* Lexington, Va.: n.p., 191–.

Vance, Rupert B. *Human Factors in Cotton Culture: A Study in the Social Geography of
the American South.* Chapel Hill: University of North Carolina Press, 1929.

Warshaw, Leon J. *Malaria: The Biography of a Killer.* New York: Rinehart, 1949.

Watkins, James L. *King Cotton: A Historical and Statistical Review 1790 to 1908.* New
York: James L. Watkins & Sons, 1908.

Weatherford, W. D. *Negro Life in the South: Present Conditions and Needs.* New York:
Association Press, 1918.

———. *Present Forces in Negro Progress.* New York: Association Press, 1912.

Wells, Ida B. *Southern Horrors and Other Writings: The Anti-Lynching Campaign of
Ida B. Wells, 1892–1900.* Edited with an introduction by Jacqueline Jones Royster.
Boston: Bedford Books, 1997.

Wilcox, Earley Vernon. "The Great White Way of Cotton." *Country Gentleman* 87
(March 31, 1922): 78.

———. *Tropical Agriculture: The Climate, Soils, Cultural Methods, Crops, Livestock,
Commercial Importance and Opportunities of the Tropics.* New York: D. Appleton,
1916.

Willis, Henry Parker. *Our Philippine Problem: A Study of American Colonial Policy.*
New York: H. Holt, 1905.

Yearbook of the New York Southern Society for the Years 1901 and 1902. New York: W. F.
Vanden Houten, 1902.

SECONDARY SOURCES

Aboul-Ela, Hosam. *Other South: Faulkner, Coloniality, and the Mariategui Tradition.* Pittsburgh: University of Pittsburgh Press, 2007.

Adas, Michael. "From Settler Colony to Global Hegemon: Integrating the Exceptionalist Narrative of the American History into World Experience." *American Historical Review* 106 (December 2001): 1692–1720.

"AHR Forum: Bringing Regionalism Back to History." *American Historical Review* 4 (October 1999): 1156–1220.

Anderson, Benedict. *Imagined Communities: Reflections on the Origins and Spread of Nationalism.* Rev. ed. London: Verso Press, 1991.

Anderson, Warwick. *Colonial Pathologies: American Tropical Medicine, Race, and Hygiene in the Philippines.* Durham, N.C.: Duke University Press, 2006.

———. "Disease, Race, and Empire." *Bulletin of the History of Medicine* 70 (Spring 1996): 62–67.

———. "Immunities of Empire: Race, Disease, and the New Tropical Medicine, 1900–1920." *Bulletin of the History of Medicine* 70 (Spring 1996): 94–118.

Angoff, Charles. *H. L. Mencken: A Portrait From Memory.* New York: Thomas Yoseloff, 1954.

Angoff, Charles, and Thomas Yoseloff. *The Man from the* Mercury: *A Charles Angoff Memorial Reader.* Madison, N.J.: Fairleigh Dickinson University Press, 1985.

Applegate, Celia. "A Europe of Regions: Reflections on Historiography of Sub-national Places in Modern Times." *American Historical Review* 4 (October 1999): 1157–82.

Aptheker, Herbert. "American Imperialism and White Chauvinism." In *Toward Negro Freedom: Historic Highlights in the Life and Struggles of the American Negro People From Colonial Days to Present,* 88–95. New York: New Century, 1956.

Arnold, David. *Colonizing the Body: State Medicine and Epidemic Disease in Nineteenth-Century India.* Berkeley: University of California Press, 1993.

———. "'Illusory Riches': Representations of the Tropical World, 1840–1950." *Singapore Journal of Tropical Geography* 21 (January 2000): 6–18.

———. "Inventing Tropicality." In *The Problem of Nature: Environment, Culture, and European Expansion.* Oxford: Blackwell, 1996.

———, ed. *Warm Climates and Western Medicine: The Emergence of Tropical Medicine 1500–1900.* Atlanta: Rodopi, 1996.

Ayers, Edward L. *Promise of the New South: Life after Reconstruction.* New York: Oxford University Press, 1992.

Ayers, Edward L., and Peter S. Onuf. *All over the Map: Rethinking American Regions.* Baltimore: Johns Hopkins University Press, 1996.

Bailey, Hugh C. *Liberalism in the New South: Southern Social Reformers and the Progressive Movement.* Coral Gables, Fla.: University of Miami Press, 1969.

Bailey, Joseph Cannon. *Seaman A. Knapp: Schoolmaster of American Agriculture.* New York: Columbia University Press, 1945.

Bardaglio, Peter Winthrop. *Reconstructing the Household: Families, Sex, and the Law in the Nineteenth-Century South.* Chapel Hill: University of North Carolina Press, 1995.

Bay, Mia. *The White Image in the Black Mind: African-American Ideas about White People, 1830–1925.* New York: Oxford University Press, 2000.

Beckert, Sven. "Emancipation and Empire: Reconstructing the Worldwide Web of Cotton Production in the Age of the American Civil War." *American Historical Review* 109 (December 2004): 1405–38.

———. "From Tuskegee to Togo: The Problem of Freedom in the Empire of Cotton." *Journal of American History* 92 (September 2005): 498–526.

Bederman, Gail. *Manliness and Civilization: A Cultural History of Gender and Race in the United States, 1880–1917.* Chicago: University of Chicago Press, 1995.

Bell, Morag. "American Philanthropy, the Carnegie Corporation and Poverty in South Africa." *Journal of Southern African Studies* 26 (September 2000): 481–504.

Bensel, Franklin. *The Political Economy of American Industrialization, 1877–1900.* New York: Cambridge University Press, 2000.

Berry, Mary Francis. "Judging Morality: Sexual Behavior and Legal Consequences in the Late Nineteenth-Century South." *Journal of American History* 78 (December 1991): 835–56.

Bertelson, David. *The Lazy South.* New York: Oxford University Press, 1967.

Bhabha, Homi K. "The Other Question: Stereotype, Discrimination, and the Discourse of Colonialism." In Bhabha, *The Location of Culture.* New York: Routledge Press, 1994.

Billings, Dwight B., Gurney Norman, and Katherine Ledford, eds. *Confronting Appalachian Stereotypes: Back Talk from an American Region.* Lexington: University of Kentucky Press, 1999.

Billington, Ray Allen. *Frederick Jackson Turner: Historian, Scholar, Teacher.* New York: Oxford University Press, 1973.

Birn, Anne-Emanuelle. *Marriage of Convenience: Rockefeller International Health and Revolutionary Mexico.* Rochester, N.Y.: University of Rochester Press, 2006.

Birn, Anne-Emanuelle, and Armando Solorzano. "The Hook of Hookworm: Public Health and the Politics of Eradication in Mexico." In *Western Medicine: Contest of Knowledge.* Edited by Andrew Cunningham and Bridie Andrews. New York: St. Martin's Press, 1997.

Bleakley, Hoyt. "Disease and Development: Evidence from Hookworm Eradication in the American South." *Quarterly Journal of Economics* 122 (February 2007): 73–117.

Bledstein, Burton J. *The Culture of Professionalism: The Middle Class and the Development of Higher Education in America.* New York: Norton, 1976.

Blight, David W. *Race and Reunion: The Civil War in American Memory.* Cambridge, Mass.: Harvard University Press, 2000.

Blum, J. Edward. "The Crucible of Disease: Trauma, Memory, and National Reconciliation during the Yellow Fever Epidemic of 1878." *Journal of Southern History* 69 (November 2003): 791–820.

———. *Reforging the White Republic: Race, Religion, and American Nationalism.* Baton Rouge: Louisiana State University Press, 2007.

Boccaccio, Mary. "Ground Itch and Dew Poison: The Rockefeller Sanitary Commission 1909–1914." *Journal of the History of Medicine and Allied Sciences* 27 (January 1972): 30–53.

Bogue, Allan G. *Frederick Jackson Turner: Strange Roads Going Down.* Norman: University of Oklahoma Press, 1998.

Bordieu, Pierre. "Identity and Representation: Elements for a Critical Reflection on the Idea of a Region." In *Language and Symbolic Power.* Edited by John B. Thompson and translated by Gino Raymond and Matthew Adamson. Cambridge, Mass.: Harvard University Press, 1991.

Borges, Dain. "'Puffy, Ugly, Slothful and Inert': Degeneration in Brazilian Social Thought, 1880–1940." *Journal of Latin American Studies* 25 (May 1993): 235–56.

Bourdaghs, Michael K. "The Disease of Nationalism, the Empire of Hygiene." *Positions: East Asia Cultures Critique* 6 (Winter 1998): 637–73.

Bowers, William L. *The Country Life Movement in America, 1900–1920.* Port Washington, N.Y.: Kennikat Press, 1974.

Bowler, Peter J. *The Eclipse of Darwinism: Anti-Darwinian Evolution Theories in the Decades around 1900.* Baltimore: Johns Hopkins University Press, 1983.

———. *The Invention of Progress: The Victorians and the Past.* Oxford, U.K.: B. Blackwell, 1980.

Brannstrom, Christian. "Polluted Soil, Polluted Souls: The Rockefeller Hookworm Eradication Campaign in Sao Paul, Brazil, 1917–1926." *Historical Geography* 2 (1997): 25–45.

Brown, Julie K. *Health and Medicine on Display: International Expositions in the United States, 1876–1904.* Cambridge, Mass.: MIT Press, 2009.

Brown, Richard E. "Public Health in Imperialism: Early Rockefeller Programs at Home and Abroad." *American Journal of Public Health* 66 (September 1976): 879–903.

———. *Rockefeller Medicine Men: Medicine and Capitalism in America*. Berkeley: University of California Press, 1979.

Buck, Paul H. *The Road to Reunion, 1865–1900*. Boston: Little, Brown, 1937.

Buettner, Elizabeth. "Problematic Spaces, Problematic Races: Defining 'Europeans' in Late Colonial India." *Women's History Review* 9 (June 2000): 277–98.

Butchart, Ronald E. *Northern Schools, Southern Blacks, and Reconstruction: Freedmen's Education, 1862–1875*. Westport, Conn.: Greenwood Press, 1980.

Butler, Leslie. *Critical Americans: Victorian Intellectuals and Transatlantic Liberal Reform*. Chapel Hill: University of North Carolina Press, 2007.

Carlton, David J. *Mill and Town in South Carolina, 1880–1920*. Baton Rouge: Louisiana State University Press, 1982.

Carrigan, Jo Ann. *The Saffron Scourge: A History of Yellow Fever in Louisiana, 1796–1905*. Lafayette: University of Southwest Louisiana, 1994.

Cassedy, James H. "The 'Germ of Laziness' in the South, 1901–1915: Charles Wardell Stiles and the Progressive Paradox." *Bulletin of the History of Medicine* 45 (March–April 1971): 159–69.

Cell, John Whitson. *The Highest Stage of White Supremacy: The Origins of Segregation in South Africa and the American South*. New York: Cambridge University Press, 1982.

Chamberlin, J. Edward, and Sander L. Gilman. *Degeneration: The Dark Side of Progress*. New York: Columbia University Press, 1985.

Chatfield, E. Charles. "The Southern Sociological Congress: Organization of Uplift." *Tennessee Historical Quarterly* 19 (December 1960): 327–48.

———. "The Southern Sociological Congress: Rationale of Uplift." *Tennessee Historical Quarterly* 20 (March 1961): 51–64.

Chernow, Ron. *Titan: The Life of John D. Rockefeller Sr.* 2nd ed. New York: Vintage, 2004.

Chomsky, Aviva. *West Indian Workers and the United Fruit Company in Costa Rica, 1870–1940*. Baton Rouge: Louisiana State University Press, 1995.

Clayton, Bruce. *The Savage Ideal: Intolerance and Intellectual Leadership in the South, 1890–1917*. Baltimore: Johns Hopkins University Press, 1972.

———. "Southern Critics of the New South, 1890–1914." PhD diss., Duke University, 1966.

Clune, Erin Elizabeth. "Emancipation to Empire: Race, Labor, and Ideology in the New South." PhD diss., New York University, 2002.

———. "'From Light Copper to the Blackest and Lowest Type': Daniel Thompkins and the Racial Order of the Global New South." *Journal of Southern History* 76 (May 2010): 275–314.

Cobb, James C. *Away Down South: A History of Southern Identity*. New York: Oxford University Press, 2005.

Conforti, Joseph A. *Imagining New England: Exploration of Regional Identity From the Pilgrims to the Mid-Twentieth Century*. Chapel Hill: University of North Carolina Press, 2000.

Cooper, John Milton, Jr. *Walter Hines Page: The Southerner as American, 1855–1918*. Chapel Hill: University of North Carolina Press, 1977.

Cox, John David. *Traveling South: Travel Narratives and the Construction of American Identity*. Athens: University of Georgia Press, 2005.

Cox, Karen L. *Dreaming of Dixie: How the South Was Created in American Popular Culture*. Chapel Hill: University of North Carolina Press, 2011.

Cueto, Marcos, ed. *Missionaries of Science: The Rockefeller Foundation and Latin America*. Bloomington: Indiana University Press, 1994.

Curtin, Philip D. *Death by Migration: Europe's Encounter with the Tropical World in the Nineteenth Century*. New York: Cambridge University Press, 1989.

Dal Lago, Enrico, and Rick Halpern, eds. *The American South and the Italian Mezzogiorno*. New York: Palgrave, 2002.

Daniel, Pete. *Breaking the Land: The Transformation of Cotton, Tobacco, and Rice Cultures since 1880*. Urbana: University of Illinois Press, 1985.

Davenport, F. Garvin, Jr. *The Myth of Southern History: Historical Consciousness in Twentieth-Century Southern Literature*. Nashville, Tenn.: Vanderbilt University Press, 1970.

Davis, David Brion. *Slavery and Human Progress*. New York: Oxford University Press, 1984.

Delfino, Susanna, and Michele Gillespie. *Global Perspectives on Industrial Transformation in the American South*. Columbia: University of Missouri Press, 2005.

Dennis, Michael. *Lessons in Progress. State Universities and Progressivism in the New South*. Urbana: University of Illinois Press, 2001.

Dickie, John. *Darkest Italy: The Nation and Stereotypes of the Mezzogiorno, 1860–1900*. New York: St. Martin's Press, 1999.

Dirks, Nicholas B. *Colonialism and Culture*. Ann Arbor: University of Michigan Press, 1992.

Doherty, Herbert J. "Voices of Protest from the New South, 1875–1910." *Mississippi Valley Historical Review* 42 (June 1955): 45–66.

Dorman, Robert L., and Charles Reagan Wilson. *The New Regionalism*. Jackson: University of Mississippi Press, 1998.

Dorr, Gregory Michael. *Segregation's Science: Eugenics and Society in Virginia*. Charlottesville: University of Virginia Press, 2008.

Doyle, Don H. *Nations Divided: America, Italy, and the Southern Question*. Athens: University of Georgia Press, 2002.

Driver, Felix, and Brenda S. A. Yeoh. "Constructing the Tropics: Introduction." *Singapore Journal of Tropical Geography* 21 (March 2000): 1–5.

DuBow, Saul. *Scientific Racism in Modern South Africa*. New York: Cambridge University Press, 1995.

Duck, Leigh Anne. *The Nation's Region: Southern Modernism, Segregation, and U.S. Nationalism*. Athens: University of Georgia Press, 2006.

Duffy, John. *The Sanitarians: A History of American Public Health*. Urbana: University of Illinois Press, 1990.

Dunn, Hampton. "Florida: Jewel of the Gilded Age." *Gulf Coast Historical Review* 10 (1994): 19–28.

Edwards, Laura F. "Southern History as U.S. History." *Journal of Southern History* 75 (August 2009): 1–32.

Edwards, William A. "Racial Purity in Black and White: The Case of Marcus Garvey and Earnest Cox." *Journal of Ethnic Studies* 15 (Spring 1987): 117–42.

Elliott, Mark. *Color-Blind Justice: Albion Tourgée and the Quest for Racial Equality from the Civil War to Plessy v. Ferguson*. New York: Oxford University Press, 2006.

Elliott, Michael A. "Telling the Difference: Nineteenth-Century Legal Narratives of Racial Taxonomy." *Law and Social Inquiry* 24 (1999): 611–36.

Espinosa, Mariola. "The Threat from Havana: Southern Public Health, Yellow Fever, and the U.S. Intervention in the Cuban Struggle for Independence, 1878–1898." *Journal of Southern History* 72 (August 2006): 541–68.

Etheridge, Elizabeth W. *The Butterfly Caste: A Social History of Pellagra*. Westport, Conn.: Greenwood Press, 1972.

Ettling, John. *Germ of Laziness: Rockefeller Philanthropy and Public Health in the New South*. Cambridge, Mass.: Harvard University Press, 1981.

Fabi, M. Giulia. *Passing and the Rise of the African-American Novel*. Champaign: University of Illinois Press, 2001.

Farley, John. *To Cast Out Disease: A History of the International Health Division of the Rockefeller Foundation*. New York: Oxford University Press, 2004.

Fee, Elizabeth. *Disease and Discovery: A History of the Johns Hopkins School of Hygiene and Public Health, 1916–1939*. Baltimore: Johns Hopkins University Press, 1987.

Feimster, Crystal N. *Southern Horrors: Women and the Politics of Rape and Lynching*. Cambridge, Mass.: Harvard University Press, 2009.

Ferguson, Jeffrey B. *The Sage of Sugar Hill: George S. Schuyler and the Harlem Renaissance*. New Haven, Conn.: Yale University Press, 2005.

Fishel, Leslie H., Jr. "The 'Negro Question' at Mohonk: Microcosm, Mirage, and Message." *New York History* 74 (July 1993): 277–314.

Fitzpatrick, Vincent. *Gerald W. Johnson: From Southern Liberal to National Conscience.* Baton Rouge: Louisiana State University Press, 2002.

————. *H. L. Mencken.* Macon, Ga.: Mercer University Press, 2004.

Flamming, Douglas. *Creating the Modern South: Millhands and Managers in Dalton, Georgia.* Chapel Hill: University of North Carolina Press, 1992.

Fleisch, Brahm David. "Social Scientists as Policy Makers: E. G. Malherbe and the National Bureau for Educational and Social Research, 1929–1943." *Journal of South African Studies* 21 (September 1995): 349–72.

Foley, Neil. *The White Scourge: Mexicans, Blacks, and Poor Whites in the Cotton Culture of Central Texas.* Berkeley: University of California Press, 1997.

Foner, Eric. *Free Soil, Free Labor, Free Men: The Ideology of the Republican Party before the Civil War.* New York: Oxford University Press, 1970.

"Forum: Empires and Intimacies: Lessons from (Post) Colonial Studies." *Journal of American History* 88 (December 2001): 829–97.

"Forum: Islands in History: Perspectives on U.S. Imperialism and the Legacies of 1898." *Radical History Review* 73 (Winter 1999): 1–146.

Fosdick, Raymond B. *Adventure in Giving: The Story of the General Education Board, a Foundation Established by John D. Rockefeller.* New York: Harper & Row, 1962.

Foster, Gaines M. *Ghosts of the Confederacy: Defeat, The Lost Cause, and the Emergence of the New South, 1865–1913.* New York: Oxford University Press, 1987.

Foucault, Michel. *The Birth of the Clinic: An Archaeology of Medical Perception.* 1973. Reprint, New York: Pantheon Books, 1994.

Fredrickson, George M. *The Black Image in the White Mind: The Debate on Afro-American Character and Destiny, 1817–1914.* Hanover, N.H.: Wesleyan University Press, 1971.

————. *Black Liberation: A Comparative History of Black Ideologies in the United States and South Africa.* New York: Oxford University Press, 1995.

————. "From Exceptionalism to Variability: Recent Developments in Cross-National Comparative History." *Journal of American History* 82 (September 1995): 587–604.

————. *White Supremacy: A Comparative Study in American and South African History.* New York: Oxford University Press, 1981.

Frenkel, Stephen. "Geographical Representations of the 'Other': The Landscape of the Panama Canal Zone." *Journal of Historical Geography* 28 (January 2002): 85–99.

————. "Jungle Stories: North American Representations of Tropical Panama." *Geographical Review* 86 (July 1996): 317–33.

Frost, David. *Thinking Progress: Academia and the Idea of Progress in the New South.* Knoxville: University of Tennessee Press, 2000.

Gadelha, P. "Conforming Strategies of Public Health Campaigns against Hookworm and Malaria in Brazil." *Parassitologia* 40 (June 1998): 159–76.

Gaines, Kevin K. *Uplifting the Race: Black Leadership, Politics, and Culture in the Twentieth Century*. Chapel Hill: University of North Carolina Press, 1996.

Gaston, Paul M. *The New South Creed: A Study in Southern Myth Making*. New York: Alfred A. Knopf, 1970.

Gellner, Ernest. *Nations and Nationalism*. Ithaca, N.Y.: Cornell University Press, 1983.

Genovese, Eugene D. *The Political Economy of Slavery: Studies in the Economy and Society of the Slave South*. New York: Vintage Books, 1965.

Gerster, Patrick, and Nicholas Cords, eds. *Myth and Southern History: The New South*. 2nd ed. Urbana: University of Illinois Press, 1979.

Gerstle, Gary. "The Protean Character of American Liberalism." *American Historical Review* 99 (October 1994): 1043–73.

Gillespie, Michele K., and Randal L. Hall. *Thomas Dixon, Jr. and the Birth of Modern America*. Baton Rouge: Louisiana State University Press, 2006.

Gilman, Stuart C. "Degeneracy and Race in the Nineteenth Century: The Impact of Clinical Medicine." *Journal of Ethnic Studies* 10 (Spring 1983): 27–50.

Ginsberg, Elaine K. *Passing and the Fictions of Identity*. Durham, N.C.: Duke University Press, 1996.

Gossett, Thomas F. *Race: The History of an Idea in America*. 1963. New ed., New York: Oxford University Press, 1997.

Grant, Susan-Mary. *North over South: Northern Nationalism and American Identity in the Antebellum Era*. Lawrence: University Press of Kansas, 2000.

Grantham, Dewey W. "The Contours of Southern Progressivism." *American Historical Review* 86 (December 1981): 1035–59.

———. *The Regional Imagination: The South and Recent American History*. Nashville, Tenn.: Vanderbilt University Press, 1979.

———, ed. *The South and the Sectional Image: The Sectional Theme since Reconstruction*. New York: Harper & Row, 1967.

———. *Southern Progressivism: The Reconciliation of Progress and Tradition*. Knoxville: University of Tennessee Press, 1983.

Gray, Richard J. *Writing the South: Ideas of an American Region*. New York: Cambridge University Press, 1986.

Green, Dan S., and Edwin D. Driver, eds. *W. E. B. Du Bois on Sociology and the Black Community*. Chicago: University of Chicago Press, 1978.

Greeson, Jennifer Rae. *Our South: Geographic Fantasy and the Rise of National Literature*. Cambridge, Mass.: Harvard University Press, 2010.

Griffin, Larry J., and Don Doyle, eds. *The South as an American Problem*. Athens: University of Georgia Press, 1995.

Guterl, Matthew Pratt. *American Mediterranean: Southern Slaveholders in the Age of Emancipation*. Cambridge, Mass.: Harvard University Press, 2008.

Gutiérrez, David. *Walls and Mirrors: Mexican Americans, Mexican Immigrants, and the Politics of Ethnicity*. Berkeley: University of California Press, 1995.

Hahn, Steven. *Roots of Southern Populism: Yeomen Farmers and the Transformation of the Georgia Upcountry, 1850–1890*. New York: Oxford University Press, 1983.

Hale, Grace Elizabeth. *Making Whiteness: The Culture of Segregation in the South, 1890–1940*. New York: Pantheon Books, 1998.

Hall, Jacquelyn Dowd. *Like a Family: The Making of a Southern Cotton Mill World*. Chapel Hill: University of North Carolina Press, 1992.

———. "'The Mind That Burns in Each Body': Women, Rape, and Racial Violence." *Southern Exposure* 12 (November/December 1984): 61–71.

Handley, George B. *Postslavery Literatures in the Americas: Family Portraits in Black and White*. Charlottesville: University of Virginia Press, 2000.

Harlan, Louis R. "The Southern Education Board and the Race Issue in Public Education." *Journal of Southern History* 23 (May 1957): 189–202.

———, ed. *The Booker T. Washington Papers*. Urbana: University of Illinois Press, 1972.

Haskell, Thomas L. *The Emergence of Professional Social Science: The American Social Science Association and the Nineteenth-Century Crisis of Authority*. Urbana: University of Illinois Press, 1977.

Haynes, Douglas M. *Imperial Medicine: Patrick Manson and the Conquest of Tropical Disease*. Philadelphia: University of Pennsylvania Press, 2001.

Hefferman, Michael. "Inaugurating the American Century: 'New World' Perspectives on the 'Old' in the Early Twentieth Century." In *The American Century: Consensus and Coercion in the Projection of American Power*. Edited by David Slater and Peter J. Taylor. Malden, Mass.: Blackwell, 1999.

Helms, John Douglas. "Just Lookin' for a Home: The Cotton Boll Weevil and the South." PhD diss., Florida State University, 1977.

Herbin, Elizabeth Ann. "Healing the Land, Healing the South: Reforming the Southern Cotton Farm, 1900–1939. PhD diss., Columbia University, 2007.

Hewa, Soma. *Colonialism, Tropical Disease, and Imperial Medicine: Rockefeller Philanthropy in Sri Lanka*. Lanham, Md.: University Press of America, 1995.

Heyman, Richard D. "C. T. Loram: A South African Liberal in Race Relations." *International Journal of African Studies* 5 (1972): 41–50.

Higham, John. "The Reorientation of American Culture in the 1890s." In *Writing American History: Essays on Modern Scholarship*. Edited by John Higham. Bloomington: Indiana University Press, 1978.

Hobsbawm, Eric. *The Invention of Tradition*. New York: Cambridge University Press, 1983.

———. *Nations and Nationalism since 1780: Programme, Myth, Reality.* New York: Cambridge University Press, 1990.

Hobson, Fred C. *Mencken: A Life.* Baltimore: Johns Hopkins University Press, 1995.

———. "The Savage South: An Inquiry into the Origins, Endurance, and Presumed Demise of an Image." *Virginia Quarterly Review* 61 (Summer 1985): 377–95.

———. *Serpent in Eden: H. L. Mencken and the South.* Chapel Hill: University of North Carolina Press, 1974.

———, ed. *South to the Future: An American Region in the Twenty-First Century.* Athens: University of Georgia Press, 2002.

———, ed. and intro. *South-Watching: Selected Essays by Gerald W. Johnson.* Chapel Hill: University of North Carolina Press, 1983.

———. *Tell about the South: The Southern Rage to Explain.* Baton Rouge: Louisiana State University Press, 1983.

Hodes, Martha Elizabeth, ed. *Sex, Love, Race: Crossing Boundaries in North American History.* New York: New York University Press, 1999.

Hofstader, Richard. *The Age of Reform: From Bryan to F. D. R.* New York: Vintage Books, 1955.

Hoganson, Kristin L. *Fighting for American Manhood: How Gender Politics Provoked the Spanish-American and Philippine-American Wars.* New Haven, Conn.: Yale University Press, 1998.

Hollandsworth, James G., Jr. *Portrait of a Scientific Racist: Alfred Holt Stone of Mississippi.* Baton Rouge: Louisiana State University Press, 2008.

Hollinger, David A. "Amalgamation and Hypodescent: The Question of Ethnoracial Mixture in the History of the United States." *American Historical Review* 108 (December 2003): 1363–90.

Hollis, Daniel Webster, III. *An Alabama Newspaper Tradition: Grover C. Hall and the Hall Family.* Tuscaloosa: University of Alabama Press, 1983.

Holloway, Jonathan Scott. *Confronting the Veil: Abram Harris Jr., E. Franklin Frazier, and Ralph Bunche, 1919–1941.* Chapel Hill: University of North Carolina, 2002.

Hoy, Suellen. *Chasing Dirt: The American Pursuit of Cleanliness.* New York: Oxford University Press, 1995.

Humphreys, Margaret. *Malaria: Poverty, Race, and Public Health in the United States.* Baltimore: Johns Hopkins University Press, 2001.

———. *Yellow Fever and the South.* New Brunswick, N.J.: Rutgers University Press, 1992.

Hunter, Tera. *To 'Joy My Freedom: Southern Black Women's Lives and Labors after the Civil War.* Cambridge, Mass.: Harvard University Press, 1997.

Hutchinson, George B. "Whitman and the Black Poet: Kelly Miller's Speech to the Walt Whitman Fellowship." *American Literature* 61 (March 1989): 46–58.

Inscoe, John C., ed. *Appalachians and Race: The Mountain South from Slavery to Segregation.* Lexington: University of Kentucky Press, 2001.

Jacobson, Matthew Frye. *Barbarian Virtues: The United States Encounters Foreign Peoples at Home and Abroad, 1876–1917.* New York: Hill and Wang, 2000.

———. *Whiteness of a Different Color: European Immigrants and the Alchemy of Race.* Cambridge, Mass.: Harvard University Press, 1999.

Jansson, David R. "American Hegemony and the Irony of C. Vann Woodward's 'The Irony of Southern History.'" *Southeastern Geographer* 44 (May 2004): 90–114.

———. "American National Identity and the Progress of the New South in *National Geographic Magazine*." *Geographical Review* 93 (July 2003): 350–69.

———. "The Haunting of the South: American Geopolitical Identity and the Burden of Southern History." *Geopolitics* 12 (July 2007): 400–425.

———. "Internal Orientalism in America: W. J. Cash's *The Mind of the South* and the Spatial Construction of American National Identity." *Political Geography* 22 (March 2003): 293–316.

Jordan, David, ed. *Regionalism Reconsidered: New Approaches to the Field.* New York: Garland, 1994.

Kaplan, Amy. *Anarchy of Empire in the Making of U.S. Culture.* Cambridge, Mass.: Harvard University Press, 2002.

———. "Romancing the Empire: The Embodiment of American Masculinity in the Popular Historical Novel of the 1890s." *American Literary History* 3 (December 1990): 659–90.

Kaplan, Amy, and Donald E. Pease. *Cultures of United States Imperialism.* Durham, N.C.: Duke University Press, 1993.

Keire, Mara L. "The Vice Trust: A Reinterpretation of the White Slavery Scare in the United States, 1907–1917." *Journal of Social History* 35 (Fall 2001): 5–41.

Keller, Richard. "Madness and Colonialism: Psychiatry in the British and French Empires." *Journal of Social History* 35 (Winter 2001): 295–326.

Kelley, Robin D. G. "'But a Local Phase of a World Problem': Black History's Global Vision, 1883–1950." *Journal of American History* 86 (December 1999): 1045–77.

Kennedy, Dane. "The Perils of the Midday Sun: Climatic Anxieties in the Colonial Tropics." In *Imperialism and the Natural World.* Edited by John D. MacKenzie. New York: St. Martin's Press, 1990.

Kermes, Stephanie. *Creating an American Identity: New England, 1789–1825.* New York: Palgrave Macmillan, 2008.

Kershner, R. B., Jr. "Degeneration: The Explanatory Nightmare." *Georgia Review* 40 (Summer 1986): 416–44.

Kirby, Jack Temple. *Darkness at the Dawning: Race and Reform in the Progressive South*. Philadelphia: Lippincott, 1972.

——— . *Media-Made Dixie: The South in the American Imagination*. Baton Rouge: Louisiana State University Press, 1978.

Kloppenberg, James T. *Uncertain Victory: Social Democracy and Progressivism in European and American Thought, 1870–1920*. New York: Oxford University Press, 1986.

Kowalewski, Michael. "Writing in Place: The New American Regionalism." *American Literary History* 6 (Spring 1994): 171–83.

Kramer, Paul A. *The Blood of Government: Race, Empire, the United States and the Philippines*. Chapel Hill: University of North Carolina Press, 2006.

——— . "Empires, Exceptions, and Anglo-Saxons: Race and Rule between the British and United States Empires, 1880–1910." *Journal of American History* 88 (March 2002): 1315–53.

——— . "Jim Crow Science and the 'Negro Problem' in the Occupied Philippines, 1898–1914." In *Race Consciousness: African-American Studies for a New Century*. Edited by Judith Jackson Fossett and Jeffrey A. Tucker. New York: New York University Press, 1997.

——— . "Making Concessions: Race and Empire Revisited at the Philippine Exposition, St. Louis, 1901–1905." *Radical History Review* 73 (Winter 1999): 74–114.

Kupperman, Karen Ordahl. "Fear of Hot Climes in the Anglo-American Colonial Experience." *William and Mary Quarterly* 41 (April 1984): 213–40.

LaFeber, Walter. *The New Empire: An Interpretation of American Expansion, 1860–1898*. Ithaca, N.Y.: Published for the American Historical Association by Cornell University Press, 1963.

Lagemann, Ellen Condliffe. *The Politics of Knowledge: The Carnegie Corporation, Philanthropy, and Public Policy*. Chicago: University of Chicago Press, 1989.

Lake, Marilyn, and Henry Reynolds. *Drawing the Global Colour Line: White Men's Countries and the International Challenge of Racial Equality*. New York: Cambridge University Press, 2008.

Lambert, David. "Liminal Figures: Poor Whites, Freedmen, and Racial Reinscription in Colonial Barbados." *Environment and Planning D: Society and Space* 19 (2001): 335–50.

Larson, Edward J. *Sex, Race, and Science: Eugenics in the Deep South*. Baltimore: Johns Hopkins University Press, 1995.

Lears, T. J. Jackson. *No Place of Grace: Anti-Modernism and the Transformation of American Culture, 1880–1940*. New York: Pantheon Books, 1981.

——— . *Rebirth of a Nation: The Making of Modern America, 1877–1920*. New York: Harper Collins, 2009.

Leidholt, Alexander S. *Battling Nell: The Life of Southern Journalist Cornelia Battle Lewis, 1893–1956*. Baton Rouge: Louisiana State University Press, 2009.

Leloudis, James L. *Schooling the New South: Pedagogy, Self, and Society in North Carolina, 1880–1920*. Chapel Hill: University of North Carolina Press, 1996.

Lemain, Gerald, Roy MacLeod, Michael Mulkay, and Peter Weingart, eds. *Perspectives on the Emergence of Scientific Disciplines*. Chicago: Aldine, 1976.

Lewis, David Levering. *W. E. B. Du Bois: Biography of a Race, 1868–1919*. New York: H. Holt, 1993.

——, ed. *W. E. B. Du Bois: A Reader*. New York: H. Holt, 1995.

Lich, Glen E., ed. *Regional Studies: The Interplay of Land and People*. College Station: Texas A&M University Press, 1992.

Link, William A. "'The Harvest Is Ripe, but the Laborers Are Few': The Hookworm Crusade in North Carolina, 1909–1915." *North Carolina Historical Review* 67 (January 1990): 1–27.

——. *The Paradox of Southern Progressivism*. Chapel Hill: University of North Carolina Press, 1992.

——. "Privies, Progressivism, and Public Schools: Health Reform and Education in the Rural South, 1909–1920." *Journal of Southern History* 54 (November 1988): 623–42.

——. "The Social Context of Southern Progressivism, 1880–1930." In *The Wilson Era: Essays in Honor of Arthur S. Link*. Edited by John Milton Cooper and Charles Neu. Baton Rouge: Louisiana State University Press, 1991.

Lisby, Gregory C. *Someone Had to Be Hated, Julian LaRose Harris: Biography*. Durham, N.C.: Carolina Academic Press, 2002.

Litwack, Leon F. *Trouble in Mind: Black Southerners in the Age of Jim Crow*. New York: Alfred A. Knopf, 1998.

Livingstone, David N. "Human Acclimatization: Perspectives on a Contested Field of Inquiry in Science, Medicine, Geography." *History of Science* 25 (December 1987): 359–94.

——. "Race, Space and Moral Climatology: Notes toward a Genealogy." *Journal of Historical Geography* 28 (April 2002): 159–80.

——. "Tropical Hermeneutics: Fragments for a Historical Narrative, An Afterword." *Singapore Journal of Tropical Geography* 21 (March 2000): 92–98.

Luker, Ralph E. *The Social Gospel in Black and White: American Racial Reform, 1885–1912*. Chapel Hill: University of North Carolina Press, 1991.

Lumley, Robert, and Jonathan Morris, eds. *The New History of the Italian South: The Mezzogiorno Revisited*. Devon, U.K.: University of Exeter Press, 1997.

Magubane, Zine. "The American Construction of the Poor White Problem in South Africa." *South Atlantic Quarterly* 107 (Fall 2008): 691–713.

Manring, M. M. *Slave in a Box: The Strange Career of Aunt Jemima*. Charlottesville: University of Virginia Press, 1998.

Marcus, Alan I. "Physicians Open a Can of Worms: American Nationality and Hookworm in the United States, 1893–1909." *American Studies* 30 (Fall 1989): 103–21.

Margolies, Daniel S. *Henry Watterson and the New South: The Politics of Empire, Free Trade, and Globalization*. Lexington: University of Kentucky Press, 2006.

McCurry, Stephanie. *Masters of Small Worlds: Yeomen Households, Gender Relations, and the Political Culture of the Antebellum South Carolina Low Country*. New York: Oxford University Press, 1997.

McElya, Micki. *Clinging to Mammy: The Faithful Slave in Twentieth-Century America*. Cambridge, Mass.: Harvard University Press, 2007.

McIntyre, Rebecca C. "Promoting the Gothic South." *Southern Cultures* 11 (Summer 2005): 33–61.

McLeod, John. *Beginning Postcolonialism*. New York: St. Martin's Press, 2000.

Meier, August. *Negro Thought in America, 1880–1915: Racial Ideologies in the Age of Booker T. Washington*. Ann Arbor: University of Michigan Press, 1963.

Miller, David C. *Dark Eden: The Swamp in Nineteenth-Century American Culture*. New York: Cambridge University Press, 1989.

Moe, Nelson. *The View from Vesuvius: Italian Culture and the Southern Question*. Berkeley: University of California Press, 2002.

Moran, Michelle T. *Colonizing Leprosy: Imperialism and the Politics of Public Health in the United States*. Chapel Hill: University of North Carolina Press, 2007.

Morris, Robert C. *Reading, 'Riting, and Reconstruction: The Education of the Freedmen in the South, 1861–1870*. Chicago: University of Chicago Press, 1981.

Morrissey, Katherine G. *Mental Territories: Mapping the Inland Empire*. Ithaca, N.Y.: Cornell University Press, 1997.

Moss, Alfred A. *The American Negro Academy: Voice of the Talented Tenth*. Baton Rouge: Louisiana State University Press, 1981.

Mott, Frank Luther. "The Magazine Revolution and Popular Ideas in the Nineties." *Proceedings of the American Antiquarian Society* 64 (April 1954): 195–214.

Nieman, Donald G., ed. *African Americans and Education in the South, 1865–1900*. New York: Garland, 1994.

Nelson, Lowry. *Rural Sociology: Its Origin and Growth in the United States*. Minneapolis: University of Minnesota, 1969.

O'Brien, Michael. "Edwin Mims: An Aspect of the Mind of the New South Considered, I." *South Atlantic Quarterly* 73 (Spring 1974): 199–212.

———. "Edwin Mims: An Aspect of the Mind of the New South Considered, II." *South Atlantic Quarterly* 78 (Summer 1974): 324–34.

———. *The Idea of the American South, 1920–1941*. Baltimore: Johns Hopkins University Press, 1979.

———. "On Observing the Quicksand." *American Historical Review* 4 (October 1999): 1202–7.

Packard, Randall M. *The Making of a Tropical Disease: A Short History of Malaria*. Baltimore: Johns Hopkins University Press, 2007.

Palmer, Steven. *Launching Global Health: The Caribbean Odyssey of the Rockefeller Foundation*. Dearborn: University of Michigan Press, 2010.

Pascoe, Peggy. *What Comes Naturally: Miscegenation Law and the Making of Race in America*. New York: Oxford University Press, 2009.

Peard, Julyan G. *Race, Place, and Medicine: The Idea of the Tropics in Nineteenth-Century Brazilian Medicine*. Durham, N.C.: Duke University Press, 1999.

Pease, Donald E. "U.S. Imperialism: Global Dominance without Colonies." In *A Companion to Postcolonial Studies*. Edited by Henry Schwartz and Sangeeta Ray, 203–20. Malden, Mass.: Blackwell, 2000.

Perdue, Theda. *Race and the Atlanta Cotton States Exposition of 1895*. Athens: University of Georgia Press, 2010.

Persky, Joseph J. *The Burden of Dependency: Colonial Themes in Southern Economic Thought*. Baltimore: Johns Hopkins University Press, 1992.

Pfeiffer, Kathleen. *Race Passing and American Individualism*. Amherst: University of Massachusetts Press, 2002.

Pick, Daniel. *Faces of Degeneration: A European Disorder, 1848–1918*. New York: Cambridge University Press, 1989.

Powell, Douglas Reichart. *Critical Regionalism: Connecting Politics and Culture in the American Landscape*. Chapel Hill: University of North Carolina Press, 2007.

Pratt, Mary Louise. *Imperial Eyes: Travel Writing and Transculturation*. New York: Routledge, 1992.

Rabaka, Reiland. *Against Epistemic Apartheid: W. E. B. DuBois and the Disciplinary Decadence of Sociology*. Lanham, Md.: Lexington Books, 2010.

Rafael, Vicente L. "Regionalism, Area Studies, and the Accidents of Agency." *American Historical Review* 104 (October 1999): 1208–20.

———. *White Love and Other Events in Filipino History*. Durham, N.C.: Duke University Press, 2000.

Rafter, Nicole Hahn, ed. *White Trash: The Eugenic Family Studies 1877–1919*. Boston: Northeastern University Press, 1988.

Ransom, Roger L., and Ritchard Sutch. *One Kind of Freedom: The Economic Consequences of Emancipation*. New York: Cambridge University Press, 1977.

Renda, Mary A. *Taking Haiti: Military Occupation and the Culture of U.S. Imperialism, 1915–1940*. Chapel Hill: University of North Carolina Press, 2001.

Rief, Michelle. "Thinking Locally, Acting Globally: The International Agenda of African American Clubwomen, 1880–1940." *Journal of African American History* 89 (Summer 2004): 203–22.

Ring, Natalie J. "Inventing the Tropical South: Race, Region, and the Colonial Model." *Mississippi Quarterly: Journal of Southern Cultures* 56 (Fall 2003): 619–32.

Roberts, Samuel K. "Kelly Miller and Thomas J. Dixon on Blacks in American Civilization." *Phylon* 41 (2nd Quarter 1980): 202–9.

Roberts, Samuel Kelton, Jr. *Infectious Fear: Politics, Disease, and the Health Effects of Segregation*. Chapel Hill: University of North Carolina Press, 2009.

Rodgers, Daniel T. *Atlantic Crossings: Social Politics in a Progressive Era*. Cambridge, Mass.: Harvard University Press, 1998.

———. "Exceptionalism." In *Imagined Histories: American Historians Interpret the Past*. Edited by Anthony Molho and Gordon S. Wood. Princeton, N.J.: Princeton University Press, 1998.

———. "In Search of Progressivism." *Reviews in American History* 10 (December 1982): 113–32.

Rose, Daphne A. *A Plague of Corn: The Social History of Pellagra*. Ithaca, N.Y.: Cornell University Press, 1973.

Rosenberg, Charles E. "Disease and Social Order in America: Perceptions and Expectations." In *Explaining Epidemics and Other Studies in the History of Medicine*. Edited by Charles E. Rosenberg. New York: Cambridge University Press, 1992.

———. "Disease in History: Frames and Framers." *Millbank Quarterly* 67 (Spring 1989): 1–15.

Rosenberg, Charles E., and Janet Lynne Golden, eds. *Framing Disease: Studies in Cultural History*. New Brunswick, N.J.: Rutgers University Press, 1992.

Ross, Dorothy. *The Origins of American Social Science*. New York: Cambridge University Press, 1991.

Russell, Edmund. *War and Nature: Fighting Humans and Insects with Chemicals From World War I to Silent Spring*. New York: Cambridge University Press, 2001.

Russell, Edmund Paul, III. "War on Insects: Warfare, Insecticides, and Environmental Change in the United States, 1870–1945." PhD diss., University of Michigan, 1993.

Rydell, Robert W. *All the World's a Fair: Visions of Empire at American International Expositions 1876–1916*. Chicago: University of Chicago Press, 1984.

Said, Edward W. *Orientalism*. 1978. Reprint, New York: Vintage, 1994.

Salman, Michael. *The Embarrassment of Slavery: Controversies over Bondage and Nationalism in the American Colonial Philippines*. Berkeley: University of California Press, 2002.

Savitt, Todd L., and James Harvey Young, eds. *Disease and Distinctiveness in the American South*. Knoxville: University of Tennessee Press, 1988.

Saxton, Alexander. *The Rise and Fall of the White Republic: Class Politics and Mass Culture in Nineteenth-Century America*. London and New York: Verso, 1990.

Schmidt, Peter. *Sitting in Darkness: New South Fiction, Education, and the Rise of Jim Crow Colonialism, 1865–1920*. Jackson: University of Mississippi Press, 2008.

Schneider, Jane, ed. *Italy's "Southern Question": Orientalism in One Country*. New York: Berg, 1998.

Sehat, David. "The Civilizing Mission of Booker T. Washington." *Journal of Southern History* 73 (May 2007): 323–62.

Shapiro, Henry D. *Appalachia on Our Mind: The Southern Mountains and Mountaineers in the American Consciousness, 1870–1920*. Chapel Hill: University of North Carolina Press, 1978.

Shumway, David R. *Creating American Civilization: A Genealogy of American Literature as an Academic Discipline*. Minneapolis: University of Minnesota Press, 1994.

Silber, Nina. *The Romance of Reunion: Northerners and the South, 1865–1900*. Chapel Hill: University of North Carolina Press, 1993.

Singall, Daniel Joseph. *The War Within: From Victorian to Modernist Thought in the South, 1919–1945*. Chapel Hill: University of North Carolina Press, 1992.

Skidmore, Thomas. *Black into White: Race and Nationality in Brazilian Thought*. New York: Oxford University Press, 1974.

Sklar, Martin J. *The Corporate Reconstruction of American Capitalism, 1890–1916: The Market, the Law, and Politics*. New York: Cambridge University Press, 1988.

Slater, David. "Locating the American Century: Themes for a Post-colonial Perspective." In *The American Century: Consensus and Coercion in the Projection of American Power*. Edited by David Slater and Peter J. Taylor. Malden, Mass.: Blackwell, 1999.

Smith, John David. "Alfred Holt Stone: Mississippi Planter and Archivist/Historian of Slavery." *Journal of Mississippi History* 45 (November 1983): 262–70.

———. "High Authority or Failed Prophet? Alfred Holt Stone and Racial Thought in Jim Crow America." *Journal of Mississippi History* 68 (Fall 2006): 195–211.

———. "'No negro is upon the program': Blacks and the Montgomery Race Conference of 1900." In *Reassessing Southerners and Their History*. Edited by John David Smith and Thomas H. Appleton Jr. Westport, Conn.: Greenwood Press, 1997.

——— . *An Old Creed for a New South: Proslavery Ideology and Historiography, 1865–1918*. Westport, Conn.: Greenwood Press, 1985.

Smith, Jon, and Deborah Cohn. *Look Away! The South in New World Studies*. Durham, N.C.: Duke University Press, 2004.

Smith, Jon, Kathryn McKee, and Scott Romine, eds. "Special Issue: Postcolonial Theory, The U.S. South and New World Studies, Part I." *Mississippi Quarterly: Journal of Southern Cultures* 56 (Fall 2003): 491–674.

——— . "Special Issue: Postcolonial Theory, The U.S. South and New World Studies, Part II." *Mississippi Quarterly: Journal of Southern Cultures* 57 (Winter 2003–2004): 5–194.

Smith, Stephen A. *Myth, Media, and the Southern Mind*. Fayetteville: University of Arkansas Press, 1985.

Sosna, Morton. *In Search of the Silent South: Southern Liberals and the Race Issue*. New York: Columbia University Press, 1977.

Southern, David W. *The Malignant Heritage: Yankee Progressives and the Negro Question, 1901–1914*. Chicago: Loyola University Press, 1968.

Stepan, Nancy Leys. *Picturing Tropical Nature*. Ithaca, N.Y.: Cornell University Press, 2001.

——— . "Tropical Nature as a Way of Writing." In *Mundialización de la Ciencia y Cultura Nacional*. Edited by A. Lafuente et al. Madrid: Doce Calles, 1993.

Stocking, George. *Victorian Anthropology*. New York: Free Press, 1987.

Stoler, Ann Laura. *Carnal Knowledge and Imperial Power*. Berkeley: University of California, 2002.

——— , ed. *Haunted by Empire: Geographies of Intimacy in North American History*. Raleigh, N.C.: Duke University Press, 2006.

——— . "Tense and Tender Ties: The Politics of Comparison in North American History and (Post) Colonial Studies." *Journal of American History* 88 (December 2001): 829–65.

Stoler, Ann Laura, and Frederick Cooper, eds. *Tensions of Empire: Colonial Cultures in a Bourgeois World*. Berkeley: University of California Press, 2002.

Strom, Claire. *Making Catfish Bait Out of Government Boys: The Fight against Cattle Ticks and the Transformation of the Yeoman South*. Athens: University of Georgia Press, 2009.

Sullivan-Gonzales, Douglass, and Charles Reagan Wilson. *The South and the Caribbean*. Jackson: University of Mississippi Press, 2001.

Sutherland, Daniel E. "Southern Fraternal Organizations in the North." *Journal of Southern History* 53 (November 1987): 587–612.

Tarr, Rodger. "Eden Revisited: Florida and the American Literary Imagination." *Mississippi Quarterly* 46 (Fall 1993): 661–66.

Taylor, Melanie Benson. *Disturbing Calculations: The Economics of Identity in Postcolonial Southern Literature, 1912–2000*. Athens: University of Georgia Press, 2008.

Taylor, William R. *Cavalier and Yankee: The Old South and American National Character*. New York: G. Braziller, 1961.

Teachout, Terry. *The Skeptic: A Life of H. L. Mencken*. New York: Harper Collins, 2002.

Tindall, George B. "The Benighted South: Origins of a Modern Image." *Virginia Quarterly Review* 40 (Spring 1964): 281–94.

———. *The Emergence of the New South, 1913–1945*. Baton Rouge: Louisiana State University Press, 1967.

———. "The Significance of Howard W. Odum to Southern History: A Preliminary Estimate." *Journal of Southern History* 24 (August 1958): 285–307.

Tomes, Nancy. *The Gospel of Germs: Men, Women, and the Microbe in American Life*. Cambridge, Mass.: Harvard University Press, 1998.

Tullos, Allen. "The Great Hookworm Crusade." *Southern Exposure* 6 (Summer 1978): 40–49.

———. *Habits of Industry: White Culture and the Transformation of the Carolina Piedmont*. Chapel Hill: University of North Carolina Press, 1989.

Turley, David. "Black Social Science and Black Politics in the Understanding of the South: Du Bois, the Atlanta University Studies, and the *Crisis*, 1897–1920." In *Race and Class in the American South since 1890*. Edited by Melvyn Stokes and Rick Halpern. Oxford, U.K.: Berg, 1994.

Twyman, Robert W. "The Clay Eater: A New Look at an Old Southern Enigma." *Journal of Southern History* 27 (August 1971): 439–48.

Tyrrell, Ian. "American Exceptionalism in an Age of International History." *American Historical Review* 96 (October 1991): 1031–55.

———. "Making Nations/Making States: American Historians in the Context of Empire." *Journal of American History* 86 (December 1999): 1015–44.

———. *Reforming the World: The Creation of America's Moral Empire*. Princeton, N.J.: Princeton University Press, 2010.

Vandiver, Frank E., ed. *The Idea of the South: Pursuit of a Central Theme*. Chicago: University of Chicago Press, 1964.

Uday, Mehta S. "Liberal Strategies of Exclusion." *Politics and Society* 18 (December 1990): 427–54.

Urban, Wayne J. *Essays in Twentieth-Century Southern Education: Exceptionalism and Its Limits*. New York: Garland, 1999.

Wald, Gayle. *Crossing the Line: Racial Passing in Twentieth-Century U.S. Literature and Culture*. Durham, N.C.: Duke University Press, 2000.

Wallenstein, Peter. *Tell the Court I Love My Wife: Race, Marriage, and Law—An American History.* New York: Palgrave Macmillan, 2004.

Warnock, Henry Y. "Andrew Sledd, Southern Methodists, and the Negro." *Journal of Southern History* 31 (August 1965): 251–71.

Warren, Kenneth S., and John Z. Bowers, eds. *Parasitology: A Global Perspective.* New York: Springer-Verlag, 1983.

Watson, Richard L. "From Populism through the New Deal." In *Interpreting Southern History: Essays in Honor of Sanford W. Higginbotham.* Edited by John B. Boles and Evelyn Thomas Nolen. Baton Rouge: Louisiana State University Press, 1987.

Watts, Trent A. *One Homogeneous People: Narratives of White Southern Identity, 1890–1920.* Knoxville: University of Tennessee Press, 2010.

Wells, Jeremy. *Romances of the White Man's Burden: Race, Empire, and the Plantation in American Literature, 1880–1936.* Nashville, Tenn.: Vanderbilt University Press, 2011.

———. "Up from Savagery: Booker T. Washington and the Civilizing Mission." *Southern Quarterly* 42 (Fall 2003): 53–74.

Wells, Jeremy Dwight. "Civilization and the South: Southern Writers and American Empire, 1866–1907." PhD diss., University of Michigan, 2000.

Wexler, Laura. *Tender Violence: Domestic Visions in an Age of U.S. Imperialism.* Chapel Hill: University of North Carolina Press, 2000.

Whisnant, David E. *All That Is Native and Fine: The Politics of Culture in an American Region.* Chapel Hill: University of North Carolina Press, 1983.

White, Richard. "The Nationalization of Nature." *Journal of American History* 86 (December 1999): 976–86.

Wiebe, Robert. *The Search for Order, 1877–1920.* New York: Hill and Wang, 1967.

Wiener, Jonathan M. *Social Origins of the New South: Alabama, 1860–1885.* Baton Rouge: Louisiana State University Press, 1978.

Williams, Arthur R. *George S. Schuyler: Portrait of a Conservative.* Knoxville: University of Tennessee Press, 2007.

Williams, William Appleman. *The Tragedy of American Diplomacy.* 2nd rev. and enlarged ed. New York: W. W. Norton, 1972.

Williamson, Joel. *The Crucible of Race: Black-White Relations in the American South since Emancipation.* New York: Oxford University Press, 1984.

———. *New People: Miscegenation and Mulattoes in the United States.* New York: Free Press, 1980.

Willoughby-Herard, Tiffany. "Waste of a White Skin or Civilizing White Primitives: The Carnegie Commission Study of Poor Whites in South Africa, 1927–1931." PhD diss., University of California, Santa Barbara, 2003.

Woodman, Harold D. *King Cotton and His Retainers: Financing and Marketing the Cotton Crop of the South*. Lexington: University of Kentucky Press, 1968.

———. *New South, New Law: The Legal Foundations of Credit and Labor Relations in the Postbellum Agricultural South*. Baton Rouge: Louisiana State University Press, 1995.

———, ed. *Slavery and the Southern Economy: Sources and Readings*. New York: Harcourt, Brace, & World, 1966.

Woodward, C. Vann. *American Counterpoint: Slavery and Racism in the North-South Dialogue*. Boston: Little, Brown, 1964.

———. *The Burden of Southern History*. Baton Rouge: Louisiana State University Press, 1993.

———. *Origins of the New South, 1877–1913*. Baton Rouge: Louisiana State University Press, 1951.

———. *The Strange Career of Jim Crow*. Edited by James S. McFeely. Commemorative ed. New York: Oxford University Press, 2001.

———. *Thinking Back: The Perils of Writing History*. Baton Rouge: Louisiana State University Press, 1986.

Wray, Matt. *Not Quite White: White Trash and the Boundaries of Whiteness*. Durham, N.C.: Duke University Press, 2006.

Wright, Gavin. *Old South, New South: Revolutions in the Southern Economy since the Civil War*. New York: Basic Books, 1986.

———. *The Political Economy of the Cotton South: Households, Markets and Wealth in the Nineteenth Century*. New York: Norton, 1978.

Wright, Susan Prothro, and Ernestine Pickens Glass, eds. *Passing in the Works of Charles W. Chestnutt*. Jackson: University Press of Mississippi, 2010.

Wright, W. D. "The Thought and Leadership of Kelly Miller." *Phylon* 39 (1979): 180–92.

Young, Alford A., Jr. "Early Traditions in African-American Sociological Thought." *Annual Review of Sociology* 21 (August 2001): 445–77.

Zackondik, Teresa. "Fixing the Color Line: The Mulatto, Southern Courts, and Racial Identity." *American Quarterly* 53 (September 2001): 420–51.

Zimmerman, Andrew. *Alabama in Africa: Booker T. Washington, the German Empire, and the Globalization of the New South*. Princeton, N.J.: Princeton University Press, 2010.

INDEX

Abbeville, La., 92

Abbott, Lyman, 145–46, 166, 171, 175

abolitionists, negative image of South by, 18–19

"acclimatization" and tropics, 88

"accommodationist racism," 192

Adams, Herbert Baxter, 204

Adler, Felix, 207

Advancing South, The (Mims), 216–17, 220

Africa, 82, 89–90, 156. *See also* South Africa

agrarian myth, 110, 121, 130–31. *See also* rural living

Agricultural Adjustment Act (1933), 134

agricultural colleges, 120, 122

agricultural conservation, 107

agricultural experiment stations, 108

agricultural Other, South as, 106

agricultural progress: importance of cotton to, 101–2; and mosquitoes, 92

agricultural reform and reformers: boll weevil as opportunity for, 119–20; as colonial project, 52; and diseased South, 116; and diversification of crops, 113, 119, 126, 128, 131; and guidance from Asian countries, 106–7, 246n34; South as laboratory for, 97, 113, 120, 127, 132–33; as tool of colonization, 108. *See also* boll weevils;

Butterfield, Kenyon L.; cotton; farm demonstration program; Knapp, Seaman A.; Poe, Clarence Hamilton

agriculture: federal intervention in, 113–14; tropical, 107, 108

Alabama: campaign against child labor in, 149–50; European settlement in, 82, 84; farm demonstration movement in, 125; public schools in, 161, 164; unequal distribution of resources to, 161

Alabama Child Labor Committee (ACLC), 150

Alabama State Board of Health, 75

Alderman, Edwin A., 7, 152, 165

Alexander, W. W., 95; *The Collapse of Cotton Tenancy, The* (with Johnson and Embree), 143, 144–45

Algeria, 82

American Academy of Political and Social Science, 182, 184, 206

American Commonwealth, The (Bryce), 205

American Counterpoint (Woodward), 223n18

American democracy, "race problem" and, 205

American Economic Association, 182, 186

American Epoch, An (Odum), 218

American Federation of Labor, 149

agricultural workers in, 133, 246n34; cotton market in, 105; Hart's study in, 53; industrious people in, 126; origin of cotton plant in, 105–6

civic diagnosticians, physicians as, 69

civilization: and American goods, 105–6; cotton as agent of, 103; decline of, in tropics, 61; degeneration and decline of, 91–92; discourse of, 43, 45–47, 232n71; and Enlightenment, 44–45; and "forgotten man," 152–53; and germ theory, 93; hookworm's effect on, 92; lack of, in South, 45–46, 52, 232n76; versus savagery, 44, 104, 105; slavery as incompatible with, 46–47; and sociocultural evolutionary theory, 44

Civilization and Climate (Huntington), 87, 90

civil rights movement, 219

Civil War, social memory of, 5–6

Clansman, The (Dixon), 25

Clash of Colour, The (Mathews), 205

"clay-eaters," 67. *See also* hookworm; pellagra; southern poor whites

"clean farming," 116, 129, 201

"clean-up" days, 65

climate and race, 88

climates, tropical, 84, 88–89

"climatic handicaps," 87

clothing: and civilization, 103, 105–6; and savagery, 104, 105; and transport of boll weevils, 249n74

Clowes, William Laird, 209

Cohn, Deborah, 11

Collapse of Cotton Tenancy, The (Johnson, Embree, and Alexander), 143, 144–45

Collier's Weekly, 203

colonial economies, 72–73, 94, 108, 133, 225n23

colonialism, 224n20, 225n24; and American exceptionalism, 225n26; and image of South as problem, 4; and Jefferson's principles, 234n101; overlap of, with sectionalism, 50–51; Reconstruction as, 54, 225n22; rhetoric of, 24, 211–13; as tool for understanding South, 10–11, 16–17. *See also* imperialism; postcolonialism

colonialism, Jim Crow, 256n68

colonial possessions: cotton growers in, 208; eradication of disease in, 94; as "laboratories," 168, 225n24; lack of public hygiene in, 87; race relations in, 206–7

colonization: and agricultural reform, 108; disciplinary strategy of, 213; models of, 52; and nationalization, 24; Reconstruction as blueprint for, 225n22; of southern blacks, 54

colonized people and poor southern whites, 143–44

color line: debate over nature of, 185–86; and education of white illiterates, 171; global implications of, 202–13; and "mulatto problem," 193–202, 214; and national reconciliation, 213–14; and passing as white, 199; poor southern whites and legitimacy of, 137; and racial degeneration of whites, 136. *See also* "race problem"

"Color Line Belts the World, The" (Du Bois), 203

Colquhoun, Archibald R., 213

Columbia, 86

Cox, Ernest Sevier, 201

"Crackers," 140–41, 143–44. *See also* southern poor whites

Craighead, Erwin, 170

Crawford, M. D. C., 109, 112

credit systems, 110

Crisis (Du Bois), 212

criticism: as hindering regional progress, 218; and Mencken, 1–2, 144, 217–18, 219–20; from North, 41–42, 216, 231n66; reactions to, of diseased South, 92–93; sectional, 48–49; South's sensitivity to, 41–42, 58, 59, 91–92

Crookman, Junius (*Black No More* character), 196–97

crop lien system, 110–11, 119, 136

Crowther, Samuel, 84

Crummell, Alexander, 183

Cuba: Archer in, 210; comparison of, with South, 53, 87; expansion of slave empire to, 17; race relations in, 179, 206; and tropical medicine, 82; yellow fever in, 241n108

cultural geographers, 53

"cultural method," 126–27

culture of reunion, 5–6, 26–27, 48–49, 177, 185, 222n8. *See also* reunification

Currie, J. H., 197–98

Curry, Jabez Lamar Monroe, 163

Dabney, Charles W., 7, 31, 161–62, 165, 172

Dallas News, 119

Darker Phases of the South, The (Tannenbaum), 33, 143, 147–48

Darwin, Charles, 45

Davis, David Bryon, 46

Davis, Jefferson, 39

debt, 110–11, 136

degeneration: and decline of civilization, 91–92; and disease, 77; as peculiar to South, 19–20; of South African whites, 158; of southern whites, 90–92, 110, 150–51; of white children, 135. *See also* racial degeneration of whites

Delaware Society, 38

democracy, multiracial, 205, 215

democratic citizens, uplift of, 129–30, 164

democratic education, reconciliation and, 162–72

demonstration farms. *See* farm demonstration program

Dershimer, F. W., 73–74

"Diagnosis of the Sick City, The" (G.T. Palmer), 69–70

Dillard, James Hardy, 165

disciplinary strategy of colonial rule, 213

disease, 58–94; as analytical tool, 59; connection of, with social environment, 60–61; descriptions of, 77–80; as distinctive to South, 19–20, 60, 62, 64, 234n4; and economic production, 74, 75, 76, 136; economy of, 71, 72–80; as geographically specific, 62, 64, 69, 73; high rate of, in South, 69; and labor, 74, 75–77, 90, 94; and land values, 75; metaphors of, 60, 61, 68, 71–72, 116–18; miasma theory of, 63, 81, 83; modes of origin of, 86–87, 89–90; and race, 80, 88–92; and racial degeneration, 61, 90–91; transmission of, through southern ports, 85; tropical, 80–88. *See also* germ theory; health reform and reformers; hookworm; malaria; pellagra; yellow fever

disfranchisement, 170, 194, 214, 265n91

Venezuela, 86

Vicksburg, Miss., 198

Victorians, 44

Villard, Oswald Garrison, 39–40

Vincent, George E., 69

Virginia, 90, 125, 234n101

Virginia Society, 38

voting, 162–63, 171

Wallace, D. D., 110

Wallace, Henry, 121

Washington, Booker T.: and global visitors, 215; as greatest man born in South, 34; hugged by Ogden, 257n89; inclusion of, at white conferences, 183; publication of, on "race problem," 178; and Tuskegee International Conference on the Negro, 207–9; and uplift, 26

Washington, Margaret Murray, 208

Washington Herald, 127

Watkins, James L., 103

Watts, Trent, 222n8

wealth. *See* economic prosperity

Weatherly, Ulysses G., 207, 265n90; "A World-Wide Color Line," 204

Wells, Ida B., 7, 198

Wells, Jeremy Dwight, 232n71

West, the, South as replacement for, 23

Westerberg, Carl, 241n101

West Indies, 82

"When Is a Caucasian Not a Caucasian" (*Independent*), 199

White, Andrew D., 188

White, John E., 45

"white blood," 200

white degeneration. *See* degeneration

"white man's burden," 206

White Man's Burden, The (Riley), 205–6

whiteness: versus blackness, 136, 196; and educational reform, 170–71; hybridity of, 141–42; and Jim Crow laws, 213; making of, 200; national identity of, 25, 136; and New South, 25–26; and racial identity, 142; salvaging of, 151; and view of blacks as objects, 215

"White question," 29–30

whites. *See* southern poor whites; southern whites

"White Side of the Southern Question, The" (Godkin), 29–30, 152

"white slavery," 147–52, 173

"White Slavery" (cartoon), 147, 148

white subversives, regulation of, 155

white supremacy: and Anglo-Saxon regression, 91–92; and degeneration of white children, 135, 151; and imperialism, 155; and inherent inferiority of blacks, 26; and interracial sex, 198–99; mixed-race subversion of, 201; and "race friction," 192; southern whites as victims, 16. *See also* degeneration

"white trash studies," 142–43

Wilcocks, Raymond W., 157, 158; "Rural Poverty among Whites in South Africa and in the South of the United States," 159

Wilcox, Earley Vernon, 99, 246n36; *Tropical Agriculture*, 107

Willcox, Walter F., 186

Wilmington, N.C., 188

Wilson, James, 114

POLITICS AND CULTURE IN THE TWENTIETH-CENTURY SOUTH

www.ingramcontent.com/pod-product-compliance
Lightning Source LLC
Chambersburg PA
CBHW010114270326
41929CB00023B/3347